# Pope to Burney, 1714–1779

## Scriblerians to Bluestockings

Moyra Haslett

First published 2003 by
PALGRAVE MACMILLAN
Houndmills, Basingstoke, Hampshire RG21 6XS and
175 Fifth Avenue, New York, N. Y. 10010
Companies and representatives throughout the world

PALGRAVE MACMILLAN is the global academic imprint of the Palgrave Macmillan division of St. Martin's Press, LLC and of Palgrave Macmillan Ltd. Macmillan® is a registered trademark in the United States, United Kingdom and other countries. Palgrave is a registered trademark in the European Union and other countries.

ISBN 0-333-69610-7 hardback
ISBN 0-333-69611-5 paperback

This book is printed on paper suitable for recycling and made from fully managed and sustained forest sources.

A catalogue record for this book is available from the British Library.

Library of Congress Cataloging-in-Publication Data
Haslett, Moyra.
    Pope to Burney, 1714–1779 : Scriblerians to bluestockings /
    Moyra Haslett.
        p. cm. — (Transitions)
    Includes bibliographical references and index.
    ISBN 0-333-69610-7 — ISBN 0-333-69611-5 (pbk.)
        1. English literature—18th century—History and criticism. 2.
    Literature and society—Great Britain—History—18th century. 3. Pope,
    Alexander, 1688–1744—Criticism and interpretation. 4. Burney, Fanny,
    1752–1840—Criticism and interpretation. 5. Literature—Societies,
    etc.—History—18th century. 6. Book clubs—Great Britain—History—
    18th century. 7. Great Britain—Intellectual life—18th century.
    8. Conversation—History—18th century. 9. Conversation in literature.
    10. Scriblerus Club. 11. Intertextuality. I. Title. II. Transitions (Palgrave
    Macmillan (Firm))

PR448.S64H37 2003
820.9'005—dc21                                                      2003045989

10   9   8   7   6   5   4   3   2   1
12   11   10   09   08   07   06   05   04   03

Printed in China

Pope to Burney, 1714–1779

**transitions**
*General Editor: Julian Wolfreys*

*Published titles*

ORWELL TO THE PRESENT: LITERATURE IN ENGLAND, 1945–2000 John
  Brannigan
CHAUCER TO SHAKESPEARE, 1337–1580 SunHee Kim Gertz
POPE TO BURNEY, 1714–1779: SCRIBLERIANS TO BLUESTOCKINGS Moyra
  Haslett
PATER TO FORSTER, 1873–1924 Ruth Robbins
BURKE TO BYRON, BARBAULD TO BAILLIE, 1790–1830 Jane Stabler
MILTON TO POPE, 1650–1720 Kay Gilliland Stevenson
SIDNEY TO MILTON, 1580–1660 Marion Wynne-Davies

BATAILLE Fred Botting and Scott Wilson
NEW HISTORICISM AND CULTURAL MATERIALISM John Brannigan
POSTMODERN NARRATIVE THEORY Mark Currie
FORMALIST CRITICISM AND READER-RESPONSE THEORY Todd F. Davis and
  Kenneth Womack
QUEER THEORIES Donald E. Hall
MARXIST LITERARY AND CULTURAL THEORY Moyra Haslett
LOUIS ALTHUSSER Warren Montag
RACE Brian G. Niro
JACQUES LACAN Jean-Michel Rabaté
LITERARY FEMINISMS Ruth Robbins
DECONSTRUCTION • DERRIDA Julian Wolfreys

*Forthcoming titles*

IMAGE TO APOCALYPSE, 1910–1945 Jane Goldman
DICKENS TO HARDY, 1837–1884 Julian Wolfreys

TERRY EAGLETON David Alderson
JULIA KRISTEVA AND LITERARY THEORY Megan Becker-Leckrone
NATIONAL IDENTITY John Brannigan
HÉLÈNE CIXOUS: WRITING AND SEXUAL DIFFERENCE Abigail Bray
HOMI BHABHA Eleanor Byrne
GENDER Claire Colebrook
IDEOLOGY James Decker
POSTMODERNISM • POSTMODERNITY Martin McQuillan
ROLAND BARTHES Martin McQuillan
MODERNITY David Punter
PSYCHOANALYSIS AND LITERATURE Nicholas Rand
SUBJECTIVITY Ruth Robbins
POSTCOLONIAL THEORY Malini Johan Schueller
TRANSGRESSION Julian Wolfreys

---

**transitions Series**
**Series Standing Order ISBN 0-333-73684-6**
(*outside North America only*)

You can receive future titles in this series as they are published by placing a standing order. Please contact your bookseller or, in case of difficulty, write to us at the
address below with your name and address, the title of the series and the ISBN
quoted above.

Customer Services Department, Macmillan Distribution Ltd
Houndmills, Basingstoke, Hampshire RG21 6XS, England

---

# Contents

# General Editor's Preface

Transitions: *transition*-, n. of action. 1. A passing or passage from one condition, action or (rarely) place, to another. 2. Passage in thought, speech, or writing, from one subject to another. 3. **a.** The passing from one note to another **b.** The passing from one key to another, modulation. 4. The passage from an earlier to a later stage of development or formation . . . change from an earlier style to a later; a style of intermediate or mixed character . . . the historical passage of language from one well-defined stage to another.

The aim of *Transitions* is to explore passages and movements in language, literature and culture from Chaucer to the present day. The series also seeks to examine the ways in which the very idea of transition affects the reader's sense of period so as to address anew questions of literary history and periodisation. The writers in this series unfold the cultural and historical mediations of literature during what are commonly recognised as crucial moments in the development of English literature, addressing, as the OED puts it, the 'historical passage of language from one well-defined stage to another'.

Recognising the need to contextualise literary study, the authors offer close readings of canonical and now marginalised or over-looked literary texts from all genres, bringing to this study the rigour of historical knowledge and the sophistication of theoreti-cally informed evaluations of writers and movements from the last 700 years. At the same time as each writer, whether Chaucer or Shakespeare, Milton or Pope, Byron, Dickens, George Eliot, Virginia Woolf or Salman Rushdie, is shown to produce his or her texts within a discernible historical, cultural, ideological and philosoph-ical milieu, the text is read from the vantage point of recent theo-retical interests and concerns. The purpose in bringing theoretical knowledge to the reading of a wide range of works is to demonstrate how the literature is always open to transition, whether in the instance of its production or in succeeding moments of its critical reception.

The series desires to enable the reader to transform her/his own reading and writing transactions by comprehending past developments. Each book in the second tranche of the series offers a pedagogical guide to the poetics and politics of particular eras, as well as to the subsequent critical comprehension of periods and periodisation. As well as transforming the cultural and literary past by interpreting its transition from the perspective of the critical and theoretical present, each study enacts transitional readings of a number of literary texts, all of which are themselves conceivable as having effected transition at the moments of their first appearance. The readings offered in these books seek, through close critical reading, historical contextualisation and theoretical engagement, to demonstrate certain possibilities in reading to the student reader.

It is hoped that the student will find this series liberating because the series seeks to move beyond rigid definitions of period. What is important is the sense of passage, of motion. Rather than providing a definitive model of literature's past, *Transitions* aims to place you in an active dialogue with the writing and culture of other eras, so as to comprehend not only how the present reads the past, but how the past can read the present.

*Julian Wolfreys*

# Acknowledgements

I would never have written a book of this kind if I had not been first excited and engaged by eighteenth-century literature through the teaching of Ian Campbell Ross. He it was who taught me to recognise the innovative, experimental and modern nature of eighteenth-century literature – the qualities which continue to draw me to the period. My first thanks then go to him as a teacher and as a friend. The writing of the book also owes more specific debts: to the series editor, Julian Wolfreys, for his continued encouragement and support; to friends and colleagues, Julian Cowley, Glynis Ridley, Ruth Robbins, and Paul Simpson in particular, for suggestions, advice, and conversations about the eighteenth century; and to former students of eighteenth-century literature at the University of Luton and Queen's University Belfast for their enthusiasm and interest. Thanks too to Gillian Russell who kindly allowed me to read a pre-publication draft of the introduction to *Romantic Sociability* (Cambridge University Press, 2002). Florence Gray, of Queen's University Library, has arranged countless interlibrary loans with exemplary efficiency and patience. That the book is completed at all is partly due to her help. I am also grateful to Margaret Bartley at Palgrave Macmillan for commissioning me to write the book, to Anna Sandeman and Sonya Barker for seeing the book through to publication and to Judy Marshall for her careful corrections of the typescript. My partner, John Brannigan, has spent more time with this book than anyone else, myself apart, and, despite claiming to know relatively little about the eighteenth century, continues to be my most acute critic. My thanks to him for always reminding me about the bigger picture – both within and without the book.

# Preface

The *Preface* can boast of an invention no antienter than Printing. The publishers of the *Classics* seldom ventured any further than a touch of the Author's life, and an *Index*, which, in most of the books I ever saw printed before 1600, stood in the same place where our *Preface* does now. But when the custom grew up of placing the *Index* at the end, then people begun to think that the book looked naked, they therefore filled up the place, where the *Index* had been, with a set of words, which, like that, had no more sense nor meaning in the place where they stood.

(Grub Street Journal, No. 318, 29 Jan. 1736)

[I]t is lamentable to behold with what a lazy scorn many of the yawning readers in our age do now a-days twirl over forty or fifty pages of *preface* and *dedication* (which is the usual *modern* stint) as if it were so much Latin. Though it must also be allowed on the other hand that a very considerable number is known to proceed *critics* and *wits* by reading nothing else.

(Swift 1986, 63)

The two quotations which serve as epigraphs to this introduction already satirise the function of book prefaces. I have chosen them to indicate from the very outset the ways in which literature of the eighteenth century tends to lampoon its own condition – what we would call today, self-reflexivity. This is the zany, experimental, fashionably 'postmodern' eighteenth century of many recent accounts. There are certainly interesting links to be made between the experimentalism of much eighteenth-century fiction and late twentieth-century forms of narrative. We might contrast Swift's *A Tale of a Tub* or *Gulliver's Travels* with Salman Rushdie's *The Moor's Last Sigh* (1995) or Umberto Eco's *The Name of the Rose* (1983), for example. Or Sterne's *Tristram Shandy* with its later sequel, Peter Carey's *The Unusual Life of Tristan Smith* (1994). The self-consciousness of eighteenth-century literature, and its interest in issues of language and of readership, have also made it open to a number of contemporary theories. These invariably find that the texts are not so much works upon which theory can be 'applied', but works which overtly comment and reflect upon contemporary literary debates.[1] This vision of the eighteenth century is in stark contrast to the periods once confidently placed as 'Augustan' and 'the age of sensibility'. Hoping, therefore, that the reader of this book will not read 'nothing else', and that its own composition will not be only to fill up so many words, I introduce this preface with a statement of this book's own intervention in these debates: how might we characterise literature of this (or indeed any) period? What are we to do with ideas of literary periodisation, which have been called into question by so many new ways of reading and yet which we still need in our teaching and study of literature?

These new ways of reading – influenced by the decentring and pluralising forces of new historicism, feminism, postcolonialism, poststructuralism and postmodernism – are sceptical of the grand narratives of traditional kinds of literary history. If we define the literary period of the early eighteenth century as 'Augustan', with all its connotations of literary decorum, balance and classicism, then we will think of Pope's imitations of Horace as exemplary and the poetry of Christopher Smart as an aberration. Compare, for example, the following excerpts of eighteenth-century poetry:

> Where'er you walk, cool gales will fan the glade,
> Trees, where you sit, shall crowd into a shade:
> Where'er you tread, the blushing flowers shall rise,
> And all things flourish where you turn your eyes.
> ('Summer: The Second Pastoral', ll. 73–6)

> For I will consider my Cat Jeoffry.
> For he is the servant of the Living God duly and daily serving him.
> For at the first glance of the glory of God in the East he worships in his way.
> For is this done by wreathing his body seven times round with elegant quickness.
> For then he leaps up to catch the musk, which is the blessing of God upon his prayer.
> For he rolls upon prank to work it in.

> For having done duty and received blessing he begins to consider
>   himself.
> For this he performs in ten degrees.
> (*Jubilate Agno*, Fragment B, ll. 695–702)

The first excerpt appears to exemplify those 'Augustan' qualities of
poise and polish, control and correctness, elegance and refinement. There is no brashness in these lines, only a harmonious balancing within and between lines. The second excerpt dispenses
with the tightly coiled energy of the heroic couplet and instead
flows into a very modern-seeming blank verse which obeys only its
own rhythm. Its erratic line lengths gesture towards a pulse of an
extended metre followed by a shorter measure, as in the liturgical
rhythms of the litany. Of course there is an obvious special plead-
ing in making such selections. The first excerpt was written by Pope
when he was sixteen. The *Pastorals* were the first poems he published, in 1709. Here Pope was consciously attempting to achieve
the kind of polished perfection and musicality typical of many
accounts of neo-classical or Augustan poetry. This is conspicuously
evident in these lines and in their best-known form, as set to music
by Handel. Later poetry would use the same heroic couplet form
for very different ends. Consider, for example, the dramatic voice
with which *An Epistle to Arbuthnot* (1735) begins:

> Shut, shut, the door, good John! fatigu'd I said,
> Tye up the knocker, say I'm sick, I'm dead.
> The Dog-star rages! nay tis past a doubt,
> All Bedlam, or Parnassus, is let out.

The abrupt opening and conversational pace and diction are just
as characteristic of the effects Pope would achieve through the
heroic couplet as the polished elegance of the famous *Pastoral*
lines.

   The second excerpt is from a manuscript of fragmentary verse
written by Christopher Smart while he was confined in a madhouse
(1759–63 are possible dates for its composition). That these verses
were not published until 1938 might confirm that the 'modernism'
of these lines – more like Allen Ginsberg, perhaps, than Alexander
Pope – could only be read as a deviation from eighteenth-century
culture. Yet, again, these lines are not necessarily typical of Smart's

entire career. The differences between Pope and Smart thus can be overplayed. Smart, for example, published a Latin translation of one of Pope's most strictly neo-classical poems, *An Essay on Criticism* (1711). This was entitled *De Arte Critica* and appeared in Smart's *Poems on Several Occasions* (1752). Smart also wrote in a wide range of verse forms which included the use of rhyme as a balancing, composed motif:

> Now the winds are all composure,
> But the breath upon the bloom,
> Blowing sweet o'er each inclosure
> Grateful off'rings of perfume . . .
> ('Hymn. St Philip and St James', 1765)

Discussions of Smart can often be found in studies of 'pre-Romantic' or 'early Romantic' poetry. Like Blake, however, Smart is as much an 'eighteenth-century' as a 'Romantic' poet. Only our inability to think of periods more flexibly prevents us from permitting them to remain where, in historical terms, they are unquestionably situated. Whether we think of Smart's liturgical rhythms in *Jubilate Agno* as the pulse of devotional rhythm or a free-thinking kind of avant-gardism is largely a matter of our reading practice, rather than any intrinsic, automatic placing.[2]

How we view a period, then, might well determine how we read its literature. If we name the eighteenth century an 'age of reason', then we will think of its literary culture as an expression of enlightenment ideals rather than as aesthetic innovations. Thinking of the eighteenth century in these terms has continued until relatively recently. In these formations of the period, critics have identified the symmetry, rhetorical poise and elegance, unity, harmony and grace of the writings they study. To overemphasise these qualities however, is to fail to register how Pope, that proponent of literary classicism, also warned against the tedium of too neat formations. We might recall, for example, his satire of landscaping in which 'Grove nods at grove, each alley has a brother, / And half the platform just reflects the other' (*Epistle to Burlington*, ll. 17–18), or, comparably, his injunction that the rules of poetry should not be followed too rigidly.[3] Pope's ideal was that a poet should master the rules, rather than slavishly follow them. Such a writing would be characterised by its flexible, varied balancing of oppositions, paradoxes and contradictions, rather than its heavy-handed use of rhyme and rhythm. Margaret Anne Doody's discussion of Augustan verse forms in *The Daring Muse* celebrated and redefined much of what was once simply labelled 'neo-classicism'. In her reading, for example, the heroic couplet is described as 'the perfect expressive form for stylistic self-consciousness' (Doody 1985, 232). She argues that the couplet permits the play of various languages and provides a 'natural pattern' for 'double-tongued statement' (263). Her thinking has done much to close the perceived gap between the form of prose and that of poetry in the period. It has also certainly influenced the presentation of literature of the period given here.[4]

Equally as influential as Margaret Doody's work have been Roger Lonsdale's ground-breaking anthologies, *The New Oxford Book of Eighteenth-Century Verse* (1984) and *Eighteenth-Century Women Poets* (1989). These suggest that the poetry of the eighteenth century is far more diverse than we had ever expected, that, for example, it certainly includes a greater number of lyrics, that apparently 'Romantic' form, than we had previously thought. No longer could we accept the convenient route of reading through the eighteenth century as the progressive narrative of how a classical period gave way to one of sensibility to one of romanticism. This teleology was parodied by Frye, who lamented that: 'Our students are thus graduated with a vague notion that the age of sensibility was the time when poetry moved from a reptilian Classicism, all cold and dry reason, to a mammalian Romanticism, all warm and wet feelings' (Frye 1956, 144). This view of the 'Augustan' period, largely associated with Pope, was quickly promulgated. In *Sense and Sensibility*, Jane Austen has Elinor mock the ways in which Marianne is ready to fall in love with Willoughby because his literary tastes agree with hers – both cannot be excited by the poetry of Pope: 'You know what he thinks of Cowper and Scott; you are certain of his estimating their beauties as he ought, and you have received every assurance of his admiring Pope no more than is proper' (Austen 1980, 40). Robert J. Griffin has traced the ways in which resistance to Pope's aesthetic came as early as the 1740s with Pope's immediate successors, Joseph and Thomas Warton and Edward Young (Griffin 1995). Thus 'warm and wet' feelings considerably predate the 1790s, the conventional dating of Romanticism, and might even be traced in the eighteenth century to Pope (in the passionate address of *Eloisa to Abelard*, 1717).

At the very least, then, it is more difficult to make the kinds of generalisations about literary periods that earlier critics made so blithely. George Saintsbury's book, *The Peace of the Augustans: A Survey of Eighteenth Century Literature as a place of rest and refreshment* (1916) and Oswald Doughty's *English Lyric in the age of reason* (1922) are easy targets because they display their critical convictions so confidently. But there is something of nostalgia, as well as rejection, in my attitude towards these books, because what is not clear, as yet, is what might replace these traditional denominations. We have problematised the generalisations upon which traditional literary history has been based as distorting, as selective, as amnesiac. But when we teach and study these periods, we still require these paradigms within which to situate even the most minute interest.

Eighteenth-century writers themselves are aware of these kinds of questions: questions of their own situation within literary history, of the tendency towards ever-greater specialisation and the separation of interests, and the temptations of intellectual refinement. Pope's attacks on scientists who pore over minutiae, while myopically missing the bigger picture, are certainly one such response. In *The Dunciad*, he rages against these scientific virtuosi and against the new kind of philology with its interest in non-canonical authors and in historicising the detail of texts. The labours of love of these philologists were scholarly editions of the classics, complete with learned commentaries, dictionaries, grammars, indexes, footnotes and emendations of difficult readings. Their attention to each precise word, or even syllable, is derisively dismissed as 'word-catching' (*Epistle to Arbuthnot*, l. 166). Traditionally, this attitude has been discussed as Augustan conservatism, the fearful rejection of new modes of knowing by those (Pope, Swift, Gay et al.) dedicated to shoring up convention and tradition. But this is to deny the Augustans some of their own polemic, particularly the judgement that it is foolish to pay attention to the particular at the expense of coherence, even if, in seeing the activity of such scholars as less than human, the argument itself is provocatively articulated:

> The critic Eye, that microscope of Wit,
> Sees hairs and pores, examines bit by bit:
> How parts relate to parts, or they to whole,
> The body's harmony, the beaming soul,

Are things which Kuster, Burman, Wasse shall see,
When Man's whole frame is obvious to a *Flea*. (Pope 1999, 306)[5]

While it is important to resist the impositions of a label, there is still
a need to discuss literature within a framework. If we think of literary periods as 'necessary fictions' and give equal weight to each of
these words, then we at least recognise the limits of our categories
before we begin.[6] In a transformed critical climate, in which more
writers are recognised as worth studying and former ways of reading are questioned, we are in a position in which we cannot accept
former generalisations about periods, but we cannot do without
some criteria for selection either, if we are to attempt to see a picture beyond the individual text. In the introduction which follows I
attempt to advance some ideas about how we might reconceive the
eighteenth century as a literary period.

## Notes

1. Many commentators have remarked on how such contemporary theories as feminism, marxism, cultural studies and deconstruction came
   to be applied to the eighteenth century much later than to other literary periods. (See Nussbaum and Brown 1987 and Damrosch 1992.)
   However, there has been much work of this kind done since the 1980s.
   See, for example (and with very different conclusions): Lund 1983,
   Atkins 1983, 1987, Rodino 1993 and Morrissey 1998.
2. Fairer and Gerrard situate *Jubilate Agno* in the mid-eighteenth century
   in reading it 'in terms of a wider mid-century search for authentic
   voices and primal experiences in the work of Chatterton and
   Macpherson' (1999, 386). Hawes 1999, situates the poem in the kinds
   of contexts sketched in this book: as interrogating the distinction
   between public and private modes of address.
3. See, for example, *An Essay on Criticism* and letter to William Walsh, 22
   October 1706 (1956, I 22–5).
4. For a defence of the heroic couplet from the kinds of modern reading
   habits which see only 'reason', 'stability' and 'order' in its form, see J.
   Paul Hunter 1996 and 2001. See also Donald Greene 1988, for the argument that stereotypes of Augustan literature are based on misreadings.
5. Compare also Pope's interest in garden design rather than the intricacy
   of individual plants (Pope 1956, III 451).

6. Suggested further reading on questions of canonicity and periodisation includes Frye 1956, Sitter 1982, Patey 1988, 1993, Griffin 1995, McGann 1996, Woodman 1998 and Siskin 1998. Among the most consistent and important interrogators of the eighteenth-century/Romantic distinction, particularly in regard to poetry is David Fairer. See for example Fairer 1984, 1996 and 1999.

# Introduction. Defining the eighteenth century: public sphere conversations

This book takes as its presiding motif for eighteenth-century literature the idea of conversation, around which there accrue associated ideas of coteries and literary groups, debates and disagreements, the public sphere and literary intertexts. Thus while 'conversation' is the dominant idea which links different parts of this book, and different aspects of eighteenth-century literature, it is not in any sense a single label. It generates a range of associated ideas, rather than necessarily imposing a determinist narrative upon the period. In this way, the book's account of the eighteenth century attempts to avoid what Hillis Miller terms '[t]he singleness of the label [which] implies the singleness of what is labelled' (1996, 197). The key term of conversation and its associated motifs are used in the awareness that they are appropriate also to other literary periods. Indeed, that is part of the attractiveness of choosing these as defining terms, in that they avoid the tendency to split off and demarcate literary periods as defined through contradistinction. The eighteenth century has especially suffered from this, as many accounts of the century are constructed as a foil by which 'Romanticism' can be identified. However, while I would agree that ideas of conversation and debate are certainly also important to other periods and other cultures, this book argues that there is a distinctiveness for these terms in the eighteenth century.

One of the most pervasive modes of approaching the century is through ideas of the public sphere, and particularly those of Jürgen Habermas. In *The Structural Transformation of the Public Sphere* (1962; first translated into English in 1989), Habermas defined an ideal model of rational, social conversation in which differences of status could be bracketed and a reciprocal and equal exchange of ideas and opinions guaranteed, at least theoretically. While Habermas acknowledged that such a public sphere was an ideal or

1

model, he also situated this public sphere in the history of eight-eenth-century Europe, and, in particular, England. Eighteenth-century society in these terms is characterised by its coffee-house culture, where men of different ranks meet freely, discuss econom-ics, politics and social customs and read and talk about newspaper reports and periodical essays. This is a culture which witnesses the growth of a general reading public, the expansion in the produc-tion of books, journals and papers, the establishment of lending libraries, reading rooms and reading societies and a whole network of clubs and groups in which the egalitarian principles of sociabil-ity and free discussion are formalised.

Habermas's theories have defended the ideals of the Enlightenment from (often poststructural) critiques of reason. Reason is defined in eighteenth-century terms, not as some kind of transcendental truth, but as a social activity, a kind of conversation, something which is endlessly open to debate and counterweight. Without dialogue and debate, rationality can only be tyrannical. Eagleton neatly summarises this argument: 'to persuade is not to dominate, and to carry one's opinion is more an act of collaboration than of competition' (Eagleton 1984, 17). Ann Kelly's account of Swift does not overtly address Habermas's terms, but her paraphrasing of Swift's attitude articulates the same kind of position: 'A single man's view is necessarily incomplete; completeness can be approached only when several minds come together' (Kelly 1988, 39). In Kelly's argument, this accounts for Swift's ambivalence towards the various clubs of which he was a member. Ideally, gatherings of mixed com-pany might produce a kind of sociable discourse in which openness towards others and tolerance of other viewpoints would be possible. In practice, however, many clubs merely fixed and entrenched error:

> [Swift] sarcastically praises the conversations of the October Club . . . for their ability 'very much [to] improve each others Understanding, correct and fix [their] Judgment, and prepare [themselves] against the Designs of the opposite Party'. . . As Swift's irony suggests, the self-reflexive members of the October Club were incapable of hav-ing enlightening discussions that might modify their crazy visions. (Kelly 1988, 39)

Swift's involvement in the Scriblerus Club was a happier one and, in place of the suspicions of self-interest and myopia which the

October Club generated, inspired warm recollections of conviviality and supportive friendship in which literary endeavours in particular might flourish.[1]

We can trace similar ideals in other key eighteenth-century writers too: Anthony Ashley Cooper, the third Earl of Shaftesbury, for example, whose essay 'Sensus Communis' (1709) celebrated communication as the expression of human sociability; or David Hume, who saw dialogue as an ideal form for philosophical texts and argued that a civilised culture might be known as one in which men and women were sociable, mixing and conversing pleasantly together (Hume 1996, 169–70).[2] However, their ideas – and those of Habermas – have been challenged by marxist, feminist and postcolonial approaches, which identify the ways in which these models are predicated on groups of white, upper-middle-class men, or, in the case of Hume, on essential differences between the sexes. That we might now see the Scriblerians as a group blinkered by self-interest, and in this every bit as ideological as the October Club Swift refused, suggests that our ideals are differently imagined. The exclusivity of the (male, middle-class, white) Scriblerians is not, for Habermas, incompatible with the ideals which he sketches, since the free conversations the Club envisages are *theoretically* possible for other (female, black, lower-class) people but it certainly questions the way in which the eighteenth century might be used as a historical model for these ideals. Such debates are important to this book's premise that the motif of 'conversation' can be used to characterise literature of the eighteenth century. If this motif excludes women writers, labouring-class writers or non-white writers, then this book will merely replicate the exclusions of older ways of considering the period. Sections throughout the book will consider the extent to which 'public sphere conversations' might be used of all writers, irrespective of their gender, class, or ethnicity.

While there have certainly been important feminist critiques of Habermas's theories, many of these take issue with a splitting of public and private, male and female, which is not true of Habermas's work, although it is true of many studies which cite Habermas as an influence.[3] Habermas's sphere of communicative rationality partakes of both the public and private spheres. While the public sphere is so defined because of its open discussion of matters of collective import, it is also characterised by the activities of private individuals outside the official zone of the state. In an excellent article on the implications of Habermas's theories for women of the eighteenth century, Lawrence Klein discusses how the eighteenth century defined 'public' in terms of sociability (Klein 1993). People at home, both men and women, therefore, were not necessarily in a 'private' sphere. Only if they were alone might they be so defined. When the bluestockings, a group of literary ladies, met in 'private' homes, then, their meetings were 'public' in so far as they were events of sociability. (That these women wrote and published also situates them there, as chapter 3 will discuss.[4]) Moreover, recent work by the historian Amanda Vickery has challenged the assumption that women were excluded from the 'public sphere', defined more traditionally as 'outdoor' spaces, or the worlds of business and politics. Vickery calls the eighteenth-century entrance of middle-class women into public places of pleasure a 'cultural revolution':

> [O]utside the house, urban entertainment flourished as never before. Most Georgian towns and cities of note experience an architectural and cultural renaissance, with rebuilding programmes, the laying-out of smart shopping streets and the creation of a recognisably modern leisure industry. . . . The impact on women's lives was nothing short of revolutionary, for what could a respectable young lady do for pleasure in the north before 1700? Precious little. Even in the grandest provincial towns like Newcastle, Manchester or York, a doctor's daughter or a merchant's wife would be lucky to find much in the way of entertainment beyond church, the races or a fair. By 1780, all that had changed. A lady could take her pick of concerts, plays, lectures, debates, exhibitions, balls and assemblies. (Vickery 2001, 2–3)

Vickery's thesis is certainly illustrated by Frances Burney's novel, *Evelina* (1778), in which her heroine, on two trips to London and one to Bristol Hot-Wells, is presented with a huge array of social activities: assemblies, the theatre, the opera, balls, museums, the pleasure gardens of Vauxhall and Ranelagh. The novel can sometimes seem like a veritable catalogue of what to do in these fashionable places. In two successive chapters, for example, the Branghtons argue over where they should go that evening: to George's (possibly the New Georgia, a tea house and garden in Hampstead, full of curiosities, or perhaps one of the many taverns in London); Don Saltero's (a coffee house and museum of curiosities in Chelsea); the Sadler's Wells, the Haymarket and Foote's theatres; the visitor attractions of the Tower of London, the Monument and St Paul's Cathedral; Vauxhall pleasure gardens where men and women might walk, listen to open-air concerts, drink tea and visit the picture room or the gardens at Marylebone which boasted in addition to these a mineral spring and, often, fireworks; taverns such as Mother Redcap's Tavern or White-Conduit House, which offered such diversions as cricket, a shrubbery maze, gardens and a fishpond; and the spa at Bagnigge Wells, which included tea arbours, a skittle alley, a bowling green, a grotto, a flower-garden, fish pond and fountain (305–13). While many of these places are too 'low' for the delicate Evelina, the complete list (or 'catechism' as Evelina calls it at one point) indicates the considerable extent of this sphere of pleasure. Evelina herself remarks at one point that public entertainments are 'almost as innumerable as the persons who fill them' (144).[5]

*Evelina* catalogues this world partly to show its dangers as well as its excitement for young and vulnerable women, such as Evelina. She is constantly besieged by preying men in many of these places and often finds herself ill equipped to behave according to the strict, unwritten rules of etiquette which dominate behaviour in such places as the public ball. This is recognisably the same world of Pope's *The Dunciad* (1728–43), a very different work which nevertheless invokes a very similar world of pantomimes, masquerades, harlequinades, fairs, operas, and pageants as its context. Many of the picaresque fictions of the eighteenth century comically transpose the travelling adventures of the *picaro* to various other kinds of travellers: a dog (in Francis Coventry's *The History of Pompey the Little; or, the Adventures of a Lap-Dog*, 1751), a coat (in *The Adventures of a Black Coat*, 1760), a guinea (in Charles Johnstone's *Chrysal; or, The Adventures of a Guinea*, 1760–5), a bank-note (in Thomas Bridges, *Adventures of a Bank-Note*, 1770–1), and a corkscrew (in *The Adventures of a Corkscrew*, 1775). In all of these works, the culture of polite society and its customs and rituals take centre stage. In Deirdre Lynch's words, these novels 'were more intent on imagining society than imagining the self' (1998, 7).[6]

This public world of conversation, debate and sociability informs eighteenth-century literature beyond that of the ostensible content of many eighteenth-century novels, or the desire for dialogue on the part of many eighteenth-century thinkers. The material conditions of literature in this period support these key terms in a particular way. The particularly public address of print; modes of publishing such as subscription publishing and the formation of powerful alliances of printers; the rise of a reading public, of which the growth in lending libraries and reading groups is an indication; and the rise of what we would now recognise as literary criticism – all of these are aspects of literary production which we accept as commonplace but which were only establishing themselves in the eighteenth century. Then there are the practices of writers themselves, the popularity of literary groups and coteries, the frequency of collaborative authorship, or the tradition of answering or continuing works by other authors and the tendency to publish revised editions of one's own or one's friends' works. At the level of literary form there is the new interest in such genres as the newspaper, the periodical and the novel; an interest in letters and in literary genres which borrow from letter writing such as verse epistles, poetic dialogues and epistolary fiction and the popularity of parodies and burlesques. All of these aspects are features of the literary history of the eighteenth century. All embody a public or conversational aspect. Existing at these three levels, then – that of publishing and reading practices, of composition and of literary form – the key motif of conversation gathers around it a cluster of associated terms and practices which together make the eighteenth century distinctively 'conversational'.

This introduction will consider each of these aspects briefly, before turning to more extensive readings and considerations of exemplary writers and texts in the chapters which follow.

## Literary groups and coteries: from the Scriblerians to the Bluestockings

Behind the authors of this book's title, Pope and Burney, lie the significant networks of friends and writers within which both worked. Although Samuel Johnson wrote up his age as an age of authors (in *Lives of the Poets*, 1779–81), this was in no way a period in which individual authors worked in lonely garrets, cut off from the rest of society with only their genius for company. While arguably no literary period might be characterised by such a stereotype, the eighteenth century in particular refuses this view of the relationship between the writer and the world. The subtitle of this book, *Scriblerians to Bluestockings*, gestures towards the 'clubbable' nature of eighteenth-century literary culture and this impulse dominates the book. Instead of choosing years in which Pope or Burney published significant works, for example, the title years hint towards their coterie influences. The years 1714 and 1779 represent significant dates for the 'Scriblerians' and 'bluestockings' respectively, the sociable contexts in which Pope and Burney might be said to have written. They do not inaugurate and end any distinct formation: no years might now be confidently said to do the kind of work which '1709' (date of Pope's first publication) or '1798' (publication of Wordsworth and Coleridge's *Lyrical Ballads*) might once have done. With the expansion of the canon and the increasing tendency to pursue rather than ignore the complexities of literary and cultural history, any choice of years would be inevitably arbitrary. The kinds of cultural mapping I construct here – of ideas of conversation and debate – cannot be demarcated in any straightforward fashion. It would certainly be possible to argue that a better starting point would be earlier (with Dryden and his circle of wits in Will's Coffee-House in the late seventeenth century) or a better finishing point later (with the final demise of the bluestockings, in the early nineteenth century). With the Scriblerians and the bluestockings, however, we have two literary groups which dominate and represent our views not only of the early and later eighteenth-century periods but also our views of male and female coteries.

The 'Scriblerians' are invariably central to our views of the early part of the eighteenth century. Scriblerian was the name given to a group of friends comprising the writers Alexander Pope, Jonathan Swift, John Gay and Thomas Parnell; the physician of Queen Anne, Dr Arbuthnot; and the Tory politician, Robert Harley, Earl of Oxford. The Scriblerians met privately, most usually at Arbuthnot's room in St James's Palace, and sometimes as often as every evening, but the original club met only for a few months (January to July 1714) before political misfortunes dispersed the group. After Queen Anne's death and the subsequent removal of the Tory party from office, Swift and Parnell returned to Ireland, Arbuthnot moved out of St James's Palace, and Oxford was impeached and sent to the Tower. Scriblerian activity continued, however, since the major collaborative project they began in 1714 continued to be written – *The Memoirs of Martinus Scriblerus* (finally published in the second volume of Pope's *Works in Prose*, 1741) – and works published independently continued the association. For example, Pope's *Dunciad Variorum* (1729) contained a prolegomena and footnotes by the same fictional pedant 'Martinus Scriblerus' and the penultimate chapter of the *Memoirs* hints towards *Gulliver's Travels*. Martinus's Travels are to an empire of pygmies, a land of giants, a kingdom of philosophers and in his fourth voyage Martinus discovers a 'Vein of Melancholy proceeding almost to a Disgust of his Species' (Kerby-Miller 1988, 165). This scheme very closely parallels Gulliver's voyages to the diminutive Lilliputians, the giant Brobdingnagians, the projectors and professors of Lagado and his fourth voyage, in which Gulliver becomes alienated from humans and in thrall to the perfections of the Houyhnhnms. While the Scriblerian Club was originally founded so as to enjoy good company together, its members quickly began writing together. Even after they had dispersed, the Scriblerians continued to regard themselves as a discrete group, with Scriblerian activity resumed in later years, particularly in 1726 and 1727, the period during and following Swift's return visits to England. Many of their writings are 'Scriblerian' in character (usually read as a mode of satire on false learning) and Brean Hammond has suggested that we ought to think of 'Scriblerian satire' as a precise kind (1988a). The context of the Scriblerians is thus an important one for a number of the following chapters (chapters 1, 4 and 5, in particular).

The apparent 'end' point of the book, 1779, gestures towards another literary group, now possibly more famous than the Scriblerians – the bluestockings. Their notoriety is a mixed one, because the word 'bluestocking' has entered common use to denote a bookish woman, more at home with learned study than with domestic chores. Bluestockings are rarely now treated seriously, their name suggests that they are merely figures of fun. This response too has eighteenth-century antecedents. In her collection of anecdotes *Thraliana* (1775–1809), Hester Thrale wrote of how the term 'bluestocking' came to be used by those who wanted to ridicule female wits. Although by the late 1770s the term 'bluestockings' was being applied only to women, it originally designated a small group of friends of both sexes. The term was coined by Admiral Boscawen, from the stockings of Benjamin Stillingfleet, who, too poor to buy evening dress, attended gatherings in his daytime blue worsteds. It was later given currency by Hannah More's poem *The Bas Bleu; or Conversation* (1786), in which More suggested that the bluestockings were the true upholders of England's Enlightenment. While 1714 is an obviously significant date in the history of the Scriblerians, since this is when the Club was first consciously formed and began working on projects together, there is no comparable date for the bluestockings. Partly this is because they were less aware of themselves as constituting a group. Their history stretches from their earliest meetings, as a group of mixed company, in the 1750s, to the death of Elizabeth Montagu in 1800. We can also speak of a first generation of bluestockings (Elizabeth Carter, Elizabeth Montagu, Hester Chapone, Catherine Talbot, Elizabeth Vesey) and a second generation (Hester Thrale, Hannah More and Frances Burney). Although Burney is not always treated as a member of the bluestockings, she did refer to herself as a bluestocking (*Diary*, June 1780) and her career intersects with the bluestockings in significant ways. The bluestockings built up a subscription list for her third novel, *Camilla* (1796), and Burney made a note in her journal of every published reference to the bluestockings she encountered, thus revealing a rare consciousness of the bluestockings as a discrete group and a cultural phenomenon. While Burney is sometimes named as a second-generation bluestocking, she also seemed to lampoon the ideals of bluestocking culture. In 1779 she wrote, but did not publish, *The Witlings*, a comic attack on the bluestocking circle with which she herself had been associated and which she alluded to in subtitling the play, *by A Sister of the Order*. The first time Hester Thrale used the term 'bluestockings' to refer to a group exclusively of women was to note that *The Witlings* was not staged because of the 'fear of displeasing the female Wits – a formidable Body, and called by those who ridicule them, the *Blue Stocking Club*' (Piozzi 1942, I 381n; annotating a passage written in 1779). In the play Lady Smatter is thought a great critic because she labours over finding faults and objections in authors such as Pope and Shakespeare, even though she has not as yet read more than halfway through their works. Mrs Sapient declares how she cares only for the mind while instructing the milliner as to her hat trimmings (Burney 1995, I 21, 15). Burney pokes fun at the vanity and egotism of these learned ladies. However, the ideal of enlightened and polite company remains despite, or even through, the satire.

Burney's satirising of fake and pretentious learning in *The Witlings* may not have been intended as an attack on the bluestockings, although both her father and closest family friend ('Daddy' Crisp) urged her not to publish the play, lest she incur the wrath of the formidable Elizabeth Montagu. As this book will show, there were many literary groups and learned coteries in the eighteenth century, any one of which may have been intended as the play's target. Burney's Esprit Club with its founding members of mixed sexes does not altogether support the anti-feminism which some commentators have seen in this play.[7] Burney may have intended to poke fun at groups in general. Club culture is as much satirised as it is celebrated throughout the century: in *The Spectator* (1711–12 and 1714), Addison and Steele imagined a club of mixed, polite company, but their periodical still included humorous pieces on such imaginary and even preposterous clubs as the Chit-Chat Club (at which Mr Spectator, their guest speaker, is permitted to speak for one minute in ten without interruption), the ugly club, the fringe-glove club, the hen-pecked club and a club of widows. The satire, however, remains and links Burney to the Scriblerians of the earlier century, with their common aim to denounce false learning. It is appropriate, therefore, that Burney signed a letter to her father at the time of writing *The Witlings* (25 July 1778) 'Francesca Scriblerus' (Burney 1994, III 51), albeit recalling the dunce Martinus Scriblerus rather than the witty Scriblerians in her typical, self-deprecating pose.

In addition to the Scriblerians and the bluestockings, there are many other literary groups. The chronology below gives the most significant of these, and, where possible, approximate dates for their existence:

1696–1709      The Kit-Cat Club. Although this Club had as much a political (Whig) as an artistic flavour, it did form an important centre for literary patronage. Its strongly aristocratic element also marks it out as distinct from its eighteenth-century successors. Its secretary was the printer Jacob Tonson the elder and members also included the writers Joseph Addison, Sir Richard Steele, William Congreve and Sir John Vanbrugh.

1710–18   The Buttonians. This group met at Button's Coffee House. Its members were all writers, including Addison and Steele (authors of *The Tatler* and *Spectator* papers), Ambrose Philips, Thomas Tickell, Henry Carey and Leonard Welsted. At their gatherings, copies of verses were presented for inspection and essays for the latest periodical planned. Although Pope was once a visitor, a rift developed between Pope and the Buttonians after Thomas Tickell reviewed his *Pastorals* in unfavourable comparison with those by Philips. The falling-out was very public.

1712–15(?1721)   The Easy Club: a club of young Scottish nationalists who shared literary interests. Their members included the poet Allan Ramsay who found a sympathetic audience for his early poems there.

1714–41   The Scriblerians.

1720–4   The 'Hillarian' circle. This literary group included Aaron Hill, Eliza Haywood, John Dyer, David Mallet, Susanna Centlivre, Martha Fowke Sansom and Richard Savage. Haywood and Savage collaborated on poems largely dedicated to 'Hillarius', a poetic persona given to Hill by Haywood and many of the poems composed and exchanged by members of the group were eventually published in *Miscellaneous Poems and Translations*, compiled by Savage and published in 1725.

1755/57–1760s   The Nonsense Club. Founded by the writer Robert Lloyd, its members also included William Cowper, George Colman, Bonnell Thornton and possibly Charles Churchill. The Club specialised in satire and parody. Colman and Thornton edited the periodical *The Connoisseur* (1754–6), in obvious imitation of *The Spectator*.

1764–94   Known as 'Dr Johnson's Literary Club' or simply 'The Club', this group existed for 30 years. Its members included the painter Joshua Reynolds, the politician Edmund Burke and the writers Samuel Johnson, Oliver Goldsmith, Bishop Percy,

Richard Brinsley Sheridan, James Boswell and the actor David Garrick. Founded as a small group of friends, with just 9 members, it grew to become a more formal Club with, eventually, 35 members.

1760s–1800    The Bluestockings.[8]

Such a list is by no means exhaustive. Samuel Johnson was involved in at least four groups, for example. In addition to the Literary Club of which he was a founding member, he was also central to the group which met at the home of Hester Lynch Thrale in Streatham. Here he met the Burneys, father and daughter, and became one of the first champions of Burney's novel *Evelina*. Then there was the literary circle in Lichfield, his home town, where he met Erasmus Darwin, Anna Seward, Thomas Day and Richard Lovell Edgeworth in the informal setting of domestic drawing-rooms. These salons had no formal name and no particular self-consciousness of themselves as groups, unlike, for the most part, those named above. However, they did operate in exactly the same manner as many of these groups, with regular meetings at which work-in-progress might be discussed. By far the greatest number of eighteenth-century literary groups operated in this more informal way. The networks of exchange, support and influence between writers were certainly considerable. In Dublin, for example, Swift met regularly with a group of friends, often assembled around the card table. In her *Memoirs* Laetitia Pilkington reports group editing sessions in Dublin at the house of Swift's friend Patrick Delany for the purpose of 'correcting . . . undigested Materials' for presentation in Mary Barber's 'Collected Poems' volume (Pilkington 1997, I 283). Despite its apparent informality, as merely a gathering of friends, their meetings did have formal club aspects. They met every Thursday evening, for example, and Swift referred to it more than once as a club.[9] Similarly productive circles of mixed company surrounded Richardson and Johnson. In addition to Samuel Richardson's circle of lady advisers – those who read his fiction in both manuscript and printed versions and commented upon its plots and characters – were the many women writers, with whom he met and worked: Charlotte Lennox, Sarah Fielding, Frances Sheridan, Laetitia Pilkington, Jane and Margaret Collier. Thomas Gray's reluctance to publish his work sprang from the desire to write only for a small audience, in effect a coterie of friends, such as Richard West and Horace Walpole, with whom he could exchange manuscript verses and thus recreate the intimacy of manuscript as opposed to the potential anonymity of print culture.

## Collaborative writing

Given the extent of literary groups and networks of literary friends, it is not surprising that eighteenth-century literature has a significant number of collaboratively or jointly written works. Thomas Gray first considered publishing only in a joint volume with his close friend Richard West and many of his early poems were written as responses to West's own poetry. While collaborative or joint authorship is most usually the result of this kind of close friendship, there are often other causes too. Because generic distinctions are fluid and not as strictly demarcated in the eighteenth century as they would later be, the early novel frequently included interpolated poems or short narratives. Thus in Delarivier Manley's *New Atalantis* (1709) there are two previously unpublished poems by Anne Finch; within Richardson's *Clarissa* (1747–8) we find Elizabeth Carter's poem 'Ode to Wisdom'; and Smollett's novel *Peregrine Pickle* (1751) includes the notorious memoirs of Lady Vane, later reprinted separately.

The most celebrated examples of both joint and collaborative writing, however, occur within circles of literary friends. Colman and Lloyd wrote burlesques of odes by Mason and Gray, supposedly at a meeting of the Nonsense Club, for example. And while the Pope and Swift *Miscellanies* (1727–32) probably originated as an attempt to foil Curll's pirated edition of their miscellaneous works (1726), they quickly became a testimony to their friendship above all else. Pope wrote to Swift of how the *Miscellanies*, in placing works by both together in one volume, would represent their intimacy:

> Our Miscellany is now quite printed. I am prodigiously pleas'd with this joint-volume, in which methinks we look like friends, side by side, serious and merry by turns, conversing interchangeably, and walking down hand in hand to posterity; not in the stiff forms of learned Authors, flattering each other, and setting the rest of mankind at nought; but in a free, unimportant, natural, easy

manner; diverting others just as we diverted ourselves. (Pope 1956,
II 426)

Pope's address is not the flattery of hailing Swift as a fellow canonical poet. Instead their joint volumes are to represent to posterity
the close amity between them. Verses will be chosen not for their
autonomous aesthetic qualities but for the ways in which they por-
tray a conversation between the two friends.[10]

While the *Miscellanies* are obviously the work of two hands, the
precise authorship of a number of Scriblerian pieces is impossible
to decipher. In its 'variorum' edition, *The Dunciad* is probably
the result of several contributors. Pope appealed to Swift to contribute to the commentary, and quite possibly included suggestions and notes from others in his circle. He also drew upon Savage
for details of the book trade, permitted Warburton to write many of
the notes for *The Dunciad in Four Books* (1743), and possibly used
epigrams sent in by readers. *The Dunciad*'s most recent editor,
Valerie Rumbold, notes the difficulty, even impossibility, of determining the authorship of its annotations, in cautioning: 'although
it is overwhelmingly likely that Pope wrote most of the notes himself, I have tried to avoid implying that any particular note is necessarily his' (Pope 1999, 2). Opponents of the Scriblerians were
fond of claiming fake sympathy with Gay because he had to bear
the shame for unpopular works (such as the stage farces *Three
Hours After Marriage* and *The What D'Ye Call It*) which, they
claimed, had been written collaboratively. Lady Mary Wortley
Montagu was so ready to perceive the Scriblerians as a group, that
she believed *Gulliver's Travels* was written by Pope, Swift and
Arbuthnot. The extent of Pope or Arbuthnot's input into these
works is unlikely ever to be known. But that they were written collaboratively was certainly the perception, or at least a motivated
misreading, of the Scriblerians' opponents.[11]

Similar questions have hovered over a significant number of
eighteenth-century texts. To what extent, if any, did Henry Fielding
help in the writing of Sarah Fielding's *The Adventures of David
Simple* (1744 and 1753)? Since Richardson discussed *Conjectures
on Original Composition* (1759) so thoroughly with its putative
author, Edward Young, to what extent is he a co-author of this work
on originality (an especially ironic example of collaborative writing)? In *The Female Quixote* (1752), the heroine's absurdities are

cured when a clergyman teaches her that fictions are not 'copies of life and models of conduct' but 'empty fictions'. Arabella's reformation is effected when she is encouraged to leave romance fiction for morally improving fiction, such as Richardson's novel *Clarissa*:

> Truth is not always injured by Fiction. An admirable Writer of our own Time, has found the Way to convey the most solid Instructions, the noblest Sentiments, and the most exalted Piety, in the pleasing Dress of a Novel. (Lennox 1980, 377)

To many commentators, this chapter ('Being in the Author's Opinion, the best Chapter in this History') is so obviously influenced by Dr Johnson that he must be its author. Or perhaps Lennox wrote this chapter in imitation of Johnson's prose style and known attitude towards fiction in general and Richardson's novels in particular.

Questions of attribution are difficult but fascinating in the eighteenth-century period because while they frustrate our attempts to fix 'authority', they exemplify the ways in which writers were coming to terms with a print culture which increasingly desired to name them. A playfulness with print culture characterises a significant number of eighteenth-century texts. Swift, for example, rarely published under his own name, using instead a variety of publishing tactics to disguise, or partially obscure, his signature, including piracy, pseudo-piracy, clandestine publication, anonymous and pseudonymous publication, misattributions and misreadings. Even Johnson, who did more than most to secure the idea of the modern, individual author, wrote a significant number of pieces which were published under the names of friends, sometimes as a personal favour to help a needy friend, sometimes to protect his own identity (as in his continuing attacks on Macpherson's forgeries of a putative third-century bard, 'Ossian').[12]

That questions of attribution were resolved, if sometimes incorrectly, by eighteenth-century readers suggests that the publishing world of this period had a confident belief in itself as a knowable community. There is certainly often the sense that literature, particularly in the early part of the century, is created out of a small number of closely affiliated writers, booksellers and publishers. While literary circles did flourish outside London, the extent of London's dominance of eighteenth-century print culture is still unquestionable. Swift suggested to Pope that he ought to annotate his poem *The Dunciad* for the benefit of those readers who lived beyond London, thinking of his own circles of friends in Dublin. The influence of powerful figures in London such as Pope, Johnson and Richardson was obviously immense. They certainly could and did make careers for friends and associates. Partly this is because of the importance of subscription publishing in the period and of the anthology or miscellany form. It was these forms which would make literary success beyond London possible in the later part of the century. Lady Miller, for example, hosted poetical assemblies and her Batheaston poetry contests in the 1770s were well known, if derided by London literati as amateur affairs. She urged Anna Seward to send verses to these competitions, which in turn were published. This method permitted Seward to publish without jeopardising respectability and to achieve fame beyond her home town of Lichfield. The following account, published in *The New Prose Bath Guide* (1778), gives us an insight into how the competition was organised, and suggests its contemporary notoriety:

> on certain Days, a great Deal of Company meet, who possess poetical Talents, and who admire them. In one of the Rooms of this Villa, stands an antique Vase, into which the Ladies and Gentlemen put Copies of Verses, written on certain given Subjects, which being drawn out, and read by one of the Company, the Majority of them determine which Piece has the most Merit, and then the Author is called upon to avow it; this being done, the LADY of the VILLA, presents the Author with the Wreath of Myrtle; and preserves the several Productions thrown into the vase, till they are bulky enough to compose a little Volume, some of which have been published . . . under the Title of 'Poetical Amusements at a Villa near Bath'.
> (Quoted in Brewer 1997, 602)

In all, four volumes of these anthologies were published (1775, 1776, 1777, 1781). By virtue of their miscellaneous collection, the gathering together of writing by different hands, anthologies of poetry, and even periodicals with their frequently diverse essayists, represent a kind of literary group or community too. A collection such as *Poems by a Literary Society: comprehending Original Pieces in the several Walks of Poetry* (1784) testifies to its origins in a literary circle, now unknown. When Richard Savage was threatened with the poorhouse, a group of friends (the 'Hillarian circle' described above) charitably subscribed and contributed to a collection of poems to save him from this fate. *Miscellaneous Poems and Translations. By Several Hands* (London: Samuel Chapman, 1726) was the result, including poetry by Savage himself and by William Congreve, Matthew Concanen, John Dyer and Aaron Hill among others. And, as Michael Suarez has argued in his recent edition of Dodsley's miscellany, *A Collection of Poems by Several Hands* (1748–58), even this significant collection was largely the result of Dodsley's gentlemen friends who acted as consultant editors, contributors and, most importantly of all, brought in contributions through their own networks of influence and friendship. Literary history has tended to think of this collection as a significant act of literary canonisation: Suarez's studies suggest that friendship played a much more central role in the choice of poets (Dodsley 1997, I 93–9). All of these anthologies are social as much as literary enterprises. Subscription publishing was also responsible for this print form of sociability, since it stamped a book with the physical presence of supporters when subscribers were listed on title pages.

### The emergence of a reading public and subscription publishing

In 1792 the bookseller James Lackington wrote of what he perceived to be a revolution in the reading habits of the British people. His claim was that the sale of books had increased fourfold since the early 1770s:

> The poorer sort of farmers, and even the poor country people in general, who before that period spent their evenings in relating stories of witches, ghosts, hobgoblins etc., now shorten the winter nights by hearing their sons and daughters read tales, romances etc., and on entering their houses you may see Tom Jones, Roderick Random, and other entertaining books stuck up on their bacon racks &c. If *John* goes to town for a load of hay, he is charged to be sure not to forget to bring home 'Peregrine Pickle's Adventures'; and when *Dolly* is sent to market to sell her eggs, she is commissioned to purchase 'The History of Pamela Andrews'. In short, all ranks and degrees now READ. (Quoted in Brewer 1997, 188)

The image of farmers hooking novels to their bacon racks is a rather idiosyncratic one, but it does convey Lackington's impression that culture is diffused throughout communities on an unprecedented scale. The picture, predictably, is more complicated than this would suggest, with literacy rates and the cost of buying books still making much of literary culture beyond the means of the labouring classes. But the eighteenth century certainly witnessed a significant increase in the numbers of those literate enough to read, wealthy enough to buy books and with enough leisure time to both read and discuss with others their reading. Thus it is to the eighteenth century that we conventionally trace the emergence of a reading public. This is defined not just as a public which reads, but a public which sees literature at the centre of its culture, and defines itself through reading. The self-image of a reader in the eighteenth century is that of one of a community of readers. The emergent genres of newspaper, periodical, novel and literary criticism made literature newly public, opened a public space for literature, a space in which it was appreciated, evaluated and even lived out. By 1724 London had three daily papers, seven papers published three times a week, and six weekly journals. This gives an indication of the appetite for news and for print which the print culture of the century fostered.

If we consider the prints of Hogarth, whose paintings are most typically used as visual records of life in eighteenth-century London, there appears to be a striking omission in his illustrations. In none of Hogarth's works do we see someone reading an English novel of the eighteenth century. In the print 'Before', there is a volume of 'Novels', probably referring to the popular amatory fictions of the early century, but not to what traditional literary history would come to term 'the novel'.[13] His prints depict people visiting masquerades, ballad operas and puppet theatres and we certainly see people reading or selling ballads, newspapers and crime and trial reports – but never a specific novel. In his series of engravings entitled *Industry and Idleness*, for example, we see only a ballad version of Defoe's work *Moll Flanders*. So if the emergence of a reading public, one particularly interested in and constituted through the reading of novels, can be traced to the eighteenth century, why is this not reflected in these images? Looking at the Hogarth prints reminds us that the reading public was still relatively exclusive. Later in the century, *The Critical Review* criticised the charity schools for placing too much emphasis on reading and writing and not enough on 'labour and industry' (Donoghue 1995,

60). Contrary to what James Lackington claimed in 1792, then, the character of the reading public in the eighteenth century is solidly middle and upper class. Lackington chooses as an image of a reader the unusual figure of the farmer. A much more representative portrayal would be the middle-class coterie. Susanna Highmore's drawing of Richardson reading a manuscript copy of his novel *Sir Charles Grandison* to a circle of friends (1751) illustrates how reading was importantly social. Although the activity of reading itself might often be solitary, fashionable circles discussed together what they read. Additionally, the earlier practice of reading aloud continued throughout the eighteenth century, especially within families and circles of friends such as those discussed above. Many of the manuals on speaking aloud (such as James Burgh's *The Art of Speaking*, 1768; Thomas Sheridan's *Lectures on the Art of Reading*, 1775, and William Cockin's *Art of Delivering Written Language; or, An Essay on Reading*, 1775) were used to instruct in the best practice of reading to friends.[14]

The correlation to these reading habits within the sphere of publishing was the important eighteenth-century method of subscription publishing.[15] Once a projected work was commissioned or encouraged, a list of supporters would be secured. They would make a financial contribution to the publishing of the work, often paying a small sum both in advance of publication and on receipt of their copy of the book. This kind of financial support was attracted in various ways: friends, acquaintances and friends of friends might be personally applied to, advertisements might be placed in newspapers, subscription tickets sold in parks or resorts, or a proposal might be included in a previous publication. Each subscriber might well pay a relatively small sum, so that for the first time the middle classes were able to support literary work in what was effectively a form of 'collective patronage', in Terry Eagleton's phrase (1984, 29). Because no one individual was responsible for the work's public appearance, literature, it was believed, was thus freed from its vulnerability to corruption, bribery and the accusation that what was being sold was only flattery. When subscription publishing replaced individual patronage as the dominant mode of publishing major works, it seemed, many interests replaced the single interest. Of course, there was still a reflected glory in being a subscriber, with your name proudly printed at the beginning of the volume. As Susan Staves has written, 'the new class of the polite is visible in Pope's subscription lists – lords, private gentlemen, doctors, lawyers, bankers, publishers, actors, ladies – mingled together in lists partly alphabetical, partly by rank, all subscribers being grouped by the initial letter of their last names and then, roughly, by rank within each letter' (quoted in Eagleton 1984, 30). This image of egalitarianism and hierarchy co-existing in the listing of the names is entirely apposite for the eighteenth century, with its increasingly bourgeois, but still gentrified culture. In practice many of the wealthiest subscribed for numerous copies, a largesse which was also often recorded on the subscription lists and thus drew attention to conspicuous wealth. (For Gay's collected poems, 1720, for example, Lord Burlington and the Duke of Chandos subscribed 50 copies each.) Even for the middle-class subscriber of one copy, however, the list played on his or her desire to be seen to be a literary reader.

Publishers obviously benefited from this type of financing, in which they ran few or no financial risks themselves. But it was also a mode which fostered, and developed out of, the kinds of networks of literary friends and supporters detailed above. Johnson and Richardson were both assiduous in encouraging subscribers for other writers, for example. Richardson helped to organise the subscriptions for James Thomson's very popular eighteenth-century poem, *The Seasons* (1730). Johnson spent over 15 years courting subscriptions for Anna Williams's *Miscellanies in Prose and Verse* (1766), which, when published, earned her £300. Elizabeth Carter's financial success in publishing her translations of the Greek philosopher Epictetus (1758) – 1200 subscribers yielded a profit of almost £1000 – permitted her to live comfortably thereafter, devoting herself to the life of the mind and the companionship of her bluestocking friends.

The publishers themselves are not excluded from the kind of collectivity I am sketching as typical of eighteenth-century culture. Many publishers founded partnerships or 'congers' to share the cost of publishing books, particularly the cost of copyrights. The word 'conger', meaning an association of booksellers, is recorded by the *Oxford English Dictionary* as appearing for the first time in 1700. In 1691, however, the publisher John Dunton had used the term to satirise greedy publishers: 'Why', he says, ''tis an *over-grown Eel*, that devours all the Food from the weaker Grigs, and when he wants other Good, swallows them too into the bargain. A *poor Fly* can't stir upon the water, but – pop, he's at him.' (*Voyage round the World*, quoted in Hill 1958, 17). Publishing congers were designed to control the trade and made publishers increasingly powerful. One aspect of this power is particularly relevant for this book's thesis: that, as Barbara Benedict's research has shown, 'these congers encouraged writers to form coteries that promoted specific literary values' (1996, 109). Smart commercial sense, then, as much as the more idealistic fostering of communities, accounts for these business practices. Because the eighteenth-century publisher was often also the bookseller, a specialisation of taste occurred around his or her shop.

Yet the printed text, unlike the manuscript copy, had no way of excluding potential readers. There are many notable and interesting examples of former strangers becoming friends just through shared reading. This is as true of the new lending libraries as it is of relations between many authors and their readers. The friendship between Richardson and Lady Bradshaigh, for example, was forged through her reading of his fiction. Distressed by the rumours that Richardson would eventually have his heroine Clarissa die, she wrote an anonymous letter to plead that he save her. Richardson replied through an advertisement in the *Whitehall Evening Post*, and thereafter she wrote directly and minutely to him of her feelings in reading further volumes of *Clarissa* and her suggestions for alternative endings. They finally met after the exchange of many letters over a period of 18 months. Many eighteenth-century authors and readers commented upon how reading was a form of conversation. The most famous of these is Sterne's comment in *Tristram Shandy* that 'Writing, when properly managed, . . . is but a different name for conversation' (87) but Diderot's letter of praise to Richardson ('Eloge de Richardson' in the *Journal étranger*, January 1762) also celebrates the intimacy between author and reader: 'O Richardson! Whether we wish to or not, we play a part in your works, we intervene in the conversation, we give approval and blame, we feel admiration, irritation and indignation. How many times have I caught myself, as happens with children being taken to the theatre for the first time, shouting out: *Don't believe him, he's deceiving you . . . If you go there it'll be the end of you. . . .*' (1994 82). The emergence of the lending library and the book club entailed that the relationship between author and reader would no longer be even theoretically a private or exclusive one.

## The circulating library, the book club and literary reviewing

One of the most famous readers of the eighteenth century is the fictional Lydia Languish in Sheridan's play, *The Rivals* (1775). She spends most of her time with her head full of the books which she has borrowed from the local library. Since it is unlikely that she could afford the number of books which she reads, borrowing from the library allows her access to a wider number of books than she could possibly buy. In Sheridan's acerbic comedy, this is not altogether to her benefit:

Act I, scene ii
Lydia Languish *sitting on a sofa with a book in her hand.*
Lucy [her maid], *as just returned from a message*
**Lucy** Indeed, ma'am, I transferred half the town in search of it. I don't believe there's a circulating library in Bath I ha'n't been at.
**Lydia** And could not you get *The Reward of Constancy?*
**Lucy** No, indeed, ma'am.
**Lydia** Nor *The Fatal Connection?*
**Lucy** No, indeed, ma'am.
**Lydia** Nor *The Mistakes of the Heart?*
**Lucy** Ma'am, as ill luck would have it, Mr Bull said Miss Sukey Saunter had just fetch'd it away.
**Lydia** Heigh-ho! Did you inquire for *The Delicate Distress?*
**Lucy** Or, *The Memoirs of Lady Woodford?* Yes, indeed, ma'am. I asked everywhere for it; and I might have brought it from Mr Frederick's, but Lady Slattern Lounger, who had just sent it home, had so soiled and dog's-eared it, it wa'n't fit for a Christian to read.
**Lydia** Heigh-ho! Yes, I always know when Lady Slattern has been before me. She has a most observing thumb, and, I believe, cherishes her nails for the convenience of making marginal notes. Well, child, what *have* you brought me?
**Lucy** Oh! here, ma'am. (*Taking books from under her cloak, and from her pockets*) This is *The Gordian Knot*, and this *Peregrine Pickle.* Here are *The Tears of Sensibility* and *Humphry Clinker.* This is *The Memoirs of a Lady of Quality, Written by Herself*, and here the second volume of *The Sentimental Journey.* . . .
**Lydia** Very well – give me the sal volatile.
**Lucy** Is it in a blue cover, ma'am?
**Lydia** My smelling bottle, you simpleton!

(Sheridan 1998, 15–16)

Lydia is obviously a figure of fun – her absurd fixation on books means that she talks about little else. It is hardly surprising after this catalogue of titles that her maid misunderstands her instruction for smelling salts to be a request for some further exotic reading (*The Sal Volatile* suggesting perhaps a French novel of shady virtue, rather like Lady Vane's rather 'fast' memoirs). The passage also suggests how the lending library creates a community of readers, each of which come to recognise each other and their tastes and foibles, if not always their personal habits.

The first libraries were founded in 1725 in Bath and Edinburgh. After the first London library (1739), libraries became a widespread means of disseminating books. By 1800 there were 122 circulating libraries in London and 268 in the provinces. They were called circulating libraries because they allowed books to be read by a wide circle of readers. Those who joined such libraries had to pay a subscription fee but this method allowed the middle classes, and even some domestic servants, to borrow a number of books relatively cheaply. Subscription was usually between half a guinea and a guinea a year. Thereafter books could be borrowed at the rate of a penny a volume or threepence for the usual 3-volume novel.[16]

Libraries were just one of the ways in which books such as novels were more extensively disseminated. Most novels continued throughout the eighteenth century to be relatively expensive, usually 6–10 shillings. Thus an average novel would cost more than a labourer's average weekly wage or the day's wage of a skilled craftsman. In the Elizabethan period, most could have afforded the penny to stand in the pit of the Globe and watch one of Shakespeare's plays. But the money required to buy an eighteenth-century novel would feed a family for a week or two. This explains why none of Hogarth's lower classes are reading novels: instead we see them reading ballads, chapbooks, stories of criminals, newspapers – all of which were cheaper.

However, there were some ways of surmounting this expense in addition to borrowing from the circulating libraries. Pirate copies of books undercut the prices of the major London booksellers. Many pirated editions came from presses in Edinburgh or Dublin, fighting the monopoly of the London publishers who usually controlled copyright. But pirated editions also came from unscrupulous

London publishers, such as Edmund Curll, who often sold cheaper abridgements of pirated copy. In addition, secondhand copies of books were sometimes sold off more cheaply at auctions. The most effective way of disseminating 'literature', however, was through the cheaper newspapers. Defoe's prose fiction *Robinson Crusoe* (1719) was originally sold for 5 shillings, quite a prohibitive price for all but the secure middle classes. But it was reprinted in the newspaper, the *Original London Post*, three times a week, as well as in cheap duodecimos and chapbooks. Newspapers were a considerably cheaper form of dissemination, not only because they could be produced and sold much more cheaply than a novel which had to be bound and attractively laid out with generous margins and heading spaces, but also because newspapers circulated much more extensively. When eighteenth-century gentlemen met in the coffee houses of London (and there were perhaps as many as 3000 of them), to gossip of politics and financial speculations, drink coffee or tea and smoke tobacco, they were also often there to read the newspapers. Addison claimed that every copy of *The Spectator* was read by 20 people in this way (No. 10; 12 March 1711).

This practice of sharing reading was formalised in the book club. This would usually include around 20 members, each of which would contribute a small sum. The total of their subscriptions permitted a number of books to be purchased and then shared between the members. Most of these clubs existed outside of London and many purchased only ephemeral works of especially topical notoriety. However, the larger clubs – such as the Huntingdon Book Club Society, established in 1742 – bought more expensively (folio and quarto editions rather than cheaper pamphlets) and more widely (novels by Sterne and Richardson).[17] These book clubs operated as intimate, exclusive kinds of circulating libraries. But they also parallel the development of literary criticism as a distinct kind of writing and response, since these groups undoubtedly discussed their reading just as much as they circulated books. Among the earliest plans to develop an exclusively literary periodical were those of a literary club which gathered around Edward Cave, the editor of the *Gentleman's Magazine*, in December 1748. The group began planning a journal that would 'give an impartial account of *every* work published, in a 12d. monthly pamphlet' to be called the *Monthly Review*.[18] This work never materialised, and it would seem to be unrelated to the first literary periodical, the *Monthly Review* directed by the bookseller Ralph Griffiths, which was established within three months of Cave's plans (in February 1749). It is suggestive, however, that these literary reviews came out of the kinds of groups of professional writers which this chapter has already identified as important to literary culture in this period. Moreover, while reading practices in the eighteenth century were undoubtedly becoming more private and individualised, the development of recognisable forms of literary criticism suggests that reader response is still imagined in terms of sociability. Readers join together as a public 'in the cultural activity of literary judgment' (Benedict 1996, 12).

All of these modes of reading meant that the individual reader would always have had a sense of him or herself as part of a reading community. Institutions such as the book club, the lending library and the rise of professional literary criticism fostered a consciousness of reading at the same time as others, and those who read the newspapers, periodicals and most recent novels, poems and plays, had the added consciousness of being up to date. This is the 'contemporaneity and simultaneity' which Gianni Vattimo sees as characteristic of modernity (1991, 10). Earlier, predominantly manuscript, cultures fostered other kinds of reading experiences and other kinds of group identity. In the eighteenth century, this new sense of being part of an imagined community of other readers made even solitary reading seem distinctly social.[19]

## Conversational circles and texts

The aspects of eighteenth-century literary culture discussed in this introductory chapter might be characterised as aspects of a material cultural history, a history of the literary production of the period. Recent research on authors, readers, publishers and the modes of publication has certainly enriched our sense of the complexity and the vitality of the period. The remainder of the book develops out of this work in tracing the ways in which ideas of sociability and public conversation extend beyond aspects of material production – in the formation of actual literary communities and groups and in the ways in which the eighteenth-century author envisages her readers as part of a reading community (chapter 1); in the important literary forms of the novel, the familiar letter, the dialogue and the periodical (chapter 2); and of the conscious interrogation of the ideals and limits of eighteenth-century circles by women writers in particular (chapter 3). These chapters illustrate that while the ideal of sociability was often present in eighteenth-century literature, authors were also acutely conscious of their failure to achieve the ideal through print. Part II of the book suggests that eighteenth-century texts might be situated in the context of a disputatious print culture, in which all published texts were open to creative misreadings, revisions and defences. Three short chapters position Pope's mock-epic poem *The Dunciad*, Swift's mock-travel account *Gulliver's Travels* and Richardson's influential prose fiction *Pamela* in this context, but examples of the 'textual conversation' I refer to in this section are legion. Gay's popular success, *The Beggar's Opera* (1728), inspired Allan Ramsay's pastoral drama, *The Gentle Shepherd* (1729), performed with a schoolboy cast; an Irish version by Charles Coffey, *The Beggar's Wedding* (1729); a pantomimic version with a Harlequin Macheath (*The Beggar's Pantomime*, 1737) and many others, including Gay's own sequel, *Polly* (1729).[20] And, within poetry, for example, there is Lady Mary Wortley Montagu's reply to Swift ('The Reasons that Induced Dr S- to write a Poem call'd the lady's Dressing Room' mimics and attacks Swift's 'The Lady's Dressing Room'), or Mary Collier's rebuke of Stephen Duck (*The Woman's Labour* replies to *The Thresher's Labour*). The 'conversations' here are not always amiable or sociable, as the last two examples in particular indicate. If not, however, they situate eighteenth-century literature in a context of public debate and argument, of noise and factionalism. In this way, they epitomise the literary communities described in the first section of the book and represent something of both the ideals and necessary tensions created in thinking about eighteenth-century communities of various kinds.

The most popular form of portraiture in the eighteenth century was the 'conversational circle' which often depicted a domestic family group or an informal gathering of mixed company. (One example, by Peter Angellis, is reproduced on this book's front cover.) But the period did not only think in terms of circles or groups, but also of cabals (with their connotations of factionalism) and coteries (with theirs of exclusivity). Habermas's ideal is one in which a public comes together in all its diversity and thus achieves a form of representativeness. Debate and dialogue rely upon mixed companies of different characters, with different attitudes and opinions. Print culture permits women, labourers and former slaves to write and to publish (albeit sometimes in compromised terms). But another problem haunts the ideal: that speakers will always only represent their own interests, and fail to be persuaded or transformed by the process of debate. In a number of issues *The Female Tatler*, for example, discusses a Table of Fame for women, one which might rival, or at least supplement, the all-male Table proposed in *The Tatler*. The captain's lady speaks on behalf of Penthesilea and other Amazonian women. The second to speak is a domineering wife, who argues that female governors should have pride of place. A widow argues on behalf of widows and takes offence at a spark's mischievous reference to the Ephesian matron (who famously consoled herself for the death of her husband with the soldier guarding his body). A lady who married a rake celebrates those women who have conquered jealousy, while the unmarried ladies of the assembled company declare chastity to be the greatest feminine virtue (Goldsmith 1999, 68). Like many eighteenth-century texts, this issue of *The Female Tatler* articulates the anxiety that the ideal social circle is often also a coterie, or, in this particular example, a collection of coteries, cabals, or special interest groups. At times, these representations remind us of the alternative philosophies of the eighteenth century and of the scandalous figure of Mandeville (and behind him, Hobbes) in particular. Against those who argued that man was inherently sociable (including Shaftesbury, Hutcheson, Smith and Hume), Mandeville argued that a successful society was one in which the 'vices' of greed and self-interest flourished because they benefited the economy. When the second, expanded edition of *The Fable of the Bees* was published (1723), a scandal ensued and Mandeville continued throughout the century to be held as a figure of immorality and ill-repute. However, he remained an influential figure, despite the notoriety and professed repudiation of his views.[21]

This book demonstrates that, for all their repudiation of Mandeville, eighteenth-century writers were also anxious about the impossibility of sustaining the sociable ideal. In her collection of anecdotes and scraps of miscellaneous writing, Hester Thrale recorded the following story:

As I plucked this Morning an Apple from a Tree I recollected the following Story & resolved to write it down. There is at Bromley in Kent
a College for Clergymens Widows, where twenty of them live retired
& are called the *Ladies* of the College: they have £20 a Year each & a
separate house consisting of three Apartments to themselves. For
many Years they had an Orchard too, which was enjoyed in common; till perceiving that their annual Disputes at the Apple Season
ran so high, & sowed such Feuds among 'em for the following Year;
they at last agreed to cut the Trees down, & Give them their Chaplain
for Fire Wood. How happy would Mandeville have been with this
Story. (Piozzi 1942, I 4)

This fragment suggestively alludes to Mary Astell's plans for an
exclusively female community (*A Serious Proposal to the Ladies*,
1694 and 1697) and to Sarah Fielding's interrogation of the ideal of
female community in *The Governess* (which opens with a squabble
among the schoolgirls over an apple). It reminds us that groups and
circles are not necessarily progressive formations. The family
reading circles which Patricia Michaelson (1989) discusses, for
example, are far from radical models of egalitarianism. Instead,
communal reading was often used as a form of censorship: only
certain kinds of books were permitted, offensive passages were qui-
etly deleted and moralistic commentaries interrupted the reading
of the text. It is important to remember that the eighteenth-century
fear of the reader was of the solitary reader, free from parental or
social control. Thus conversational circles and literary communities
might enable or prohibit women's writing; might provide a safe
venue in which experimental, innovative writing could be attempted or might seek to reinforce literary conventions and encourage
only imitations; might fold any or all readers into fictional communities or might seek to exclude all except the privileged few of the
coterie. In short, the meanings of such key terms as 'public conversations', 'literary communities' and 'conversational texts' are not
certain, only that these were crucial ideas for eighteenth-century
writers, whether they were embracing or refuting these as ideals.

**Notes**

1.  Though invited to dine with them, Swift never did become a member
    of the Tory October Club, because of their opposition to Harley's min-

istry. He was, however, a member of the Brothers Club, formed as a Tory counterpart to the Kit-Cat Club. Swift became disillusioned with this Club because of its extravagance, its failure to accomplish anything of note (such as the encouragement of poetry) and because, in growing from 12 to 20 members, it had, in Swift's opinion, become too large a society.

2. Shaftesbury's essay was reprinted in *Characteristicks*, 1711, which went through at least ten editions in Britain between 1711 and the 1790s. The bluestockings Montagu, Carter and Talbot all read and commented upon the *Characteristicks*. For its importance to the eighteenth century, see Klein 1994, and to the bluestockings, Heller 1998.

3. For representative feminist critiques of Habermas, see Pateman 1989, Fraser 1992 and Landes 1998. For an account of criticisms of Habermas which nevertheless defends his continuing relevance, see Backscheider 1996.

4. For a very interesting account of the bluestockings in relation to Habermas and theories of social space, see Heller 1998.

5. For useful cultural and social histories of public entertainments, associations and clubs, see Stallybrass and White 1985, Borsay 1989, Barry 1994, Brewer 1997, and Clark 2000.

6. For discussions of these 'circulation' narratives see Douglas 1993, Lynch 1998 and Bellamy 1998.

7. Compare the comic satire of a *conversazione* of learned ladies debating Shakespeare in Sarah Fielding's *David Simple* (Book II, ch 2).

8. For accounts of the Kit-Cats, see Solkin 1992, 27–47 and Brewer 1997, 40–4; for the Easy Club, see Law 1989; for Johnson's Club, see Brewer 1997, 44–50; for the Nonsense Club, see Bertelsen 1986.

9. Swift 1963–5, I 121; II 67; III 191.

10. Schakel 1993 argues that Pope increasingly attempts to imitate Swift's mode of poetry, inspired by the editing of these *Miscellanies*. Scouten 1981 argues that Swift attempted to imitate the poetry of Pope in the late 1720s. Both are very persuasive arguments!

11. For Wortley Montagu on *Gulliver's Travels*, see Wortley Montagu 1965–7, ii 71–2. Edward Young also thought the work was collaboratively written. For attacks on the collaborative writing of the Scriblerians, see chapter 1 below.

12. For the ironies of Johnson – author of *Lives of the Poets*, a work which created the modern idea of individual, canonical authorship – writing collaboratively, see Woodmansee 1994.

13. See Wagner 1995, 13–20.

14. Hunter's very persuasive account of the novel discusses its rise in terms of the development of a 'culture of the closet', which marked a modern shift towards silent solitary reading (1990, 157). However,

recent work on eighteenth-century reading practices suggests many more communal reading practices than was previously thought. (See Michaelson 1989, Tadmor 1996, and Raven 1996.)

15. Subscription publishing was much used in the seventeenth century for scientific, theological and law publishing. However, the first subscription for English poetry was Tonson's posthumous edition of *Paradise Lost* (1688) and the first subscription for a living poet was his edition of Dryden's *The Works of Virgil* (1697).

16. See Porter 1982, 253 and Watt 1957, 43.

17. On book clubs, see Fawcett 1968, Kaufman 1969, 36–64, Oldfield 1989, Brewer 1997, 182–3 and Manley 1999.

18. See Carlson 1938.

19. On the transition from a manuscript to print culture, see Kernan 1989, Love 1993 and Ezell 1999.

20. *Polly* was banned by the Lord Chamberlain for its perceived political satire, although it was published by subscription.

21. For example, Adam Smith explicitly attacked Mandeville at the end of *The Theory of Moral Sentiments* (1759), but as Gillian Skinner has argued, there is considerable proximity between Mandeville and Smith (Skinner 1999, chapter 4). See also Bellamy 1998, *passim.*

# Part I

# Conversational Forms

# 1 Literary Communities

The more . . . refined arts advance, the more sociable men become: nor is it possible, that, when enriched with science, and possessed of a fund of conversation, they should be contented to remain in solitude, or live with their fellow-citizens in that distant manner, which is peculiar to ignorant and barbarous nations. They flock into cities; love to receive and communicate knowledge; to show their wit or their breeding; their taste in conversation or living, in clothes or furniture. Curiosity allures the wise; vanity the foolish; and pleasure both. Particular clubs and societies are everywhere formed: both sexes meet in an easy and sociable manner; and the tempers of men, as well as their behaviour, refine apace. So that, beside the improvements which they receive from knowledge and the liberal arts, it is impossible but they must feel an increase of humanity, from the very habit of conversing together, and contributing to each other's pleasure and entertainment.

(Hume 1996, 169–70)

In this passage from his essay 'Of Refinement in the Arts', David Hume identifies the 'spirit of the age' as one of sociability. Men, and women, meet in polite and easy company and together they create a revolution in manners and thinking. Crucially, they need one another: men can educate and elevate female understanding, women can refine and make more polite the behaviour of men.[1] Although Hume's is the more famous, Henry Fielding's essay 'On Conversation', published in his *Miscellanies* (1743), makes broadly similar points: 'Man is generally represented as an Animal formed for and delighted in Society' (DeMaria 1996, 825). Similarly, if more briefly, Samuel Johnson referred to his own period as a 'clubbable' age (1775). Clubs, societies, coteries, conversational circles, literary groups, salons, coffee houses – all of these are ideas and spaces we associate with the eighteenth century. Eighteenth-century literature also associated these ideas with its own culture. While other cultures and histories have just as good a claim on many of these terms, it is the eighteenth century that presents these ideas as its own dominant self-image. The very term 'sociability' was coined by natural law theorists in the early eighteenth century as a response to the sense that 'society' existed outside of the state. This is the foundation on which Habermas builds his theory of an eighteenth-century public sphere.

This chapter takes the theme of 'literary communities' as a deliberately capacious trope in which various aspects of eighteenth-century society and literature can intertwine. Literary communities here include historical literary groups, writers meeting together, formally or informally, inspiring and encouraging each other's work; literary representations of community; and the interactions between readers and writers. All of these different kinds of literary formation figure in this chapter as a way of considering eighteenth-century self-representations. However, the idealised consensus of Habermas's public sphere is also under challenge in the eighteenth century, as writers and artists fear the splintering as much as they celebrate the consolidation of community. Eighteenth-century literature self-consciously adopts the task of representing society to itself, but this then entails showing the splits, factions and divisions which characterise society as much as the ideals of community. Hume's and Fielding's 'sociable' and Johnson's 'clubbable' era resonate with Gay's much darker vision of eighteenth-century society in *The Beggar's Opera* (1728), especially in Lockit's expression of it: 'Lions, wolves, and vultures don't live together in herds, droves or flocks. Of all animals of prey, man is the only sociable one. Every one of us preys upon his neighbour, and yet we herd together' (Gay 1986, 98–9). Similarly, while many books dedicated to the art of conversation presented talk as a sociable and ethical ideal, they also articulated anxieties about the talker's capacity to lie to and to bully others.[2] The tropes of textual conversations and literary groups that underlie this book, then, are not always ideal formations, but they present debates that are distinctive to the eighteenth century in their pervasiveness and significance. Central to the ideas and practices of literary sociability are the literary groups – real and fictional – which pervade eighteenth-century literature.

## Literary groups

When Virginia Woolf imagined her hero/heroine Orlando returning to eighteenth-century London, she represented her as being mesmerised by the image of Dryden, Addison and Pope together at the Cocoa Tree chocolate house. Woolf's own footnote draws attention to the obvious historical error here which can be corrected with reference to 'any textbook of literature'. (Dryden died in 1700, when Pope was only 12, too young to drink chocolate in public places.) The error is never corrected however, because the names of the three writers function as an 'incantation' to Orlando, awakening her own aspiration to be a writer. This ambition will also draw her to the social parties of the Countess R——, where, it is reported, Pope occasionally visits. Woolf's cameo portrait attempts to represent the era, even if only in caricature. Her talismanic image of the eighteenth century is of writers meeting together, in coffee houses and in drawing rooms. Eighteenth-century literary clubs and writers often drew upon the images of the circle of wits surrounding Dryden which met at Will's Coffee-house or of Addison's 'little Senate' at Button's or of Pope's group of Scriblerians meeting around St James's Palace. Steele announced in the first issue of *The Tatler* (12 April 1709) that accounts of poetry would be dated from Will's Coffee-house, in obvious allusion to Dryden's circle. *The Guardian* set up a famous lion's head at Button's, through which readers might post letters to the periodical (No. 98 3 July 1713). Fielding and Sterne drew on aspects of Scriblerian culture: Fielding signing many of his plays as 'Scriblerus Secundus', Sterne rewriting the Scriblerian work of *The Memoirs of Martinus Scriblerus* in *Tristram Shandy*. Other writers also paid homage to the Scriblerian name: Bonnell Thornton published occasionally under the pseudonym 'Martin Scribbler, Jun', Burney signed herself in a whimsical letter to her father as 'Francesca Scriblerus' and the labouring poet James Woodhouse published *The Life and Lucubrations of Crispinus Scriblerus* (c.1795). The appeal of the literary group was obvious. Whether literary or not, groups certainly offered writers an immediate audience for their works, a supportive and safe environment in which to experiment and to innovate, a group of friends who might aid in the publication and positive reception of their books.

Of the formal literary groups, the Scriblerians are certainly the most significant. Their interaction fostered writings and publications that are now central to our ideas of early eighteenth-century literary culture. In addition to the support and inspiration which they gave to one other, there are a number of collaboratively written works. The most interesting of these is *The Memoirs of Martinus Scriblerus*, the account of the education of an eccentric pedant, brought up by his father Cornelius according to a slavish devotion to the ancients. Although the full text was not published by Pope until 1741, its origin can be dated to early 1714, when the Scriblerians met as a club in Arbuthnot's rooms in St James's Palace. Martinus is first introduced to us as 'a certain Venerable Person, who frequented the Out-side of the Palace of St James's' (Kerby-Miller 1988, 91), as if a Scriblerian-manqué. Accused of criminal conversation by a Spanish man – when, Martinus claims, he had looked upon his wife's inner thigh only in the interests of the purest science, to study the miraculous pomegranate which blossomed there – Martinus Scriblerus now roams the world, out-cast from society, trusting in the editor of the memoirs to make known his discoveries. In an introduction addressed to the reader, Pope assumes the guise of Scriblerus's historiographer, he who found the manuscript of the memoirs on the pavement of Pall-Mall (haunt of the Scriblerians who met at least once in a Pall-Mall coffee house outside St James's). This introduction immediately frames Martinus as a central figure for the Scriblerians as a group:

> he for some years continued his Correspondence, and communi-
> cated to me many of his Projects for the benefit of mankind. He sent
> me some of his Writings, and recommended to my care the recovery
> of others, straggling about the world, and assumed by other men.
> The last time I heard from him was on occasion of his Strictures on
> the Dunciad; since when, several years being elaps'd, I have reason
> to believe this excellent Person is either dead, or carry'd by his vehe-
> ment thirst of knowledge into some remote, or perhaps undiscov-
> er'd Region of the world. (93–4)

The explicit allusion to Scriblerus's commentary on Pope's *Dunciad*, the implicit allusion to Swift's *Travels into Several Remote Nations of the World*, and the correspondence of projects by which to reform mankind all point to the Scriblerian circle. Within the *Memoirs* itself, the account of Martinus's birth, education and early life draws upon the knowledge and interests of all the Scriblerians. For example, Martinus's birth prefigures the rage against hack writing: 'on the night before he was born, Mrs Scriblerus dream'd she was brought to bed of a huge *Ink-horn*, out of which issued several large streams of Ink' (98) and such quarrels as that of Cornelius Scriblerus with his son's wet-nurse over her eating beef (105–7) draw upon Arbuthnot's knowledge and interests in medical debates. Not only does the penultimate chapter hint at Martinus's voyages to those lands Gulliver would explore, but as a child his father invented for him 'a Geographical suit of cloaths' to help him understand the world: 'He had a French Hat with an African Feather, Holland Shirts and Flanders Lace, English Cloth lin'd with Indian Silk, his Gloves were Italian, and his Shoes were Spanish: He was made to observe this, and daily catechis'd thereupon, which his Father was wont to call "Travelling at home" ' (107). Pope later noted that the character of Martinus Scriblerus was chosen as that of 'a man of capacity enough; that had dipped into every art and science, but injudiciously in each' (Sherburn 1934, 76). Martinus as an individual stands as an inverse image of the group (who would see themselves as having dipped judiciously into many arts and sciences). Martinus's fractured, contradictory nature is invoked as a satire on Locke's theories of the discontinuities of identity, because the self is constituted by a consciousness which can always alter:

> Crambe would tell his Instructor, that All men were not *singular*, that Individuality could hardly be praedicated of any man, for it was commonly said that a man *is* not the same he *was*, that madmen are *beside themselves*, and drunken men *come to themselves*; which shews, that few men have that most valuable logical endowment, Individuality. (119)

Passages of this sort satirise theories of individual identity and figure Martinus, appropriately, as many-selved. In this way, Martinus can be seen as an inverted image of his many creators and a mirror of the medley form of *Memoirs* themselves in which 'whenever [the Reader] begins to think any one Chapter dull, the style will be immediately changed in the next' (94).[3]

Pope's conversations with Spence concerning *The Memoirs* suggest that its collaborative publication was important to the Scriblerians' self-image as a group. He spoke, for example, of how the project 'was begun by a club of some of the greatest wits of the age. Lord Oxford [Robert Harley], the Bishop of Rochester

[Francis Atterbury], Mr Pope, Congreve, Arbuthnot, Swift, and others. Gay often held the pen; and Addison liked it very well, and was not disinclined to come in to it' (Sherburn 1934, 76). Here, Pope extends the image of collaboration beyond the Tory interests of the formal Scriblerian group (Pope, Swift, Parnell, Arbuthnot, Gay and Oxford). He boasts how '[t]he Deipnosophy consisted of disputes on ridiculous tenets of all sorts', alluding to the art of learned discussion while dining which takes its name from Athenæus's *Deipnosophistae* (written after A.D. 228). This recounts imagined discussions at a series of fictitious banquets attended by a varied and extensive cast of prominent intellectuals. These discussions are riddled with quarrels and conversations on a wide variety of subjects, ranging from the dishes before them to literary criticism. The Scriblerians were certainly proud of their status as a group, or 'deipnosophy'. They wrote many joint letters to fellow members, composed humorous poetic invitations to club meetings and referred to themselves as a club long after they had all dispersed from St James's Palace. The following playful invitation, each couplet written by a different contributor, illustrates the self-consciousness of the Scriblerians as a club:

> The Invitation                         [April 10?, 1714]
>
> My Lord, forsake your Politick Utopians,
> To sup, like Jove, with blameless Ethiopians.
> > > > > Pope.
>
> In other Words, You with the Staff,
> Leave John of Bucks, come here and laugh.
> > > > > Dean.
>
> For Frolick Mirth give ore affairs of State,
> To night be happy, be to morrow great.
> > > > > Parnell.
>
> Give Clans your money, us your smile
> your Scorn to T[ownsh]end & Ar[g]ile
> > > > > Doctor.
>
> Leave Courts, and hye to simple Swains,
> Who feed *no* Flock upon *no* Plains.
> > > > > Gay.

The Reply                                    Apr: 10: [1]714

You merry five who filled with blisful nectar
Can Phillips sing as Homer chanted Hector
I wil attend to hear your tuneful Lays
And wish yr merits meet with one who pays –
(Kerby-Miller 1988, 353–4)[4]

Each couplet names the club member by handwriting, signature and theme. Pope echoes his translation of *The Iliad* (in which the Greek gods do not deign to 'grace / The Feasts of *Aethiopia*'s blameless Race'); Swift uses the most comic rhyme ('Staff'/'laugh') and, like Parnell, exhorts Oxford to leave politics and join their fun; the Scottish Arbuthnot writes of the topical case of the government giving money to the clans; and Gay was to publish his mock-pastoral series, *The Shepherd's Week*, just five days later (15 April 1714). In turn Oxford's reply alludes to the Scriblerian feud against Ambrose Philips, whose pastorals had been praised in *The Guardian* at the seeming expense of Pope's. Although this was initially Pope's battle, it quickly became a Scriblerian one too. Philips told his friends at Button's Coffee-house, according to Pope's own report, that Pope 'was entered into a cabal with Dean Swift and others to write against the Whig interest, and in particular to undermine his own reputation and that of his friends Steele and Addison' (Pope 1956, I 229).

In addition to sharing literary feuds and cultural values – a disdain for shallow or arcane knowledge, contempt for what they perceived as populist writing – we can find countless textual echoes among their works. Both Swift and Pope use the image of the spider to symbolise the modern hack writer (in the *Battle of the Books* and *An Epistle to Dr Arbuthnot*). In the introduction to *A Collection of Genteel and Ingenious Conversation*, Swift invokes 'bamboozle' and 'bite' as colloquialisms still in use (Swift 1995, 113); in *The Beggar's Opera*, Lucy laments how she has been 'bamboozled and bit' (Gay 1986, 91). References in their letters and reported conversations also make explicit the extent to which they inspired and encouraged each other's work. The inspiration for Gay's ballad opera, *The Beggar's Opera*, is usually traced to Swift's suggestion that he write a 'Newgate Pastoral' (1963–5, II 215). In Pope's poem *An Epistle to Dr Arbuthnot* (1735), Pope dramatises himself as in deep conversation with Swift (ll.272–8) and Pope's later dialogue poems might be read as attempts to recreate the context of the

Scriblerian club after its demise. Pope's comments to Spence about the writing of *The Memoirs of Martinus Scriblerus* suggest a nostalgia for the heady days of 1714 when the group met regularly in London: 'The design [of *The Memoirs*] was carried on much farther than has appeared in print; and was stopped by some of the gentlemen being dispersed or otherwise engaged (about the year 1715)' (Sherburn 1934, 76).

Many later groups might be cited as continuing the kind of literary camaraderie evident among the Scriblerians. The Nonsense Club, for example, fostered collaborative writing. Colman and Thornton's joint editing of the essay journal *The Connoisseur* with contributions from other club members and the *Two Odes* (1760) which burlesqued the poetry of William Mason and Thomas Gray and which were written by Colman and Lloyd are the most notable examples. They also produced many works inspired by the group and addressed to group members, such as Robert Lloyd's many verse epistles to his friends. The club also had its own literary ethos, a 'cultivated flippancy' which delighted especially in burlesque (Bertelsen 1986, 56). Hannah More's argument in 'The Bas Bleu: or, Conversation' (1787) is that the mixed company at Elizabeth Vesey's parties, which included Edmund Burke, Horace Walpole, Samuel Johnson, Lord Lyttleton, Elizabeth Carter and Elizabeth Montagu, is a company which fosters knowledge, taste and the arts. Here the visitors 'strike new light by strong collision' (l. 323). This poem echoes the many paeans to conversation that were published in the eighteenth century. Like Fielding's 'An Essay on Conversation', for example, it depicts the social exchange of learning and wit as not only the most important use of talents but also the most virtuous. More's poem is specifically female-centred: Montagu, Boscawen and Vesey are credited with reforming conversation; the virtues of Conversation, Mind and Attention are all addressed as female; and the poem functions throughout as an extended compliment to Elizabeth Vesey. Vesey's position within the bluestocking circle is exclusively as a friend and hostess. Unlike others of the group, she did not publish, did not even 'write' (if we exclude her letters to bluestocking friends and a sentimental correspondence with Laurence Sterne). But Vesey's parties were celebrated within the group, especially because, by 'breaking the circle', she checked the tendencies to boredom, detraction and staring which characterised companies which sat in a complete circle. More concludes her poem by arguing that the kindness and patience of Vesey's 'attention' represented a 'moral beauty' which makes her social parties a model of good company in distinction from the noisy sparring of wit found, for example, in the famous French salon, the Hôtel de Rambouillet.

Literary groups such as the Scriblerians, the Nonsense Club and the bluestockings survive in the writings which they inspired and in the representations of coterie and salon life which they influenced. Fictional representations of clubs of authors or literary critics appear in a number of eighteenth-century texts: in Thomas Gordon's *Humourist* (1720), Sarah Fielding's *The Adventures of David Simple* (1744), David Fordyce's *Dialogues concerning Education* (1745) and in Tobias Smollett's *The Adventures of Humphry Clinker* (1771), for example.[5] That writers were commonly thought to work together in supportive relationships can be seen in Goldsmith's account of the society of authors in *The Citizen of the World* (1760–1). Goldsmith's fictional Chinese traveller, Lien Chi Altangi, is intrigued by the huge number of books which he sees crowding from the press. To explain this phenomenal publishing rate, his English friend, the Man in Black, takes Lien to a club of authors where he meets doctor Nonenity, Tim Syllabub, Mr Tibs and Lawyer Squint. All are writers of various kinds: the doctor, despite his silence, writes indexes, essays on the origin of evil and philosophical enquiries on just about anything; Tim Syllabub writes riddles and bawdy songs; Mr Tibs writes anything from receipts for the bite of a mad dog to Eastern tales; and Lawyer Squint, writer of political speeches for hire, can also write the history of every new play and is full of 'seasonable thoughts upon every occasion' (Goldsmith 1969, 100). The account is primarily an attack on hack, commercial writing: few writers appear on Lien's first visit because the bailiff calls and, on his second visit, the poet who attempts to read work-in-progress is made to pay for the privilege, as enshrined in the club's laws. It suggests, however, that even mediocre writers imitate the successes of such predecessors as the Buttonians and Dr Johnson's Club, of which Goldsmith himself was a member.

The conceit of the literary group also underpins many eighteenth-century periodicals: later issues of *The Female Tatler* (1709–10) are ostensibly written by a 'Society of [six] Modest Ladies' and *Letters of the Critical Club* (1738) is composed of letters from each of the seven club members. The use of the club device in periodicals is often perfunctory. In *The Female Spectator* (1744–6), for example, the female club is only occasionally mentioned. However, all these depictions of literary groups form part of a strong tradition throughout the eighteenth century of satirical and comic depictions of club life. This tradition is particularly evident in the essay-periodicals, and in *The Spectator* (1711–12, 1714) in particular. *The Spectator* certainly contains the most significant collection of fictional clubs among the periodicals. Examples include the Everlasting Club (No. 72; 100 men ensure that the club is always in session by taking turns to retain a 24-hour vigil), the She-Romps (217; rowdy club meetings permit women to attack prudish behaviour, sometimes by literally attacking a prude), the Rattling Clubs (630; men who interrupt church services), even a club formed to reread *Spectators* (553). In all, some 38 societies are mentioned in *The Spectator*. A few are real clubs (such as the notoriously rowdy Mohocks and the Tory club of which Swift wrote, the October Club), but most are imaginary.[6] That they were a popular feature of *The Spectator* is suggested by the imitation of these clubs in *The Guardian*: in accounts of a Short Club (91–2), Tall Club (108), Silent Club (121), Dumb Club (132) and Terrible Club (143). We know that Pope wrote the two essays on 'The Club of Little Men' for *The Guardian* (25 and 26 June, 1713). These essays were published under the pseudonym of 'Bob Short' and detailed how the door of the club room was made lower, so as to admit no man of above 5 foot, and how the statutes decreed immediate expulsion to anyone caught standing on tiptoe, wearing tall hats or wigs, riding a horse above 14 hands or wearing heels of more than one and a half inches. Other comic fictional clubs in later periodicals include the 'Fiddle-Faddle' club of ladies, who write to *The Grub-Street Journal* (No. 176; 10 May 1733) that women are not sufficiently esteemed, but who spend all their time gossiping about fashion and beaux and complaining about the *Grub-Street*'s tendency to report on politics; the 'Eating Club' who complain of extravagant diets in *The Connoisseur* (No. 87; 1755); the club of virtuosos, a society of anti-social pedants each of whom obsessively collects different curiosities, halfpennies, *Gazettes*, English books printed in the black character, as described in Johnson's *Rambler* (No. 177; 26 Nov. 1751); and Goldsmith's description of various clubs in *The Busy Body* (13 Oct. 1759) – the choice spirits club (who sing popular songs until the drink runs out and they disband for the evening), the muzzy club (who smoke their pipes in silence), the club of fashion (who compete in flattering two titled gentlemen) and the society of moral philosophers (whom the writer finds arguing, not about religion or priesthood, but about who has not paid their membership).

One extended and especially detailed example of club life is Alexander Hamilton's three-volume *History of the Ancient and Honorable Tuesday Club*. Although there was a historical Tuesday Club in Annapolis (1745–56), the minutes of which survive, Hamilton wrote up the 'History' of the club as a comic fiction. This account delights in club culture, most conspicuous in the proliferation of its club vocabulary: clubical, clubific, clubarians, clubically. Club activities are recorded in detail, such as anniversary speeches, mock trials of members, letters, club conundrums and other riddles, poems and songs, pseudo-learned essays and digressions, and toasts. The book is necessarily then both hybrid, or 'puzzlementationful' in Hamilton's term, and comic. The club's anonymous historian sketches club culture as intrinsically light-hearted:

> none but your merry, droll, facetious, Jocose, good humored, risible companions, punsters, comical Story tellers, and *Conundrumifiers*, ought to be members of those nocturnal assemblies, called Clubs, for the Quintessence, marrow and main fulcrum of Clubs consists in gayiety, Jollity, pleasantry and Jocosity. (Hamilton 1995, 22)

Among the most important laws of their constitution is the 'Gelastic Law', by which men are laughed down should they raise contentious issues of religion or government. In his essay 'Sensus Communis: An Essay on the Freedom of Wit and Humour' (1709), the Earl of Shaftesbury identified raillery as the key reflex around which groups could cohere, as the spontaneous laughter of the group would make their agreement explicit. The Gelastic Law of the Tuesday Club might almost have been created in conscious imitation of Shaftesbury's theory. The law, however, is not sufficient to prevent the demise of the club, through luxury, pride and ambition. For example, the club almost dissolves after 'sederunt' (or meeting) 112, when Mr Quircum Comic writes a letter insulting cats (the President's favourite pets) in retaliation for the President's disapproval that he host the sederunt at the School House (130–2). The book is ultimately unfinished, as Hamilton died while still writing the history. In its existent state, of 14 books, it marks the rise and fall of the club. Key to this narrative is the struggle between the club's President and the Chancellor: President Nasifer Jole wanting to arrogate supreme power to himself, the Chancellor Philo Dogmaticus attempting to foster rebellion against the President. The climax of this struggle comes when the Chancellor orders the President to be searched to recover the Seal, of which he is the keeper. When the President storms out of the sederunt, he begins the 'interregnum' of 15 weeks. The political satire here is explicit: the President argues for absolute authority, the Chancellor calls himself a 'republican' (275–6). The narrator, meanwhile, is typically inconsistent. At one point he compares the President and the Chancellor to Caesar and Pompey who pretended to fight for liberty, but really fought for power and dominion (243). However, when the Chancellor is expelled from the club, the narrator scolds the club's treatment of him as inconsistent with what was due to him as a subject of 'true Patriotism and worth' and one who contended for the club's 'liberties and privileges, against the arbitrary proceedings and tyranny of the Chair' (309). Alexander Hamilton enters the text as the Secretary, Loquacious Scribble, who is one of the members suspected by the history of fomenting trouble and discontent. As a depiction of club life, then, *The Tuesday Club* mimics and mocks the rituals and customs of these coteries and suggests their fun and high spirits if also their plays for power and privilege. The club, as depicted in *The Tuesday Club*, is certainly a microcosm of society beyond its elite membership.[7]

Literary groups, like other clubs and gatherings, were always as much factions as idealised social communities, largely because these self-selecting groups tended to be formed along homogeneous party-political lines. The Scriblerians in general, and certainly Pope in particular, seemed to have tried to cross party-political lines. The young Pope had visited the Whig circle which gathered around Addison in Button's coffee house and consistently depicted himself as an honest friend of both Whigs and Tories: 'In moderation placing all my glory, / While Tories call me Whig, and Whigs a Tory' (Pope 1993, 267). And when he included the leaders of both Whig and Tory parties on his subscription list for the translation of the *Iliad*, he was able to display his much-vaunted political 'neutrality' for all to see. Pope's self-image was of belonging to the 'Patriot Opposition', that cross-party allegiance which united against Robert Walpole, although the extent to which he supported the Opposition in practical terms is much debated.[8] Pope's own later account of the Scriblerians, as dictated to Spence, attempted to make it a more inclusive gathering of intellects than was certainly the case, including writers (Addison and Congreve) thought of as Whig. The literary group, however, was more likely to reflect social divisions than to aspire to the ideal of relative egalitarianism associated with the coffee house. And in reflecting the splits and factions of society, the intimate, exclusive group also offered an escape from them. These ideas are evident in the philosophy of sociability associated with the Earl of Shaftesbury's writings. In his *Characteristicks* (1711) in particular, he sketched how ideals of sociability could be fostered most successfully in a contracted society. Thus 'that social love and common affection which is natural to mankind' ends in more and more 'intimate' conversations and 'conspiratorial' associations. Far from exemplifying how 'sociable' or unified the eighteenth century was, then, the existence of clubs, polite assemblies and literary groups might represent the failure of social cohesion just as much as its glue. That literary groups constantly drew the fire of their opponents is just one example of this. The Scriblerians, for example, frequently found themselves under attack specifically as a group. In *The Twickenham Hotch-Potch, For the Use of the Rev. Dr Swift, Alexander Pope, Esq; and Company* (1728), Nicholas Amherst attacks the Scriblerians as an assembly comprising 'an impertinent *Scotch*-Quack [Arbuthnot], a Profligate *Irish*-Dean [Swift], the Lacquey of a Superanuated Dutchess [Gay], and a little virulent Papist [Pope]' (Guerinot 1969, 110). The association of the characters makes the inference of identity here absolutely clear. That writers are formally and publicly associated together in such clubs made them easy targets for enemies and rivals. Sherburn argues that Gay's comedy *Three Hours After Marriage* failed to maintain its original popularity due to the opposition of the (Whig) wits at Button's coffee house. Gay's hint in the advertisement to the play that he had been helped by Pope and Arbuthnot only resulted in abuse such as the following: 'I rather think this Issue from the United Powers of a *Triumvirate* of Authors more resembles the old Fable of the three *Heathen Gods*, who clubbed their Urine in a Hide to produce one dirty, nasty Bantling' (*A Letter to Mr John Gay* 1717, 6–7).[9] Attacks on group identity were frequent even when the attackers themselves were members of a group. In *The Scribleriad* (1742), for example, an anonymous defence of *The Dunciad*, the dunces are envisaged at their club:

> the Club despair,
> Till they the Snuff-box smell, and see the Chair.
> Then all the Dunciad d – n, and, grown elate,
> Prick up their Ears, and bray, 'To the Debate!
> 'The Chiefs were sate, the Scriblers waited round
> 'The Board with Bottles, and with Glasses crown'd,'
> (Sambrook 1967, 16)

Images of social and literary circles recur in eighteenth-century literature. This much has already been claimed. However, it might be more correct to argue that eighteenth-century literature is full of images of factions and cabals. Sarah Fielding's account of the theatre in *The Adventures of David Simple* (1744), for example, is of the tendency of the 'cabal' or group pre-organised to cry up or down a play or player or author. In Smollett's *Adventures of Humphry Clinker*, Matthew Bramble describes an encounter between two writers from different cabals who have been at open war for 20 years (105) and he and his nephew Jery Melford visit a society of writers in which formality and reserve dominate the proceedings. Jery writes of how the writers 'seemed afraid and jealous of one another, and sat in a state of mutual repulsion, like so many particles of vapour, each surrounded by his own electrified atmosphere' (116). Fictional representations of assemblies, tea-table groups, levées and other kinds of social gatherings are, most usually, similarly negative. Among countless references to the tea-table as a place of malicious scandal-mongering is Gay's poem 'The Tea-table' (1716). Among the most famous representations of the eighteenth-century levée is Hogarth's depiction in the second engraving of *The Rakes Progress* (1735), in which numerous hangers-on seek the rake's patronage, including a fencing master, prizefighter, several musicians, dancing master, landscape gardener, tailor, milliner and poet. The dangers and corruptions of such public spaces as balls, pleasure gardens, assemblies and masquerades are anxiously detailed in innumerable conduct books and prose fictions. Smollett's Matthew Bramble bewails an exhaustive catalogue of degenerate and repellent public spaces, including the King's Bath and a public ball at Bath and a duke's levée, a reception at court and the public entertainments of Vauxhall and Ranelagh at London (*Humphry Clinker*, 1771). Among Fielding's satirical depictions of fashionable society in *Tom Jones* is one that characterises it as a club, with its own rules (every member must tell a lie) and official positions (it is rumoured that the devil acts as president; Fielding 1996, 692–3). Thus while many literary groups and networks thought of themselves as supporting and enabling their writers, literary representations were more likely to depict groups as divisive and exclusive. Literary groups might inspire ideas for their writers, help revise each other's work or enable collaborative publishing ventures. They might help writers make connections with influential publishers, printers or reviewers. They might provide financial support, helping an author find a patron or a body of subscribers, and moral support, in providing the author with a sympathetic first audience. But from other perspectives, literary groups merely exacerbated tensions and rivalries with other writers, only stoked political partisanship, only inflated reputations and made authors complacent. Thus, depending on your point of view (or whether you were a member of the said community or not), literary groups might represent an escape from or an exacerbation of the schisms of the wider community.

What is true of the literary club is true also of any kind of perceived community. For Shaftesbury, the ideals of sociability could be practised only among an exclusive gathering. For David Hume, the question was why such ideals could not be mapped onto society itself: 'But why, in the greater society or confederation of mankind, should not the case be the same as in particular clubs and companies' (Hume 1966, 281). That places like White's, Brooke's, Almack's and Boodle's in London began as chocolate and coffee houses, in which any man might enter for the price of a penny, but ended as exclusive clubs, might then only typify the ways in which ideals of sociability were doomed to fail in practice. In Smollett's *The Adventures of Humphry Clinker* (1771), Matthew Bramble supports the Society for the Encouragement of Arts, but fears it will degenerate from 'democratical form' into 'cabal and corruption' (1984, 115). Mullan identifies this problem, of mapping the culture of a select gathering onto the wider community, as one of the key concerns of moral philosophy in the eighteenth century, the problem of 'projecting a sympathetic alignment of feelings seen as the rule in limited companies of the enlightened on to a more inclusive model of society' (Mullan 1990, 25). This problem could be 'solved' only in the realms of fiction, and in the sentimental novel in particular, in which the eighteenth-century novelist could create a relationship with her reader that might approximate to the kind of social virtue absent from the world beyond the text. It is thus to the construction of readers and spectators that the chapter will shortly turn. This section concludes, however, by considering a play that dramatises the fractures and divisions of contemporary society and a possible overcoming of these. That play is Susannah Centlivre's *A Bold Stroke for a Wife* (1718).

Anne Lovely is the ward of four guardians whose consent, her father's will dictates, must be secured before she can marry. Anne's life is literally divided between these four guardians: she spends three months with each one in turn and is forced to comply with their values and behaviours. When the play opens Anne has just returned from fashionable Bath, where she has been staying with the elderly rake, Sir Philip Modelove. She is thus dressed in hoop petticoat, low-cut dress and face patches. Her next quarter must be spent with Obadiah Prim, a strict Quaker, who dictates that she should wear a pleated cap, concealing hood and handkerchief modestly positioned over her neck and chest. Other guardians who must also be placated are the eccentric virtuoso Periwinkle, with his dilettantish obsession with science, natural history and exotic curiosities, and the ruthlessly capitalistic Tradelove, whose days are spent in talking up shares in the London coffee houses. Anne desires to marry Colonel Fainwell but also to keep her fortune of £30,000. This she can only do if all four guardians agree to accept Fainwell as her husband. The fop and the devout Quaker, the science enthusiast and the stockjobber are already incommensurate parties. But Centlivre also adds hints of their political differences. Sir Philip and Periwinkle with their titled families, their natural wealth and, in Sir Philip's case at least, enjoyment of the West End, are Tory influences over Anne; Prim, the Quaker hosier, and Tradelove, with his paeans to trade and the glory of the merchant, are both evidently Whig. In 'A Description of a City Shower' (1710), Swift satirically identified a sudden downpour as the only event which might reconcile feuding Whigs and Tories. In *A Bold Stroke for a Wife*, only the intricate and careful plotting of Colonel Fainwell (and his creator) can effect a resolution. Fainwell dupes each guardian in turn by appearing to them as the incarnation of their own desire. He appears to Sir Philip as the echo and embodiment of his own narcissistic self, disguised as a fashionable, skirt-chasing Frenchman. He appears to Periwinkle as an Egyptian collector of curiosities, including the miraculous belt that can make its wearer invisible. (Although when a chance remark by the landlord exposes the deception, Periwinkle must be tricked more prosaically: he is duped into signing his consent to the marriage of Fainwell and Anne by thinking he signs a document making him the wealthy executor of a dying uncle's will.) Tradelove too is tricked in his own terms: thinking he tricks Fainwell's Dutch merchant, he finds himself in debt to him and able to pay only with the price or commodity of his ward, Anne. And Obadiah Prim, Fainwell's most daunting challenge, is duped when Fainwell disguises himself as a visiting Quaker preacher, Simon Pure, and, in a hilarious scene of religious/sexual fervour, 'converts' Anne to Quakerism by having her become his wife.

Centlivre's play suggests that the fractures and tensions within society can be overcome only through clever, comedic plotting. The impossible can happen, consensus can be fashioned out of disparate factions and loyalties. But this is only an illusory, manufactured community, lacking true consensus. The only consensus possible is that manufactured through the convenient fiction of community. Theatre itself, as we will see, constructs an illusory form of community. Spectators laugh at the same joke while often sitting beside a stranger. In his Preface to *The Rivals* (1775), Sheridan wrote of how 'the scope and immediate object of a play is to please a mixed assembly in the representation' (Sheridan 1998, 3). Despite differences of rank, colour or gender, responding to the same literary work creates a sense of shared experience, even if that experience will always be at least partially marked by whether the stage is above or below one's sight-lines and by the class perspective segregated seating imposes. *A Bold Stroke for a Wife* represents the divisions and tensions within English society but it also comically resolves these differences through stage play. It might be seen then as an exemplary play for the theatre, for its audience and for the attempts of eighteenth-century literature in general to negotiate the attempts and dangers of manufacturing community.

The play admits that there is no such thing as a consensual community – Anne's guardians cannot agree on such issues as how a woman ought to dress and what makes a good husband. But simultaneously the play expresses an urge towards reconciliation and consensus – the hero must overcome the political and other fractures which make his lover's guardians incommensurate if he is to marry the heroine. This chapter has already suggested that literary groups can provide a sense of community where in fact there is fracture and discontinuity. The next section explores the activity of reading as providing an idea of community, especially when the act of reading is made a self-conscious one.

## Communities of readers and spectators

In 1704 Defoe wrote: 'The Preaching of sermons is speaking to a few of mankind[;] printing books is talking to the whole world' (cited Watt 1987, 103). In identifying print as a form of public conversation, Defoe anticipates recent work on ideas of nationhood and particularly that of Benedict Anderson, who famously argued that the nation is an 'imagined community' in which people separated by geographical distance could come together through the medium of print. For Anderson it is the form of the newspaper in particular which fosters community, defining newspaper reading as an 'extraordinary mass ceremony: the almost precisely simultaneous consumption ("imagining") of the newspaper-as-fiction' (Anderson 1991, 35). Ernest Renan defined the nation as a 'daily plebiscite'. For Anderson, the newspaper permits the manifestation of this idea of a daily plebiscite, as each reader joins with others through a common language and common readership. While Anderson does not refer specifically to the eighteenth century – indeed, most theories of nationhood agree in dating its rise to the end of the eighteenth century – his work reminds us of the major shift in ideas of reading which newspapers undoubtedly inaugurated. The rise of the newspaper can confidently be situated in the eighteenth century: originating with the official government publication, the *London Gazette* (founded in 1695), the newspaper flourishes thereafter. Between 1730 and 1770, for example, it is estimated that around 346 new titles – of newspapers, essay journals, reviews and magazines – appeared in England and Michael

Harris has estimated that in 1746 newspaper readership was nearly half a million people (Harris 1987, 190). In the introduction I considered the ways in which the institutions of the circulating library, the book club and the literary review inaugurated a sense of a reading public and with it the combination of 'simultaneity' and 'contemporaneity' which Vattimo associates with modernity. These ideas obviously accrue around our understandings of the early newspaper, as they do with Anderson's conception of the nation as an 'imagined community'. An alternative narrative, of relatively low literacy rates in the eighteenth century, reminds us that we ought not to overestimate the extent of these kinds of reading community. Much recent empirical research calls into question the idea of a mass 'reading public' in the eighteenth century. In this view the reading public is still an elite, exclusive coterie, rather than an open, inviting community. However, while it may be wrong to talk too simplistically of an eighteenth-century rise of the reading public, we can see in this period a culture beginning to think of itself as a culture of reading. The period itself obviously wrestled with the idea of the democratisation of literature, even if the term 'democratisation' itself was never used. This was now a print culture in which readers could not theoretically be excluded, even if cultural practices often tried to safeguard elite culture from a threatening 'vulgarisation'.

That literary culture was now a culture of print, rather than of manuscript, was thus often as much a matter of concern as it might be of celebration. Gone was the intimacy which manuscript seemed to offer. Gone too was the authenticity which manuscript seemed to guarantee. Many eighteenth-century texts aspire towards, or at least gesture towards, scribal form. Topical pamphlets on the case of Mary Blandy, who was executed for parricide in 1752, advertised that the original manuscripts, in Blandy's own handwriting, could be consulted at the publisher's shop by any interested parties. Print in itself could not guarantee such authenticity. Richardson attempted to make moments of intensity all the more realistic in his first novel by having his heroine comment on the physical evidence of her emotions, the materiality of her script: in her account of her mistress's death, Pamela's tears wet the page ('O how my Eyes run! – Don't wonder to see the Paper so blotted!'; 11); when Mr B arrives at the Lincolnshire estate, her fingers tremble ('I can hardly write; yet, as I can do nothing else, I know not how to forbear! – Yet I cannot hold my Pen! – How crooked and trembling the Lines! – I must leave off, till I can get quieter Fingers!'; 182); as they also do when she hurriedly tries to transcribe a letter from Mr B to Jewkes without her knowledge ('You'll see how tremblingly by the Lines . . .'; 197). Once the letters are printed, they are beyond such possibilities of authenticity, although Richardson holds onto the trace of the idea of manuscript legitimacy in subsequent challenges to spurious sequels: as the 'real' editor he possesses papers they do not. However, the authenticity of print as opposed to manuscript can only be asserted, not demonstrated. Similarly, Gray's reluctance to publish his own poetry sprang from his fear of the publicity which publication would inevitably bring and its inability to exclude undesirable, unwanted, unknown readers. Writing to Walpole in 1768 he lamented: 'When you first commenced an author, you exposed yourself to pit, box and gallery. Any coxcomb in the world may come in and hiss, if he pleases; aye, and (what is almost as bad) clap too, and you cannot hinder him' (Gray 1971, III 1009).

To argue that the eighteenth century consolidates the culture of print is to risk ignoring the extensive print culture that precedes the century. It also ignores the continuation of manuscript writing, especially significant within the literary groups I have been considering. The Scriblerian verses of invitation quoted above were exchanged privately, in handwritten form. Gray circulated verses in manuscript among his gentlemen friends, his sonnet on the death of Richard West remained in his commonplace book until published posthumously by William Mason (1775). And all of the bluestockings read and discussed each other's writings prior to their publication and, often, when they were not published at all.[10] What is distinctive about the eighteenth century, however, is its self-consciousness as a print culture. *The Spectator*, for example, confidently claimed print as 'this great Invention of these latter Ages' (No. 166).[11] The self-consciousness, and self-reflexivity, of eighteenth-century literature will emerge as a distinctive aspect of this book's focus on conversations and literary communities and chapter 4 in particular will focus on ideas of proliferating texts which haunted the eighteenth-century literary imagination. This chapter continues by examining the ways in which the reception of literary texts is figured within eighteenth-century literature, the ways in which literature of this period imagines and calls its readers into its own space. Of the many conversations taking place in eighteenth-century literature, then, the conversations between writer and reader or, in the case of the theatre, between writer and spectator, are among the most significant. These two kinds of conversation are different, of course, in that the reader is not always part of an actual community, such as any particular theatre audience represents. Spectators in the theatre cannot escape the consciousness of being in a community, made real by their reactions and intensified when, as we shall see, the spectators look at each other as well as look at the stage. Readers, in contrast, often form an imagined community, made present only in the consciousness of belonging to a print culture. We need to refine this model however, to take the experiences of reading groups into consideration. As the introduction argued, evidence of reading practices in the eighteenth century suggests that reading aloud continued to be an important aspect of literary culture and reading aloud in company is itself depicted in a number of books, as in the case of the interpolated story in *Joseph Andrews* (1742) of 'Leonora, the Unfortunate Jilt'. This is told by a lady in the coach, with interruptions and reflections from Parson Adams and the other passengers (Fielding 1980, 90–115). In addition to this practice are the many conversations about reading which pervade eighteenth-century literature. Both of these modes – reading aloud and conversations about reading – are juxtaposed when, in *The Progress of Romance* (1785), Clara Reeve has her two female conversationalists discuss memories of *Pamela*:

> **Euphrasia**  I remember my mother and aunts being shut up in the parlour reading *Pamela*, and I took it very hard that I was excluded.
> **Sophronia**  I can remember the time when this book was the fashion, the person that had not read *Pamela*, was disqualified for conversation, of which it was the principal subject for a long time. (Kelly 1999, VI 219)

Whether real or imagined, all of these silent readers, reciting readers, debating readers and theatre spectators perform ideas of community. The following sections consider three specific aspects of performed communities: the tradition of writing poems on the reception of one's poetry, typical of lower-class writers in particular; the theatrical conventions of the eighteenth-century stage with their direct appeals to the audience; and the idea of a reading public for fiction.

## The poetry of reception

Among the traditions of poetry emerging in the eighteenth century is that of poetry by lower-class or peasant writers. Between 1717 and 1800 the following poets published work: Jane Holt (née Wiseman, a domestic servant), Robert Dodsley (weaver and servant), Stephen Duck (a farmworker who was patronised by Queen Caroline's court), Constantia Grierson (midwife), John Bancks (weaver), Mary Collier (a laundress and occasional fieldhand), Henry Frizzle, Mary Masters (who prefaced her collection by referring to her lack of education), Robert Tatersal (bricklayer), Henry Jones (bricklayer), James Eyre Weeks (shoemaker), Mary Leapor (daughter of a gardener, she worked for a time in the kitchen of an estate), George Smith Green (who published as a 'tradesman'), Joseph Lewis (ivory turner), William Falconer (sailor), James Woodhouse (the 'shoemaker poet'), Phillis Wheatley (black slave), John Bennett (shoemaker), Susannah Harrison (a domestic servant), Ann Yearsley (a milkmaid, described by Hannah More as 'a Milker of Cows, and a feeder of Hogs, who has never even *seen* a Dictionary'), Robert Burns (son of a peasant or 'cottar', he worked for a time as a farmer), John Bryant (tobacco-pipe maker), Ann More Candler (a 'Suffolk cottager'), Elizabeth Hands (domestic servant, later wife of a blacksmith), Elizabeth Bentley (daughter of a journeyman cordwainer), Janet Little ('the Scotch milkmaid') and Robert Bloomfield (farm labourer). In 'An Introductory Essay on the Lives and Works of Our Uneducated Poets' (1831), Robert Southey identified John Taylor (the seventeenth-century waterman poet) as the first uneducated poet and undoubtedly poetry by labouring-class writers, often under the alias of 'anonymous', predated the eighteenth century. But it is only in the eighteenth century that such poets are situated within a discourse of 'natural genius' and come to represent a distinct tradition, a particular community, of writers. This self-consciousness is evident in the title pages of many of their publications in which their lower-class origins are clearly advertised: for example, John Bancks's volume of poetry was entitled *The Weaver's Miscellany* (1730), Robert Tatersal's *The Bricklayer's Miscellany* (1734) and Joseph Lewis published under the pseudonym of 'Lancelot Poverty-struck' (as in *The Miscellaneous and Whimsical Lucubrations of Lancelot Poverty-struck*; 1758).

Within this tradition is a subgenre of 'reception poems' in which the poet imagines and portrays the reception of her poetry. Mary Leapor and Elizabeth Hands in particular published a number of this kind of poem.[12] Although Leapor's poetry was published only after her death, her poems demonstrate how her writing made her an object of curiosity and gossip in her local community. They show a poet keenly aware of the attitudes of a range of readers – polite and labouring class – to her work. In 'An Epistle to Artemisia: On Fame', for example, Mira, Leapor's poetic pseudonym, finds herself continually interrupted by a stream of noisy visitors:

> So soft *Pappilia* o'er the Table bends
> With her small Circle of insipid Friends;
> Who wink, and stretch, and rub their drowsy Eyes,
> While o'er their Heads Imperial Dulness flies.
> 'What can we do? We cannot stir for Show'rs:
> Or what invent, to kill the irksome Hours?
> Why, run to *Leapor's*, fetch that idle Play:
> 'Twill serve to laugh at all the live-long Day.'
>     Preferment great! To beat one's weary Brains,
> To find Diversion only when it rains! (ll. 169–78)[13]

The boredom of Pappilia's circle, who come to read Mira's poetry only because they have nothing else to do, is here the 'Imperial Dulness' which suggests that 'An Epistle to Artemisia' is a kind of *Dunciad* for its poet. In place of the hack writers who besiege the poet in Pope's *Dunciad* is the stream of poor readers who force their shoddy readings upon the poet: Mira is visited by Delpho, an inscrutable critic whose cryptic pronouncements pass for profundity; Cressida, a flighty, vapid neighbour who is only really interested in how becoming she looks; Vido, whose praise is empty because it is bestowed indiscriminately on anything he reads; and Parthenia and Sophronia, who both scold Mira for neglecting housework. Poor readers of the poet Mira and of the woman, Mary Leapor, abound in her poems. In 'Minutius. Artemisia. A Dialogue', for example, the critic Minutius studies but does not read Mira's poems because he cannot decipher her handwriting and punctuation, the stylistic marks of her uneducated status. In 'The Epistle of Deborah Dough', the dairymaid writes to her cousin of the scribbling Mary and complains of the false airs she assumes. For Deborah Dough, the country poet is no match for her own daughter who is 'better learned (as people say); / Can knit a stocking in a day'. Although Leapor did not live to see any of her writings in print, plans for a subscription publication were fairly advanced before her death. ('Upon her Play being returned to her, stained with Claret', for example, is inspired by the actual event of her play having been refused in London.) The subscription proposal argued that Leapor was a poet 'who could borrow no Helps from the Converse of her Country Companions' (quoted in Greene 1993, 20). The ideal audience which the subscription plans aim to create is exemplified by Bridget Freemantle, the supportive woman who, as Artemisia, is just as present in Leapor's work as obtuse country bumpkins and scolding working women. While these reception poems, then, satirise the inability of her neighbours to read her poetry, in doing so they gesture towards other communities of readers. In the 'Epistle to Artemisia', Mira is also visited by Codrus, a 'rival' poet whose attempts are mocked in the poem: 'In shocking *Rhimes* a Nymph's Perfections tells, / Like the harsh Ting-Tong of some Village-Bells' (ll. 139–40). His visit comes immediately after Mira has fretted anxiously that her own poems 'smell / Too much of *Grub-street*' (ll. 127–8), Vido's empty praise having made Mira all the more unsure of the quality of her work. There is an implicit suggestion then that poetic confidence is fostered through an appreciative, sympathetic reading community. As we shall see in discussions of the novel, the dependency of literary writing on the idea of a reading community is not limited to lower-class writing, though it is made especially acute there.

The most obvious Popean echo in 'Epistle to Artemisia' is to Pope's *Epistle to Dr Arbuthnot*, in which the poet is also besieged by importunate visitors and timewasters, while drawing resilience from the support of a friend. In both poems, the sharp exchange of conversation is folded sharply into heroic couplets, as in the following brusque words between Mira and Sophronia:

'Go, ply your Needle: You might earn your Bread;
Or who must feed you when your Father's dead?'
She sobbing answers, 'Sure, I need not come
To you for Lectures; I have store at home.
What can I do?'
    '—Not scribble.'
        '—But I will.'
'Then get thee packing — and be aukward still.'
    Thus wrapp'd in Sorrow, wretched *Mira* lay,
Till *Artemisia* swept the Gloom away:
The laughing Muse, by her Example led,
Shakes her glad Wings, and quits the drowsy Bed. (ll. 156–66)

Leapor wrote that 'seeing myself in Print would give me the same Uneasiness as being stared at' (Griffin 1996, 202). Although she never lived to see these poems in print, they dramatise that staring and perhaps exorcise it. Leapor's self-consciousness, unlike Pope's, is stamped with a class-consciousness which argues that writing is an inappropriate form of labour. Freemantle's biographical note to the first volume suggests that Leapor was forced to accept an image of herself as eccentric: 'she always chose to spend her leisure Hours in Writing and Reading, rather than in those Diversions which young People generally chuse; insomuch that some of the Neighbours that observ'd it, expressed their Concern, lest the Girl should over-study herself, and be mopish' (quoted in Greene 1993, 10). This self-consciousness is then more than a matter of literary self-reflexivity. It is also the awkwardness of feeling oneself to be a cynosure, the centre of attention, a talking-point. The writer is acutely aware of being read.

### Theatrical performances

Many of the most popular dramas of the eighteenth century figured the formation of new communities through the joining of families in marriage. In Fielding's *The Modern Husband* (1730), for example, the social circles of Bellamant, his wife, his daughter (Emilia) and his son (Captain Bellamant) and of Lord Richly, his daughter (Charlotte Gaywit) and his nephew (Mr Gaywit) are closely linked in marriage as the play unfolds: Mr Gaywit marries Emilia and Captain Bellamant marries Charlotte Gaywit. These solutions exclude the 'modern husband' of the title and his wife (Mr and Mrs Modern) whose pimping and prostituting debar them from the play's happy ending. However, even the rakish Lord Richly, who, Don Juan-like, attempted to exploit an outdated *droit de seigneur* over the ladies of his social circle but who failed to seduce the virtuous Lady Bellamant, is redeemed in the virtue of his nephew and his choice of wife in Emilia. In Goldsmith's *She Stoops to Conquer* (1773), the Marlow and Hardcastle families are finally reunited through the marriage of the son (Charles Marlow) to the daughter (Kate Hardcastle), although here it is Charles's extreme bashfulness in the presence of a respectable lady such as Kate which is the obstacle to be overcome. The functioning of marriage as plot resolution is not, of course, particular to the eighteenth century. But theatre practice then neatly incorporated the audience into the play itself, as part of its own community. To understand why this was the case, we need to turn to the material context of the eighteenth-century theatre.

Unlike the bipartite theatre with which we are now familiar, the theatre of the eighteenth century was divided into the 'house' or auditorium, the 'platform' and 'the scene' (Figure 1). The scenic stage was that part of the stage which recessed behind what we would now call the proscenium arch, then a much less significant divide. Most stage business took place on the platform, which thrust into the auditorium. Stage-doors through which actors made their entrances and exits were just in front of the proscenium frame, and thus part of the 'platform'. The scenic stage allowed for changes of scene and 'discoveries'. Later in the century, after changes in lighting illuminated the scenic stage, the split stage permitted contrasting representations of intimate and social spaces: the relative intimacy of the platform could be contrasted with scenes of spectacle or wonder on the scenic stage. Melinda Finberg notes that Hannah Cowley exploited the depth of the Covent Garden stage by splitting her scenes in *The Belle's Stratagem* (1780) between intimate domestic scenes, staged on the platform, and larger scale public scenes, such as a bustling auction house and a spectacular masquerade, on the scenic stage (Finberg 2001, lv). Similarly, Elizabeth Griffith's play *The Times* (1779) used the scenic stage for the fashionable world of the card-party, with the platform stage being used for the more intimate worlds of the drawing and dressing rooms in which the main characters interact

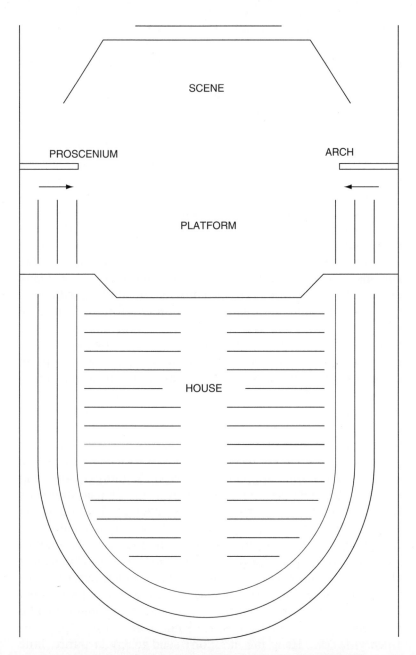

**Figure 1**    A Schematic Diagram of the Tripartite Theatre

in smaller groups. In general, too, the split stage could accommodate different kinds of dramatic genre. The scenic stage was appropriate for the more spectacular forms of heroic tragedy, which often involved important discovery scenes and histrionic acting styles. The platform stage suited comedy, where more naturalistic acting styles and the illusion of intimacy prevailed.

Possibly the most significant distinction between the two kinds of theatre, however, is that the clear divisions between the audience and actors which mark the bipartite theatre are not characteristic of the tripartite, in which spectators sat in stage-boxes (at the wings of the platform) or even, in some cases (especially on crowded benefit nights) on the platform itself or at the back of the scenic stage. With such a theatre design, no member of the audience could avoid looking at both the stage and other spectators. The spectators were inevitably part of the spectacle, part of the evening's entertainment. It is not surprising then that so many descriptions of the theatre in contemporary fiction satirise the tendency of spectators to attend plays in order not to see but to be seen. Mr Lovel in Burney's *Evelina* (1778), for example, freely admits that he pays little attention to the play and comes merely 'to meet one's friends and shew that one's alive' (182). The absorption of the audience into the play's drama was most spectacularly managed when the Duke of Bolton courted (and later married) the actress who first played Polly Peachum in Gay's *The Beggar's Opera* (1728). The seduction of the Duke by Lavinia Fenton in her performance as Polly is dramatised in Hogarth's painting of the first production, in which Polly's appeal to her father is also Lavinia Fenton's to the watching Duke of Bolton. Repertory actors and actresses certainly became well known to the regular audiences who attended their performances. This made casting of parts all the more significant, as productions could rely upon audiences to remember actors from other roles. In the first performances of Hannah Cowley's play, *The Belle's Stratagem* (1780), the character of Hardy was played by Quick. At one point in the play, Hardy tells his audience that he will borrow a masquerade costume from his old friend, the actor Quick, specifically his Jewish costume which he wore playing the character of Isaac Mendoza in Sheridan's play, *The Duenna* (1775): 'Hang me, if I don't send to my favourite, little Quick, and borrow his Jew Isaac's dress. I know the dog likes a glass of good wine, so I'll give him a bottle of my forty-eight, and he shall teach me' (Finberg 2001, 244). Thus Cowley enjoys a joke with the theatregoing audience: Quick as Hardy plays Hardy playing Quick playing Isaac Mendoza!

That eighteenth-century audiences shared the stage with the actors is also dramatised in the many prologues and epilogues which explicitly address the audience. In the first epilogue which Goldsmith wrote for *She Stoops to Conquer* (1773), Mrs Bulkley and Miss Catley quarrel as to which of them is due to recite the epilogue. They decide the audience should determine, but because Bulkley appeals to her supporters (the critics and wits, the young men who follow French fashions, gamesters, barristers and doctors) and Miss Catley to hers (the old gallants and the Scottish and Irish spectators), the epilogue is inevitably 'unspoken' and the epilogue which is performed is taken up entirely with the attempt to decide who should speak it. In Colman and Garrick's play, *The Clandestine Marriage*, the epilogue's traditionally explicit turn to the audience is anticipated within the play, as, in the last lines, Lovemore appeals to the benediction, not just of his wife's father and patron, but of the play's audience (Colman and Garrick 1928, 333).

As in the example of Goldsmith's epilogue, these turns to the spectators usually dramatise their difference and stratification as much as any communality they may possess as audience. The major divide within eighteenth-century theatre was undoubtedly that of class or status. Seating at the theatre was determined by class status, with the wealthy and fashionable spectators of the boxes cut off from the tradesmen of the middle gallery and the servants and impecunious professionals of the upper galleries. Although they might have been able to speak to the intellectuals associated with the pit, whose back rows were almost on a level with the boxes, here too there was a rigid physical distinction. Different seating areas created different perspectives of the stage, different experiences of the production. The seemingly obvious community of the audience was then internally fractured, a condition of which drama of the period was itself aware. These separations of rank are clear in Garrick's Epilogue to Arthur Murphy's *All in the Wrong* (1761):

> What shall we do our different tastes to hit?
> You relish satire (*to the pit*), you ragouts of wit (*to the boxes*),

> Your taste is humour and high-seasoned joke (*first gallery*).
> You call for hornpipe and for hearts of oak (*second gallery*).
> (Thomas 1989, 408)

Although in practice seating might sometimes be more mixed than these distinctions imply, the system of graduated pricing did tend to ensure that the poorest would sit in the cheapest gallery seats. In addition to the segregation of class by seating, there is also evidence that the composition of the audience varied on different nights. During much of the eighteenth century, Tuesdays and Saturdays were 'opera nights' and on these nights the upper classes were under-represented at the playhouses.

In stratifying its audience according to class or rank, of course, the eighteenth-century theatre merely mirrored its society. Acting styles also confirmed these distinctions. Before the rise of a more naturalistic acting style, emerging only gradually with the performances of Garrick in the mid-eighteenth century, dramatic convention called for studied and mannered styles. Hogarth wrote of how a foreigner visiting England would recognise the class status of any theatrical character merely from the way the actor stood. Rigid distinctions between the ranks were made in life, as in theatrical performances, by differences in dress, gesture, ways of speaking. That social roles are as much performances as any stage performance is made explicit in Eliza Haywood's amatory fiction *Fantomina* (1725). The heroine tricks a naturally promiscuous lover into remaining faithful to her by assuming a diverse range of identities: a prostitute, an inexperienced countrygirl (the 'Fantomina' of the narrative's title), a rustic maid (Celia), a middle-class widow (the Widow Bloomer), and a mysterious, amorous, and aristocratic lady (Incognita). Anticipating her readers' scepticism, the narrator argues that 'Fantomina' is such a consummate actress that 'all the comedians at both Playhouses are infinitely short of her Performances' (Backscheider and Richetti 1996, 238). But her convincing performances rely upon a society strictly defined by its codes of conduct. As Celia, for example, she dresses plainly ('a round eared Cap, a short Red Petticoat and a little Jacket of Grey Stuff'; 234), speaks differently (in 'a broad Country Dialect'), blackens her hair and eyebrows and behaves with 'a rude unpolished Air'. Part of this behaviour, crucially, is accepting payment for sex.

*Fantomina*, then, represents the ways in which behaviour, dress and accent are 'speaking' parts in eighteenth-century culture. But it also hints that modes of behaviour are influenced by the stage and by fiction. 'Fantomina' continually refuses the role of the victim which popular amatory fiction sketches for other fictional women. Toni O'Shaughnessy Bowers defines the genre according to its most typical plot in which 'an innocent young girl is seduced by an experienced, older man who promises her everlasting love but abandons her ruthlessly once his physical desires have been sated' (Bowers 1994, 52). 'Fantomina' continually reminds herself, and us, of this plot as she works to avoid it. Her triumph is ultimately taken from her: pregnant, she is unable to call upon the argument of victimhood to shame Beauplaisir into marrying her. Her mother 'commanded her to reveal the Name of the Person whose insinuations had drawn her to this Dishonour' (247), but 'Fantomina' can only confess that Beauplaisir is the innocent party, she the guilty. Playing the roles of others has entailed that 'Fantomina' has become others, including, as Beauplaisir had initially cruelly predicted, the prostitute: 'He had no reason to distrust the Truth of this Story [that she is a country lady called 'Fantomina', not a prostitute], and was therefore satisfied with it; but did not doubt by the Beginning of her Conduct, but that in the End she would be in Reality the Thing she so artfully had counterfeited' (231).

The perceived blurring of identity and mask is a pervasive theme in eighteenth-century writing and a continual cause of concern for many. That the eighteenth century was a culture of literal and metaphorical masquerade has been most persuasively argued by Terry Castle (1986). Castle's work examines the significance of masquerade entertainments, those evenings of controlled licence, when, for the price of an admission ticket, eighteenth-century people dressed in costumes of their own choosing: shepherdesses, nuns, priests, prostitutes, birds, harlequins, Turks and hussars. These flourished in London between the 1720s and 1780s and, as Castle has shown, haunted the eighteenth-century fictive imagination. That a number of theatres, such as the King's Theatre at the Haymarket, also hosted masquerades is only the most obvious example of the intimacy between the masquerade and the theatre. Contemporary approaches to issues of gender and other forms of identity have taught us to think of identity as a performance. At times, too, eighteenth-century drama turned self-consciously to just this issue. In Goldsmith's epilogue to Charlotte Lennox's comedy *The Sister: A Comedy* (1769), for example, the reciting actor appears to mock (although in reality praising) the play's author for having written a moral play when she ought to have written a 'speaking masquerade'. Turning to the audience he announces:

> Well, since she thus has shewn her want of skill,
> What if I give a masquerade? I will.
> But how! Ay, there's the rub! (*pausing*) I've got my cue:
> The world's a masquerade! The masquers, you, you, you.
> 　[*To Boxes, Pit, Gallery*
> Lud! What a groupe the motley scene discloses!
> False wits, false wives, false virgins, and false spouses
> (Goldsmith 1975, 177)

The young coquette, the angry spark, politician, patriot, critic – all are severally addressed and mimicked. All, he claims, play roles.

In one of the many introductory chapters of *Tom Jones* (1749), Henry Fielding set himself the task of 'A Comparison between the World and the Stage'. Here Fielding notes how the same language – of 'stage', 'scene' and 'transactions behind the curtain' – is used of theatre and of life, not because dramatists so faithfully represent life that the terms are shared, but because so many people 'play' their characters. The hypocrite is only the most obvious of these. While many writers have drawn these kinds of parallel, however, Fielding's narrator can recall no authors who have compared the world with the theatre *audience*. His comparison is between the diverse readers of his own fiction and the factions of the theatre audience. Tom has defended and selflessly protected his friend Black George who in turn betrays Tom's generosity by stealing £500 from him. How should we judge Black George, the narrator asks:

> Those who sat in the world's upper gallery, treated that incident, I am well convinced, with their usual vociferation; and every term of scurrilous reproach was most probably vented on that occasion.
>
> If we had descended to the next order of spectators, we should have found an equal degree of abhorrence, though less of noise and scurrility; yet here the good women gave Black George to the devil, and many of them expected every minute that the cloven-footed gentleman would fetch his own.

The pit, as usual, was no doubt divided: those who delight in heroic virtue and perfect character, objected to the producing such instances of villainy, without punishing them very severely for the sake of example. Some of the author's friends cried, 'Look'ee, gentlemen, the man is a villain; but it is nature for all that.' And all the young critics of the age, the clerks, apprentices, &c., called it *low*, and fell a-groaning.

As for the boxes, they behaved with their accustomed politeness. Most of them were attending to something else. Some of those few who regarded the scene at all, declared he was a bad kind of man; while others refused to give their opinion till they had heard that of the best judges.

Now we, who are admitted behind the scenes of this great theatre of Nature (and no author ought to write anything besides dictionaries and spelling-books who hath not this privilege) can censure the action, without conceiving any absolute detestation of the person, whom perhaps Nature may not have designed to act an ill part in all her dramas; for in this instance life most exactly resembles the stage, since it is often the same person who represents the villain and the hero; and he who engages your admiration to-day, will probably attract your contempt tomorrow. (Fielding 1996, 285)

This passage rehearses a number of the features represented as typical of the eighteenth-century theatre: the tendency of the fashionable to attend the theatre but to fail to attend to the play; and the stratification of seating, with the noisiest spectators in the upper gallery (associated with the servant classes), superstitious women in the middle gallery (associated with tradesmen and their wives), critics and friends of the author in the pit (associated with just these categories) and the polite gentry of the boxes (associated with the wealthiest spectators). The final paragraph, of course, draws a distinction between the theatre spectator watching and the writer or reader who is able to go 'backstage'. A number of literary historians have argued for a causal link between the decline of drama after the 1737 Licensing Act and the rise of the novel.[14] In its incorporation of dialogue, its reliance upon dramatic characters and scenarios, and its frequent awareness of itself as a work realised in the audience of its readers, the novel continues a generic conversation with theatre throughout the eighteenth century. The ways in which the novel confronted its own readers as spectators is the subject of the next section.

## Novel readers

In the opening pages of *Tom Jones* (1749), Fielding introduces his narrative to possible readers as a 'bill of fare to the feast' and announces the publicity which is inevitable in print culture in general, and novels in particular: 'An author ought to consider himself, not as a gentleman who gives a private or eleemosynary treat, but rather as one who keeps a public ordinary, at which all persons are welcome for their money' (29). Fielding's famous opening was a reworking of a chapter heading in *The Adventures of David Simple* (1744) by his sister, Sarah Fielding: 'Containing such a Variety, as makes it impossible to draw up a Bill of Fare, but all the Guests are heartily welcome; and I am in hopes every one will find something to please his Palate' (Sarah Fielding 1987, 251). Both quotations suggest the self-conscious nature of many eighteenth-century fictional narrators, who dramatise their address to the novel's readers as a form of sociability. Readers are invited to participate in the novel's imaginative order, and are encouraged to reflect upon their complicity in the narrative's address. They reflect what Walter Ong has called the 'new fashionable intimacy' between author and reader in the early eighteenth century (1975, 14). At times the participation of the reader is so literal as to parody itself: as when the narrator of *Tom Jones*, for example, cautions the reader of his description of Squire Allworthy's house in chapter 4. The chapter heading anticipates the danger: 'The reader's neck brought into danger by a description; his escape, and the great condescension of Miss Bridget Allworthy' and pursues it within the chapter itself:

> Reader, take care, I have unadvisedly led thee to the top of as high a hill as Mr Allworthy's, and how to get thee down without breaking thy neck, I do not well know. However, let us e'en venture to slide down together, for Miss Bridget rings her bell, and Mr Allworthy is summoned to breakfast, where I must attend, and, if you please, shall be glad of your company. (Fielding 1996, 37)

When the narrator self-consciously addresses his or her readers, they in turn become self-aware as readers and such explicit addresses turn even the most apparently 'private' reading, of the solitary reader in her closet, into a public affair.

The opening section of this chapter concluded with a discussion of how eighteenth-century literature is as much about the fracturing of community as it is about its formation. In imagining its own reader, the eighteenth-century novel is often just as conscious that its readers will disagree, will argue with each other. Haywood's late novel, *The History of Miss Betsy Thoughtless* (1751), for example, imagines both sympathetic and sceptical readers of its heroine. One chapter heading conjures up these different responses: *'Cannot fail of exciting compassion in some readers, though it may move others to laughter'* (Haywood 1997, 200), but such polarised responses are often encouraged by the narrator's own shifting stances and deliberate ambiguities. Her flighty, 'thoughtless' heroine begins to feel some regret when her preferred suitor, Trueworth, disappears. The narrator is designedly coy, however, about whether this regret is a sign of Betsy's reformation (regretting that she has toyed with the one man she esteems) or continuing vanity (regretting to lose one of her many suitors, whose collective attentions feed her egotism and imperiousness): 'whether [her inquietude] proceeded in reality from the first shootings of a growing inclination, or from that vanity, which made her dread the loss of so accomplished a lover, cannot be easily determined' (286). These explicit ambivalences only reinforce the depiction of Betsy throughout the first volumes: unreasonable, spoilt, vain and sometimes cruel, she is also kind, generous, and intelligent.

For Henry Fielding, incorporating differences becomes a comic way of satisfying market demand. Some readers enjoy tender scenes, some do not. The narrator of *Amelia* (1751) attempts to cater for both tastes by placing the account of Booth's sorrowful parting from his pregnant wife Amelia in a separate chapter and by scaring off any unsympathetic readers: 'we will, according to our usual custom, endeavour to accommodate ourselves to every taste, and shall therefore place this scene in a chapter by itself, which we desire all our readers who do not love, or who perhaps do not know the pleasure of tenderness, to pass over; since they may do this without any prejudice to the thread of the narrative' (Fielding 1987, 94). Earlier in the same novel, Fielding writes two accounts of the same conundrum to accommodate the literary preferences of Tory and Whig critics. The conundrum is how an apparently gentle and sensitive woman such as Miss Matthews could also be a murderess, or, in the terms of the chapter heading, how 'it is possible for a woman to appear to be what she really is not' (33). The (Tory) reader might compare this behaviour with how the weather changes between one day (say, the birthday of the Stuart pretender, Bonnie Prince Charlie) and the next or how the fair Celia might change her political colours as it suits her company. Another (Whig) reader might think of how Betty Careless, the apparently innocent and modest maiden seen at the theatre, is the same girl 'discovered in bed with a rake at a bagnio, smoking tobacco, drinking punch, talking obscenity, and swearing and cursing with all the impudence and impiety of the lowest and most abandoned trull of a soldier' (36). Not only is the simile different between the two accounts, so too is the style. The passage written to please the Tory critic is consciously poetic, elevated, absurdly grandiose: 'it is the same English climate, in which on the lovely 10th of June, under a serene sky, the amorous Jacobite kissing the odoriferous Zephyr's breath, gathers a nose-gay of white roses to deck the whiter breast of Celia' (36). The Whig account is plain speaking and direct, as in the quotation above. Although the narrator offers the two accounts in order to please all kinds of readers, the differences in style betray the author's own loyalties. The Tory reader who identifies herself as such only finds a comic reflection.

While this example shows Fielding's comic twist on different readers, it is typical of many eighteenth-century texts which depict print culture as one of endless proliferation in the attempt to satisfy imperious readers. The London newspaper, the *British Mercury*, in 1715 announced that it would try to accommodate all tastes by adding miscellaneous pieces to its news format:

> there are solid Readers, who read for Information; and there are others more Mercurial, who value not a Book any farther, than for the Diversion and Amusement it affords. The Design of this Paper, is, as far as practicable, to please all Readers; which cannot be hop'd but by a Succession of Variety. *The History of the World* in it, was acceptable to many, and at last grew tedious to some. It was follow'd by *the Rover*, an entertaining Piece, not disagreeable to others. Next follow'd *Geography*, an abridgement, not without its Use, and *Algier*, could not but please some. It is intended now to find such Subjects, as may be short and pleasing; so that by constant Change, something may touch every different Genius. (*British Mercury*, 11 June 1715)

Although the *Mercury*'s strategy failed (the newspaper folded shortly after this very announcement), its attempt to please many readers was taken up by later journals which would increasingly include a mixture of essays among their news features (Harris 1987, 180). Writing for a wide audience was evidently the aspiration of the newspaper printers and writers; satisfying such diverse tastes and opinions was quite another matter. To an extent then, we can see the playful addresses to different kinds of reader by Haywood and Fielding as a comic reworking of the commercial printer's dilemma. The always potentially fickle reader is buttonholed and addressed directly in their fictions.

While not all eighteenth-century novels have self-conscious narrators, all perceive and situate themselves as being didactic as well as entertaining, in offering both instruction and pleasure. To this extent all eighteenth-century novels are oriented towards their readers. The 'hailing' of the reader in eighteenth-century fiction has recently been discussed in work by Richard Barney and Leah Price in which the true subject of the eighteenth-century novel is located in the reader, or, more specifically, in the process of the reader's education. Readers are called upon to observe and to judge characters – criminals who repent (Defoe's Moll Flanders, for example), flawed heroes who reform (Fielding's Booth), heroes and heroines who prove their moral worth (Richardson's Pamela, Fielding's Joseph Andrews). In turn, these books also judge the reader. This is most explicit in the case of the novels of Samuel Richardson. For William Warner, Richardson's *Pamela* (1740) attempted to reform reading practices and to 'elevate' the novel out of the popular romance tradition with which it was most associated in the early eighteenth century. Warner argues that the new mode of reading which *Pamela* inaugurated was important to 'the long-term institutionalization of novel reading' (Warner 1998, 223). This mode might be summarised as the 'sympathetic identification with and critical judgement of fictional characters', although Warner lists a number of characteristics of this kind of reading: reading fictional characters as if they were real people; seeing the reader's response as part of the same moral universe, and thus conferring a moral seriousness upon the novel; reading in newly detailed ways in which the reader is encouraged to imagine details where they may be missing, to make connections or adjudicate between different aspects, to try to interpret the author's intentions; and to judge what is 'proper' and 'improper' in a text.[15] This kind of highly 'qualified' reading is, Warner suggests, the reading to which Habermas refers in defining a critical public sphere composed of private subjects:

> The relations between author, work, and public changed. They became intimate mutual relationships between privatized individuals who were psychologically interested in what was 'human', in self-knowledge, and in empathy. Richardson wept over the actors in his novels as much as his readers did; author and reader themselves became actors who 'talked heart to heart'. . . . The reality as illusion that the new genre created received its proper name in English, 'fiction': it shed the character of the *merely* fictitious. The psychological novel fashioned for the first time the kind of realism that allowed anyone to enter into the literary action as a substitute for his own, to use the relationships between the figures, between the author, the characters, and the reader as substitutes for reality. (Habermas 1989, 50)

The form of the (elevated) novel, then, becomes a kind of community, in which the response of readers becomes a measure of their worth. Richardson's fictions certainly provoked a range of different responses, not least because they themselves anticipated and dramatised in advance such differences. That Richardson's fiction already folds within itself any possible criticism is noted in Sarah Fielding's *Remarks on Clarissa* (1749), when Bellario defends *Clarissa* by pointing out how the novel anticipates and censures criticism:

> There is one Thing has almost astonished me in the Criticisms I have heard on *Clarissa's* Character; namely, that they are in a Manner a Counterpart to the Reproaches cast on her in her Lifetime.
> She has been called perverse and obstinate by many of her Readers; *James Harlowe* called her so before them. Some say she was romantic; so said *Bella*; disobedient; all the *Harlowes* agree in that; a Prude; so said *Salley Martin*; had a Mind incapable of Love; Mr *Lovelace's* Accusation; . . . Others say, she was artful and cunning, had the Talent only to move the Passions; the haughty Brother and spiteful Sister's Plea to banish her from her Parents Presence. I verily think I have not heard *Clarissa* condemned for any one Fault, but the Author has made some of the *Harlowes*, or some of Mrs *Sinclair's* Family accuse her of it before. (Fielding 1985, 41)

Richardson's novels anticipate criticism in so far as they dramatise different perspectives upon their heroines (and, in the case of Charles Grandison, hero). These perspectives are not overtly legitimised by the novels. Instead such critics and readers find themselves pulled into the terms of the novels and the debates which they set out.

One implication of Sarah Fielding's comment on the ways in which Richardson's novels subsume potential criticisms within their own frame, then, is to make the critics and the characters who surround Richardson's heroines occupy analogous spaces. While much has been written on the ways in which Richardson's fiction initiates the novel as a genre which explores the psychology of the individual, there has been little discussion of how it folds the readers into the fictional communities of the novels.[16] While the 'realism' of Richardson's fiction is not today discussed in terms of its provoking discussion of his characters as of 'real people', it was certainly thus discussed by his own correspondents. Lady Bradshaigh reassured Richardson that critics who attacked the lasciviousness of *Clarissa* revealed only their own depravity: 'it must be a very unvirtuous mind that can form any other ideas from what you relate than those of terror and pity for you' (Richardson 1804, II 27). Similarly, the authors of *Pamela's Conduct in High Life* attacked *Pamela Censured* for finding a scene of attempted rape a scene which might excite: 'How do the Fright, the Terror and Apprehensions of a defenseless Virgin kindle Desire?'[17] If readers choose to read as antipathetic characters do, the reading reveals more of the reader than of the text. For William Warner, it is this positioning of the reader which gives the novel a moral seriousness which earlier fiction did not. Unlike the entertainment unashamedly offered by the novels of Aphra Behn, Delarivier Manley and Eliza Haywood, Richardson's *Pamela* elevated the novel, by appropriating that entertainment in the guise of didactic instruction.

Eighteenth-century anxieties about the activity of reading novels, especially when the reader is female, are well documented. In Sheridan's *The Rivals* (1775), Sir Anthony Absolute, having observed Lady Languish's maid returning from the library, remarks to Mrs Malaprop, 'Madam, a circulating library in a town is as an ever-green tree of diabolical knowledge! It blossoms through the year! And depend on it, Mrs Malaprop, that they who are so fond of handling the leaves will long for the fruit at last' (Sheridan 1998, 20). Pamela's main stipulation for the new post she envisages taking up after leaving Mr B is that it allow her 'a little Time for Reading' (Richardson 2001, 77). In *Gulliver's Travels* (1726), the fire in the empress's apartment is started when a maid of honour falls asleep reading a romance. And in *The Female Quixote* (1752), Arabella's obsession with romance fictions makes her unable to act in or judge the world appropriately. However, recent empirical work on eighteenth-century reading practices suggests that these fears were exaggerated. There is no evidence, for example, that the novel-reading public was predominantly female and we should remember that, when Richardson defined his project in publishing *Pamela* as an explicitly moralistic one, he did not foreclose the tendency of novel readers to identify with fictional characters, as the cultural conservatives feared, but rather exploited this very tendency. Indeed, sentimental fiction encourages and even trains its readers to empathise with the sorrow and sufferings of the vulnerable characters it represents. Almost invariably, the sentimental hero or heroine performs the appropriate responses of sympathetic weeping and generous charity that are recommended to the reader. In this and in other ways, the eighteenth-century reader is always 'in training'. In Lynch's terms, that reader is taught to participate in 'a social world that was being reconceived as a transactional space, as a space that held together through the circulation of fellow feeling' (Lynch 1998, 89). In what is perhaps the exemplary novel of this kind, MacKenzie's *The Man of Feeling* (1771), Harley is presented as the man of feeling continually in terms of his responsiveness to the narratives of others. When we see Harley weep on hearing the story of the beautiful lunatic of Bedlam (of how her father refused to allow her to marry her lover, her lover's subsequent death at sea, and her endurance of a loveless, forced marriage) or the story of Edwards (who returns from war to find his grandchildren orphaned, destitute, but stoical), we are encouraged to weep too. Similarly, in *The Adventures of David Simple* (1744), David moves from being the focus of the narrative to becoming the listener of others' narratives, in short, he becomes a reader of sensibility as much as its hero. David listens to the stories of Cynthia and of Camilla and Valentine sympathetically and benevolently. With his help Cynthia is enabled to escape the tyranny of the woman who keeps her in subjection as a servile companion and

Camilla and Valentine are rescued from near-death by starvation. In so doing, it is implied, David does only what the sympathetic reader in his place would do, what any reader ought to do. John Mullan, Janet Todd and Betty Schellenberg have all written of the significance of sensibility as a literary mode in the eighteenth century, as a response to the perceived fracturing of society. Shared feeling comes to form the only kind of the social consensus possible within a world of economic and social fragmentation. The ideals of sociability were to be realised in sentimental fiction only as a form of wish-fulfilment, as the impersonality of the market and the greed and selfishness which it was seen to promote threatened traditional family and social ties.[18] As we will see from the example of *David Simple*, however, even when novels of sensibility depict an ideal of community, they also reveal how hard won and fragile it can be.

The title of Sarah Fielding's novel – *The Adventures of David Simple, containing an account of his travels through the cities of London and Westminster in the search of a real friend* (1744) – announces its hero's great project as the search for true friendship. The novel also defines this journey as the search for community: 'a little Community, as it were of two, to the Happiness of which all the Actions of both should tend with an absolute disregard of any selfish or separate Interest' (Fielding 1969, 26). When David finally finds a community of true friends – Camilla, whom he marries; her brother Valentine and his wife Cynthia – the narrator constantly refers to them as 'our (little) Society'. Such an ideal society, the pronoun suggests, can incorporate sympathetic and like-minded readers, standing against the world. More darkly, however, the novel also implies that goodness can lead to error, and from this danger the reader, too, may not be exempt.

While David Simple appears as the sympathetic man of feeling of the novel, its obvious hero, his 'simplicity' is also increasingly questioned, particularly in the novel's sequel, *Volume the Last* (1753). Here David comes to recognise his own tendency to be naïve and too trusting of others and the novel is increasingly explicit about how David's selflessness permits him to be exploited. That David is an untrustworthy guide, however, is also hinted in the original novel. Narrative irony paints David as a comically mock-heroic figure, as 'an Enthusiast . . . in this point only as mad as Quixote himself could be with Knight Errantry' (27) and the language of comic 'knight errantry' underpins subsequent descriptions such as the following: 'My Hero . . . was to begin the World again. And the next Fancy he took into his Head, was to dress himself in a mean Habit, take an ordinary Lodging, and go amongst the Lower Sort of People, and see what he could make of them' (125). David's inability to see that Orgueil, Spatter and Varnish are untrustworthy is also implicitly contrasted with the more knowing reader, who recognises that these names advertise their unreliability. It comes as little surprise to us that 'Orgueil' tends to be proud, 'Spatter' to be severe on all faults, and 'Varnish' to wink at them. To this extent, the reader is always more knowing and wise than David Simple. But 'speaking' names in eighteenth-century convention always speak to *us*, not to characters within the fictional scheme. David's difficulty in adjudicating between Spatter and Varnish is defended by the narrator when she steps in to caution the reader against complacency:

> If the Reader has a mind to have a lively idea of this Scene, let him imagine to himself a Contention between a Painter, who is finishing his favourite Piece, and a Man who places his Delight in throwing Dirt; as fast as the one employs his Art to make it beautiful, and hide its Blemishes, the other comes with Shoals of Dirt, and bespatters it all over. And poor *David* was in the Situation of a Man who was to view the Piece, which had thus alternately been touched by the Pencil, and daubed with Mud, till it was impossible to guess what it originally was. Or if this will not give him an adequate Idea of it, let him fancy a vain Man giving his own Character, and a revengeful one giving that of his most inveterate Enemy. (94)

David's quest to find a true friend is thus as much a quest in finding someone to believe, someone whose word he can trust. This most apparently moralistic novel, then, is also typical of eighteenth-century fiction in its self-reflexivity. Who to credit, whose story to believe: these are the questions of fiction itself.[19]

The eighteenth century might be said to have had a heightened awareness, and often fear, of the relativity of judgement. That questions of judgement and interpretation are constantly open to question, determined by perception and prejudice as much as by the innate fitness of the subject, is returned to again and again in countless literary and philosophical texts. As we have seen, a number of eighteenth-century dramatists and novelists imagine how

their audiences might well fail to agree. Typical of this consciousness is Fielding's Mr Gaywit who announces in *The Modern
Husband*: 'Ask a man's character of one of his party, and you shall
hear he is one of the worthiest, honestest fellows in Christendom;
ask it of one of the opposite party, and you shall find him as worthless, good-for-nothing a dog as ever was hanged' (1882, IX 98).
Competing versions of the truth unsettle not just how we might
decide between versions but how we might judge at all. Within
*David Simple*, the reader is confronted with the paradox that to
trust others may be foolish or virtuous. David's goodness resides at
least partly in his trusting nature and the narrator presents an
apparently robust defence of just this aspect of David Simple in the
sequel:

> If, from judging of others by himself, such a Man is imposed on,
> by the false Colours hung out to deceive him, and thereby becomes
> the Sacrifice of his own Simplicity, he is thought the proper Object
> of Ridicule, and the Words *simple* and *silly* are immediately made
> synonimous: but if, after some Experience of the World, he should,
> in his future Transactions, be guided by that Experience, to act con-
> sistently with it, and should thereby avoid those Evils to which his
> Inexperience rendered him liable, he is suddenly metamorphosed
> into a *cunning* Fellow; and those very persons, who had before
> laughed at his Folly, can now clearly enough distinguish the
> Meaning of the Word *Simplicity*, to blame him for his Want of it;
> without considering the essential difference there is between the
> proper Caution built on Experience, and that unjust Suspicion of all
> Mankind, which often, if not always, arises from the Knowledge of
> harbouring in our own Bosoms a false and malignant Heart. (324)

Yet even here, where the narrator seems to be at her most didactic,
there is a narrative irony which undercuts such reflections: David
has just agreed to be guided by Mr Ratcliff in continuing to pursue
a lawsuit which is steadily depleting his fortune. While the narrator
overtly defends David's 'simplicity' in the passage above, the name
'Simple' continues to speak of a number of interpretative possibilities. The *Oxford English Dictionary* suggests that such different
readings of 'simple' as 'honest', 'unpretentious', 'homely' and 'lacking acuteness or quick apprehension' were all current in the mid-
eighteenth century. In 1785, Grose's *Dictionary of the Vulgar Tongue*
recorded the sense of 'Simple Simon' as 'a natural, silly fellow'.

Thus, while the use of speaking names tends to foreclose different interpretations, the moral of *David Simple* is not an obvious one. We might know how we ought to feel about such characters as 'Orgueil', 'Spatter' or 'Varnish'. How we should judge David Simple is not nearly so self-evident. Instead, the novel makes demands of its readers, demands we might not usually associate with eighteenth-century didactic fiction. Sarah Fielding's novel may be said to weigh aspects of cynicism, scepticism and trust against each other and ultimately to counsel, not the negativity and even self-indulgence of cynicism, nor the blind or naïve foolishness of timid or unquestioning trust, but a benevolent scepticism – perhaps of the kind represented by Cynthia, who might be constructed as the heroine of the novel, although she is not overtly positioned as such.

Cynthia's obvious intelligence makes her the target of Mrs Orgueil's spite and a focus of narrative anxiety. Her wit, like the narrative's constant return to questions of interpretation, stretches the novel's conventional morality. The narrator explicitly contrasts the two sets of couples in their different responses to the shopkeeper's wife who is crying because her husband has paid off his debts rather than buying her the luxuries she desires. While Cynthia laughs and she and Valentine talk of the incident as 'ridiculous', David and Camilla look grave and ponder why anyone could be so concerned about such trifles (192). Cynthia's laughing response is dangerously improper for a sentimental heroine (however proper it might have been for Shaftesbury's club gentleman). But even though the novel does not present Cynthia as its heroine, significantly it is she alone who survives. To contrast the behaviour of Cynthia and Camilla in *Volume the Last* is to see Cynthia's scepticism as a form of wisdom and Camilla's trust as mistaken: while Cynthia would have had them drop friendship with Mr and Mrs Orgueil, Camilla encourages Cynthia to allow Mrs Orgueil to take her ailing daughter to Bath, where Mrs Orgueil's cruelty effectively kills her. Perhaps then the novel only ostensibly celebrates David Simple as its protagonist and obvious hero, while simultaneously reflecting ironically upon him. In his place as exemplar we might choose Cynthia, the female wit.

If the ideal of community is presented in *The Adventures of David Simple*, it is presented only obliquely, as something precious to be wrought from the corruption and malice in which it must make its way. Negotiating that terrain is shown to be difficult but not impossible. And the reader is taught that skill of negotiation through reading and adjudicating between the obviously unreliable (such as the Spatters, Varnishes or Orgueils of the world), the morally attractive but ineffectual (the Davids and Camillas) and the outspoken, even at times improper, but wise (the Cynthias). The final chapter of the sequel recounts David's death-bed sentiments: the unworldly man of feeling faces death with joy and piety. Of the 'Society' of two couples and six children, only Cynthia and her eldest niece, Camilla, survive. While the book does not close with them, the very fact of Cynthia's survival remains as an alternative ending, from which the reader might draw some obvious conclusions. Despite its apparent morality, then, it is the reader who must 'complete' the meaning of *David Simple*, who must weigh up the benevolence and kindness of David against his naïvety and otherworldliness.

It is in the necessary participation of the reader that common ground might be found between such ostensibly different fictions as *The Adventures of David Simple, Tristram Shandy* and Smollett's *The Adventures of Humphry Clinker* (1771). In Smollett's epistolary novel, many voices dispute over the meaning and value of the people and places visited on a tour of England and Scotland. In the eyes of Matthew Bramble, for example, Bath is 'the very center of racket and dissipation', a 'national hospital' where 'none but lunatics are admitted', a place of frightening social mixing, where, for example, 'Even the wives and daughters of low tradesmen, who, like shovel-nosed sharks, prey upon the blubber of those uncouth whales of fortune, are infected with the . . . rage of displaying their importance' (Smollett 1984, 34, 37). For his niece Lydia Melford, Bath is 'an earthly paradise', 'a new world', where '[a]ll is gayety, good-humour, and diversion' (39) and for her brother Jery, the social mix of Bath that his uncle detests is only 'a source of infinite amusement' (49). Consensus is moulded in this novel through a series of recognitions: Bramble acknowledges the affection he feels for his extended family and recognises Humphry Clinker as his illegitimate son; Jery and Lydia come to recognise Bramble's authority and accept his views as just. In the specific example of judging Bath, Jery and Bramble's difference of view is put to the test when they attend a social experiment. The wealthy Jack Holder hosts a general tea-drinking in one of Bath's assembly rooms at which the ladies can grab free sweetmeats and nosegays when he rings a bell. Holder, Bramble, Jery, together with their friend the actor Quin, watch from a gallery above:

> The tea-drinking passed as usual; and the company having risen from the tables, were sauntering in groupes, in expectation of the signal for attack, when the bell beginning to ring, they flew with eagerness to the desert, and the whole place was instantly in commotion. There was nothing but jostling, scrambling, pulling, snatching, struggling, scolding, and screaming. The nosegays were torn from one another's hands and bosoms; the glasses and china went to wreck; the tables and floor were strewed with comfits. (52)

By the end of the novel, Bramble, Lydia, Jery and Humphry Clinker in particular have expressed their love and concern for each other and, bound by affection and loyalty, they, together with the newly married couple of Tabitha Bramble and Mr Lismahago, constitute what Bramble calls, in an echo of *David Simple*, 'our little society' (339). But fractures and differences of opinion remain and are ultimately unresolved. The novel ends with the younger generation of Jery, Lydia and her new husband George Dennison, returning to Bath instead of accompanying Bramble and Humphry Clinker back to the idyllic retreat of rural Monmouthshire.

Betty Schellenberg ends her account of fictional 'conversational circles' with considerations of *Humphry Clinker* and *David Simple*: 'the communal ideal does not succeed in transforming the rapaciously egotistical social climate. Rather, the potential for consensus has been transferred to an extra-textual and extra-social dimension: that of reader response' (1996, 118). For Schellenberg, the fractures of *Humphry Clinker* are resolved only in the synthesising response of the reader, a response that is inevitably also that of Matthew Bramble. Her reading differs from mine only in placing the resolution of Sarah Fielding's sequel in a religious afterlife, whereas I read Cynthia as the oblique heroine, whom the reader might substitute in the place of David. Both arguments agree however, in suggesting that it is the reader who is called upon to respond to the novel appropriately.

### Testing sociability: speaking to strangers

While generalisations about eighteenth-century literature in general, and the novel in particular, are increasingly difficult to make, it might be said that a considerable number of literary texts articulate or imply a self-consciousness about their own status as texts.

Often this takes the form of direct addresses to the reader. Thinking about the eighteenth-century novel in particular allows us to make connections between the different kinds of prose fiction written by Defoe, Swift, Haywood, Sarah Fielding, Henry Fielding, Burney and Sterne. The last of these is often the greatest challenge to any attempt to synthesise eighteenth-century fiction within a common perspective. *The Life and Opinions of Tristram Shandy, Gentleman* (1759–67), in its idiosyncratic narration of eccentric life, can seem utterly resistant to any attempt to 'tame' it within a grander narrative – despite Victor Shklovsky's famous remark that it is the 'most typical novel in world literature'. And its portrayal of opaque characters, wrapped up the solipsism of eccentric 'hobby horses', seems to refute the possibility of community. However, it does share with the other novels discussed in this book a sensitivity to its reader's participation and may be said to literalise many aspects of the eighteenth-century novel in general. Tristram Shandy hails his reader as 'my dear friend and companion', thus making the 'conversational' aspect of eighteenth-century literature particularly explicit: 'As you proceed further with me, the slight acquaintance which is now beginning betwixt us, will grow into familiarity; and that, unless one of us is in fault, will terminate in friendship' (10). The conversational ease with which Tristram addresses the reader is evident here and in casual chapter openings such as the following: 'There will be just time, while my uncle Toby and Trim are walking to my father's, to inform you, that Mrs Wadman had, some moons before this, made a confident of my mother' (537). The relationship between writer and reader is explicitly modelled on one of friendship and sociability. This friendship, and the reader's increasing intimacy with Tristram himself, offers a way of overcoming the solipsism so obvious in all of the novel's characters. This intimacy is also the narrative trait which *Tristram Shandy* shares with many other eighteenth-century texts. For example, in his introduction to a modern edition of *Tom Jones* (Fielding 1996), John Bender describes Fielding's novel as inviting the sociable reader to enter into polite conversation with the narrator and as legitimising the novel as a forum for critical discussion. Fielding's narrative is seen to encourage the existence of a reader ready for public-sphere exchange, a reader capable of participating in rationally informed public discussion. John Richetti has also made broadly similar points in discussions of the way in which eighteenth-century fiction negotiates a rational public consensus within the public sphere (1992, 1999).

*Tristram Shandy* does not ask its readers to judge characters and morals to anything like the extent of novels by Defoe, Richardson, Sarah Fielding or even Henry Fielding. Instead it draws its readers into happy complicity with its own playfulness and moral seriousness. Readers are asked to meet the narrator halfway, by bringing their own understandings and imaginations into play. Thus in order to understand Uncle Toby's feelings for the Widow Wadman, readers must sketch her figure themselves, according to their own desires, and Tristram helpfully provides a blank page within his book for them to draw upon (377). Readerly licence such as this ensures the reader understands Toby more fully and 'respects' the reader's own imagination. But it will also protect the book from harsh criticism: 'Thrice happy book! Thou wilt have one page, at least, within thy covers, which MALICE will not blacken, and which IGNORANCE cannot misrepresent' (378). In giving readers so much freedom to form their own opinions and judgements, Sterne wrote a book which would be radically individualistic. Readers would read themselves, as much as the book (see Ross 2001, 411). They might enjoy the book's passages of bawdy humour (such as the story of Tristram's circumcision by sash-window or Slawkenbergius's tale with its many innuendos concerning large 'noses'), its moral instruction (such as Yorick's sermon on conscience), its contemporary satire of arcane learning (as in the theological discussion, quoted in French, of whether a foetus might be baptised) or its passages of pathos and sentiment (such as the death of Le Fever). Initial reviews tended to divide along these fractures, entirely as Sterne himself anticipated ('"Tis enough if I divide the world'; cited in Ross 2001, 258). When Sterne was writing the first two volumes of *Tristram Shandy*, he worried that readers would not share his humour (Ross 2001, 202) and, like Fielding, his novel is full of swipes against literary critics and professed connoisseurs and experts who might misjudge his book. In one attack, Tristram reflects on his desire for a reader who would give up his imagination into his hands: 'I would go fifty miles on foot, for I have not a horse worth riding on, to kiss the hand of that man whose generous heart will give up the reins of his imagination into his author's hands, ——be pleased he knows not why, and cares not wherefore' (144). Such a wish is oddly counter to Tristram's often cited desire that his reader exercise his own imagination, free of authorial control:

> Writing, when properly managed, (as you may be sure I think mine is) is but a different name for conversation. As no one, who knows what he is about in good company, would venture to talk all; – so no author, who understands the just boundaries of decorum and good breeding, would presume to think all. The truest respect which you can pay to the reader's understanding, is to halve this matter amicably, and leave him something to imagine, in his turn, as well as yourself. (87)

The eighteenth-century reader is thus a fitting paradigm for the wider problems of sociability. Readers are often befriended, flattered and welcomed in eighteenth-century novels. But readers are also seen as potentially distracted, wayward, dissenting, imperious – often in the same novels.[20] The same kinds of concerns expressed by moral philosophy – Shaftesbury's caution that only in exclusive groups would true sociability prevail, Hume's disappointment that the ideals of club culture could not be applied to society more generally – are replayed in the relationship between the eighteenth-century author and his/her reader. While eighteenth-century literature, then, might often lack images of communities happily bound together through love, loyalty and unselfishness, its texts constantly interrogate the nature of the relationship between author and reader. This relationship can sometimes be just as acrimonious as the failure of families and coteries to integrate into society, more dangerous and corrupt. Publishing obviously entails speaking beyond one's own friends and family. Speaking to strangers, as literature implies, will always be the more exacting test of sociability.

## Notes

1. See Hume's early essay 'Of Essay Writing' (1742; Hume 1996, 1–5).
2. See Warren 1983.
3. The multiple nature of individuality is also explored through Martinus's romantic entanglement with the conjoined twins, Lindamora–Indamira. For interesting discussions of this episode see Todd 1995 and Hawley 1998.

4. 'John of Bucks' denotes the Tory politician John Sheffield, Duke of Buckingham. Townshend and Argyll, both Whigs, had opposed payment to Scottish clans on the basis that these funds supported Jacobitism.

5. See the satirical examples of Sarah Fielding 1969, 82–91; Smollett 1984, 116–17; Goldsmith 1969, 98–105. Gordon's first essay in *The Humourist* describes 'news-writers' as forming the 'most populous Society within the Liberties' of London (1720, 1). The rural academy described in Fordyce's work is repeatedly called a 'Poetical Club'.

6. The figure of 38 includes the Spectator club itself – the framing fiction of the periodical. The use of the club motif as a framing device for the periodical is discussed in chapter 2.

7. See Somerville 1996 and compare Swift's 'A Character, Panegyric, and Description of the Legion Club' (1736) for an additional literary example of the motif of the club as a political assembly, in this case the shambolic and corrupt parliament in Dublin.

8. For important discussions of Pope's political affiliations, see Goldgar 1976, Gerrard 1994 and Erskine-Hill 1996.

9. Attacks on the club's supposed collaborative writing were also frequent. In *The Confederates* (1717), J. D. Breval pictured Pope gloating secretly over his skill in making Gay take responsibility for the 'failure' of their play, *Three Hours After Marriage*. See also Leonard Welsted, *One Epistle to Mr A. Pope* (1732) in Welsted 1965, 17.

10. Elizabeth Carter failed to persuade Hester Chapone to publish the writings of her 'green book' (see Carter 1817, I 342–50). David Shields's excellent account of sociability in eighteenth-century British America argues that manuscript dominated the writings associated with coffee houses, clubs, balls, salons, colleges and gaming tables (Shield 1997). See Ezell 1999 for the argument that we have underestimated the significance of a continuing manuscript culture among literary writers of the early eighteenth century.

11. Harold Love argues that the reign of George I (1714–27) might be dated as the moment at which a transition occurred from a scribal to a print culture as the medium of ideological debate (1993).

12. See Leapor's poems 'The Headache: To Aurelia', 'An Epistle to Artemisia: On Fame', 'Minutius. Artemisia. A Dialogue', 'The Epistle of Deborah Dough', 'Upon her Play being Returned to her, stained with Claret', 'The Proposal' and 'To Lucinda'; and Elizabeth Hands's poems 'A Poem, on the Supposition of an Advertisement appearing in a Morning Paper, of the Publication of a Volume of Poems, by a Servant Maid' and 'A Poem, on the Supposition of the Book having been published and read' (both published in *The Death of Amnon*, 1789). See also Janet Little's poem 'Given to a Lady Who Asked me to Write a

Poem'. Poems of imagined reception are a feature of women's writing in general, as, for example, in Mary Jones's dramatised attempt to gain a patron in 'An Epistle to Lady Bowyer' (1750). Jones gives up the attempt when she finds the lord's footman act as literary critic. (This poem is reprinted in Fairer and Gerrard 1999.) Gray's 'A Long Story' is an example by a male poet who shared a timidity and caution of print with many eighteenth-century women writers.

13. The complete poem is reprinted in Fairer and Gerrard 1999.

14. The Licensing Act restricted legitimacy to only two theatres in London as a result of increasing tension between the government, primarily Robert Walpole, and the theatres which staged satirical performances, openly critical of government in general and Walpole in particular. Among the most notable of these were several plays by Fielding, whose turn to fiction in the 1740s is widely interpreted as a response to this censorship. For the relationship between the theatre and the novel, see Brown 1981, Hunter 1984, Marshall 1986, Campbell 1995, and Allen 1998.

15. Warner notes that reading fictional characters as if they were real is not new in the eighteenth century (and he refers to the debates concerning *La Princess de Clèves*, 1678), but that these discussions have a new level of importance in the eighteenth century. See Warner 1998, 224 n.21.

16. Ian Watt's discussion of 'formal realism' in relation to *Pamela* tends to associate this novel with the emergence of modern subjectivity. The reading of Pamela as inaugurating the 'depth' psychology of modern subjectivity is evident in those readings which see the complexities and contradictions in Pamela's behaviour and thinking as part of her psychology. That Pamela is in love with Mr B, for example, is seen to be unrecognised by Pamela, but transparent to us. (Why is she so apparently angry when Mr B suggests she marry Williams? Why does she delay in Bedfordshire to complete Mr B's waistcoat? Why do two cows appear to Pamela as two bulls?) Pamela questions why she is so concerned when she learns that Mr B almost drowned ('What is the Matter, with all his ill Usage of me, that I cannot hate him?'; Richardson 2001 179) – the readers supply the answer. That Pamela suppresses a truth known to us (that she desires Mr B) only seems to increase the 'truthfulness' of the account.

17. Quoted in *Pamela Censured*, 67–8 (in Keymer and Sabor 2001, II).

18. Compare Dowling's argument that the verse epistle also constructs an ideal reader who might join the community of the poet and his friends in refusing the corruptions of the world (1991).

19. These are also questions of commerce in the new financial culture of symbolic value of stocks, shares and paper money. When David

applies to Mr Nicols for a loan, using Valentine's wealth accrued in Jamaica as security, Mr Nichols refuses to accept only Valentine's word as sufficient security (368–70). For important accounts of the links between fiction and finance in the eighteenth century see Nicholson 1994, Sherman 1996, Thompson 1996, Lynch 1998 and Ingrassia 1998.

20. For discussions of potentially distracted and partial readers, see Barrell 1983, Bender 1987, and Warner 1998. For recent work on eighteenth-century readers, see Warner 1998 and Fergus 2000. Hunter 1977 discusses the direct address to the reader as an attempt to counter increasingly private modes of reading.

# 2 Social/Textual Forms

Much contemporary work on eighteenth-century literature defines it as a discursive space in which writers can imagine and challenge the social order. Indeed this statement might summarise the vast amount of work on the novel in the 1980s and 1990s: John Bender's discussion of the novel as prefiguring changes in prison design and legislation (Bender 1987), John Mullan's argument that eighteenth-century writing in general, and the sentimental novel in particular, attempts to stage society as a scheme of consensus (Mullan 1988) and John Richetti's account of the reciprocal definitions of fictional self and society (Richetti 1999) are prominent examples of this tendency. For John Richetti (1992 and 1999) and Paula Backscheider (2000), eighteenth-century prose fiction is the genre in which a textual public sphere becomes possible. And, as we have seen in chapter 1, John Bender links Fielding's style of narration with the negotiation of a rational public consensus within the public sphere. This chapter further develops these arguments by examining how literary forms in the eighteenth century, including the novel, might be said to continue the ideals of sociable, critical discussion and to extend those ideals into a specifically literary sphere.

Habermas is again an explicit presence behind these kinds of argument, for the public sphere that he discusses is one prefigured in print. In *The Structural Transformation of the Public Sphere*, the literary public sphere is the precursor of a political public sphere and the public is always, from the outset, a reading public.[1] The sociable spaces of coffee house, club, salon, tavern, and reading society grew in significance only because of the growth of the press associated with them. The published word was 'the decisive mark' of the 'new domain of a public sphere' (Habermas 1989, 16). Habermas opens the book with an examination of the etymological links between ideas of 'a public', 'publication', and 'publicity'. Timothy Dykstal captures these overlapping associations when he defines the Habermasian public sphere as 'that space in participatory societies where citizens talk about – where they "publish" – their opinions, to make them known to themselves as well as to others' (Dykstal 1996, 27). That this language is not altogether unfamiliar to eighteenth-century readers themselves is suggested by Frances Burney's self-conscious 'Preface' to *Evelina* (1778): 'The following letters are presented to the public – for such, by novel writers, novel readers will be called' (Burney 2000, 95).

However, that Burney's address is partly ironic, implying a pretension that novelists bequeath upon themselves, is also significant. It is at least a reminder to us not to overestimate or idealise the extent to which literature might create a political democracy, one of the wilder claims of enthusiastic commentators. Eighteenth-century literature rarely allowed such self-congratulation to go without criticism. While *The Spectator* boasted of its 'Threescore thousand Disciples' (No. 10; Bond 1965, I 44), Swift warned: 'It is the Folly of too many to mistake the Echo of a London Coffee house for the Voice of the Kingdom' (1711, 47). And although Tristram Shandy defended the detail of his memoirs as not wanting to disappoint 'any one soul living', he also conceded that 'I know there are readers in the world, as well as many other good people in it, who are no readers at all' (Sterne 1983, 7). Many eighteenth-century literary texts do celebrate the potential of writing in general, and publication in particular, to create a new kind of community. Writing in *The Guardian* (172; 28 Sept. 1713), for example, Pope claims that writing makes 'the Voice become visible' so that 'what is spoken and thought at one Pole, may be heard and understood at the other'. Such confidence, of course, overlooks the small matter of different languages, as it does of contrary readers, who may misread as much as agree. Pope himself knew that readers might well misunderstand his words, even when they lived in the same city space, as chapter 4 will explore in more detail. The gap between aspiration and reality regarding eighteenth-century readers mirrors that discussed in chapter 1 – between a society that prided itself on its polite sociability and one that also routinely castigated its own inability to create or sustain this ideal.

This chapter then will consider whether it is at the level of textual form that the ideals of open, critical discussion and the social virtues of respect, toleration and understanding can be located. As chapter 1 has shown, too many eighteenth-century texts question and challenge the idea that these ideals already exist to allow us to think there is a seamless fit between the polite society sketched by historians of eighteenth-century society and philosophy and the depictions of that society we see in its literary texts. Perhaps then, it is in the literary modes and genres of the periodical, the novel and the incorporation of conversational ideals into other genres such as the dialogue, the familiar letter and the verse epistle, that eighteenth-century literature responds to the ideal self-representations of its own culture.

## The novel

In chapter 1, the relationship between novelist and reader was considered as a type of literary sociability. In the novel of sensibility, the reader is idealised as a sympathetic friend of the tender-hearted hero or heroine, and, by implication, of the novelist herself. In novels by Fielding, Haywood and Sterne, the reader is directly addressed, as if buttonholed in a conversation with the imperious, garrulous narrator. Even where the reader is imagined as wayward, cynical or just distracted, these novels foster the sense of a direct conversation, which establishes a kind of virtual community, between author, characters and readers in the absence of real association. At its most dangerous, these conversations are figured as too intimate, too private. This is certainly the response of countless eighteenth-century men and women who feared the unregulated tendencies of the novel, particularly when read by the solitary reader in her closet. Images of novel reading in the eighteenth century are thus split between those of sociable groups, reading aloud together and discussing their reading amicably, and the silent, individual reader, wrapped up in her own sympathetic engagement with the book.

These diverse pictures neatly illustrate the contrary implications of the novel as a 'public' or 'conversational' genre. The novel has traditionally been regarded as the form through which modern ideas of subjectivity and individualism are established. The solitary reader is only the reflected image of the private self explored in the novel, according to this view. However, just as the image of the solitary reader has been called into question – by empirical research into reading communities and by new interpretative approaches to

eighteenth-century literary texts, which trace the explicit construction of readers as part of these texts' meanings – so too the meanings and definitions of this 'individual' self have been much
revised. We have tended to think of subjectivity as the purest definition of a 'private' sphere. And traditionally – or at least since Ian
Watt's important study *The Rise of the English Novel* (1957) – the
novel has been seen as the account of a highly particularised, individual self, told through the new mode of psychological realism.
The tendency of critical work on the novel in the 1990s, however,
was to question the absolute distinction between 'public' and 'private' life which Watt's account of individualism implicitly relied
upon. Novelistic individualism is now seen as a socialised individuality, rather than the trans-historical interiority that Watt's formal
realism appeared only to unveil.[2]

The critical history of the eighteenth-century novel since Watt
might be summarised as mirroring the development of the
approaches of new historicism and cultural studies out of the 'older'
historicist and more purely marxist interpretations of the novel.
Many of these approaches agree that the individualism sketched by
Watt is too abstract and that the very idea of the individualised self
was problematised within eighteenth-century fiction. Terry Castle,
for example, focuses on fictional representations of the masquerade
as dramatising the very nature of the novels in which they occur,
including the ways in which the novel parodies ideas of unique individuality (Castle 1986) and Richetti argues that despite the intense
focus on character subjectivity in the work of Defoe, Richardson, and
Burney, 'even those novels are about the limitations (and moral dangers) of individualism' and novels by authors such as Fielding and
Smollett 'are deeply critical (and hilariously satirical) of this emerging modern self and the new kind of society that encourages it'
(Richetti 1996, 8). In short, for eighteenth-century fiction, 'individuality itself is the issue' (Richetti 1999, 16). For Watt, the psychological
realm of fiction is a private, intimate space. For a host of more recent
critics, the psychological realm of fiction is also a public and
socialised space. For Nancy Armstrong (1987), a 'unique', inter-
nalised personality is created only from the social pressures exerted
by early modern conduct books and the novels which are their counterparts; John Mullan (1988) and Aileen Douglas (1995) focus upon
the body as the point of intersection between the social and the individual; Betty Schellenberg (1996) discusses the ways in which the fic-

tional conversational circle, so common among mid-century novels, serves as an alternative to the bourgeois individualised self; and Richard Barney (1999) argues that Watt overlooks the 'public' dimension of Lockean thinking, particularly evident in his work on pedagogy in which personal behaviour is moulded so as to conform to social norms.

What is true of studies of the eighteenth-century novel in general, is also true of the sentimental novel in particular. In 1974, Brissenden wrote that the 'one basic notion' of sentimentalism was the idea that 'the source of all knowledge and all values is the individual human experience' (4) and the view that sentimentalism was radically individualistic was unquestioned until more recent studies of sensibility, when, for example, Van Sant (1993) located sentimentalism within the context of contemporary sciences; Benedict (1994) argued that novels of sensibility framed models of social feeling and traditional values from which their readers could learn; and Ellis (1996), Bellamy (1998) and Skinner (1999) all argued for the political significance of novels of sensibility. The first of these more sociological approaches to sentimental fiction was that of John Mullan (1988), who examined the ways in which sentimental fiction attempted to create a more ideal space of social relations, as figured in the relationship between writer and reader. The arguments of Benedict and Mullan in particular link an important point within this chapter's discussion (namely, that eighteenth-century fiction was deeply suspicious of ideas of modern individualism, the very ideas which critics such as Watt have hailed as part of the novel's innovative representation) with the arguments of the first chapter (that eighteenth-century readers were called to participate in the imaginative space of the novel). As Benedict's work argues, for example: 'By portraying the virtue of the individual as the ability to sympathize with fellow humans, sentimental fictions moralize private experience in an attempt to counter the threat that novelistic individualism offers conventional social relations' (Benedict 1994, 6).[3] In all of these accounts, the novel assumes a cultural centrality because in this form, more than any other, we see the importance of private feeling to the public sphere. For Habermas, individuals bring to the public sphere the identity they have developed 'in private'. The egalitarianism offered by the public sphere is one in which everyone shares an abstract humanity that encompasses and is defined by each person's individually validated identity:

The sphere of the public arose in the broader strata of the bour-geoisie as an expansion and at the same time completion of the inti-mate sphere of the conjugal family. Living room and *salon* were under the same roof; and just as the privacy of the one was oriented toward the public nature of the other, and as the subjectivity of the privatized individual was related from the very start to publicity, so both were conjoined in literature that had become 'fiction'. (Habermas 1989, 50)

If we contrast some approaches to Defoe's *Robinson Crusoe* (1719), we can also see something of these major shifts in critical interpretations of the novel, something of how Watt's ideas have been challenged and refined over the past 40 years. *Robinson Crusoe* has often been situated as the first novel in English, and cer-tainly this is where Watt's narrative of the rise of the novel begins. Feminist criticism has challenged the way in which this narrative ignores the amatory fictions of Aphra Behn, Delarivier Manley and Eliza Haywood, which either preceded, or, in the case of Haywood, appeared simultaneously with, Defoe's belated turn to fiction in the final decade of his own writing career. *Robinson Crusoe* figures as the 'first' novel in Watt's account, however, not explicitly because its author was a man, but because this text, above all others, has been read as the account of a unique identity, of a psychological interi-ority seen as constitutive of the novel as a genre. (The female-authored fictions which do not appear to depict individual personalities in any 'depth' are then omitted from these kinds of narrative.) Defoe's use of fictionalised Puritan autobiography in the writing of *Robinson Crusoe* certainly makes the book one of intense introspection. What novel could be more fitting to show the genre's emphasis on particular, individualised identity than the story of a sailor shipwrecked and living alone on a desert island for much of the account? And if we consider the relationship between the novel and ideas and ideals of community as a significant aspect of how literary form engages with social forms, how can we account for a novel with, for the most part, just one character?

For Watt, individualism is a modern concept, defined by the ways in which each person is seen as independent from any other and free from tradition. Such individualism is possible because of the rise of industrial capitalism, which relies upon the economic separation of individuals, and because of the spread of Protestantism, especially in the form of Puritan individualism. And since Robinson Crusoe amasses a private wealth from his desert island while examining his own conscience through the intensity of his spiritual diary, he can be seen as the very epitome of these two impulses. Even if we restrict our focus to those sections of the book in which Crusoe is alone on the island, however, we can see that defining individualism in terms of independence and innovation cannot fully account for this work. For example, the novel continually tests individuality against the norms of community. This is evident in Crusoe's frequent comparisons between his experiences and those of 'the world': deliberating how he should turn his grindstone to sharpen his tools costs him as much thought as 'a Statesman would have bestow'd upon a grand Point of Politicks, or a Judge upon the Life and Death of a Man' (Defoe 1994, 61) and birds who steal his corn are treated as thieves would be in England, namely shot and hung as a warning to others (85). At the level of form, the diary that Crusoe records also continues the sense of continual testing:

> *Why has God done this to me? What have I done to be thus us'd?*
> My Conscience presently check'd me in that Enquiry, as if I had blasphem'd, and methought it spoke to me like a Voice; WRETCH! *dost thou ask what thou hast done!* Look back upon a dreadful misspent Life, and ask thy self *what thou has not done? Ask,* Why is it *that thou wert not long ago destroy'd?* Why *wert thou not drown'd in* Yarmouth Roads? *Kill'd in the Fight when the Ship was taken by* the Sallee man of War? *Devour'd by the wild Beasts on the* Coast of Africa? Or, *Drown'd HERE, when all the Crew perish'd but thy self?* Dost thou ask, *What have I done?*
> I was struck dumb with these Reflections, as one astonish'd, and had not a Word to say, no not to answer to my self, but rose up pensive and sad . . . (68)

This is not a journal of textual solipsism. Instead, Crusoe's self-questioning and examination always open his character to a critique and confession that reaches beyond introspection. This is partly because Crusoe's identity is always already a socialised identity. His refusal to be naked, despite his solitariness and the heat, is one obvious example of this (98). Additionally, the diary is framed by Crusoe's recollections of his experiences, in which the diary's ostensible address to God and to himself is replaced by an obvious address to the reader. Crusoe is a 'Memento' to others, a warning and a reminder of sinfulness (140–1). Defoe used the third volume of his work, *Serious Reflections during the Life and Surprising Adventures of Robinson Crusoe* (1720), to restate the importance of the book as primarily didactic. In defending the veracity of the book as a real 'history', Defoe hints that the account is based on his own experiences of imprisonment and in reading Crusoe's confinement on the island as an allegory, the reader might make application to other kinds of experience, since ''tis as reasonable to represent one kind of Imprisonment by another, as it is to represent any Thing that really exists, by that which exists not' (242). This is a definition of representation and a defence of its potential to be both realistic and symbolic at once. It is also an admission that reading supplies and applies meaning. Thus *Robinson Crusoe*, no less than the novels discussed in chapter 1, gestures towards its readers throughout and folds them into its own space.

For Defoe, readers need not experience shipwreck, confinement or even imprisonment, his own experience. In the essay 'On Solitude' in *Serious Reflections*, he writes of how man can be just as isolated and alone in the midst of the crowds of London as he might be on a desert island: 'I enjoy more Solitude in the Middle of the greatest Collection of Mankind in the World, I mean, at *London*, while I am writing this, than ever I could say I enjoy'd in eight and twenty Years Confinement to a desolate Island' (245). Solitude is defined in this essay, not in the more usual sense of being alone, but as being in a state of contemplation. Contemplation, peace, tranquillity and being with God are suggested as the true ends of solitude, rather than apartness, and such a solitude, it is implied, is more likely to be achieved amidst the crowds of London than in a hermit's cell or on a desert island. Tempting as it might be to think of the island experience as permitting an advantageous retreat into the self, Defoe's essay stresses that it does not have that effect. And because solitude can be achieved more successfully in a crowd than when alone, Defoe implies a model of selfhood which is relational rather than absolutist. Defoe's own commentary upon his fiction in the *Serious Reflections* might then lend support to Novak's argument that *Robinson Crusoe* does not idealise solitary life on a island, but rather dramatises the fear and insecurity of living outside civilisation, the punishment which isolation represents (1963).

Watt's argument that *Robinson Crusoe* represents an individualism characteristic of the eighteenth-century novel is also challenged in Richard Barney's more recent account of the ways in which the novel emerged as a form of popular education (Barney 1999). His chapter on *Robinson Crusoe* argues that the story is about the 'eventual *effacement* of strictly private selfhood in favor of lucidly public and political identity' (252). This is not only because Crusoe becomes the 'Lord and Lawgiver' of a community comprising Friday, Friday's father and the Spaniard (Defoe 1994, 174) rather than the earlier community of Crusoe, his parrot, dog and two cats (108), but also because he comes to recognise that 'private' or personal promptings are part of a larger providential order. His individuality, in Barney's terms, is 'shaped by being eminently legible – both to the eyes of Providence and those of the viewer/reader' (203). *Crusoe* is an exemplary case within Barney's treatment of the eighteenth-century novel because it embodies the eighteenth-century sense of subjectivity as improvised, as an entity both public and private, created through both social orchestration and individual agency. To this extent, Barney's specific treatment of the relationship between educational and fictional texts echoes John Richetti's more general reflections on the eighteenth-century novel, such as that: 'Novelistic specificity focuses on social relationships that promote self-awareness in characters balanced (or torn) between individualism and communal identity. The effect is to render individuals as (potentially) both socially constructed and individually defined' (Richetti 1999, 8).

Frances Burney's *Evelina* (1778) has also figured centrally in critical accounts of the novel because it, like *Robinson Crusoe*, seems to represent an acute interiority. Evelina, while shy, embarrassed and properly retiring in company, writes explicitly of her feelings and fears in letters to her guardian, the Reverend Villars, and to her close friend, Miss Mirvan. Indeed, most accounts of the phenomenal popularity which *Evelina* enjoyed on its first publication suggest that it was because the novel gave access to the thoughts of a young girl on her 'entrance into the world', as the novel's subtitle highlights. Evelina is 'entering into the world' in two ways. As a girl just turned 17 she is 'coming out' in society as a young woman, one who can put childhood behind her, who can now move in the sphere of adulthood and, crucially, one who might now marry. Evelina is also 'entering the world' of London society after 16 years retirement in the country at Berry Hill. Evelina marks the absolute distinction between country and capital when she writes of how their group must '*Londonize*' themselves (Burney 2000, 116). These rituals of 'coming out' into the world of high society might be mapped onto the ways in which Habermas defined the public sphere. A specific kind of public emerges out of the lives of private individuals, out of a reading public. People bring their experiences of intimacy and privacy to test out that self in relation to a public culture. However, in testing out individuality within a public culture, that individual identity is shown to be provisional. This is the implication of eighteenth-century fiction, although it is not something which Habermas, with his focus upon political spheres and the emergence of democracy, pursues. *Evelina* certainly shows identity to be provisional, always improvised through experiences in and encounters with the world.

In one reading of the novel, Evelina experiences a life split between public and private selves. Social decorum insists that Evelina behave politely to those who make her feel uncomfortable and hide her true estimation and feelings on countless occasions. One of the first lessons Evelina learns, for example, is that ballroom etiquette prohibits a young lady from choosing whom she can refuse and accept as a dance partner. The novel is full of situations in which Evelina must dissemble or be silent and her inability to speak her mind because of the conventions of properly feminine behaviour is compounded by her own shyness and delicacy. At her first visit to a public ball at the Ridotto, Evelina had wriggled out of dancing with Sir Clement Willoughby by hinting of a pre-engagement with Lord Orville. Wanting to apologise to Lord Orville for this 'impertinence', Evelina finds herself unable to speak:

> the conversation became calmly sociable, and politely cheerful, and, to every body but me, must have been highly agreeable: – but, as to myself, I was so eagerly desirous of making some apology to Lord Orville . . . and yet so utterly unable to assume sufficient courage to speak to him . . . that I hardly ventured to say a word all the time we were walking. . . . So . . . I continued silent, uncomfortable, and ashamed. (159)

Continually Evelina is silent and bashful in company, eloquent and open in her letters to Villars and Miss Mirvan. The distinction between how Evelina feels and how Evelina behaves is continually being underscored. When Lord Orville visits Evelina after seeing her at Marybone Gardens, Evelina can tell Villars how she feels but she cannot show these feelings to Lord Orville:

> the next moment, he appeared himself.
>
> If formerly, when in the circle of high life, and accustomed to its manners, I so much admired and distinguished the grace, the elegance of Lord Orville, think, Sir, how they must strike me now, – now, when, far removed from that splendid circle, I live with those to whom even civility is unknown, and decorum a stranger!
>
> I am sure I received him very awkwardly; depressed by a situation so disagreeable, could I do otherwise? (367)

J. Paul Hunter notes that the first readers of *Evelina* loved the novel because they felt they were 'being let in on secrets' (1996, 33). And the intimacy which the letter form creates between heroine and reader is undoubtedly still a large part of the pleasure of this novel. However, the discreet veiling of her emotions in public is also the key dilemma for the eighteenth-century heroine: properly reserved, she is also inevitably conscious of being 'read', her behaviour being interpreted in ways over which she has little control. She is constantly concerned how Lord Orville, in particular, will judge her actions, a concern for how she is 'read' that is literalised when Villars calls her 'a book that both afflicts and perplexes me' (394).

A number of critics have discussed the novel as dramatising reading practices and, in particular, as delineating in Lord Orville the paradigm of an ideal reader.[4] The novel traces the reform of Lord Orville as reader, as he changes his opinion of Evelina during the course of the novel. At first he thinks her 'a poor, weak girl', either 'ignorant or mischievous' (128–9). Later, reminded of this initial judgement by Sir Clement, he traces the change in his opinion:

> I knew not, then, how new she was to the world; at present, however, I am convinced, that whatever might appear strange in her behaviour, was simply the effect of inexperience, timidity, and a retired education, for I find her informed, sensible, and intelligent. She is not, indeed, like most modern young ladies, to be known in half an hour; her modest worth, and fearful excellence, require both time and encouragement to shew themselves. She does not, beautiful as she is, seize the soul by surprise, but, with more dangerous fascination, she steals it almost imperceptibly. (486–7)

Evelina, not to be known in half an hour, comes thus to be truly known only by Villars, Miss Mirvan, Lord Orville – and the novel's readers. And this resistance is the mark, not only of Burney's fictional heroine, but of proper femininity as defined by eighteenth-century conduct books. Nancy Armstrong has written of how the bourgeois model of female interiority, developed in the eighteenth century, displaced the previous model, based on aristocratic public display (Armstrong 1987). That women possess a heightened emotional sensibility, that theirs is an overwhelmingly inner life, becomes the hallmark of bourgeois female subjectivity. Thus the eighteenth-century woman comes to figure as the 'first' middle-class person and as the locus for the development of the novel, with its interest in subjectivity. For literary history, this means that the novel is a relentlessly 'feminised' form, not just because increasing numbers of women writers openly publish novels, but because the genre itself takes as its subject the 'interiority' which is a feature of femininity. To recognise that this 'private self' is a feminised self is also to recognise that 'interiority' is fashioned by its public representations.

If woman is the ultimate 'private' person, then domesticity is the ultimate private space. The intimacy and affection of the idyllic home becomes the site of the eighteenth century's ideal form of sociability, the affectionate couple becomes the community which can face and refuse the corruptions of a rapacious, divisive world. While bad marriages merely reflect the selfishness of an individualistic society, happy marriages, like harmonious societies, preserve the ideals of wider consensus within a coterie, or, in this case perhaps, a couple. That the eighteenth-century novel valorises a retreat from a 'public' world into the private spaces of home or country is evident in a significant number of novels, many of which draw back from the corruptions and dangers of 'the world', usually London society, to position their family groups more safely in the retreat and privacy of the countryside. Fielding's *Amelia* (1751), Smollett's *Humphry Clinker*, and Burney's *Evelina* certainly idealise the countryside as a space of quiet virtue and security and return their characters to its protection at the close of the narrative. *Amelia*, in particular, juxtaposes the urban world of gambling, corruption, debt, lawsuits and sexual infidelity into which Booth's waywardness leads him with the idyllic countryside of Amelia's childhood to which they are restored in the final chapter.

Explaining the subsequent fortunes of his characters, Fielding's narrator notes that Booth returned to London for two days to pay off his final debts but 'hath never since been thirty miles from home' (Fielding 1987, 545). For James Thompson, such novels serve to construct and consolidate the ideology of separate spheres, in which the 'masculine' sphere of publicity and finance is ranged against the essential 'femininity' of privacy and emotion (Thompson 1996).

But, as the discussion of the 'public' nature of interiority suggested above, this kind of distinction – between 'public' and 'private', between 'personal' and 'political' – cannot be defined in such absolute terms. It has certainly been open to many challenges, mostly feminist, in the 1990s. For Patricia Meyer Spacks, for example, the novel by the end of the eighteenth century has become a 'feminized part of the new public sphere, in which discussions of politics and of private life could meet' (Spacks 1990, 233). Partly this is because feminism has taught us that, if 'the personal is the political', then boundaries between what is 'political' or even 'public' need to be redrawn so as to incorporate issues of family and emotional life, in short issues of sexual politics. It is also because we have learnt to look for issues of finance and power in our reading, not merely expecting that women novelists (or indeed novelists in general) will write about interiority and private subjectivity. Gillian Skinner opens her discussion of sentimental fiction with the premise that: 'it is perfectly possible to address "public" issues of contemporary economic or political debate within the framework of a sentimental exploration of the "private" world of feeling' (Skinner 1999, 3).

The ultimate impossibility of splitting the 'public' from the 'private' is also made apparent in *Evelina*. Although Evelina attempts to shun publicity and cast herself into shade, her modesty, shyness and delicacy themselves court attention because these are qualities celebrated and valued in young ladies. In other words, the more retiring her behaviour, the more she attracts comment. As Lady Howard notes in a letter to Villars: 'she has a certain air of inexperience and innocency that is extremely interesting' (111). Even after she has been acknowledged by her father and engaged to Lord Orville, Evelina still wants to avoid drawing attention to herself. She marvels, for example, at the behaviour of young ladies at Bath: 'At the pump-room, I was amazed at the public exhibition of the ladies in the bath: it is true, their heads are covered with bonnets, but the very idea of being seen, in such a situation, by whoever pleases to look, is indelicate' (539). (Lest we think Evelina is shy of exposing herself in revealing bathing-costume, we might remember from Lydia Melford's account of Bath in *Humphry Clinker* that ladies bathing wear 'jackets and petticoats of brown linen'; Smollett 1984, 39.) However, Evelina finds herself the centre of attention on numerous occasions. At the theatre, Evelina listens as the gentlemen with her party discuss whether her colour is due to attractive blushing or the application of rouge (180–1). At the Pantheon, Evelina finds herself openly stared at by a gentleman who, in an '*audible whisper*' asks Sir Clement: 'who is that lovely creature?' (211). The gentleman, Lord Merton, then joins Lord Orville, Sir Clement and Captain Mirvan in a general discussion which compares the beauties of the ladies in their party with the beauties of architecture (212–13). Evelina finds herself the centre of attention at Bristol when a copy of verses praising her beauty is circulated in the pump-room and strangers openly measure her against the claims of the poem:

> We went first to the pump-room. It was full of company! and the moment we entered, I heard a murmuring of, '*That's she!*' and, to my great confusion, I saw every eye turned towards me. I pulled my hat over my face, and, by the assistance of Mrs Selwyn, endeavoured to screen myself from observation: nevertheless, I found I was so much the object of general attention, that I entreated her to hasten away. . . .
> . . . But we had not gone three yards, before we were followed by a party of young men, who took every possible opportunity of looking at us, and, as they walked behind, talked aloud, in a manner at once unintelligible and absurd. 'Yes,' cried one, ''tis certainly she! – mark but her *blushing cheek!*'
> 'And then her *eye*, – her *downcast eye!*' cried another.
> 'True, oh most true,' said a third, '*every beauty is her own!*'
> 'But then,' said the first, 'her *mind*, – now the difficulty is, to find out the truth of *that*, for she will not say a word.'
> 'She is *timid*,' answered another: 'mark but her *timid air*.' (464)

In a culture that valorises the private introspection and modest retirement of the young lady, those qualities are also on 'display'. Richard Barney neatly captures this paradox when he writes of how women were represented as 'publicly private figures' (1999, 319).

*Evelina* can be seen as thematising this paradox in numerous plot details, such as the circulation of the anonymous verses on Evelina, referred to above, or in the way in which Evelina's attempt to keep her name secret from Lord Orville's retinue only makes her companions reveal it (372). It is also suggested throughout in the novel's deployment of the epistolary mode. The letter is the literary form which more than any other confounds the distinction of public and private. In this regard, it corresponds with the novel. Both forms appear to be resolutely private (both are most associated with single readers and the letter is rarely published) and individualistic (the creation of fictional, three-dimensional character in the novelistic hero or heroine; the autobiographical absorption of the letter-writer). However, like the novel, ideas of privacy and individualism are played out in forms of public conversation.

## Textual letters: the familiar letter, the verse epistle and epistolary fiction

In 1751, Johnson lamented that so few writers had distinguished themselves by publishing their letters (*The Rambler*, 152, 31 August, 1751). One year later, in his biography of Swift, John Boyle, Earl of Orrery, deplored 'that license which of late has too much prevailed of publishing epistolary correspondences' (1752, 156). The apparent contradiction between the two statements illustrates the ambivalence with which the eighteenth century confronted the publication of letters, perhaps even, publication itself.[5] In 1739, Pope had been the first writer to oversee the publication of his own letters, but the scandal of such self-promotion had had to be disguised through elaborate and complicated play with Curll. (Pope had deftly engineered a pirated edition of his personal letters so that he could then bring out an authorised, corrected edition without impropriety.) Few writers followed such a scandalous precedent: the letters of Lady Mary Wortley Montagu, Thomas Gray, Laurence Sterne, Horace Walpole and Samuel Richardson were all published posthumously. Sometimes letters might be inadvertently published as part of another's correspondence, but to publish one's own letters was to make public what was supposedly private. Despite their reluctance to publish their own letters, however, we know that Wortley Montagu, Sterne, Walpole and

Richardson all prepared their letters for publication and anticipated their being made public, even if only after their own deaths,
when accusations of vanity could not so easily be made. The letters
of Horace Walpole began to appear one year after his death, but
Walpole himself had already seemed to aspire to their publication:
he had previously bound all his letters to Mann in eight volumes.
Eighteenth-century writers certainly developed a new sense of how
they might be read by posterity. As John Brewer has argued, Pope's
careful negotiations were only one example of a new trend – 'the
process of making private correspondence a genre of publication,
of recognizing that if one's privacy was to be publicly represented,
it was better to do it oneself than to rely on (often unreliable) others' (Brewer 1995, 14). The familiar letter is an authentic letter written for a private audience, generally a friend or friends of the writer,
in distinction from the many works of philosophy, science, travel,
and history which adopted the letter as their form.[6] But although
the familiar letter is defined as an exchange between friends, many
eighteenth-century writers also envisaged the publication of their
'private' letters. Such letters then address several audiences simultaneously – or rather, the address to the intimate friend in manuscript becomes a way of forging a relationship with the more
anonymous, unknown, reader of print. Like the novels discussed in
chapter 1, then, the address to the single reader is, implicitly, an
address to other readers too. In this way, and, as we shall see, in
others, distinctions between 'private' and 'public' correspondences
break down.

We tend to think of the letter as an essentially 'private' genre,
among the most personal of written expressions (where it might be
compared with the diary or journal). Johnson defined it in this
sense when he wondered if the lack of published letters might be
because of a 'due sense of the dignity of the publick?':

> We do not think it reasonable to fill the world with volumes from
> which nothing can be learned, nor expect that the employments of
> the busy, or the amusements of the gay, should give way to narra-
> tives of our private affairs, complaints of absence, expressions of
> fondness, or declarations of fidelity. (Johnson 1969, V 43–4)

If the letter is by definition personal, inconsequential and relatively
unimportant, why then should Johnson desire that more great

writers publish their private letters? The answer takes us to one of the many ways in which the letter as 'personal' expression is a problematic idea in eighteenth-century terms. Personal letters were frequently read aloud. Swift joked about this practice when he wrote to Lord Bathurst: 'When I receive a letter from you, I summon a few very particular friends, who have a good taste, and invite them to it, as I would do if you had sent me a haunch of venison' (1963–5, V 253). And personal letters were always liable to be opened by the government-run Post Office in London. After the pirating of some of his letters, Pope wrote to Swift that he was not ashamed of those letters which, while they might be dull, were not immoral. He then added a parenthetical aside for the benefit of such government spies: 'as for instance, if they printed this letter I am now writing, which they easily may, if the underlings at the Post Office please to take a copy of it' (Pope 1956, III 80). Eighteenth-century letter-writing was also a 'public' form in so far as it was held to be a craft, one best cultivated by careful imitation of well-written examples. This last is the reason Johnson so desires writers to publish their correspondence: well-written, published letters might teach us all how to write well too. If the eighteenth century is thought of as the great age of the familiar letter, then, it is because letter-writing was cultivated as an art. Letter-writing manuals and collections of 'model' letters, both historical and fictional, abound in the period. Robert Dodsley's advice on letter-writing in *The Preceptor* (1775), for example, includes models by ancient writers (Cicero, Pliny), seventeenth-century exemplars (Voiture, Temple and Balzac) and more contemporary models (Pope and Gay). Richardson's *Letters Written to and for Particular Friends* (1741) is among the best known of the collections of fictional model letters among students of the eighteenth century, because compiling it led Richardson to write his first epistolary novel, *Pamela*. Such letter-writing manuals encouraged writers of all ranks to perfect epistolary technique. Moreover, at a time when the recipient paid for the cost of the correspondence, careful, deliberative letter-writing was only polite.

The debate as to whether letter-writing should be natural, artless, spontaneous and unaffected or careful, deliberative and composed is the debate which has dominated discussions of the eighteenth-century familiar letter, both then and now. Pope, Swift and Sterne all wrote of how important it was to appear natural and unaffected in writing a letter. Pope repeatedly wrote that writing a letter was just like 'talking upon paper' and Sterne wrote to his daughter Lydia 'never let your letters be studied ones – write naturally, and then you will write well'.[7] The air of spontaneity, however, was something which had to be created, as Pope and Sterne also knew. Both took extreme care over the writing of letters. The drafts of a number of Sterne's letters survive in his notebooks and the repetition of apparently 'spontaneous' passages also illustrates the deliberative nature of his familiar letters. Dodsley's essay on letter-writing, while ostensibly teaching how 'natural' and 'unaffected' such writing ought to be, indicates that the ideal letter was a compromise between sincerity of feeling and the decorum of its correct, not intuitive, expression:

> Set Discourses require a Dignity or Formality of Stile suitable to the Subject; whereas Letter-writing rejects all Pomp of Words, and is most agreeable when most familiar. But, tho' lofty Phrases are here improper, the Stile must not therefore sink into Meanness: And to prevent its doing so, an easy Complaisance, an open Sincerity, and unaffected Good-nature, should appear in every Place. A Letter should wear an honest, cheerful Countenance, like one who truly esteems, and is glad to see his Friend; and not look like a Fop admiring his own Dress, and seemingly pleased with nothing but himself. (Quoted in Redford 1986, 4)

The language of Dodsley's advice itself betrays the deliberate cultivation of ease: 'an easy Complaisance . . . *should appear. . .* '. While Sterne's fictional writings suggest a writer deeply conscious of the constructedness of (written) feelings, they also exemplify the maxims of many eighteenth-century letters: to express spontaneity is to write artfully. The best letters aspire to the condition of conversation, but then, as we have seen, conversation itself is properly seen as correct and decorous. Johnson's essay on epistolary writings in *The Rambler* (1751), like most writings on the letter, addresses the question of correct style. The essay refuses to make rules for letter-writing, because different subjects will require different kinds of voice and style:

> The qualities of the epistolary style most frequently required, are ease and simplicity, an even flow of unlaboured diction, and an artless arrangement of obvious sentiments. But these directions are no

sooner applied to use, than their scantiness and imperfection become evident. Letters are written to the great and to the mean, to the learned and the ignorant, at rest and in distress, in sport and in passion. Nothing can be more improper than ease and laxity of expression, when the importance of the subject impresses solicitude, or the dignity of the person exacts reverence.

That letters should be written with strict conformity to nature is true, because nothing but conformity to nature can make any composition beautiful or just. But it is natural to depart from familiarity of language upon occasions not familiar. Whatever elevates the sentiments will consequently raise the expression; whatever fills us with hope or terrour, will produce some perturbation of images and some figurative distortions of phrase. Wherever we are studious to please, we are afraid of trusting our first thoughts, and endeavour to recommend our opinion by studied ornaments, accuracy of method, and elegance of style. (Johnson 1969, V 45–6)

Johnson's most consistent advice is one of propriety, of fitting language appropriately to its subject-matter. To do so is never merely to 'emote' on paper.

That the question of the correct style for letter-writing still dominates our own period is evident in modern responses to the letters of Ignatius Sancho. These are studied in a number of university courses as a way of representing the experiences of the eighteenth century's 'others': the experience of black slaves. In many accounts, however, the letters sit rather problematically as representations of slave experience, especially compared to other black writers of the time, Olaudah Equiano in particular. Sancho's style is one of heightened emotion, of sentiment at its most self-conscious. It is an obviously 'artificial' style, and one that can tell us a great deal about sensibility as a literary mode in the latter half of the century. Consciously modelled on Sterne's style, the letters address issues of slavery, commercialism and imperialism in the language of deliberate emotion. But it is the letters' obvious 'affectation' that has troubled many and, at first glance, Equiano's autobiographical account of his life – *The Interesting Narrative* (1789) – can seem the more radical, even revolutionary work. In using the refined and self-consciously literary style of sensibility, Sancho's *Letters* are certainly unlike other African writings of the period.

Born on a slaveship crossing the Atlantic, Ignatius Sancho endured servitude in London before, with the help of the Duke and

Duchess of Montagu, becoming a self-employed, respectable member of the bourgeoisie as a shopkeeper in Westminster. He became renowned for his friendships with the wealthy and the famous in London society. He corresponded with Sterne, became a friend of Garrick and was painted by Gainsborough. His letters – published in 1782 as *Letters of the Late Ignatius Sancho: an African* – were tremendously popular. The first edition had over 1160 subscribers, and the two volumes of letters went through five editions before 1803, bringing Sancho's family a great deal of money. (Indeed, his son, Billy, became the first Black British publisher.) Sancho became famous beyond Westminster in his own lifetime when his letter to Sterne (27 July 1766) was included in Sterne's *Letters* of 1775. Sancho writes to Sterne as a stranger, someone who had enjoyed both *Tristram Shandy* and his Sermons, and appreciating Sterne's condemnation of slavery in the latter, asks him to write again on the subject:

> That subject, handled in your striking manner, would ease the yoke (perhaps) of many – but if only of one – Gracious God! – what a feast to a benevolent heart! – and, sure I am, you are an epicurean in acts of charity. – You, who are universally read, and as universally admired – you could not fail – Dear Sir, think in me you behold the uplifted hands of thousands of my brother Moors. – Grief you pathetically observe is eloquent; – figure to yourself their attitudes; – hear their supplicating addresses! – alas! – you cannot refuse. – Humanity must comply . . . (Sancho 1994, 86)

Sancho's style here is consciously sentimental. The free use of the dash is one indicator of this style, representing the immediacy of strong feeling, a kind of 'hesitatingly fluid style', in Markman Ellis's description (1996, 82). It tries to capture the way in which the mind naturally proceeds, flitting between phrases, and constructs the appearance of artlessness, of naturally occurring speech. Sancho here depicts himself as one man of feeling appealing to another: both are 'epicures' of charity. Significantly, then, Sterne's reply to the 'good-hearted Sancho' mirrors the first, in both subject-matter and in style:

> There is a strange coincidence, Sancho, in the little events (as well as in the great ones) of this world: for I had been writing a tender tale of the sorrows of a friendless poor negro-girl, and my eyes had

scarce done smarting with it, when your Letter of recommendation in behalf of so many of her brethren and sisters, came to me – but why *her brethren*? – or your's, Sancho! any more than mine? It is by the finest tints, and most insensible gradations, that nature descends from the fairest face about St. James's, to the sootiest complexion in Africa: at which tint of these, is it, that the ties of blood are to cease? and how many shades must we descend lower still in the scale, 'ere Mercy is to vanish with them? – but 'tis no uncommon thing, my good Sancho, for one half of the world to use the other half of it like brutes, & then endeavour to make 'em so. (July 1766; Sterne 1935, 285–6)

Sterne's reply attempts the same kind of conversational immediacy as that of Sancho (the qualification of 'why her brethren?', the abbreviated "'em'). Sancho's initial letter had conjured up the sight of the supplicating slave as a spectacle, as an affecting tableau, to arouse his reader's pity. This kind of highly visual vignette is typical of sentimental writing. Sterne's reply is a more indirect scene: he has just finished writing the affecting scene of the 'friendless poor negro-girl' which was published the following year (1767) in Volume IX of *Tristram Shandy*.[8] Sterne does not repeat the story because more significant for the familiar letter are his own feelings in regard to it. There is a curious solipsism here as Sterne weeps over the image he has deliberately composed, as his sentimental traveller will later do.

This consciously sentimental style is repeated in many letters by both Sancho and Sterne. Indeed, Ellis suggests that, such is the extent of Sancho's pastiche of Sterne, his letters might more properly be read as an 'epistolary novel' rather than a 'biography in letters' (81). Throughout the *Letters*, sensibility is expressed through sentiment, as a way of feeling ('I hope you cultivate the good-will and friendship of L—. He is a jewel – prize him – love him – and place him next your heart'; 29 Nov. 1778, or 'A tear of joy dancing upon the lids is a plaudit not to be equalled this side death!'; 1778) and as expressive style ('You must excuse blots and blunders – for I am under the dominion of a cruel head-ach – and a cough, which seems too fond of me'; 11 Oct. 1772). The self-consciousness of this style is everywhere apparent: in figuring himself as the supplicating slave in the letter to Sterne, for example, we see a self-dramatising, theatrical, perhaps even self-indulgent, persona being created. In *A Sentimental Journey* (1768), the exaggeration of sensibility suggests irony, and thus the book is often read as much as a satire on sensibility as it is an exemplary instance of it. Sancho, however, in the context of discussions of slavery is unlikely to be sending sensibility up. And commentators then and now have been divided over the implications Sancho's exaggerated sensibility raises. Thomas Jefferson, for example, argued that as a sentimentalist, Sancho problematically relies on feeling rather than argument in challenging slavery, and he was troubled by Sancho's imitations of Sternean (or 'Shandean') style:

> His letters are more honour to the heart than to the head. . . . He is often happy in the turn of his compliments, and his stile is easy and familiar, except when he affects a Shandean fabrication of words. . . . His imagination is wild and extravagant, escapes incessantly from every restraint of reason and taste, and, in the course of its vagaries, leaves a tract of thought as incoherent and eccentric, as is the course of a meteor through the sky. His subjects should often have led him to a process of sober reasoning: yet we find him always substituting sentiment for demonstration. (1787; quoted in Ellis 1996, 82–3)

Sancho's modern editor – Paul Edwards – is also troubled by the way in which the apparently artless, unpolished style of the letters only reveals the studied calculation of artlessness. In his introduction to the modern edition of Sancho's *Letters* (1994), Edwards comments closely on that famous letter to Sterne:

> when he calls Sterne 'an epicurean in acts of charity', enjoying his generous impulses as 'a feast to a benevolent heart' at the release 'if only of one – Gracious God!', we might detect behind the generosity of heart something of a self-indulgent benevolism as much concerned with enjoying the virtue of its own conduct as with the cruelties it sought to alleviate. The letter achieved great popularity in its day, and it is not hard to see why: it invites a comfortable moral glow and a generous tear, while keeping the bare brutalities of slave-ownership and the trade at a 'civilised' distance. (Sancho 1994, 7)

These criticisms echo many made of sensibility in general. George Starr, for example, describes the 'curious paradox' of sensibility as its tendency to replace the ostensible object of sympathy with one's own feelings (Starr 1994, 192). They also reflect concerns over the 'spontaneity' or 'naturalness' of letter-writing, as well as its ostensible egotism. Can a letter be both a carefully crafted imitation of Sterne, for example, and also a heartfelt expression of personal feeling? However, it is exactly this combination – of 'spontaneity' with 'refinement', of the 'unaffected' with the polish of politeness – which characterises the eighteenth-century familiar letter. Such a letter should claim to be artless, but therein lies its artfulness. It is written as a private exchange, but the public loves to read exchanges between friends and in crafting their own portraits, writers often have an eye as much on the anonymous, unknown readers of the future as they do on their closest friends. It is these characteristics, I would argue, that make Sancho an 'eighteenth-century' writer as opposed to the 'Romantic period' writing of Olaudah Equiano, even though their writings were published within seven years of each other.

The same paradox underlies the eighteenth-century verse epis-tle. This form may lay claim to being the dominant poetic genre for women writers in particular. (Almost a third of the selections in Roger Lonsdale's important anthology – *Eighteenth-Century Women Poets* – are kinds of verse epistle.) This is a genre through which female poets can assume modesty. There are no special poetic privileges accorded to the verse epistle: it does not require elevated diction or classical learning, nor does it rank highly in the hierarchy of poetic genres. When Laetitia Pilkington published a verse epistle by Constantia Grierson, she did so, she argued, to show how Grierson's writing could 'descend from its sublime Height to the easy epistolary Stile' and Susanna Blamire wrote to her friends that she 'scrawls' her poetic epistle at her leisure because 'sublimity of style / Takes up a most prodigious while'. Her verse letter – 'Epistle to her Friends at Gartmore' (written circa 1772) – is a conversational, intimate account of her typical day. It easily incorporates gossip and 'inconsequential' chat, and confi-dently addresses close friends:

> When breakfast's done, I take a walk
> Where English girls their secrets talk;
> But as for you, ye're modest maids,
> And shun the house to walk i' the shades;
> Often my circuit's round the garden,
> In which there's no flower worth a farthing.
> I sit me down and work a while,

> But here, I think, I see you smile;
> At work! quoth you – but little's done,
> Thou lik'st too well a bit of fun.

This is consciously informal poetry. It establishes a firm intimacy with its addressees not only by directly hailing them and dramatising their imagined responses within the verse, but also by its colloquialisms and light-hearted rhyming (such as 'garden'/'farthing'). Although Blamire downplays her own artistry throughout, the poem, like much eighteenth-century poetry, hides its skill beneath the appearance of 'easy', conversational writing.

The motif of the modest, unassuming writer is found repeatedly in verse epistles by women. In 'Epistle to Mrs Anne Griffiths', for example, Jane Brereton dramatises herself in exactly these terms: 'For me, who never durst to more pretend / Than to amuse myself, and please my friend'. Although these poems, by Blamire and Brereton, were not published in their own lifetimes, many women writers were attracted to the verse epistle because of the way in which it could negotiate the dangers of print culture. In addressing a friend, they could escape the anonymity and alienation of print. If published, these poems wore the appearance of being only inadvertently made public. And they created a knowable community within print culture by having the anonymous reader assume the position of the friend. The same kind of paradox which we have considered in relation to the familiar letter, then, provides a possibility for the woman writer. For Julia Epstein the familiar letter is 'a genre by definition – but not in fact – destined for private audiences only' (Epstein 1985, 400); for J. Paul Hunter: 'Some verse epistles are quite personal, although (by definition) they are not really private' (Hunter 2001, 30). The verse epistle permits the poet to envisage and depict her own ideal audience or community of readers. And this dramatised community exerts a strong pressure upon any actual, probably unknown reader to read as a friend too.

It would be wrong, however, to overemphasise the 'informality' or lack of prestige of the verse epistle. Many eighteenth-century women poets consciously imitate Pope in their poetic epistles. In his works we can see the flexibility of the verse epistle: from occasional poems to poems of moral philosophy; from expressions of flirtatious gallantry to those of satirical denunciation and anger. The 'Epistle to Miss Blount, On her leaving the Town after the Coronation' (1717) light-heartedly commiserates with the young lady's boredom in the country and intimately addresses Teresa and Martha by their epistolary pen-names. The 'Epistle to Robert Earl of Oxford' (1721) sends condolences on the death of Parnell and sympathises with Oxford on his exile from political influence. These early, almost 'occasional', poems echo the familiar letter in their specific, intimate address to close friends. The later epistles extend their subjects to matters of philosophy and ethical debate (the proper use of riches in the *Epistle to Bathurst*; the nature of man in the four extended epistles to Bolingbroke of *An Essay on Man*), but they often retain the same conversational, 'easy' style. Typical of these features are dramatic addresses (as in the openings of *An Essay on Man*: 'Awake my St John' or *Epistle to Bathurst*: 'Who shall decide, when doctors disagree, / And soundest casuists doubt, like you and me?'), allusions to other conversations (the *Epistle to Cobham* begins: 'Yes, you despise the man to books confined', *An Epistle to a Lady* with 'Nothing so true as what you once let fall') and parenthetical asides ('Next please his Excellence a town to batter; / (Its name I know not, and it's no great matter)' in *Epistle 2 of Book II*, a free translation from Horace). As with the verse epistles of female poets, the form permits a special kind of relationship between writer and ostensible reader. In addressing *An Essay on Man* to Bolingbroke, for example, Pope can 'engage in asides, provoke objections, recapitulate and wander, in the certainty that his good-natured listener will sanction these things' (Rogers 1975, 64). Rogers's discussion of the verse epistles illustrates how the personality of Pope's addressee colours the idiom and style of each one: sometimes bawdy in addressing Bathurst, a close friend, Pope is more formal with Burlington, who is more acquaintance than friend. Irrespective of the element of formality, however, all of these verse epistles create a sense of community, at the most literal level between Pope and his addressee and, at a symbolic level, between Pope and his epistolary audience beyond his own, known, community.[9] The attraction of constructing an ideal audience in this way extended beyond Pope to the many practitioners of verse epistles in the eighteenth century.

When the editors of eighteenth-century periodicals published letters from readers, often only fictional, they did so at least partly to evoke the impression of a community of readers. The same dynamic, in which distinctions between publicity and privacy are played out through print, is evident in epistolary fiction. This is most apparent in those fictions which explore female character. Richardson's *Clarissa* (1747–8) opens with the publicity which has greeted events in the Harlowe family, particularly the duel between Clarissa's brother and her suitor, Lovelace, as Anna Howe asks Clarissa to write to her of the affair:

> I am extremely concerned, my dearest friend, for the disturbances that have happened in your family. I know how it must hurt you to become the subject of the public talk; and yet upon an occasion so generally known it is impossible but that whatever relates to a young lady, whose distinguished merits have made her the public care, should engage everybody's attention. I long to have the particulars from yourself . . . (Richardson 1985, 39)

In the same letter Anna Howe hints that, should events take a tragic turn, the record of Clarissa's own innocence in her private letters will protect her from accusation (40). Publicity is not courted; to do so would be improper for a young lady. But publicity may ultimately be the safeguard of Clarissa's virtue. The publication of *Clarissa* allows the reader to weigh the principal accounts against each other, those of Clarissa, her friend Anna Howe, her suitor and eventual rapist Lovelace, and his friend Belford. Twentieth-century readers have not always accepted Clarissa's perspective. In this regard they only fulfil her early awareness that 'there would hardly be a guilty person in the world, were each *suspected* or *accused* person to tell his or her own story, and be allowed any degree of credit' (172).[10] Readers of *Clarissa*, as of other polyphonic letter-novels (such as Smollett's *Humphry Clinker*), must discriminate between diverse accounts of the same events, must exercise their own judgement without the aid of a narrator to guide them. In the multiple correspondences of *Humphry Clinker* every perspective is judged and interpreted by everyone else. In *Clarissa*, Clarissa and Lovelace give contrasting accounts of the rape. These novels require the reader to read as if they were the inadvertent recipient of genuine letters. They blur the distinction between the reader within the text and the reader of the text. As in the verse epistle, this blurring makes the print reader less anonymous. The reader can be known through his or her sympathy with Clarissa, Anna Howe, Lovelace, Belford or any number of other characters and perspectives. Richardson himself wrote to Lady Bradshaigh of how 'undecided Events' permit the reader to participate in the novel: 'It is not an unartful Management to interest the Readers so much in the Story, as to make them differ in Opinion as to the Capital Articles, and by Leading one, to espouse one, another, another, Opinion, make them all, if not Authors, Carpers' (Richardson 1964, 296).

Clarissa and Lovelace are similar only in their great propensity for writing letters. When Anna Howe writes to Clarissa concerning Mrs Fortescue's opinion of Lovelace, the account is dominated by his love of writing, but writing clandestinely: 'Mrs Fortescue says that, in the great correspondence by letters which he holds, he is as secret and careful as if it were of a treasonable nature – yet troubles not his head with politics' (74). Anna Howe is careful to distinguish between his fondness of writing letters and theirs:

> That you and I, my dear, should love to write is no wonder. We have always from the time each could hold a pen delighted in epistolary correspondencies. Our employments are domestic and sedentary, and we can scribble upon twenty innocent subjects and take delight in them because they *are* innocent; though were they to be seen, they might not much profit or please others. But that such a gay, lively young fellow as this, who rides, hunts, travels, frequents the public entertainments, and has *means* to pursue his pleasures, should be able to set himself down to write for hours together, as you and I have heard him say he frequently does, that is the strange thing. (74–5).

Here letter-writing is seen to be inevitably trivial and, because of that, the special province of women. The 'innocent subjects' of such scribbling are also to be found in thousands of epistolary fictions published in the eighteenth century. In Frances Sheridan's *The Memoirs of Miss Sidney Bidulph* (1761), long sections of the correspondence between Sidney and her friend Cecilia are omitted as 'nothing material' to the main story of Sidney's suppressed love for Orlando and his painful attempts to please her. At one point Sidney apologises that the journal she is writing for her friend is so trifling: 'for these last fourteen days, had I kept a journal for my cat, I think I should have had as much to say for her' (Sheridan 1995, 294). Out of the 'inconsequentialities' of family relationships, courtships and marriage, however, is the eighteenth-century novel forged. And out of the ostensibly 'private' nature of the personal letter is the female novelist authorised to write, and publish. In doing so, she also questions the distinction between the 'public' or 'political' world of parliamentary elections and business transactions and the 'private' or purely 'domestic' world of the home. Long before modern feminism coined the phrase, such fictions make the personal political.

In her study of epistolary fiction, Elizabeth Cook discusses the relationship between public and private constructed through this specific form. This relationship is a paradoxical one, in that public and private intersect and are differentiated in epistolary fiction. The way in which public and private reciprocally define each other is summarised by Cook as follows:

> [Epistolary fictions show] how the thematics of the domestic and the erotic can be made to encode and even to regulate ostensibly public matters; in the everted structures of epistolary narratives the private is thoroughly colonized by the public. At the same time, the genre also demonstrates how registers of knowledge that seem to belong to a public discursive domain are anchored, guaranteed and authorized by aspects of the private . . . that letter-fictions helped to invent and naturalize. (Cook 1996, 177–8)

Not only, then, are the 'private' subjects of relationship and family thoroughly politicised, but ideas of subjectivity and selfhood – the 'private' at its purest definition – are themselves made meaningful through the paradigm of the public.

This is the claim made for the novel in general in the opening section of this chapter. It is in epistolary fiction, however, that the paradoxical necessity that the 'private' be 'publicised' is most apparent. It is not surprising, therefore, that some of the most explicit discussions of the literary public sphere, and the relationship between the literary and political public spheres, sketched so vaguely in Habermas's own work, have occurred in recent work on the epistolary novel (Cook 1996; Carnell 1998). A reading of one letter from *Evelina* – the heroine's first – illustrates many of these aspects. In this letter, Evelina tentatively asks her guardian, the Reverend Villars, if she might be allowed to visit London with the Mirvan family. The letter exemplifies the way in which subjectivity is in formation *through* text, as Evelina is torn between a number of impulses: her obedience to the Mirvans in making the request but her fear of seeming ungrateful to her guardian, her desire to go to London but her desire also to please her guardian, not least in thinking as he does:

Well but, my dear Sir, I am desired to make a request to you. I hope you will not think me an incroacher; Lady Howard insists upon my writing! – yet I hardly know how to go on; a petition implies a want, – and have you left me one? No, indeed.

I am half ashamed of myself for beginning this letter. But these dear ladies are so pressing – I cannot, for my life, resist wishing for the pleasures they offer me, – provided you do not disapprove of them.

They are to make a very short stay in town. The Captain will meet them in a day or two. Mrs Mirvan and her sweet daughter both go; – what a happy party! Yet I am not *very* eager to accompany them: at least, I shall be contented to remain where I am, if you desire that I should.

Assured, my dearest Sir, of your goodness, your bounty, and your indulgent kindness, ought I to form a wish that has not your sanction? Decide for me, therefore, without the least apprehension that I shall be uneasy, or discontented. While I am yet in suspense, perhaps I may *hope*, but I am most certain, that when you have once determined, I shall not repine.

They tell me that London is now in full splendour. Two Playhouses are open, – the Opera-House, – Ranelagh, – and the Pantheon. – You see I have learned their names. However, pray don't suppose that I make any point of going, for I shall hardly sigh to see them depart without me; though I shall probably never meet with such another opportunity. And, indeed, their domestic happiness will be so great, – it is natural to wish to partake of it.

I believe I am bewitched! I made a resolution when I began, that I would not be urgent; but my pen – or rather my thoughts, will not suffer me to keep it – for I acknowledge, I must acknowledge, I cannot help wishing for your permission.

I almost repent already that I have made this confession; pray forget that you have read it, if this journey is displeasing to you. But I will not write any longer; for the more I think of this affair, the less indifferent to it I find myself. (Burney 2000, 113–14)

Some readers have seen 'emotional blackmail' in this letter. Certainly the letter ends with Evelina praising her guardian and alternating expressions of obedience with hopes that he will allow her to go. But this would be to make Evelina more calculated than she seems from such an inconsistent letter. The letter articulates Evelina's contradictory feelings and impulses and it foregrounds how the very writing of the letter itself takes over these feelings – bewitched by her pen, 'or rather [her] thoughts'. In this letter, subjectivity does not precede the writing of the letter but is produced and organised by it. When John Brewer discusses the letter form in relation to Habermas's theories of the public sphere, it is the particular capacity of the letter to make the private public which makes it a paradigmatic form for the period:

> as Habermas stresses, one of the key issues debated in the public sphere was that of freedom and subjectivity, of what it meant to realize oneself as a person. The forms this discussion took, he emphasizes, were frequently literary and usually rendered through the medium of print. This sense of pure humanness was a public construction which depended both on the representation of the intimate sphere and on the public elaboration of its values. In short, the public sphere produced an unprecedented discussion and unparalleled public exposure of private life. (Brewer 1995, 6)

Evelina's first letter exemplifies the ways in which selfhood was constructed through its 'public' rehearsal: not only in the validation of self in relation to society which the trip to London will permit, but also in the very act of writing as a mode of self-reflection.

*Evelina* figures here as the culmination of several genres: the epistolary and the novelistic. Both are recognised as distinctive eighteenth-century forms and both are now being read in new ways, largely in the light of the work of Habermas and of the feminist interest in ideas of public and private life. The genres discussed in the following sections – dialogue and periodical – are more obviously related to the public sphere. Little argument concerning their 'social' nature seems to be necessary. We need only think of the intersubjectivity which all dialogue presumes or the public address of the periodical. What these sections argue, therefore, is the surprising pervasiveness of 'conversational form' in the period and the significance of the periodical for ideas of community and sociability.

## The dialogue and other conversational forms

The word 'dialogue', or words synonymous with it, occur in thousands of eighteenth-century titles and the dialogue form is found across a wide range of kinds of texts: philosophical works, political allegories, science textbooks, satiric dialogues and matrimonial dialogues.[11] The dialogue form certainly appears a significant feature of eighteenth-century literature once we think about the importance of ideas of sociability and conversation to the period's self-image. In his excellent account of the philosophical dialogue, Michael Prince writes: 'Often set in coffee-houses, public walks, salons, stage coaches, and the like, dialogue was one of the genres that represented the public exchange of ideas taking place among subjects who were (at least in theory) free and equal' (Prince 1996, 16). As we will see, the parenthetical aside ('at least in theory') is crucial. Before considering more than the ideal self-image of the dialogue, however, I will consider three major genres in which ideas of dialogue play a part: Augustan poetry, literary biography and literary criticism.

In addition to ostensibly 'transcribed' conversations there are a variety of forms in which ideas of conversation and debate also play a part. These might include the miscellany, which juxtaposes writings by a collection by authors; the emergence of the genre of published anecdotes and tabletalk, often identified by the suffix '-iana' (as in Hester Thrale's *Thraliana*, begun in 1776); the digressive tendencies of eighteenth-century fiction and poetry; the popularity of such 'sociable' forms as the epigram, anecdote, joke, impromptu, toast, bon mot, witticism and compliment; and the poetic form of the heroic couplet.[12] This last example is persuasively argued both by Margaret Doody in her important study of eighteenth-century poetry, *The Daring Muse* (1985), and by J. Paul Hunter in an essay entitled 'Couplets and Conversation' (2001). In the twentieth and twenty-first centuries, we have tended to expect poetry to be about emotion, to give a voice to private feelings and intense subjectivity. The broad context for Hunter's argument is that eighteenth-century expectations of poetry were that it should be about public issues and only later in the century would a shift towards a conception of poetry as meditative, solitary and private arise. This is the kind of narrative for eighteenth-century poetry to which we have become accustomed: the argumentative, social and discursive poetry of the early decades gives way to a more lyrical, rhapsodic, sublime and imaginative poetry associated with the Wartons, Gray, Collins and other poets problematically identified as 'pre-Romantic'. Like all narratives, this one too is open to challenges. Poetry by women, for example, does not in general follow this trend, with Pope remaining the dominant influence on women's poetry across the century.[13]

Within the larger argument that eighteenth-century poetry is committed to public conversation, Hunter's specific focus is upon the ways in which poetry written in heroic couplets can seem so conversational. Hunter's essay builds upon Doody's argument that the heroic couplet is energised by its ventriloquism of two voices, voices responding to and often crossing each other (Doody 1985, 263). Despite the overtly poetic techniques used by many eighteenth-century poets – the couplet and its associated characteristics of zeugma, antithesis, chiasmus and syllepsis – their poems attain an informality and conversational ease, surprising in poetry so apparently 'formal'. Hunter directly asks and answers this apparent paradox:

> How can the aims of poetry be so 'formal' on the one hand and so colloquial and informal on the other?
> The short answer is that couplets never try to deny that they are artful, calculated, rhetorical, and 'artificial' even when they strive to be smooth, accessible, colloquial, and conversational. They don't try to emulate talk *exactly* – just provide a tone and simplicity of vocabulary and syntax that make them as understandable as a clear spoken sentence. (25)

In the same volume of essays, John Sitter argues that the use of regular rhyme in the heroic couplet permitted poets such as Pope to be much less formal in the diction they used. Since rhyme elevated the poem above the prosaic, the poet was free to unbutton him or herself in relaxed conversation (Sitter 2001, 152). Sitter and Hunter, in arguing that the language of eighteenth-century poetry is characterised by play and flexibility, echo Margaret Doody in *The Daring Muse*. All three stress that the more eighteenth-century poetry we read we will discover rhyme permits rather than inhibits freedom. Thinking in this way can at first seem counter-intuitive, but only because rhyme is now primarily associated with song lyrics and greeting card verses. There is perhaps a danger here that 'conversational form' becomes such a capacious term that it might include all kinds of text. Courting that danger, however, the remainder of this section considers dialogue to be an important feature not just of those works which identify themselves as dialogues, or of the emerging novel (as chapter 1 suggested in discussing the relationship between author and reader) but also of such forms as literary biography and literary criticism.

Boswell begins his *Life of Johnson* (1791) with a defence of his method, in which, he argues, the 'peculiar value' of his book is 'the quantity that it contains of Johnson's conversation' (Boswell 1980, 23). Certainly the Johnson who emerges from his famous biography is primarily Johnson the conversationalist and speaker of aphorisms. At one point Boswell remarks how 'I never could discover how he found time for his compositions. He declaimed all the morning [with his levée of morning visitors], then went to dinner at a tavern, where he commonly staid late, and then drank his tea at some friend's house, over which he loitered a great while. . . . I can scarcely recollect that he ever refused going with me to a tavern, and he often went to Ranelagh' (437). Johnson's talk, as recorded by Boswell, is not always that of polished brilliance, of rounded phrases and florid eloquence. Boswell also records the occasional *longueurs*, inconclusiveness and apparent trivialities of conversation, defending this meticulousness as the truest form of biography. Any random selection from the *Life* reveals a huge diversity of topics. To take just one day – 31 March 1772, for example – Johnson talks about whether marriage is natural to man (to which the answer appears to be that it is not), whether there is beauty independent of usefulness and about swearing in conversation; several books are then reviewed (Goldsmith's *Life of Parnell*, Ruffhead's *Life of Pope*, Warton's *Essay on Pope*), before Johnson's talk continues with the proper use of riches and the character of Bayes in Buckingham's play *The Rehearsal* (1672); the Pantheon and Ranelagh are then compared as places of entertainment, before the day finishes with a discussion of the balance of crown and government and the appointment of bishops to the House of Lords (Boswell 1980, 473–8). In his recording of such detailed conversations, Boswell is as much a social historian as he is a biographer. In the attempt to transcribe Johnson's conversation so meticulously, Boswell also records the talk of many of the later eighteenth-century's most famous characters. The title page of the *Life* recounts that it exhibits 'a view of literature and literary men in Great Britain for near half a century'. Boswell's ultimate defence of his detail, however, is like that of the periodical essayists and novelists we encountered in chapter 1 – the variety of his readers:

> Of one thing I am certain . . . I am justified in preserving rather too many of Johnson's sayings, than too few; especially as from the

diversity of dispositions it cannot be known with certainty before-
hand, whether what may seem trifling to some, and perhaps to the
collector himself, may not be most agreeable to many; and the
greater number that an authour can please in any degree, the more
pleasure does there arise to a benevolent mind. (26)

Two significant texts which we would now think of as kinds of literary criticism also take the form of dramatised conversations:
Sarah Fielding's *Remarks on Clarissa* (1749) and Clara Reeve's *The
Progress of Romance* (1785). Fielding's text is a celebration of
*Clarissa* in the form of a fictionalised assembly, who meet after
each publication of volumes to discuss their response to the
unfolding narrative, and, in a concluding section, in an exchange of
letters between two of the main conversationalists, Miss Gibson
and Bellario. The mixed company differ in their judgements of the
novel and its characters, often revealing only their own foibles and
predilections. The old man's imperious behaviour towards his
daughter, for example, echoes the harshness of Mr Harlowe
towards his wife and disproves his criticism that such tyranny was
'unnatural' (Fielding 1985, 10–12). The mother with three daughters of marriageable age defends the sober and worthy
Mr Hickman from the charge of being insipid because he 'has
Qualities that Mothers would be fond of in a Husband for their
Daughters' (26). The gentlemen are bemused that Richardson's
loyal female readers refuse this aspect of the novel. In this regard,
free and open discussion is not particularly capable of changing
attitudes: Miss Gibson drops the subject of Mr Hickman rather
than confess she remains unpersuaded that he could be an agreeable husband (29). Similarly, while Miss Gibson delights in the
'conversion' of Bellario, his reformation is wrought by the process
of reading successive volumes of *Clarissa* as much as by the conversation of the assembly. At the first of the meetings he attends,
Bellario is unconvinced that Clarissa is capable of love and is concerned by reports that the novel will end with the catastrophe of
her death. By the last meeting, Bellario can only praise Clarissa and
the plotting of her creator, praise which he repeats and develops in
his letter to Miss Gibson. But Bellario has always announced his
intention to reserve judgement until the ending of the novel.
Similarly, in advancing their opinions of the novel, many of the
speakers use the multiplicity of voices within *Clarissa* to quote in

support of what they say. When the mother defends Hickman, for example, she quotes Clarissa's praises because Clarissa is Miss Gibson's great 'favourite'. And Miss Gibson's tenderness for Clarissa is expressed by quoting the parting words of Belford: 'Farewell, my dear *Clarissa!*' In this way, the *Remarks on Clarissa* ventriloquises the voices within the novel. For Sarah Fielding, this is a form of literary criticism which is fair and impartial because views are so evidently deduced from the text (3, 56). The assembly's failure to agree on the character of Mr Hickman appears a minor diversion within the greater scheme of praising the novel and its heroine, which the concluding letters reiterate. However, it is this lack of consensus that ultimately makes conversation the appropriate scheme for the critical discussion. Neither the novel nor the responses to it can absolutely fix or resolve this interpretative crux.

Reeve's *Progress* uses the frame of a dialogue between three friends because, she claims in the preface, ideas for the work came out of conversations with friends, because it would permit a 'more full and accurate examination' of opposing views and because it would enliven a potentially dry work (Kelly 1999, VI 164). The friends – Sophronia, Hortensius and Euphrasia – set aside each Thursday to meet and discuss the nature of prose fiction. Euphrasia, like Miss Gibson in *Remarks on Clarissa*, often appears to speak on her author's behalf. She it is who leads the conversation, defining the history of the romance genre and defending it from its critics, of whom Hortensius is one. And because the romance was, and still is, largely associated with femininity, the debate takes on a sexual colouring, heightened by Hortensius's often gallant and flirtatious responses. That *The Progress of Romance* is concerned about sexual as much as textual politics is evident in numerous exchanges: in Euphrasia's complaint, for example, that 'Others having seen a few of the worst or dullest among [romances], have judged all the rest by them; – just as some men affect to despise our sex, because they have only conversed with the worst part of it' (211) or in that of Hortensius: 'You are ready enough to pay due respect to writers of your own sex, but you are rather severe upon some of ours' (223). Using the dialogue form here permits Reeve both to write a form of literary criticism and to reflect upon the authority of criticism itself. The female critic in particular is one whose authority cannot be taken for granted, as the responses of Hortensius suggest. The dialogue also gives glimpses of the necessity of its own compromises. Defences of Fielding and Rousseau are given to Hortensius, for example, as too risqué for a female reader to articulate. Yet when Euphrasia reveals that she has been recording all their conversations and will seek public opinion through publishing these, it is Hortensius who is shy of such publicity, asking that his identity be kept in 'masquerade' (261). Only the threatened 'feminisation' of Hortensius's weekly discussions with these two ladies might explain such reticence.

Although one of the ideals of textual dialogue is that of representing heterogeneity, of articulating a range of voices and opinions, dialogue itself is just as capable of closing down differences of opinion, of using many voices only in order to promote one. This might be said of *Remarks on Clarissa*, in which objections to Richardson's novel are quickly refuted and in which the only competition between the two concluding letters would be that of which letter more effusively praises Richardson's grand design. Similarly, in *The Progress of Romance*, Sophronia, who is given the task of adjudicating between the stances of Euphrasia and Hortensius, is always obviously going to comply with Euphrasia. Her summary of their stances represents only a foregone conclusion: '*Hortensius* would prohibit the reading all Novels in order to exclude bad ones. – *Euphrasia* would make a separation in favour of works of Genius, taste, and morality' (260). Her ultimate verdict – 'bad books are bad things; – but shall we therefore prohibit reading?' (261) – reveals Euphrasia's stance as being the moderate stance, which did not discountenance Hortensius's objections but resolved them. In his account of the philosophical dialogue, Daniel Brewer unveils dialogue as monologue in disguise, as only pretending to represent difference in order to convince the reader of its own designs all the more (Brewer 1983). However, the form of dialogue more usually complicates any attempt at interpretative tyranny. Even in those dialogues which intended and attempted to resolve differences in a resounding, concluding, transcendent argument – dialogues Michael Prince terms 'metaphysical' – the very act of incorporating dissident voices into the text can often rebound. In contrasting the 'metaphysical' dialogues of Shaftesbury and Berkeley with the more sceptical dialogues of Hume and Ramsay, Michael Prince writes that even in the first of these kinds: 'the attempt to ameliorate opposition through its partial representation instigates a dynamic of its own' (Prince 1996, 16–17). In the case of the *Remarks on Clarissa*, the lack of consensus on how to judge Mr Hickman and, in *The Progress of Romance*, the tension between gendered positions which continually resurfaces, remind us that dialogues can unleash tensions and indeterminacies, or at least permit them to be articulated.

Fielding's and Reeve's texts are not typical of literary criticism in the eighteenth century, in so far as it is first institutionalised in the essay-periodicals and increasingly in the literary reviews of dedicated journals. But that Fielding and Reeve write literary criticism in the form of dialogues is appropriate. Literary criticism emerges in the eighteenth century out of conversation: the conversations of Addison's circle at Button's coffee house, the tendency of polite company to discuss their reading together, the gossip and infighting of the publishing worlds of London, Dublin, Edinburgh and, increasingly, of other provincial towns. Countless 'literary' texts embed aspects of this pervasive 'literary critical' culture into their own forms: when fictional characters discuss books and theatre performances, when periodical essayists report on their reading and theatregoing, when works of all kinds are written purposefully to attack or defend other writers and texts. Literary criticism in the eighteenth century is inseparable from gossip and from the ways in which people – both fictional and real – incorporate their reading preferences into their conversations and self-perceptions. This makes eighteenth-century literary culture one of intertextuality and of sequels and counter-fictions in which the 'literary' and the 'literary critical' cannot be so easily separated.[14] The representation of talk in the periodical also fulfils a literary critical aspiration – as in the *Spectator*'s essays on *Paradise Lost*, for example. But its significance to ideas of sociability transcends the merely literary. Among the papers of the early periodical we can see the ways in which the literary and the political public spheres interact.

## The periodical

One of the most explicit considerations of the ways in which social and textual form interact is a recent essay by Scott Black entitled 'Social and Literary Form in the *Spectator*' (1999) in which the periodical is linked with the convergence of three related phenomena: a new use of print technology (the newspaper), a new literary form (the essay) and a new social space (the city). It is not surprising that Black's focus should be on the eighteenth-century periodical, since, of those studies which situate eighteenth-century culture in relation to ideas of the public sphere and sociability, by far the most extensive are studies of the periodical.[15] That the periodical essay can be seen as imaginatively occupying the space of the coffee house was something which eighteenth-century commentators themselves remarked. In an essay in *The Bee* (1790–1), for example, the writer sketched the following domestic scene of a family reading a periodical together: 'A man, after the fatigues of the day are over, may thus sit down in his elbow chair, and together with his wife and family, be introduced, as it were, into a spacious coffee-house'.[16] The equivalency of the coffee house and of the periodical is also evident in the way in which eighteenth-century periodicals used the figure of the club as a framework. Dunton's question-and-answer journal, *The Athenian Mercury* (1691), was only the first to announce a club as its sponsor. Charles Gildon claimed in his *History of the Athenian Society* (1693) that this society was comprised of twelve members, including a divine, a lawyer, a civilian, a surgeon, an Italian, a Spaniard, a Frenchman, and a Dutchman (the last four used as interpreters) and included an engraving showing the society in session. This was most probably a fiction, designed to allow a wide range of questions to be answered. Similarly, *The Tatler* (1709–11) was dated from a variety of public places so as to permit variety of subject matter and narrative styles: accounts of gallantry, pleasure and entertainment are sent from White's Chocolate House, accounts of poetry from Will's coffee house, learning from The Grecian and foreign and domestic news from St James's (associated with the Whigs). All other features are sent from Mr Bickerstaff's own apartment. Increasingly the section from 'My Own Apartment' comes to dominate *The Tatler*, thus initiating what would be the periodical's predominant form, the single essay periodical, and its characteristic voice, the polite tone of the urbane gentleman.

*The Spectator* (1711–12, 1714) maintains the ideals of variety and comprehensiveness by circulating around the fiction of the Spectator's club, which included such famously diverse friends as Sir Roger de Coverley, a Tory rural squire; Sir Andrew Freeport, a Whig city merchant; Will Honeycomb, a 'well-bred fine gentleman' who delights in fashion and gossip and is a great favourite with ladies; the Templar, a young law student who is more interested in studying the theatre; Captain Sentry, a stout virtuous former soldier; and a relatively undifferentiated clergyman, his minor status reflecting the secular nature of *The Spectator's* project to reform manners. Unlike the 'Fat' (No 9), 'Lazy' (320) or 'Lawyer' (372) clubs which recruit members because of the things they hold in common, the Spectator club is specifically formed as an ideal society in which political (Tory/Whig), social (town/country) and professional differences are resolved in the harmony of polite company. That these figures were designed by Steele and Addison, the periodical's main writers, to represent a variety of readers is made evident when the Spectator contemplates the demise of his club and the possibility of creating a new club (No. 550; 1 Dec. 1712). One country gentleman tries to bribe his way into Sir Roger's position with a barrel of October ale; a shareholder wants to take Sir Andrew Freeport's place, thinking this would raise the credit of his fund; soldiers write in hoping to replace Captain Sentry and clergymen wanting to replace the Spectator's clergyman friend. Even the incorporation of women, so important as readers of the early periodical, is at least flirted with, though never achieved: some ladies argue that Will Honeycomb should be replaced with a woman because he did not take sufficient care of their interests.[17] In an earlier paper, the Spectator confidently announced how his club is so formed that it can represent all ranks and report on everything that passes not only in the city but in 'the whole Kingdom' (No. 34; 9 April 1711).

Other periodicals would imitate the framing device of the club. *The Lay Monk* (1713) presented itself as the transactions of a society of unmarried gentlemen, as recorded by their secretary; *The Plain Dealer* (1724–5) was peopled with the Plain Dealer himself, his sweetheart Patty Amble, a clergyman, a critic, Major Stedfast, and Ned Volatile – a club in all but name; *The Grub-Street Journal* (1730–7) sketched a satirical club, including Mr Bavius, secretary; Mr Quidnunc, the scholiast and news critic for the group; Mr Poppy, the poet, who is 'ready to compose Panegyrics or Satires, Copies of verses from friends of Authors, Odes, Epithalamiums, Funeral Elegies, Anagrams and Acrostics, and annual Salutations from the City Bell-men to their worthy masters and mistresses, – at reasonable rates'; and Giles Blunderbuss, Esquire, historiographer to the society. Mr Noodle and Mr Numbscull are later elected to

membership.[18] Although these characters are scarcely individu-
ated, several numbers of the *Journal* do present club meetings (for
example, Nos 3, 6, 15), one issue is devoted to proposals for erect-
ing a college for Grub-Street authors (No. 33), articles are introduced as being first read to the Club and letters are addressed to
the society's secretary, Mr Bavius. A number of other periodicals
replaced the formal club with different kinds of community. In *The
Guardian* (1713) and *The Grumbler* (1714), for example, the essays
were ostensibly arranged around family groups: Nestor Ironside
and his friends, three generations of the Lizard family; and Squire
Gizzard and his family. The device of a club or community as the
framing trope of the periodical continued to be used throughout
the eighteenth century.[19] However, its use was increasingly casual
and certainly no periodical ever sustained the fiction of the club as
consistently as *The Spectator*. There is rarely a sequence of more
than half a dozen numbers into which the club does not somehow
enter and the club is maintained until the final issue. The society is
dissolved with the death of Sir Roger de Coverley (517), the marriage of Will Honeycomb (530), the Templar's farewell to his studies
(541), Captain Sentry's withdrawal to the country (544) and Sir
Andrew Freeport's renunciation of town life in favour of a meditative, philanthropic existence on his estate (549). The tentative plans
of the Spectator for forming a new society (549, 550, 553) never
appear serious; the periodical ends with the passing of the original
club. However, the majority of periodicals in the eighteenth century were the work of a group of contributors and this allows us to
think of their enterprise as 'clubical' to an extent. Steele and
Addison, and Pope and Swift, certainly spoke of their collaborative
work as being public memorials to their friendships.[20]

In addition to reflecting the 'clubbable' spirit of the age in its
framework and collaborative writing, the periodical also extends,
perhaps even inaugurates, the address of narrator to reader which
we have already noted in eighteenth-century prose fiction. Walter
Ong's comment concerning the 'new fashionable intimacy'
between author and reader in the early eighteenth century, quoted
in chapter 1, specifically referred to Addison and Steele as
authors.[21] The self-consciousness of the narrator's address to the
reader supplements the kind of direct response which the newspaper and periodical press encouraged by printing letters from readers, even if some of those letter-writers were obviously fictional (as

the Spectator himself acknowledges in issue 542). It has been estimated that around 25 per cent of the first series of *The Spectator*
was made up of letters. In addition to the letters are the comments
which the Spectator, silent and retiring in company, overhears and
records in his journal. Thus, as Scott Black argues, *The Spectator*
defines its public 'as much by listening to it as speaking to it' (35).
This was to be a consistent aspect of the eighteenth-century periodical more generally. *The Gentleman's Magazine*, for example,
often printed readers' effusions, especially in verse, and both it and
Fielding's *Covent-Garden Journal* were often largely made up of letters. Although many were fictitious, these letters did promote the
perception of a reading community for their journals. Newspapers
and periodicals, then, often blurred the distinction between writer
and reader. The eighteenth-century periodical, by reaching out to
its readers and incorporating them into its frame, makes the form
a meeting-place for writers and readers alike. Readers could even
buy *The Tatler* with a blank half-sheet to enable them to send on
copies to friends and, should they wish, write to them with news,
reflections on that issue, or bits of gossip. This literalises the way in
which the reader of the periodical was also envisaged as an author
and suggestively anticipates Sterne's more famous incorporation of
a blank page into *Tristram Shandy*.

*The Spectator* dramatises this transfer of authority, from writer to
reader, when letters are incorporated into, or even make up entire
runs of, the papers and when the Spectator overhears comments
upon his own journal. Among the most interesting of these is an
essay in which the Spectator listens while readers argue about the
true intention of his paper. In Essay 568 (16 July 1714), the
Spectator enters a coffee house near the Royal Exchange, and seeing three men 'in close conference over a pipe of tobacco', the
Spectator fills his own pipe and joins them, after the preliminary
overture of a few puffs. Such is the easy manner in which men associate in coffee houses: 'I need not tell my Reader, that lighting a
Man's Pipe at the same Candle, is looked upon among Brother-
smokers as an Overture to Conversation and Friendship' (Bond
1965, V 539). The Spectator initiates the discussion of his journal by
picking up the latest issue and commenting on how witty this
paper was. Soon the three men are quarrelling over how to judge
the journal: one thinks it more witty than wise, the other is
offended by its political implications, the third thinks it suitably

cautious. The previous issue had mostly concerned the writing of an imaginary political libel. This was uncharacteristic of *The Spectator* which, in reforming manners, always claimed to satirise social types, never individuals, a method of satire which permitted the Spectator to retain his demeanour as polite and moderate, never angry or vindictive. However, *The Spectator's* implied reader should see immediately that, rather than a political libel, the issue is a satire on such, and that the Spectator in judging it 'witty' is the most correct of the coffee-house readers:

> If there are *four* Persons in the Nation who endeavour to bring all things into Confusion and ruin their native Country, I think every honest *Engl-shm-n* ought to be upon his Guard. That there are such every one will agree with me, who hears me name *** with his first Friend and Favourite *** not to mention *** nor ***. These People may cry Ch—rch, Ch—rch, as long as they please, but, to make use of homely Proverb, The Proof of the P—dd—ng is in the eating. This I am sure of, that if a *certain Prince* should concur with a *certain Prelate*, (and we have Monsieur *Z—n*'s Word for it) our Posterity would be in a sweet P—ckle. (No. 567; V 538)

Lest the reader overlook the satire, the paper opened with the Spectator's decision to 'season' the journal with some political scandal on the advice of a friend. The best thing to make a book sell, the friend recommended, is to scatter it with controversial words (such as *Faction, Villain,* or *Frenchman,* conspicuously dressed in italics) and with insinuations (such as 'M —— h', with which readers could flatter their own percipience in recognising the allusion to the Duke of Marlborough while the author is freed from accusations of libel). Thus the Spectator's attempt at political satire typically divides readers. The offended reader is scandalised because he thinks himself sure of how to decipher the asterisks and recognises a satire against the Church in referring to it in the same sentence as 'Pudding'. The sympathetic Whig gentleman who defends the paper is forgotten as the Spectator leaves the coffee house, frustrated by 'that gross Tribe of Fools' who always read particular allusions into general reflections and see political treason in the most innocent words. In concluding the paper, he tells an anecdote in which a reading of Allestree's *The Whole Duty of Man* (1658) led to unforeseen consequences:

I remember an empty pragmatical Fellow in the Country, who upon reading over *the whole Duty of Man*, had written the Names of several Persons in the Village at the Side of every Sin which is mention'd by that excellent Author; so that he had converted one of the best Books in the World into a Libel against the Squire, Church-wardens, Over-seers of the Poor, and all other the most considerable Persons in the Parish. This Book with these extraordinary marginal Notes fell accidentally into the Hands of one who had never seen it before; upon which there arose a current Report that Some-body had written a Book against the Squire and the whole Parish. The Minister of the Place having at that Time a Controversy with some of his Congregation upon the Account of his Tythes, was under some Suspicion of being the Author, till the good Man set his People right by shewing them that the satirical Passages might be applied to several others of two or three neighbouring Villages, and that the Book was writ against all the Sinners in *England*. (541)

The Minister's function in this story is similar to that of the Spectator. Both guide and correct errant readings. There is little ambiguity in *The Spectator* and much authorial control. Ultimately, however, there is no certainty that readers will oblige. Despite the obvious moral to which the paper points in its concluding paragraphs – that readers should not 'over' interpret – the motto attached to the paper suggests that readers can always resist and escape the author's control: 'When you rehearse my verse, it is not mine but thine'.[22] As we will see in Part II, the awareness that readers can always read otherwise is characteristic of much eighteenth-century literature.

This paper gives us a glimpse of the way in which *The Spectator*'s attempts to fashion a community could be seen to fail, something which, here at least, the journal is prepared to admit. This is a failure in so far as the address to readers in these periodicals is implicitly one to fellow club members, thus attempting to collapse club culture into that of society at large. The periodical itself certainly lays claim to the ideal of a community of readers, synthesised by their reading of and responses to the paper. The intimacy between writer and reader which the style constructs is used to create a sense in which readers join writers in a kind of 'club' society in all but name. After the announcements of the paper's demise, one gentleman writes of a new club he has formed with some friends in order to reread all previous issues of *The Spectator* (No. 553; 4 Dec.

1712). This club is never named, but as a 'Reading *The Spectator*' club, it serves as an apt image of how the paper creates a reading community, and one which is recognised as such by its participants. *The Spectator* may then be said to attempt the translation which Hume desired, of the friendship and intimacy of the coterie or group transferred to the threatened anonymity and selfishness of society beyond the circles of friends and family. This project, to paraphrase Michael Ketcham, permits *The Spectator* to embrace an expanding readership while creating the illusion of an intimate community (Ketcham 1985, 676). Such a community can only be achieved if the fracturing forces of political, social, and sexual difference are dissolved or in some way neutralised. This *The Spectator* attempts to do through the persona of the Spectator himself, a man who resolves 'to observe an exact Neutrality between the Whigs and Tories, unless I shall be forced to declare myself by the Hostilities of either Side' (No. 1; 1 March 1711). This parity is ostensibly dramatised in the balancing of Sir Roger de Coverley with Sir Andrew Freeport, both virtuous and polite gentlemen whose differences of political opinion are never acrimonious. The Spectator claims his own impartiality on the basis of his status as perpetual 'looker-on'.

The Spectator is sociable but silent in company. He is at the coffee house by six o'clock in the morning, often dines at a common ordinary, and loves to ramble about London. As he does so he watches and reflects on all he sees, always curious and eager to instruct his readers and contrive schemes for the public good. Unlike his fellow club men, he is not defined by his occupation, but by his being a witness of his society, by being only a spectator. This allows him to transcend any particular identity and become a representative for all. Some of the most explicit of these claims appear in the first issue in which the Spectator announces his universalism:

> Thus I live in the World, rather as a Spectator of Mankind, than as one of the Species; by which means I have made my self a Speculative Statesman, Soldier, Merchant, and Artizan, without ever medling with any Practical Part in Life. I am very well versed in the Theory of an Husband, or a Father, and can discern the Errors in the Oeconomy, Business and Diversion of others, better than those who are engaged in them; as Standers-by discover Blots, which are apt to escape those who are in the Game. (Bond 1965, I 4–5)

That the Spectator's knowledge is 'speculative' or 'theoretical', notwithstanding this defence, can be problematic. At one point he confesses that he knows nothing of women but what he has deduced from seeing plays (No. 51; Bond 1965, I 217). Reading the many papers on occupations while the Spectator himself is at leisure also points up the disjuncture between his passivity in the world and his engagement with it. In Essay 454 for example, the Spectator describes almost 24 hours in London. Most obvious is the way in which life in the city is split between different classes and professions, differences as great, he explains, as those between people born in different centuries. Early in the morning market-stall vendors sail the Thames and begin business at Covent Garden. By mid-morning, bourgeois ladies flirt in hackney carriages and, in our terms, 'window shop'. By noon, the fashionable classes begin to awake and showy equipages supplement the more mundane hackney carriages (more mundane because they are hired by those who cannot afford their own). By afternoon, the Spectator visits first the Royal Exchange, where merchants congregate amid almost 200 shops and boutiques, then a coffee house, where traders buy and sell shares. The evening is spent at Will's coffee house, where people talk of gambling, love, learning and politics. Thus the city is divided not just geographically but also temporally: 'Men of Six a Clock give Way to those of Nine, they of Nine to the Generation of Twelve, and they of Twelve disappear, and make Room for the fashionable World, who have made Two a Clock the Noon of the Day' (Bond 1965, IV 99). The Spectator remains detached from the bustle and activity he observes and he implies in his opening paragraph that it is this detachment which is essential to an impartial view: 'they who enjoy [Speculation], must value things only as they are the Objects of Speculation, without drawing any worldly Advantage to themselves from them, but just as they are what contribute to their Amusement, or the Improvement of the Mind' (98). His detachment is literalised when he looks down upon the ground floor arcade from the first floor of the Exchange, where all the voices from below 'rose up in a confused Humming' and allow the Spectator to reflect more philosophically on the world, '*What Nonsense is all the Hurry of this World to those who are above it?*' (102). Yet the Spectator's leisure, the very thing which allows him to ramble at will in London, marks him, not as a man above class interests, but as a man of fortune. His pretence to impartiality, to spectatorship, is absolutely dependent on financial independence, as the contrast between those who busily work in London with the freedom and passivity of the Spectator makes clear. This tension would also shortly underlie Gay's *Trivia* (1716) in which the Walker, like the Spectator, watches and judges the city. And, because the Royal Exchange and the trading of shares are described so positively in this and other papers, the Spectator would have been recognised immediately by contemporary readers as a sympathetic Whig. The Spectator's political neutrality, his status as universal representative, is always just as much a fiction as his ideally harmonious club of mixed company.[23]

In its use of the club device, its easy informal style and conversational manner, and its incorporation of readers into its own frame, *The Spectator* exemplifies a kind of textual sociability unrivalled by any other eighteenth-century text. Later periodicals developed some of these aspects in a more attenuated form but *The Spectator* continued its influence throughout the century. In 1779, Vicesimus Knox wrote: 'There is scarcely an individual, not only of those who profess learning, but of those who devote any of their time to reading, who has not digested the Spectators'.[24] At the moments of their first printing, *The Tatler* and *The Spectator* served as mirrors in which an early reading public could see itself reflected. Almost all recent commentators on the early periodical are agreed on this point. For Habermas, the public reflected in the mirror of *The Tatler*, *The Spectator*, and *The Guardian* came to self-understanding 'through entering itself into "literature" as an object' (Habermas 1989, 43). For Hammond, these three journals '*produce* a readership that was simultaneously represented to be the *actual* readership' (1997, 184). And for Scott Black, the periodical essay provided 'the formal condition by which the metropolitan world became self-reflective' (Black 1999, 38). The direct address of author to reader inaugurated in the periodical certainly created a kind of conversation which might challenge and even potentially overcome the anonymity and indeterminacy which print culture seemed to threaten. Simultaneously, too, the way in which the early periodical offered a polite model – both in the depiction of social friendships among the periodical's characters and the friendship developed between essayist and reader – refuted the aggression, profanation, vulgarity and general impoliteness associated with 'Grub Street', the print market at its worst. For Scott Black, *The*

*Spectator* consolidates the use of the essay form as a form of fictional conversation, in which an 'easy', apparently casual and unmethodical voice is the ideal. The essay's self-presentation is one of thoughts just as they occur, the speaker talking with unbuttoned ease. Such 'conversation' also attempts to transcend the divisions of party politics and social rank which will always threaten to fracture the social sphere. David Shields makes this point in his discussion of the colonial American journal, but his argument is true of the English periodical too: 'By refiguring the intercourse of society at large as the exchanges of a friendly circle, the party animosities that troubled the public spirit were elided, and, in their place, a politics of sympathy was established' (Shields 1997, 267). Although, as we have seen, the extent to which such consensus was achieved can be debated, the whiggish *Spectator* did incorporate writings by writers identified with the Tory party, Swift, Pope and Parnell among them, and there is evidence that the periodical was read by both Whigs and Tories.[25] Although this consensus was to be short-lived – none of the essays in the resumed *Spectator* (1714) were written by any other than Whig figures – it did give a fleeting glimpse of the possibilities of the way in which fictions could make all of society participate in a form of coterie culture.

## The republic of letters

All of the genres and forms discussed in this chapter are 'social/textual' forms in so far as they inscribe aspects of sociability as an ideal within their form: whether through the interrogation of public/private distinctions and of the nature of subjectivity in the novel or the letter, in the transcription or capture of conversation in forms of dialogue, or the ways in which the periodical fashioned its own reading public, and, in doing so, attempted to reimagine society as a kind of community. Literary genre might be defined, to paraphrase Fredric Jameson, as a social contract between a writer and a specific public. What makes the genres discussed here more distinct, however, is the eighteenth century's own suggestion that literature might form a kind of (literary) public sphere, in which debates could freely be made, writers could 'speak' as relative equals and individuals could situate themselves in relation to others.[26] If this is to idealise the idea of a print culture, it is an idealisation shared with at least a number of eighteenth-century writers, when so many of them adopted the term the 'republic of letters'.[27]

Throughout the genres discussed in this chapter, we have seen how women writers availed themselves of the possibilities of modern print to enter into 'publicity'. To write in the form of letters, for example, was not to aspire to literary greatness; to write about the concerns of the individual, of feelings and moral dilemmas, often in a domestic setting, as the novel increasingly did, was to debate issues which were not debarred from women and, indeed, were increasingly to become identified with them. The dialogue forms used by Fielding and Reeve permitted them to articulate a range of opinions and to hint at sexual differences without being too adversarial. Because the dialogue lacked a clear authorial voice, it may have appealed to women writers who were anxious that aspiring to authorship was too presumptuous.[28] The periodical depended upon its female readers, a dependency which it acknowledged from the outset (even if disparagingly, as in the 'honour' to the ladies of the title *The Tatler*), and which shaped their ethic of polite behaviour. And, as the further examples of Ignatius Sancho and the labouring-class poets discussed in chapter 1 suggest, the 'republic of letters' was a more egalitarian space, in admitting women, slaves and labourers to its ranks, than the political public sphere. The most consistent criticism of Habermas's work on the public sphere has always been that his idealisation of a theoretical public sphere, in which an abstract humanity makes all equal, blinds him to its real exclusions. The debate between liberal and radical feminisms has always paralleled this debate: can existing structures accommodate difference, correcting errors of the past, or are those structures intrinsically discriminatory?

For Elizabeth Cook, the prevailing view in the eighteenth century was the first of these: 'whether as actual event or enabling fiction, the egalitarian model of the public sphere had wide appeal in the eighteenth century, even – or perhaps especially – for those who did not fully participate in it' (Cook 1996, 114). We might recall here the example of Ignatius Sancho, whose letters so consciously, so 'artificially' imitated the fashionable sentimental style of the age. Many contemporary readers have preferred the apparently direct, plain-speaking of Olaudah Equiano's account, praised even in its own time for the 'artless manner' and the 'truth and simplicity' with which it was told (*The Monthly Review*, June 1789 and *The General Magazine and Impartial Review,* July 1789). But these readers overlook the ways in which Equiano's style is itself a convention, a rhetoric (and the irony that modern scholarship by Ogude 1982, and Carretta 1999, has cast doubt on the authenticity of Equiano's account). Sancho achieved gentlemanly status by assimilation. Although the politics of this manoeuvre might be problematic – suggesting as it does that the white, middle-class values of sentimentalism and commercialism are justly normative – it does suggest that the literary public sphere was able to offer at least some freedoms denied in the political sphere. A number of contemporary feminist critics have argued that the 'virtual' public sphere which literature offered gave women access to a form of political participation, that their exclusion from such spaces as the coffee house was compensated for by their involvement in print culture, whether as writers, publishers or readers. In the tenth issue of *The Tatler,* for example, the fictional Mrs Jenny Distaff writes of how ladies can learn about the politicians who frequent the Clubs by reading her brother's journal. And a significant number of specifically female periodicals – such as *The Female Tatler, The Female Spectator,* and *The Lady's Museum* – challenge the exclusion of women as editors and writers from the dominant periodicals.[29]

As chapter 1 has argued, however, we cannot accept the century's own, often idealised, self-representations. Significant numbers of women did publish in the eighteenth century. Judith Phillips Stanton calculates that by 1800 the numbers of women authors could be assessed in the following categories: 97 playwrights, 263 published poets, 201 published novelists, 170 religious writers, 247 letter or autobiographical writers (1991, 325) and these kinds of figures are often in need of constant revision, tending always to be underestimations. However, it is worth remembering that the women most central to the bluestocking circle published only in the most 'respectable' genres: Elizabeth Carter's published volumes of poems (1736, 1762) and translation of Epictetus (1758); Elizabeth Montagu's *Essay on . . . Shakespear* (1769) and the three dialogues she contributed anonymously to Lyttleton's *Dialogues of the Dead* (1760); Hester Chapone's conduct book, *A Letter to a New-Married Lady* (1777); and the anonymous contributions to Johnson's periodical *The Rambler* by Carter (Nos 44 & 100), Chapone (10) and Catherine Talbot (30). While many of these show some daring at venturing into the 'masculine' genres of classical translation, literary criticism and satire, it is significant that none of these women published a novel or a play, that Talbot published only one essay during her lifetime, and that so many of these works were published anonymously. Similar ambivalences surround the career and writings of Ignatius Sancho. As a respectable grocer and fashionable man about London, Sancho eventually achieved the status of an insider, a 'proper' English gentleman. *The Monthly Review*, for example, complimented Sancho as being 'what is very uncommon for men of his complexion, *A Man of Letters*' (1783, 492–7). Celebrated in London society, the apotheosis of his gentlemanly status was undoubtedly the portrait by Gainsborough (1768). A sympathetic and warm portrait, this shows Sancho, not wearing servant livery, but dressed in fashionable waistcoat with gold brocade edging and black necktie. He is not shown holding an object, as was common in images of black slaves or servants, making them of secondary importance. Instead he is portrayed in the gentlemanly 'hand-in-waistcoat' pose. This pose signified the modest reserve of an English gentleman and although the pose was very common, it confirmed Sancho's image as a respectable Englishman. Gainsborough's portrait might be described as the first proper portrait of a British black person since, although black servants were frequently depicted in portraits of the aristocracy, they tended to disappear into the background, included only as exotic accessories. Gainsborough's portrait certainly provides a visual image of Sancho's cultural assimilation. But running like a thread throughout the letters is Sancho's sense of himself as an outsider. Often this sense is underplayed. For example, on one occasion, a family outing, Sancho records 'we went by water – had a coach home – were gazed at etc etc but not much abused' (Sancho 1994, 104). We need to read the letters with care, to see how the fashionable pose of polite and refined sensibility co-exists with strong, if also sometimes muted, protests against inhumanity and injustice.

The example of Ignatius Sancho suggests that we cannot prejudge or predetermine these kinds of issues, that each writer needs to be considered on his/her own terms. Neither particular genres nor particular writers can be presumed to fit models of sociability, egalitarianism or publicity. Many eighteenth-century writers, among them countless women, refused the publicity which print suggested. And genres, such as the dialogue, were never intrinsically generous to the appeals of difference. Dialogue might just as easily promote monologue, disguised only through the appearance of genuine conversation in which different viewpoints are weighed (despite Prince's qualification, noted above, that the voicing of such difference, even if ultimately denied, retained a rhetorical force). Goldsmith complained of Johnson that, in so dominating his social circles, he was 'for making a monarchy of what should be a republick' (Boswell 1980, 545). To carry opinion might be to dominate or to persuade. Ultimately, the 'republic of letters', like Habermas's public sphere, may be more ideal than real – but none the less important for that. The following chapter interrogates further the relation between literary and political public spheres in addressing the specific issue of women writers in relation to the dominant themes of this book: ideas of sociability and literary community and the ways in which print culture offers – or prohibits – a kind of freedom for a specifically female voice.

## Notes

1. See Habermas 1989, 23, 29, 51.
2. See, for example, Jill Campbell 1995, for a discussion of how public- and private-sphere values intertwine, how the gendered spheres of the domestic and public do not stay neatly in their separate places; Liz Bellamy 1998, argues that eighteenth-century novels articulate a tension between public and private versions of identity; James Thompson 1996 sees the eighteenth-century novel as attempting to separate a domestic, private sphere from a public, economic sphere of finance, but argues, in Marxist terms, that this separation is always only a constructed one, one developed only during the eighteenth century. For criticisms of Watt's 'ahistoricism', see, for example, Lynch 1998, 4.
3. For a comparable discussion of the poetry of sensibility as committed to a social as much as a personal vision, see Spacks 2001.
4 See, for example, Campbell 1990 and Allen 1998.
5. For the argument that the popularity of the letter form was in part due to an ambivalence over print itself, see Marshall 1986, 13–33.
6 Examples include *Letters Concerning Clay Roads* (1755), *Roman History in a Series of Letters* (1774), *Letters on Materialism* (1777), and *Letters on the Force of Imagination in Pregnant Women* (1765).
7. See Pope 1956, I 105, 238, 353; III, 433 and Sterne 1935, 302.

8. See Ellis 1996, 55–67 and 79–86 for an important discussion of this exchange of letters. Ellis suspects that the *Tristram Shandy* episode was inspired by Sancho's letter, rather than accidentally coincidental with it, as Sterne's letter claims.

9. See Dowling 1991, for the argument that the Augustan verse epistle attempts to reconstitute community in a world threatened by fragmentation and alienation. In this account, the verse epistle parallels the novel of sensibility, as discussed by Mullan, Todd and Schellenberg. See chapter 1 of this book.

10. See, most famously and controversially, Warner 1979. Cook 1996 argues that Richardson contains the potentially radical effects of his novel by having Belford edit and publish the letters, while Clarissa herself rejects the publicity of the law-courts in refusing to prosecute Lovelace for rape. See Carnell 1998, for a contrary reading to this.

11. Examples include Berkeley's *Alciphron, or the Minute Philosopher*, 1732, and Hume's *Dialogues Concerning Natural Religion*, 1779; the debate between Stuart and Williamite positions in *A Dialogue Between an Oak and an Orange-Tree*, 1716; John Harris's *Astronomical Dialogues Between a Gentleman and a Lady*, 1719, and Algarotti's *Sir Isaac Newton's Philosophy Explain'd for the Use of the Ladies*, translated into English in 1739 by Elizabeth Carter; Lord Lyttleton's *Dialogues of the Dead*; Edward Ward's *Nuptial Dialogues and Debates*, 1710 and *Modern Midnight Conversation, or Matrimonial Dialogues, Adapted to the Times*, 1775.

12. For an interesting essay on eighteenth-century digressions, see Barrell and Guest 1987. For a definition and discussion of 'sociable' forms, including the dialogue, see Shields 1997, 33 and *passim*.

13. See Thomas 1994.

14. See Part II for a further discussion of this issue.

15. See for example Goldsmith 1975, Gordon 1995, Copley 1995 and Prescott and Spencer 2000. Mackie 1997, 17–29 discusses the periodical in relation to Habermas's ideas of the public sphere, questioning the ways in which his model occludes questions of power and ideology. Hammond 1997, 145–91 discusses the periodical's creation of polite refinement from disparate influences.

16. Quoted in Klancher 1987, 23.

17. Among the most significant recent studies of *The Tatler* and *The Spectator* are three which specifically explore aspects of gender in these works: see Shevelow 1989, Mackie 1997, Maurer 1998.

18. Bavius was a poet who attacked Horace and Virgil. Nothing of his own work survives. Pope annotates 'quidnunc' in *The Dunciad* as 'a name given to ancient members of certain political clubs, who were constantly enquiring *quid nunc?* what news?'.

19. British-American examples include the *South-Carolina Gazette* (Meddler's Club), the *Virginia Gazette* (Monitor Club) and the *Weekly Rehearsal* (Society of Gentlemen). See Shields 1997, 267.
20. See the final issue of the first series of *Spectators* (555; 6 Dec. 1712); the dedication of Steele's *The Tender Husband* (1705) and Pope 1956, II 426, quoted in the introduction to this book.
21. He also added that it was 'achieved largely by casting readers as well as writer in the role of coffeehouse habitués'; 1975, 14.
22. The epigraph is from Martial's *Epigrams*, here translated by *The Spectator's* modern editor, Donald Bond 1965, V 539.
23. See Maurer's argument that Sir Andrew Freeport is pre-eminent among the club members (1998, 180ff) and the debate between Sir Andrew and Sir Roger in *Spectator*, No. 174, which Sir Andrew seems obviously to win.
24. Quoted in Bond 1965, I xcix. Bond also discusses Hugh Blair and Samuel Johnson as important celebrators of Addison's prose style in particular. Blair's lectures at Edinburgh University in the 1760s and 1770s hailed Addison's writing as the perfection of English style. He set students the task of analysing *Spectator* essays and himself gave 'critical examinations' of Nos 411–14.
25. Bond notes that the subscription list for the collected octavo edition of *Spectators* (1712–13) included a 'respectable' number of Tories (Bond 1965, I xxvciii).
26. Habermas himself does not explain how the literary public sphere is related to the (political) public sphere. For considerations of this connection, and critiques of Habermas, see Eagleton 1984, Cook 1996 and Carnell 1998.
27. See, for example, *The Spectator*, Nos 445, 470, 494, 529 and the early review magazine, *The Present State of the Republic of Letters*, ed. Andrew Reid (1728–36). In Fielding's *Covent-Garden Journal*, Sir Alexander Drawcansir establishes a Court of Censorial Inquiry which hears and determines 'all manner of Causes, which in anywise relate to the Republic of Letters' (Fielding 1988, 45). Griffin 1993 surveys the idea of a 'republic of letters'.
28. See Brant 2000, 302 and Marshall 1986, 29–32. Cook notes that, although the phrase 'the republic of letters' is used much earlier, it is appropriated by polite literature in the eighteenth century (Cook 1996, 184 n.5).
29. See Habermas 1989, 56; McDowell 1998, 258, discussing Delarivier Manley; Schellenberg 1996, 91; Berry 1998; Backscheider 2000. Mrs Jenny Distaff writes issues Nos 10, 33, and 36–38. That these issues – and many of *The Female Tatler* – were not written by women does not cancel the significance of the *claim* to female authorship.

# 3 Female Communities

In 1779 the painting exhibition at the Royal Academy included a group portrait of prominent female artists, entitled *The Nine Living Muses of Great Britain*. The nine women represented there were the singer Elizabeth Linley Sheridan, the painter Angelica Kauffman, the poet and critic Anna Lætitia Barbauld, the scholar and poet Elizabeth Carter, the novelist Charlotte Lennox, the educator and writer Hannah More, the writer and actress Elizabeth Griffith, the bluestocking literary patron, writer and critic Elizabeth Montagu, and the historian Catherine Macaulay. While this group included notable bluestocking figures (Carter, More and Montagu), in reaching beyond members of that circle it represented an imaginary or virtual coterie of female artists. That these ladies might form a female artistic tradition or 'club' was picked up by Elizabeth Carter, writing of an earlier engraved form of this painting to her friend Elizabeth Montagu:

> One thing is very particularly agreeable to my vanity, to say nothing about my heart, that it seems to be a decided point, that you and I are always to figure in the literary world together, and that from the classical poet, the water drinking rhymes, to the highest dispenser of human fame, Mr. Johnson's pocket book, it is perfectly well understood, that we are to make our appearance in the same piece. (Carter 1817, III 47–8).

Carter's allusion here is to *Johnson's Ladies New and Polite Pocket Memorandum for 1778*, in which an engraved version of the painting was first circulated. The popularity of this engraving may well have influenced the exhibition of the painting, by Richard Samuel, at the Royal Academy in 1779. The kind of cultural confidence which Carter's letter displays is because she is able to situate herself within an established group of female friends. In 1784 Elizabeth Montagu seemed to hint at the notoriety conveyed by this painting when she wrote to Elizabeth Vesey, another blue-stocking hostess, of the significance enjoyed by the bluestockings in their own time: 'After supping Helicon with the nine do they not often condescend to drink tea in Bolton Street or Hill Street? We have lived much with the wisest, the best, and most celebrated men of our Times, and with some of the best, most accomplished, and most learned Women of any times' (Montagu 1923, II 7).[1]

Samuel's painting and its engraving by Walker are virtually unprecedented in the history of portraiture. No other group portrait of female writers exists to compare with these. They suggest that the significance of women artists is such that they might be represented together. Of course, partly this is a matter of serendipity. The classical legend of the nine Muses of the various arts is the obvious rationale for a painting of nine female artists. But the image's existence and popularity lends to these women a *collective* importance which is greater than their individual significance. It suggests that against the many famous literary clubs (most prominently the Scriblerians and Johnson's Club) – almost male by definition – there is another grouping possible, if only in the realms of art. The distinction between the real and the imaginative club is central to this chapter, in which I will consider ideas of female community in the eighteenth century. But let us begin with a return to Habermas, key theorist of ideas of group culture in this and any period.

## Women's place in the public sphere

One of the most controversial aspects of Habermas's definition of the public sphere is its exclusion of women, an exclusion which some feminist critics have argued is essential, rather than historically contingent, to Habermas's construction.[2] Habermas's definition is based on an idealised model which he locates in the eighteenth century. Habermas openly acknowledges the idealism of his account, while simultaneously discussing elements of this ideal public sphere in relation to the history of eighteenth-century Europe. The history which Habermas sketches presents only a flawed model, but within this actually occurring history lies the possibility of the theoretical ideal. Critiques of Habermas's work have thus tended to challenge the concept of a public sphere from either historicist or theoretical perspectives. This chapter begins with a consideration of some of the most important historicist replies and ends with the question of the theoretical usefulness or otherwise of Habermas's work for feminism. If women were excluded from the domain of the historical, imperfect, public sphere, as defined by Habermas (and this 'if', as we shall see, is an important one), is the theoretical, ideal public sphere necessarily also exclusivist?

The exclusion of women from Habermas's theoretical construction of the public sphere seems to compound the historical exclusion of women from the exemplary site of public-sphere life, the coffee house. Habermas implies that women were antithetical to coffee-house culture when he suggests that discussions of consequence on such matters as politics and economics were possible in the coffee house because women were absent: 'Critical debate ignited by works of literature and art was soon extended to include economic and political disputes, without any guarantee (such as was given in salons) that such discussions would be inconsequential, at least in the immediate context. The fact that only men were admitted to coffee-house society may have had something to do with this' (Habermas 1992, 33). Habermas also cites pamphlets attacking the coffee houses purportedly written by women as evidence of their exclusion. For example, *The Women's Petition against Coffee* (1663) presents itself as a lament by wives abandoned by their coffee-house-consorting husbands and unsatisfied by husbands made impotent by excessive coffee drinking. Its full title bawdily alludes to the second of these complaints: *The Women's Petition against Coffee, representing to Public Consideration of the Grand Inconveniences according to their Sex from the Excessive Use of that Drying, Enfeebling Liquor*. If women are excluded from the public sphere, their site then becomes that of a 'private' sphere, where they are conveniently settled away from the 'significant' domains of politics, economics and public discussion and debate. The model of 'separate spheres' in which men are associated with and situated within a public sphere, and women with a private sphere, is a model which dominated thinking about gender until, arguably, the late 1980s. Only in the final decade of the century did feminist thinking chafe against its confines and challenge the ways in which, as Linda Kerber has argued, the model of the separate spheres was 'a trope which hid its instrumentality even from those who employed it' (Kerber 1988, 30). Paula McDowell (1998), for example, criticised the idea of one public sphere, masculine and bourgeois in Habermas's formation, and argued that we ought to think in terms of overlapping public spheres, in which non-élite women writers and printers certainly have a place. Amanda Vickery has documented women's extensive involvement in public, social activities and has argued that eighteenth-century prescriptions that women should remain in private, domestic interiors were only reactions to women's highly visible publicity (Vickery 1993, 1998). While Vickery does not discuss the particular space of the coffee house, the paradigmatic site of public-sphere activity for Habermas, many other accounts dovetail with Vickery's own work, in questioning the real exclusion of women from even this most apparently homosocial space of public sphere life.

Habermas's work on the public sphere was first published in 1962 and inevitably bears traces of older, and increasingly outdated, historical accounts of the period. More recent histories of the later seventeenth and eighteenth centuries have stressed, contra Habermas, that women were not entirely excluded from the coffee house. Steven Pincus 1995 and Helen Berry 1998 both cite evidence which suggests that women frequented coffee houses – at least in the late seventeenth century. For example Pincus cites Lady Giffard, sister to Sir William Temple, as a known habitué of coffee houses in the late Restoration period in addition to the many women who ran and owned coffee houses throughout Britain. Lillywhite's 1963 list of London coffee houses confirms that women were associated with the ownership and management of coffee houses throughout the eighteenth century. Pincus also argues that Habermas's reliance upon the pamphlets criticising coffee-house culture is misplaced. Three Restoration pamphlets claim to be written by women: *The Women's Petition against Coffee* (1663), *The Maiden's Complaint against Coffee* (1663) and *The Ale-Wives Complaint against the Coffee-Houses* (1675) but Pincus finds these pamphlets motivated by the religious criticism of nonconformity as much as by any specifically female perspective. They are just as likely to have been commissioned by rival vintners and brewers, losing trade to the coffee-sellers, as by disgruntled wives. Markman Ellis's essay 'Coffee-women, "*The Spectator*" and the public sphere' (2001) focuses on the women who were always present in coffee houses and taverns: those who served at the bar and often owned the coffee shop itself. One famous literary example is Lockit's daughter Lucy in Gay's *The Beggar's Opera*, who has been trained by her father in the arts of 'serving' men at the bar. Peachum's use of his daughter is similar, and similarly sketched, as he notes: 'A handsome wench in our way of business is as profitable as at the bar of a Temple coffee-House who looks upon it as her livelihood to grant every liberty but one' (Gay 1986, 50). Ellis argues that the flirtatious, immoral serving girl has been excluded from many accounts of coffee-house culture because she does not conform to the sobriety and seriousness of the coffee house as it is idealised by Habermas and by many eighteenth-century accounts. Even if we accept the idyllic depiction of sobriety and communality sketched by supporters – both eighteenth-century and modern – of the coffee-house ideal, this ideal was predicated upon virtues and values which its culture associated with femininity (see Clery 1991). Already we can see that in accounts of the public sphere, cultural (mis)perceptions are as significant as actual conditions. Historical coffee houses were never as polite or as exclusively male as idealising accounts would have them be.

All of these counter-arguments to Habermas's depiction of the coffee house, however, tend to refine his model rather than to challenge it. Pincus and Berry demonstrate that female attendance in the coffee house was not unknown – but their evidence testifies only to the late seventeenth century. Markman Ellis's account proves that while women were not absent from the coffee houses, 'ladies' certainly were: no woman of respectable character could be seen to visit such a place. That the coffee house exists as a site by which respectable femininity might be known and defined is evident from many of the early eighteenth-century accounts of women frequenting the coffee house. Among the mock 'ads' of *The Female Tatler*, for example, is the following: 'The young lady in the parish of St Laurence, near Guildhall, that lately went to the Coffee-House in man's clothes with the two 'prentices, called for a dish of Bohee, smoked her pipe, and gave herself abundance of straddling masculine airs, is desired to do so no more' (Morgan 1992, 88). In 1755, the landlord of the Golden Head Coffee House in London advertised a forthcoming attraction thus: 'Mr Vetter at the Golden Head . . . has opened his Coffee House to accommodate Ladies and Gentlemen with the sight of his large piece of Artificial Rock and Grotto Work twenty six feet round and nine feet high. There is a passage for the Ladies without going through the Coffee House' (cited from an unnamed paper in Lillywhite 1963, 700). Even Mary Davys inveighs against female attendance in the coffee house: 'how ready are we . . . to call that Man a Mr *Maiden*, who spends his Mornings in dress at a looking glass, and his Afternoons in making visits, drinking tea, and criticising upon the nicety of Good-breeding? On the contrary, it would be every whit as ridiculous for us Women to be every day at a Coffee-house, talking politics and reading Gazettes' (Davys 1725, I 257). When Davys revised the work in which this comment is found, *The Merry Wanderer*, she had become a coffee-house owner herself since its first publication 20 years earlier. But while she revised the text, she did not cut this passage, perhaps because her respectability as a proprietor necessitated her repeating the prescriptions concerning correct femininity. Similarly, while Smollett's Lydia Melford intriguingly refers to a female coffee house in Bath, she is forbidden to visit such a space: 'my aunt says, young girls are not admitted, inasmuch as the conversation turns upon politics, scandal, philosophy, and other subjects above our capacity' (Smollett 1984, 40). In these ways we can see the operation of 'separate spheres' in eighteenth-century culture: men attend coffee houses and gaming clubs; women frequent India Houses, tea shops with a large female clientele, while at the dinner tables of the polite, ladies withdraw to a separate room to permit the gentlemen to discuss the 'consequential' issues of politics, business, current affairs.

Amanda Vickery's thesis of women's enjoyment of public activities, in mixed companies, is overlaid with an alternative model, then, of segregated zones. However, finding specifically female spaces in the public sphere, places which might function as feminine equivalents of the coffee house, is more difficult. Historical examples of exclusively female public clubs, for example, are hardly common. Even the bluestockings, remembered now as an all-female group, were never in practice made up solely of women. That their very name testifies to one of the male associates of the group – Benjamin Stillingfleet's tendency to wear informal blue worsted stockings to meetings – provides a neat metaphor for the gender aspects concerned here: a group often thought of as exclusively female is known by a name which bears the traces of its mixed company. The 'Shakespeare Ladies Club', who waged an anonymous campaign to promote performances of Shakespeare in late 1736, seems to suggest the promise of an exclusively 'female club'. But beyond some brief references to this club in epilogues and newspaper commentary (for example, the *Daily Advertiser* envisaged how Shakespeare would return from the grave to thank the Shakespeare Ladies Club and praise their good judgement), we know very little of their existence and whether, indeed, there was such a society.[3] The *Oxford English Dictionary* suggests a definitional link between the idea of the 'coterie' and women in the eighteenth century: 'A friendly or fashionable association. It has of late years been considered as meaning a select party, or club, and sometimes of ladies only' (1818). All of the dictionary's eighteenth-century citations refer to gatherings of women. But beyond the many slighting references to the proverbial tittle-tattle and scandal-mongering of tea-tables, there seems little evidence of an exclusively female culture in what we might term the public sphere.

While men certainly dominate the history of public communities in the eighteenth century, then, evident in the spaces of parliament, coffee house, the debating society and the influential periodicals *The Tatler* and *The Spectator*, there are no exclusively female counterparts. As Joseph Lew has suggested, it may well be that the key distinction in eighteenth-century terms is not that between men and women's spaces but between exclusively male and shared spaces (Lew 1991). Women's involvement in mixed company is an issue this chapter will return to. But it would be too precipitate to close the issue of all-female groups, since the *idea* of specifically female communities was such a significant one in the eighteenth century. References to Protestant nunneries, tea-tables, female academies and circles proliferate in the period. Most of these were imaginative rather than real. Often they were pejorative rather than aspirational. But together they suggest a counterpoint to the paradigmatic coffee house, if only in imaginative terms.

## Imaginative female communities

Images of female communities often seem to exist as extravagantly fictional images, created to counterpoise the dominance of men-only groups. When 'Corinna, A Country Parson's Wife', for example, publishes her *Critical Remarks on the Four Taking Plays of this*

*Season* (1719), she dedicates the work to the Wits at Button's coffee house before proposing the creation of 'a Society of Female Wits' who will 'depose' the Wits from their 'Usurpt Authority'. This context – of an associative link between ladies and the reformation of the stage – casts doubt on the authenticity of the 'Shakespeare Ladies Club' as a real entity. But it also exemplifies how female groups proliferate as an idea and how the circulation of that idea keeps it open as a possibility.

Many eighteenth-century images of female groups are satirical or derogatory. The female 'tea-table', for example, is almost invariably invoked as an image of gossip, scandal, silly chatter and malicious innuendo. Thus when Swift concludes his *Polite Conversation*, the women who begin the final dialogue gossip in the vapid manner of meaningless clichés and empty folkloric tags. Swift also wrote elsewhere that 'A Knot of Ladies got together by themselves, is a very School of Impertinence and Detraction' ('Letter to a young lady on her marriage'; Swift 1948, IX 88). Among the many clubs sketched in *The Spectator* is Kitty Termagant's 'Club of She-Romps': 'We are no sooner come together than we throw off all that Modesty and Reservedness with which our Sex are obliged to disguise themselves in publick Places . . . As our Play runs high the Room is immediately filled with broken Fans, torn Petticoats, Lappets of Head-dresses, Flounces, Furbelows . . . once a month we *Demolish a Prude*' (Bond 1965, II 345–6). Here an exclusively female group is an excuse only for transvestite behaviour: these 'she-romps' behave more like rowdy men than the image of demure femininity sketched elsewhere in *The Spectator*. Similarly, the image of a female parliament was often invoked only to satirise the idea of a female tyranny – as it was in Charles Johnson's *The Wife's Relief* (1712), and Henry Fielding's *The Modern Husband* (1732), for example.[4] 'Petticoat' rule was invoked to satirise the Duchess of Marlborough in *The Petticoat Plotters, or the D[uches]s of M[arlboroug]h's Club* (1712) and the putatively female community of Queen Anne and her ladies-in-waiting was lampooned in many satires which lewdly depicted a lesbian court. But recuperative images also circulated, responded to and even challenged these stereotypes. John Dunton's *Petticoat-Government* (1702) praises the 'pettycoat government' of Queen Anne and argues that 'Government is not only lawful and tolerable in women, but *justly*, *naturally*, and *properly* Theirs' (6); the anonymous Gaelic text, the

*Parliament na mBan* ('The Parliament of Women', 1703) criticises male chauvinism which has relegated women from public life to the domestic periphery; and the fictional Pamela wishes for 'a Parliament of Women' (Richardson 2001, 450). Satiric images of female communities, then, often have aspirational counterparts. In many cases the connection between the satiric and the imagined ideal is one of inspiration or direct dialogue. Budgell's unflattering depiction of the 'club of She-Romps', for example, may well have been inspired by Delarivier Manley's depiction of 'The Ladies of the New Cabal' in *The New Atalantis* (1709). Budgell's She-Romps behave like gentlemen and thus suggest that the very idea of a female club is an absurdity. More equivocally, the ladies of Manley's cabal laugh at their ease and hold possessions in common but are throughout associated with lesbianism despite, or because of, the narrator's futile attempts to protect them.[5]

One of the ways in which we can see satirical and desired images as deeply connected is within the instability of the satiric view itself. The ridicule of female-only communities always permits a gap in which readers might be excited as much as amused by the depiction. In Centlivre's *The Basset-Table* (1705), for example, Lady Reveller mocks Valeria's learning by suggesting she found 'a College for the Studies of Philosophy, where none but Women should be admitted' (Centlivre 1872, I 218). Valeria's reply – that 'What you make a Jest of, I'd execute, were Fortune in my Power' – is a reminder that while female schools might be a joke to some, it is an ideal to others. This is especially so in a context in which this very issue – of female schools – had been much debated. Mary Astell's scheme of a female college in *A Serious Proposal to the Ladies* (1694) had been followed by Defoe's largely approving 'Academy for Women' (in *An Essay upon Projects*, 1697) and by an attack on Astell in *The Tatler* (No. 32; 1709) while satire of Astell possibly lies behind the jibe at Valeria in Centlivre's play too. Similarly, when *The Connoisseur* devoted two issues to a scheme for a 'female parliament' and to debates in that parliament (Nos 44 and 62, 1755), it did so to ridicule the very idea it proposed: the female parliament passes the ultimately rather trivial motion that female dress is inclined to popery, for example. But the inevitable interpretative slippage which is possible in reading satire would always suggest that derogatory images, presented mock-earnestly, could also inspire.

Partly what I am attempting to do here is to sketch an imaginative pre-history for the bluestockings, the most significant and famous of female groups. While their actual gatherings were always of mixed companies, their most deeply felt association was as a kind of virtual community, meeting and conversing through exchanged letters. The status of the bluestockings as a female club is felt at the level of the imagination. It seems entirely fitting then, to sketch a pre-history not in terms of actual, empirical gatherings, but in terms of imaginative visions, even when these are satirical. Gary Kelly has situated the bluestockings in relation to the most well-known and extensive account of an all-female society – the novel *Millenium Hall* (1762) by Sarah Scott, who was associated with the bluestocking circle through her sister, Elizabeth Montagu. Here we have a full-scale imaginative vision of a female society, composed of widows and single women, who live together, sharing wealth and talents and devoting themselves to the genteel pursuits of art, industry and charity. Towards the end of the narrative, Scott's male narrator exclaims:

> All that romance ever represented in the plains of Arcadia, are much inferior to the charms of Millenium-Hall, except the want of shepherds be judged a deficiency, that nothing else can compensate; there indeed they fall short of what romantic writers represent, and have formed a female Arcadia. (Scott 1995, 223)

The narrator forgets that the first person he and his travelling companion, Mr Lamont, met was a shepherd, playing upon his flute in conventional pastoral fashion:

> When we had walked about half a mile in a scene truly pastoral, we began to think ourselves in the days of Theocritus, so sweetly did the sound of a flute come wafted through the air. Never did pastoral swain make sweeter melody on his oaten reed. . . . Our pleasure was not a little heightened, to see, as the scene promised, in reality a shepherd, watching a large flock of sheep. (56)

These passages suggest the obviously utopian element of Millenium Hall. Here we see an aristocratic pastoral idealism which, together with aspects of humanist classicism and Christianity, make up the work's particular kind of utopian thinking. Despite the feminocentric aspect of *Millenium Hall*, the conventional shepherd is still required as part of a utopian tradition. The presence of the shepherd, however, also reminds us that beyond the community or 'family' of ladies at the Hall are many other communities, those either nurtured or inspired by the Hall itself. These include the female haymakers and their children, seen happily at work in the fields (57); the charity cottages in which 12 women rescued from poverty live as neighbours and work co-operatively together (65–8); the society of the disabled and deformed who tend gardens enclosed from the public eye (70–6); a neighbouring community of ladies with small or no fortunes, modelled exactly on the plan of Millenium Hall and soon to extend to a second, larger house (114–21 and 219–22); schools for young girls and boys, alms-houses for the old, settlements of furniture and stock for young married couples, settlements of income and furnishings for a clergyman's widow and her children, and a carpet and rug making industry which employs 'several hundreds of people of all ages', all instituted and funded by the Millenium Hall ladies (159, 195–8, 243–4), in addition to sundry other charities, caring especially for destitute children (247–8). Despite the ways in which Millenium Hall is figured as a retreat from the world, then, it is also at the centre of its own complete world, in which different classes happily co-exist and even neighbours with no direct link to the Millenium Hall society, such as the clergyman and his wife (222–3), embody the contentedness and simplicity associated with the Christian morality of the Hall. This society does not exclude men – successive stewards at the Hall have been male, a smaller school accommodates boys until they are apprenticed and the society of the deformed is a mixed community – but its charity and refuge is offered to those who seem to need it most and those are women and children buffeted by inheritance laws, economic vulnerability and sexual objectification. These oppressions are dramatised in the inset narratives of the Millenium Hall ladies. Their escape into a different kind of society is evident in the extended descriptions of the Hall and its surrounding community.

Beyond *Millenium Hall* there are a significant number of texts which similarly imagine communities of women. These include Jane Barker's partly fictional, partly autobiographical work, *A Patch-Work Screen for the Ladies* (1723). This tells the story of Galesia, interspersed with other narratives, recipes, medicinal remedies and poetry. The formal diversity of the work is framed and given cohesion by the overarching female society upon which Galesia accidentally stumbles and to which she contributes her multiple narratives as part of its own 'patch-work' of artistic works. Like the society of Millenium Hall, this community is made up of 'poor Gentlewomen', employed at the House 'to keep them from Distress, and evil Company, till Time and Friends could dispose Things for their better Settlement' (Barker 1997, 74). The framing device thus suggests the same kind of genteel charity which later characterises Scott's *Millenium Hall*, where the female community also figures as a frame for the inset narratives of its members. In both texts, the idyllic community provides little narrative of its own – its static perfection provides a backdrop to the stories, mostly unfortunate, which make up the greatest part of the narrative. Indeed, at one point in Barker's sequel, *The Lining of the Patch-Work Screen* (1726), a female character is unable to tell Galesia a story from her experiences in a French convent, saying: 'nothing remarkable had appeared there, but extraordinary Vertue and Piety, the Religious performing their Devotions in exact Regularity, and the Seculars as perfect in their Respect and Obedience' (267). When she does tell Galesia a story she once heard outside the convent it is the more obviously fictional tale of a governess possessed of supernatural powers, able to run up chimneys and fly. The idyllic female communities depicted in these texts do not offer narratives but representations of ideal life. They are thus at once backdrops to the narratives and enabling contexts in which these female narratives can be told. In Barker's fiction, the community is much less of a presence – we do not have the extended descriptions of the estate which introduce and then punctuate the stories of *Millenium Hall* and much of the social interaction at the House is in groups of mixed company. However, it is the lady and her female servants or friends working together on the patch-work who provide the rationale for Galesia's miscellaneous pieces of literary work. (When the making of the patch-work is first described, it is the lady and her maids who busy themselves with completing the screen; 74. Later, it is the lady's female guests who take up the patch-work; 151.) While Barker's sequel, *The Lining of the Patch-Work Screen*, finds Galesia living in London, the context of female circles continues. Among the diverse pieces introduced in this work are stories introduced merely by glancing at books lying open and stories told by visitors, male and female, to Galesia's home. Many of these stories take the feminised form of 'gossip' among friends, and while gentlemen callers to Galesia's home tell her many such stories, it is significant that, when Galesia and her friends go to dinner at Lady Allgood's, it is only after dinner, when the ladies retire to their own tea-table, that the stories continue (221). There they 'pass'd the short Winter's Afternoon, in Tea and Chat' (238). When the book closes it does so with a reminder of the society Galesia enjoyed in *The Patch-Work Screen*, as the lady's waiting-woman arrives in London to escort Galesia back to the country hall (290). A seemingly abrupt ending, the final paragraphs of *The Lining of the Patch-Work Screen* remind us of the frame narrative of the prequel and gesture towards the utopian dimension it would later share with *Millenium Hall*.

The 'little Society' of nine schoolgirls and their teacher, Mrs Teachum, in Sarah Fielding's *The Governess* (1749) represents another significant, imaginative, female community. As a 'little female academy', this is necessarily only a temporary society. Indeed the narrative ends with the sad departure of the eldest girl, Jenny Peace, who returns to live with her aunt. Yet *The Governess* plots how the girls improve from a collection of envious, squabbling children, to a harmonious and virtuous circle of friends, and in this regard, however temporary their society, the book embodies the ideals of female community. When the girls are invited to tour a stately home, one exclaims: 'I wish we could all live here for ever' (Fielding 1987, 114). Although Polly Suckling's desire is partly because she is entranced by the finery of the great house, her expression also testifies to the perfect amity in which they now live together. The ideal which the book presents, however, often seems more troubled than it cares to admit. The relationship between Mrs Teachum and the nine girls is obviously hierarchical. She is the instructor and guide of their behaviour, but, in the opening pages, she is also their discipliner. After the girls fight and bicker over who should have the most desirable apple, Mrs Teachum punishes them. The anonymous narrator is overtly coy about this punishment, however: 'Mrs *Teachum*'s Method of punishing I never could find out' (5).[6] And the following day the girls fight just as much over who is most to blame for the punishment itself. This puts Mrs Teachum's authority into question. Throughout the narrative, Mrs Teachum is a constraining presence: the girls are too abashed to confess to their past faults in her hearing and thus Jenny is instructed to write down the stories of their short lives for Mrs Teachum to read later (40) and all the girls are timid and shy when Mrs Teachum asks them to retell their reading of the play so that she 'may see whether [they] give the proper Attention to what [they] have heard' (101). All stories must be morally edifying and Jenny's first story of the giants is criticised for its supernatural elements and inflated language (34–5). The book appears to support Mrs Teachum's strictures, in the overt didacticism of many of its passages and its explicit reformism. *The Governess* alludes to its own status as educator when the narrator ends the book with the suggestion that this narrative will continue to serve succeeding generations of girls at the school: 'All Quarrels and Contentions were banished her House; and if ever any such Thing was likely to arise, the Story of Miss *Jenny Peace*'s reconciling all her little Companions was told to them' (125). In this way, the book is both 'the governess' and 'the little female academy' of its title and subtitle. But while the book does not overtly challenge the model of Mrs Teachum, there are a number of places where her authority is contrasted with the love which Jenny Peace, the eldest of the girls, inspires in the others. When Jenny leaves, this contrast is explicit: Polly Suckling cries 'I'm sure we shan't, nor we can't, be half so happy, when you are gone, tho' our Governess was ten times better to us than she is' and Jenny urges the girls to dry their tears, anxious that Mrs Teachum 'might take it unkindly, that they should be so afflicted at the Loss of one Person, while they still remained under her indulgent Care and Protection' (123). In other places, the contrast between Jenny and Mrs Teachum is only implicit. When Polly Suckling, for example, complains of the triviality of fairy stories, Jenny is amused by the affectation of only seven years. She tells a story from her own childhood – of how she disdained to go with her family to see a raree show, thinking herself above such childish things, but came to regret her self-consequence when her mother spoke of her own delight in the event. Here Jenny defends 'innocent amusement[s]' even if they cannot be recuperated by moralism (63). (No moral agenda for attending raree shows is offered!) In contrast, Mrs Teachum, as her 'speaking name' suggests, cannot be anything other than a teacher. Although we see her attempt to put the children at their ease in her presence ('Come, my Dear, throw off all Fear and Reserve; imagine me one of your Companions, and tell me the Story of the Play you have been reading'; 102), she only reproves Sukey's reading of the play by drawing out the moral which the child has forgotten in her account (104–5). One other passage challenges Mrs Teachum's authority. When the girls hasten to give their pocket-money to a beggar man, Mrs Teachum cautions them against someone who might be a fake. Dolly boldy replies to her schoolmistress and the episode ends abruptly, without obvious closure:

> [Mrs Teachum] told them, she approved of their Readiness to assist the poor Fellow, as he appeared to them: But oftentimes those Fellows made up dismal Stories without much Foundation, and because they were lazy, and would not work. Miss *Dolly* said, Indeed she believed the poor Man spoke Truth; for he looked honest; and, besides, he seem'd almost starved. (60)

Mrs Teachum's precepts and the central story of the book, that of 'The Princess Hebe', counsel obedience to parents and guardians, even when the reason for their strictures is not understood. The fairy of the story moralises thus: 'True Obedience consists in Submission; and when we pretend to choose what Commands are proper and fit for us, we don't obey, but set up our own Wisdom in Opposition to our Governors' (74). However, as the episode with the beggar suggests, this maxim may not always be trustworthy.

*The Governess* is overtly addressed to young readers and implicitly to young girls. It is thus easy to read it as a conservative work, an equivalent for children of the popular conduct books for women which dominate considerations of gender in the period. *Millenium Hall* has certainly been read as a conservative vision of class and gender relations. (The girls whom the Millenium Hall ladies care for, for example, walk with the housekeeper every day 'lest their being always in our company should make them think their situation above a menial state'; Scott 1995, 160). The Millenium Hall ladies advocate piety, marriage and many of the values which their own culture deemed properly 'feminine': but they also practise a kind of female homosociality which protects them from unhappy marriages and patriarchal laws. Moreover, in both *The Governess* and *Millenium Hall*, the more radical aspects of the societies they depict are a consequence of their informal constitutions. The ideal commonality which the Millenium Hall ladies exercise leads them to share wealth and time in acts of radical altruism and benevolence and to re-envisage commercial society, with its instrumental desires for profit and wealth-creation, as a maternalistic society in which the sick, the elderly and abandoned children are cared for and the poor given employment. In *The Governess*, the implicit critique of Mrs Teachum and the moral conservatism which she embodies takes place because she is ultimately outside the ideal society which the nine girls themselves construct, under the guidance of their equal, if slightly older, schoolfriend Jenny Peace. Even after she leaves, Jenny is still the harmonising force: 'All Quarrels and Contentions were banished her House; and if ever any such Thing was likely to arise, the Story of Miss *Jenny Peace*'s reconciling all her little Companions was told to them; so that Miss *Jenny*, tho' absent, still seemed (by the bright Example which she left behind her) to be the Cement of Union and Harmony in this well-regulated Society' (125).[7]

That both of these texts offer a significantly muted form of protest is also true of Mary Hamilton's *Munster Village* (1778), the last of the utopian fictions I will consider. In this account, Lady Frances uses her father's estate and wealth, bequeathed to her rather than to her brother who married against their father's wishes, to create the ideal community of the text's title. Although her eventual gift of this estate to her nephew ensures the continuity of patriarchal inheritance, Lady Frances's transformation of the estate is a radical manoeuvre within this conventional patrimony. It is also an intervention, not only in the community which she creates, but in the reformation of the male inheritor, for the young Lord Munster is kept ignorant of the wealth he will inherit from her on his sixteenth birthday in order that he can develop the virtues of industry, education and thrift which he might otherwise refuse. Munster Village is situated in the rural retirement of Shropshire, but Lady Frances's ambition is to create 'works of national magnificence' (Hamilton 1987, 29). Her centre of learning – like Astell's proposed academy – is ambitious rather than retiring. Her works include a village for artisans, with endowed cottages designed by the famous Capability Brown, a charitable hospice, an Academy of sciences and arts, a library open to all, an astronomical observatory, an anatomy theatre and painting, sculpture and architecture galleries. While only 20 young girls are educated (compared to 200 young boys), the traditional female education of wifely accomplishments is disdained in favour of whatever activity – manual or mental – seems best to suit each girl. The community then is seen in terms of its variety: 'buildings of great utility and much fancy, groves inspiring different sensations, from the lucid summits that wake the mind to gaiety, to the dark brown of *clair obscure* of trees crowding their branches together in the vale, which possess the soul with home-felt contemplation' (130). At heart this variety is also an attempt to unite aesthetics and utility. The more conservative glimpses of an ordered, determined society, such as Lady Frances's prescriptions even for what the young women of the village might wear, are overlaid with this ideal of beauty and use synthesised: 'A country girl returning from the spring with a pitcher of water on her head, perfectly resembles those figures which the most exquisite antiques represent in the same attitude' (28). Lady Frances as the muse and patron of this society is herself an artist, founder and initiator of the community. Appropriately, then, in the midst of the Academy stands a statue of Lady Frances herself as Muse and foundress, representing a power which is both symbolic and real.[8] Her project is repeatedly invoked as an artistic one. During the masquerade pageant of the book's final scenes, for example, artists throughout history (such as the Renaissance painter Raphael, the Restoration writer the Duke of Buckingham and the pseudo-ancient poet Ossian) compliment Lady Frances and her community. Thus we have hyperbolic sentences such as the following: 'Michael Angelo, that celebrated restorer of the arts of painting, sculpture, and architecture, expressed how infinitely he was charmed with Munster Village!' (132). The cross-dressing of the pageant – with the novel's heroes and heroines parading as the revered writers, artists and philosophers of history – reminds us of the important ways in which literature, and more specifically fiction, enables the transcendence of limitations. The pageant, organised to commemorate the wedding anniversary of Lady Frances and Lord Darnley, is also the moment at which the various subplots are resolved, with separated lovers reuniting in the conscious resolution of literary plot. To a greater extent than the other texts considered, then, *Munster Village* relies upon aesthetics rather than politics to resolve the tensions of its context and to achieve its idealised community.

As in *Millenium Hall*, it is the inset narratives which speak of women's real oppressions: the unhappy marriage of Mrs Lee makes her an outspoken advocate for divorce; the figure of the unmarried mother, Miss Harris, is depicted sympathetically; the Duchess's husband is cruel and unfaithful to her and her ward is abducted by him and only just escapes being forced to marry him. In short, forced and unhappy marriages abound in *Munster Village*. Lady Frances is happily affianced but refuses marriage when she inherits her father's estate in order to establish the village. She finally marries the faithful Lord Darnley and dedicates her project to him:

> It is true, the great works I have carried on, the encouragement I have given to learning, the manufactories I have introduced into this kingdom, etc etc have procured me the suffrage of the world, and may transmit my name down to posterity. But what flatters me most is, that if I have acquired any fame, it is derived from the man I love. . . . Unassisted by Agrippa and Mecaenas, where should we have placed Augustus? (57)

However, the apparent self-deprecation of this passage is offset in a number of ways by alternative voices within the text. For example, it is Lord Darnley who is here situated in the position of the inspirer – the patron Maecenas to whom Lady Frances is herself also compared (131). In *Munster Village*, the inspiring Muse is also always the creator. Moreover, this passage is juxtaposed with the scepticism of Mrs Lee's arguments on marriage, still present in the final page of the book. Despite the happy reunions of the final section of the book, Mrs Lee refuses to marry Mr Villars, the man whom she had covertly loved while unhappily but faithfully married. There is some narrative attempt to resolve this gap between Mrs Lee's scepticism and Mr Villars' suit: 'these differences were soon settled, agreeable to their mutual wishes' (150). This abrupt settling of differences remains ambiguous, however, and continues to be unsettled by Mrs Lee's outspokenness:

> To me it is terrible to reflect, that it is a strangely unequal conflict, in which the man only ventures the loss of a few temporary pleasures, the woman the loss of liberty, and almost the privilege of opinion. – From the moment she's married she becomes the subject of an arbitrary lord; even her children, the mutual pledges of their affection, are absolutely in his power, and the law countenances him in the use of it – and a woman finds no redress for the indelicate abuses of an uncivil, a passionate, and avaricious, an inconstant, or even a drunken husband – from matrimonial decisions there is no appeal. (150)

This is a voice which the novel cannot seem to accommodate entirely within its frame, just as the narratives of the ladies of Millenium Hall comment tangentially on their professions of faith in eighteenth-century marriages and wifely propriety. To an extent this kind of double-voice is inevitable in the representation of a retreat, a place which is both an escape from the world but also a way of inhabiting that world. When Mary Astell sketched her plan for a 'religious retirement' for ladies (1694), this paradox, or what Astell herself called 'a double aspect', was already evident: '[it] shall have a double aspect, being not only a Retreat from the World for those who desire that advantage, but likewise, an institution and previous discipline, to fit us to do the greatest good in it' (Astell 1996, 18).

All of these texts – *The Patch-Work Screen for the Ladies, Millenium Hall, The Governess* and *Munster Village* – envisage forms of female community in significantly hybrid literary forms. Barker's *Patch-Work* combines short stories, autobiographical reminiscences, recipes in verse, poems, allegories and supernatural events; Scott's *Millenium Hall* combines the romance conventions of victimised women, oppressed by unsuitable, forced marriages and unwanted, rakish attentions, with the obviously utopian depiction of a community, described through the eyes of two (male) outsiders, travelling through England; Fielding's *The Governess* describes a school for girls while instructing children to improve their behaviour and to enjoy the fanciful, if often also moralistic, stories of fairytales and enchanted happenings; Hamilton's *Munster Village* combines romance plots of separated lovers, unhappy and enforced marriages with an interest in erudition and practical schemes – its many inset asides, digressions and footnotes include references to the history of silk manufacture (34–5), an account of contemporary Denmark (82–3) and extended satires on female fashions (109–13). These hybrid genres enable continuing conversations and are certainly partly why current readings find so many different kinds of complex, often competing, ideologies and messages at work within their variety.

None of these texts could be described simply as a 'novel'. In many ways they resemble the collections of female biographies which were especially popular in the seventeenth century as much as they do new kinds of eighteenth-century prose fiction. Hagiographic works on historical women continued to be published throughout the eighteenth century – the 'Table of Fame' of illustrious women in *The Female Tatler* (1709–10), George Ballard's *Memoirs of Several Ladies of Great Britain* (1752), a collection of *Biographeum Faemineum* (1766) and William Alexander's *The History of Women from the Earliest Antiquity, to the Present Time* (1779) are all important examples of the genre in the period under consideration here. The *Female Tatler's* collection of famous women was written as an explicit rebuff to the *Tatler's* 'Chamber of Fame', which had included no women, and insinuated that if, as its female readers desired, Lucretia was to be included, it might provide 'a small Tea-Table' for illustrious women, provided enough women could be found to fill it.[9] Ballard's collection was inspired by Elizabeth Elstob, once a famous Anglo-Saxon scholar, but discovered by Ballard living in obscurity and poverty. His commemoration of learned ladies included in its second volume the eighteenth-century poets Mary Lady Chudleigh, Anne Finch Countess of Winchilsea and Constantia Grierson. Inspired by these encyclopaedias of eminent women, Thomas Amory commemorated many women, unknown to history but met by him in his travels through England in his *Memoirs: Containing the Lives of Several Ladies of Great Britain* (1755) and *The Life and Opinions of John Buncle, Esquire* (1756, 1766). In these highly idiosyncratic texts, Amory recounts countless examples of virtuous women, all significantly Unitarians like himself and several of whom he claims to have married. These women are the 'choice things' of what he calls his '*Kimelia*, or literary Miscellany', made up of relations of antiquities and nature, philosophical observations, accounts of men, things and books (Amory 1755, xiii–xiv). As Amory himself acknowledges, then, while the accounts of ladies are not the most substantial part of his *Memoirs*, they are its most significant. It is impossible to know whether these ladies are historical or not, and their possibly fictive nature makes Amory's text a fantasy which is similar to the collection of women depicted in *Millenium Hall*.[10] This is especially true of the account of Mrs Harcourt's house of religious ladies which admits 24 women, extending also to 12 female boarders and a school for 12 girls. Amory recommends such a society – in which women live as recluses from the world but are free to re-enter society whenever they wish – as a plan for all women to follow. As with the Millenium Hall ladies, these women read, reflect, pray, practise music and painting, and pool financial resources to live communally together (1755, 139–433). Amory's status as observer is similar to that of Lamont in Scott's fiction in his complete recommendation of such a society: 'They are without all peradventure the happyest society on this globe, and if I were a woman, born with talents and money enough, to fit me for this claustral house, I had rather be a member of it, than reign a queen upon the greatest throne' (Amory 1755, 417).

These collections of female biography represent 'virtual' or imaginative communities. In this regard they parallel other diverse forms, such as anthologies of women's writing and poems in honour of women writers. The most significant of these were Colman and Thornton's collection of *Poems by Eminent Ladies* (1755), John Duncombe's poem in praise of women writers, *The Feminiad: A Poem* (1754), and Mary Scott's reply to Duncombe, *The Female Advocate; a Poem, Occasioned by Reading Mr Duncombe's Feminead* (1774). While anthologies of poetry for female readers were increasingly common, relatively few matched audience and author by gender. Colman and Thornton's was certainly the most significant of these.[11] Colman and Thornton's preface, like Carter's letter on *The Nine Living Muses*, recognises the significance of their being grouped: 'there can be no doubt of their appearing to advantage together, when they have each severally been approved by the greatest writers of their times' (1757b, I iii). Duncombe and Scott's poems also commemorate women poets, although Scott's poem is written to challenge Duncombe's selection as too narrow. Where Duncombe's list begins after the Restoration, Scott's begins in the Renaissance; Duncombe's selection praises only 15 women poets, Scott's honours 50 women writers. Both poems draw upon the eighteenth-century predilection for biography, and especially grouped biographies which concentrate on a single theme (here, the theme of eminent women).[12]

The fictional communities of Sarah Scott, Sarah Fielding, Mary Hamilton, Jane Barker and Thomas Amory are 'private', in the sense of being retreats and rural idylls, far removed from the circles of court, parliament and fashionable urban life. They embody the neo-classical ideal of rural retirement from the corruption of the city, modern counterparts to the *beatus vir* of Horace and Virgil. In their quiet retirement, they resemble a number of actual female communities of the eighteenth century, such as Astell's school for girls in Chelsea (established in 1709), Sarah Scott's attempts to found a Millenium Hall community at Hitcham, Berkshire (1768), Elizabeth Inchbald's stay at a house for single and separated women, and Mrs Cholmley's charitable community for old and married servants who are obliged to retire.[13] However, in being published, the texts (and the associated genres of collected female biographies and anthologies) represent communities of women in the public sphere – the public sphere of print. The remainder of this chapter will consider the ways in which print culture might be said to represent a form of public sphere for women writers.

### Women's involvement in the creation of the 'public sphere'

Thus far, this chapter has concentrated on images of predominantly or even exclusively female company. The most significant response to Habermas's apparent exclusion of women from the public sphere, however, is the reminder that the 'masculine' public sphere was always feminised and indeed came to be constituted through female participation. The polite codes of the coffee house and the periodical, for example, were based upon a way of behaving which would not give offence to the most polite and refined – women. A significant body of writing in the eighteenth century emphasised the civilising influence women exercised upon men: from Judith Drake, the anonymous writer of the *Essay in Defence of the Female Sex* (1696), to the Scottish philosopher David Hume, from Jonathan Swift to Hester Chapone and Mary Wollstonecraft.[14] For all of these writers, the company of both sexes is necessary to challenge the social stereotypes which confined intellectual debate to male gatherings and condemned exclusively female gatherings, such as the tea-table, to trivial topics. Elizabeth Montagu casually referred to this theory in reflecting upon society:

> To speak sincerely, I think no society completely agreable if entirely male or female. The masculinisms of men, and the feminalistics of the women, if the first prevail they make conversation too rough, and austere, if the latter, too soft and weak. (Montagu 1923, II 358)

These arguments rely, however, upon a sharply demarcated distinction between masculinity and femininity. Paradoxically, then, advocates of segregated and of mixed company relied upon the same kinds of thinking. That men are brutish and coarse or pedantic and overly intellectual without female company is used to support the mixing of the sexes. But, in other arguments, it urges the necessity of gender separation.

*The Guardian* clearly envisages separate spheres for its male and female readers when it suggests it might design a separate posting box for those female correspondents too timid to post their letters at the lion's head:

> There is a Notion generally received in the World, that a Lion is a dangerous Creature to all Women who are not Virgins, which may have given occasion to a foolish Report, that my Lion's Jaws are so contrived, as to snap the Hands of any of the Female Sex, who are not thus qualified to approach it with Safety. I shall not spend much time in exposing the falsity of this Report, which I believe will not weigh any thing with Women of Sense, I shall only say, that there is not one of the Sex in all the Neighbourhood of *Covent Garden*, who may not put her Hand in the Mouth with the same Security as if she were a Vestal. However that the Ladies may not be deterred from corresponding with me by this Method, I must acquaint them, that the Coffee-Man has a little Daughter of about four Years old, who has been virtuously educated, and will lend her Hand, upon this Occasion, to any Lady that shall desire it of her.
>
> In the mean time I must further acquaint my fair Readers, that I have Thoughts of making a Provision for them at my Ingenious Friend Mr *Motteux's*, or at *Corticelli's*, or some other Place frequented by the Wits and Beauties of the Sex. As I have here a Lion's Head for the Men, I shall there erect an Unicorn's Head for the Ladies, and will so contrive it that they may put in their Intelligence at the top of the Horn, which shall convey it into a little Receptacle at the bottom prepared for that purpose. Out of these two Magazines I shall supply the Town from time to time with what may tend to their Edification, and at the same Time carry on an epistolary Correspondence between the two Heads, not a little Beneficial both to the Public, and to my self. (Stephens 1982, 388).[15]

The coffee-man's four-year-old daughter – 'virtuously educated' – may well allude to the more commonplace idea of the 'service' which coffee-house girls perform. This essay is also coloured by the gallantry it adopts so consciously as a mode of communicating with its female readers: that women need instructions in how to deliver a letter through the lion's head without getting their fingers caught seems to represent as much a rhetorical gesture on the essayist's part as it does any real timidity by *The Guardian*'s female readers. But we also see the creation of a distinction between male and female writing and reading which parallels the increasingly overt separation between the sexes in the context of the coffee house. In the reading rooms of Theophilus Shrimpton at Bath, separate areas for men and women were set apart (Raven 1996, 182), a physical arrangement which mirrors the increasing prescriptions as to 'proper' feminine reading. Hortensius in Reeve's *The Progress of Romance* (1785), for example, can recommend Richardson and Addison as writers fit for women readers, but *Tristram Shandy*, with its bawdy playfulness, 'is not a woman's book' (Kelly 1999, VI 235).

The separation of the sexes in terms of physical spaces, then, has its potential corollary in literary terms. One aspect of this is that women writers found their work increasingly defined by their gender. For the late seventeenth- and early eighteenth-century female authors and publishers of Paula McDowell's study (1998), for example, their gender is inconsequential. Within the career of Delarivier Manley, however, we see a shift towards increasing gender-consciousness: 'In her writings from 1705 to 1715, Manley's allegiances and identities had been multiple: royalist daughter, Tory supporter, ruined woman, party writer. After 1714, she suggested, her new allegiance in her writing must be to her gender: to her femaleness and to "feminine" writing . . .' (McDowell 1998, 283). Susan Wiseman discusses how Catharine Macaulay's reputation switched from being the author of a republican history of the seventeenth century (*History of England*, 1763–83) to being the author of the more properly 'feminine' subject of education (*Letters on Education*, 1790). What is lost, is not just the situation of the woman writer in the context of political historiography, but also in the context of a tradition in which gender is not an issue and 'certainly not the very foundation on which women can claim entry to the political sphere' (Wiseman 2001, 195).

The issues here are complex because much of the evidence is conflicting or contradictory. Some male writers apparently published poetry under pseudonymous female names in the later eighteenth century (to escape 'ungallant' reviewers), but Frances Burney was still afraid of revealing herself as the author of *Evelina* (1778) to her family and the wider public, for example. The eighteenth century certainly witnessed a hugely significant proliferation of women writers publishing their own work and under their own names. And many have argued that literature itself was increasingly feminised as the novel rose in cultural prestige and modes of sensibility dominated literary genres. Indeed, when Habermas discusses women's participation in the public sphere, he distinguishes between political and literary spheres:

> Women and dependents were factually and legally excluded from the political public sphere, whereas female readers as well as the prentices and servants often took a more active part in the literary public sphere than the owners of private property and family heads themselves. (Habermas 1989, 56)

Habermas's exclusion of women from the political public sphere has been challenged by social histories of the eighteenth century which demonstrate that women's political role in society did not end with their lack of franchise.[16] Habermas, however, did argue that women were among the most significant members of the literary public sphere, as the quotation above illustrates. The conversational community which Habermas depicts – created through print above all – was open to both genders, and women's participation, as writers, publishers, reviewers and readers, bequeathed to them a cultural authority which they lacked in other aspects of eighteenth-century life.

In the following section I consider the career of Lady Mary Wortley Montagu as an illustrative example of the tensions and paradoxes which eighteenth-century club culture caused for the woman writer.

### 'Almost a Scriblerian': the case of Lady Mary Wortley Montagu

This section focuses on the relationship between Lady Mary Wortley Montagu and the Scriblerians as a figure for the relations between the woman writer and male literary club culture. While the Scriblerians were supportive of many women writers on an individual level, their one literary portrait of a woman writer is that of Phoebe Clinket in *Three Hours After Marriage* (1717), that mediocre writer of absurdly hyperbolic plays and poems. Whatever their individual support for women writers then, it was this portrait which would be the more influential. The bluestocking Catherine Talbot, for example, later wrote of her fear that she'd be thought a 'Phoebe Clinket': she 'is a Character admirably drawn', she wrote 'and I live with the dread of her before my Eyes' (Kelly 1999, III 6 & 16n). But Wortley Montagu, it would seem, was a woman writer obviously aware of the power which male club culture wielded. She certainly had an early lesson in that culture. A popular story concerning Wortley Montagu is recorded in her grand-daughter's biography, and commemorated in two later paintings: Andrew Garrick Gow, *The Duke of Kingston introducing his Daughter, Lady Mary Wortley Montagu as Toast to the Members of the Kit-Cat Club* (1873) and Aubrey Hammond, *Lady Mary Montague toasted by Members of the Kit-Cat Club* (1925).[17] This is the story of how, when she was only seven, Wortley Montagu had the unprecedented experience of attending a meeting of the Kit-Cats, the famous Whig club. At this meeting her father suggested that his daughter be included among the female toasts of that year, and the Kit-Cats demanded that they must first see this beauty. Thus, in very compromised terms, Wortley Montagu became the only woman ever to attend a meeting of the Kit-Cats. This was a 'trifling incident, which Lady Mary loved to recall', her grand-daughter wrote: 'Pleasure, she said, was too poor a word to express her sensations; they amounted to ecstasy; never again, throughout her whole future life, did she pass so happy a day' (Wortley Montagu 1977, 9).

In this section, I want to interrogate the sexual politics of the literary coterie through the figure of Lady Mary Wortley Montagu, because, while she was certainly never a member of the Scriblerian group, she was, in Valerie Rumbold's suggestive phrase, 'almost a Scriblerian' (1989, 134). She became a close friend of Pope, Gay and Arbuthnot, at the very moment in which these three were the only Scriblerians to remain in London.[18] She also recognised and wrote about the Scriblerians as a group, particularly in later satires at their expense. Indeed, so ready was she to perceive them as a group, that she believed *Gulliver's Travels* was written by Pope, Swift and Arbuthnot.[19] But most crucially, she wrote the *Town Eclogues* in some kind of collaboration with Pope and Gay and found a number of them not only pirated by Curll with the title *Court Poems* in 1716, but introduced to the public through a teasing advertisement which suggested that the author might be Gay, or Pope, or Lady Mary Wortley Montagu. In addition to their possibly collaborative authorship, these poems are also part of Scriblerian culture at this time because they intervene in the debate between Pope and Ambrose Philips concerning the nature of pastoral poetry. While this argument was principally Pope's, it was also, necessarily, a Scriblerian argument, with the Scriblerians being drawn into the feud. As their earliest literary feud, it was also an importantly crystallising one for the Scriblerians. This context, then, situates the *Town Eclogues* as a Scriblerian work and their author, Lady Mary Wortley Montagu, as 'almost a Scriblerian'.

Philips and his supporters argued for a modern aesthetic for pastoral poetry. The *Town Eclogues* literalise this theory for comic effect. The Virgilian conventions of singing-contests and love-laments are bathetically 'updated' in the *Town Eclogues*, used for fashionable, fickle, courtly London. Contemporary life does not poetic beauty make, these poems insinuate, and as such they support the kinds of argument Pope proposes: for example, that 'pastoral is an image of what they call the Golden age. So that we are not to describe our shepherds as shepherds at this day really are, but as they may be conceiv'd then to have been; when the best of men follow'd the employment' (Pope 1961, I 25). In contrast to this manifesto, Thomas Tickell praised the pastorals of Ambrose Philips in *The Guardian* by arguing for greater realism and calling upon English authors to alter the classical models of pastoral in the interests of probability. In this mode of pastoral, English fairies would replace classical gods, hyacinths and 'Paestan' roses would be replaced by king-cups, endives and daisies, and Hobbinol, Cuddy and Colin Clout would replace Daphnis, Alexis and Thyrsis as names of shepherds. The shepherd of Tickell's pastoral should speak as English peasants do, should sing of English peasant sports and customs and, instead of an idyllic carefree existence, should be troubled by such anxieties as a thorn in the foot or a stolen lamb. The flawed characters of the *Town Eclogues*, with their vanities, narcissism and general immorality, in contrast, suggest what 'realism' might do to the pastoral genre – make it only comic.

Women's writing is part of the cultural economy of the pastoral because so much of women's writing of this time operates within pastoral modes. But it is not an unproblematic economy for the woman writer. Pastoral is the genre in which male poets learn their craft: Pope's later insistence on his being only 16 when he wrote the *Pastorals* is part of this kind of general depreciation. The adoption of

pastoral by early eighteenth-century women writers, then, is hardly
a symptom of poetic ambition – quite the contrary. When in her own
earliest writings, Wortley Montagu wrote traditional pastorals and
satires upon pastoral, she may have been both advancing her sense
of herself as a poet and distancing herself from the perceived limitations of the pastoral. When, over ten years later, Wortley Montagu
writes the 'town eclogues', she adopts a similarly equivocal position
in relation to the genre. But in situating herself within the circle of
Pope, she is also staking a claim to the particular kind of pastoral aesthetic which that circle espouses. And that aesthetic is one which is
deeply embedded in ideas of tradition and authority. In this way,
Wortley Montagu drew upon the authority and prestige which the
association with the Scriblerians seemed to offer to her.

However, for the woman writer, literary collaboration was also
problematic. When Pope transcribed the eclogues into an elegant
manuscript edition, for example, he made changes to the text, such
as an alternative ending for 'Wednesday'. In this poem, Dancinda
refuses her lover at length, fearful of abandonment, but Dancinda
is gently satirised when her husband's return shows her not to be
the coy nymph she had pretended to be. Pope's alternative ending
has Dancinda scolding her lover for permitting her to refuse him at
such length when he might have spent the moments before her
husband returned more opportunely:

> The Lady with a Look, and cries
> Ah thoughtless Youth! What moments have you mist?
> You have but listen'd when you should have kist! (ll. 90–2)

Wortley Montagu's Dancinda is anxious that if she yields her
lover will abandon her. Pope's Dancinda, with a twist in these three
concluding lines, reveals herself as only acting the coy nymph, now
angry that his patience and her performative verbosity have wasted
their snatched minutes together. In a characteristic gesture, then,
three concluding lines are able to ironise the entire poem, are
able to change a poem expressing considerable sympathy for
Dancinda to one mocking her. This edition is certainly a collaboratively authored text, and, as I've argued here, should be situated
within Scriblerian debates, but it is, in Isobel Grundy's term, one of
'contested collaboration' (1999, 107). Pope's lines in the manuscript
are not entirely legible, Wortley Montagu having struck them out.

Similarly, Pope's attacks on Curll, the publisher of the pirated edition of *Court Poems*, changed from an accusation that Curll had pirated the texts to the accusation that Curll tried to pass off a lady's work for his own.[20] All the possibilities of anonymous, transvestite and masqueraded authorship were quickly vexed with questions of ownership and reputation. One thread throughout Wortley Montagu's writing career is an attempt to disguise her gender: whether writing a political periodical in the guise of the male essayist (*The Nonsense of Common-Sense*, 1737–8), ventriloquising Pope's voice in verse satire (as in the *Dunciad* satires and 'P[ope] to Bolingbroke') or in writing anonymously for *The Spectator* (the only woman ever to do so in 555 issues). Added to these modes of publishing is that of collaborative writing, and collaborative association with literary circles is one mode within which women can attain an authority they otherwise lack in that literary culture. In the contact culture of the coffee house, for example, women can be excluded. In print culture, they can negotiate, sometimes through masqueraded authorship, the very reasons for that exclusion. But while literary clubs and circles, unlike the coffee houses, could, at an informal level, include women writers, these women were never admitted without invoking their gender difference. In an age of playful authorial signature, writing is the space where identities can be negotiated, although, increasingly, the gap between published signature and gendered identity would be closed.

Writing in 1978, Pat Rogers argued that: 'those few eighteenth-century ladies who achieved some independence rarely displayed clubbable tendencies; the lone scholar is a more natural product of frustration and repression. There were collections of educated women, notably the bluestockings . . . ; but it seems reasonable to say that comparatively little female resentment was directed against the clubs and coffee houses' (47). Rogers's argument, written before the considerable current interest in eighteenth-century women's writing, is still, I think, premature: for there is much more work to be done on the relationship between women and literary club culture. When, in one of the town eclogues, two rakes engage in a Virgilian singing-contest, they boast of their sexual conquests. Silliander attempts to trump his adversary at one point by claiming: 'Yet I could tell – but that I hate to boast – / A *Club of Ladies*, where 'tis me they toast' (ll. 28–9; my emphasis). If we add this allusion to other aspects of Wortley Montagu's life – her extraordinary introduction to a Kit-

Cat meeting when she was only seven, for example, or her reference to the Turkish bagnio as the 'ladies coffee-house' or her later insistence to her daughter that she wished she might have been an Abbess of a Protestant nunnery[21] – we see a woman at least conscious of her sex's exclusion from contemporary club culture.

There was never any question of Lady Mary Wortley Montagu being a member of the Scriblerus Club – her gender was even more of a bar than her political (Whig) tendencies. How could she think about her exclusion from male club culture without invoking the very gender she so frequently attempted to leave behind in her writing? Critics of Habermas's theory of the public sphere have long argued that its ideal universalism serves only to mask exclusions of class, race, gender. Literary clubs and circles – unlike the coffee houses – could, at an informal level, include women writers. But women writers were never admitted without invoking their gender difference. In theoretical terms, these kinds of issues have been recently considered by Joan Scott, in an essay with pertinent parallels to the concerns of my argument here. Scott is addressing what she calls the 'impossible choice' for feminists between equality and difference:

> But when women (among others) were denied citizenship on the grounds of their difference, how could they demand change as human individuals without invoking the difference that excluded them? . . . How could discrimination, which ascribed group characteristics to individuals on the basis of their sex, be fought without raising the question of sexual difference? How could the question of sexual difference be raised without reproducing the terms on which exclusion was based in the first place? (Scott 1997, 17)

Joan Scott's essay addresses questions of positive discrimination in contemporary political nominations, but it also maps onto our current ways of thinking about eighteenth-century literary culture, and specifically how to figure women within that culture. In 1718 Curll published yet another volume of poems which included *Court Poems II* – not by Lady Mary Wortley Montagu, but by now associated with her. This volume was entitled *The Ladies Miscellany*. Poems forged in the excitement of collaboration and association with the most notorious authors of their day – the Scriblerians – were already becoming part of a female tradition, towards which their author felt such ambivalence.[22]

## The public emergence of the woman writer

This chapter, while seeming to refer only to a particular aspect of eighteenth-century print culture (the participation of women writers within that culture), is also an important intervention in the concerns of the book as a whole. The first chapters of this book revolve around the ideal and the failure of community, and both these aspects are particularly visible in the case of women writers. There is no absolute conclusion to be drawn here. Women were excluded from almost all forms of formal clubs and societies in eighteenth-century Britain and America, including the societies of the coffee house and the tavern. However, many women did feel included within informal literary societies and did participate in the community of letters. It is worth recalling that, although Smollett's Lydia is not allowed to visit the ladies' coffee shop in Bath, she does add that she is permitted to visit the booksellers shops:

> where we read novels, plays, pamphlets, and news-papers, for so small a subscription as a crown a quarter; and in these offices of intelligence (as my brother calls them) all the reports of the day, and all the private transactions of the Bath, are first entered and discussed. (Smollett 1984, 40–1)

Such an argument is of course complicated by the continuing pressures of being a woman author, and the compromised terms under which female entry to the republic of letters was often held. An example of this complexity is the unusual trait of male authors publishing poetry under female pseudonyms in the 1770s and 1780s. Contradicting our commonplace associations of female authorship in the past, usually drawn from the dominant examples of George Eliot and the Brontës, all of whom published under masculine pseudonyms, this fact may ultimately, however, reinscribe the motif of the disadvantaged woman writer. These gentlemen published under female pseudonyms probably so as to resist critical reviews and to court the gallant, decorous, but condescending response of the male reviewer to the female writer. Goldsmith assumed this kind of condescension when he aligned women's writing with the Grub Street of the later eighteenth century: 'Yet, let not the ladies carry off all the glories of the late production ascribed to them; it is plain by the style, and a nameless somewhat in the manner, that pretty fellows, coffee-critics, and dirty-shirted dunces have sometimes a share in the achievement. We have detected so many of these imposters already that in future we shall look on every publication that shall be ascribed to a lady as the work of one of this amphibious fraternity' (*Critical Review*, August 1759).[23]

In the eighteenth century, we see examples of women writers recognised and honoured by society: Charlotte Lennox presented with an apple pie decorated with bay leaves and a crown of laurel by Dr Johnson and his club of 'Ivy Lane' gentlemen or Frances Burney publicly saluted by the King at Drury Lane Theatre when the epilogue to Holcroft's *Seduction* (1787) praised the female critic of Shakespeare (Elizabeth Montagu) and the author of *Cecilia* (Burney). Whether praised or condemned, the woman writer was a figure of immense interest in the eighteenth century. She might be aligned with the best of moral values and seen as integral to the formation of a polite public sphere (as the bluestockings were often regarded) or she might be associated with the mediocrity of hack, inferior writing (as Haywood certainly was). Perhaps her voice was needed to refine the republic of letters or perhaps rather she would always be an adjunct to the main centres of literary activity, only the toast of the literary club, rarely its member, or requiring the intercession of a brother or husband to ensure publication. But whatever the response, she was always regarded as a woman writer. It is therefore not an exaggeration to say, despite the innumerable examples of earlier woman writers, that the eighteenth century witnessed the emergence of the woman writer into the public sphere of letters. Publicity and gender were thus always intertwined. It was (only) as a *woman* writer that she emerged as a public literary figure. And that was both her triumph and her handicap.

## Notes

1. Vesey's soirées were held at her home in Bolton Row, Elizabeth Montagu's at Hillstreet.
2. For an overview of feminist responses to Habermas see Fraser 1992 and Landes 1998. Habermas himself in 'Further Reflections' was to concede: 'Unlike the exclusion of underprivileged men, the exclusion of women had structuring significance' (1992, 428).

3. See Avery 1956.
4. 'Cou'd we a Parliament of Women call, / We'd vote such Statutes as shou'd Tame you all' (Johnson 1712, epilogue); Mrs Modern: 'what empty politicians men are found, when they oppose their weak heads to ours! On my conscience a parliament of women would be of very great service to the nation' (Fielding 1882, II 129).
5. See Wahl 1999, 117–29.
6. Jane Collier defended Fielding's coyness regarding Mrs Teachum's punishment in a letter to Richardson as pleasing all readers who have decided views on such points. Richardson, it would seem from this letter, wanted Fielding to be more specific on this point (Richardson 1804, II 61–4).
7. For a more sympathetic reading of Mrs Teachum see Suzuki 1994, 328. Suzuki also stresses the sociable and communal models which the book proposes (328–32) and notes how Sherwood's 1820 rewriting of the novel omits the original's attention to sociability and gentility (332).
8. For a discussion of the representation of a 'community' of female artists who exercise symbolic and real cultural power, see Elizabeth Eger's 2001 essay on the painting of the 'nine living muses'.
9. See Aitkin 1970, II 247 (*The Tatler* 84; 22 Oct. 1709). For *The Female Tatler*'s Table of Fame of illustrious women, see Nos 68, 86, 88, 88*, 90, 92, 96 as numbered in the modern Thoemmes Press edition (Goldsmith 1999).
10. Amory consciously compares his work on these ladies with the more renowned examples of Ballard's collection. For example, of Mrs Marinda Benlow Amory writes: 'She is at this day a philosopher in pettycoats. There is nothing superior to her in *George Ballard's* Collection' (1755, 11).
11. Other miscellanies of exclusively female writers include Delarivier Manley's compilation of elegies on the death of the poet Dryden, *The Nine Muses* (1700), with poems by Sarah Fyge Egerton, Mary Pix, Catherine Trotter and Susanna Centlivre; *The Virgin Muse*, published by J. Greenwood (1717; reissued in 1722 and 1731) and Edmund Curll's *Ladies Miscellany* (1718) which included, for example, pirated copies of Lady Mary Wortley Montagu's *Town Eclogues*.
12. Horace Walpole in *A Catalogue of the Royal and Noble Authors of England* (1758) claims his grouping is no stranger than the odd volumes collecting specimens of mortals who have demonstrated a love of statues, died laughing, studied at Oxford, or proved illustrious bastards. See Stauffer 1941, I 501–8.
13. For Scott's scheme, see Rizzo 1994, 318–9 and Bree 2000. For Inchbald, see Hill 1987, 124. I do not include here societies of only two

women, such as Sarah Scott and Lady Barbara Montagu's living together or the famous 'Ladies of Llangollen' who lived together for 50 years (1779–1829).

14. See Hume, 'Of Essay Writing' and 'Of the Rise and Progress of Arts and Sciences' (1742); Swift, 'Hints towards An Essay on Conversation' (1957, 85–95); Chapone, 'On Politeness and Accomplishments' (1773; Kelly 1999, III 326–37). Wollstonecraft disapproved of girls' boarding schools and standing armies alike.

15. The ladies' post-box was never erected, though spoken of again in *The Guardian* Nos 120 and 123. *Corticelli's* and *Motteux's* were both fashionable shops.

16. See Colley 1992 and Foreman 1998 for accounts of women's participation in political campaigns and issues. Other feminist work argues that we should extend our definitions of 'politics' to include issues of gender and of family life. See, for example, Armstrong 1987 and Backscheider 2000.

17. See Pointon 1993, 144 for reproductions of these paintings.

18. Her friendship with Pope began in early 1715 and by the summer only Pope, Gay and Arbuthnot remained in London: Parnell had followed Swift to Ireland; Oxford was in the Tower accused of high treason; and in March Bolingbroke, not a member of the Club, but friend to most of its members, had fled to France. Wortley Montagu's literary friendships are thus centred in what remains of the original Scriblerian club and they overlap with continuing Scriblerian projects. (The 'Double-Mistress' episode of *The Memoirs* is substantially written in early 1716, for example; *Three Hours After Marriage* is written during 1716 and first performed in January 1717.)

19. For Wortley Montagu on *Gulliver's Travels*, see Grundy 1999, 272. Wortley Montagu's later satires against her former friends demonstrate that she recognised them as a grouping: the dunces of 'Her Palace placed beneath a muddy road' are Swift, Gay, Arbuthnot, and Pope, in a verse pamphlet which mimics and inverts the *Dunciad*; and in her attack on satirical writers in *The Nonsense of Common-Sense*, IX (1738) she juxtaposes allusions to Pope, Swift and Gay as a 'Club'. (See Wortley Montagu 1977, 148.)

20. See *Dunciad* (1729) II, 54 n: Curll 'meant to publish [this volume] as the work of the true writer, a Lady of quality; but being first threaten'd, and afterwards punish'd, for it by Mr *Pope*, he generously transferr'd it from *her* to *him*, and has now printed it twelve years in his name.' See *The Curliad*, for Curll's jibe that Pope had accused him falsely here, since this is not an exact account of the *Court Poems* episode.

21. Wortley Montagu 1965–7, III 97 (To Lady Bute, 20 Oct. 1755). Recalled in a letter to her daughter in reflecting on *Sir Charles Grandison*, and

selecting only that hero's project of an English Monastery for ladies for compliment.

22. See Dykstal's summarisation of this issue, especially as articulated by Monique Wittig: 'The discursive model of the public sphere has a revisionary power that comes precisely from this principle of universality. In our own day, the feminist theorist and novelist Monique Wittig reveals this power when she declares that, "in spite of the harsh law of gender and its enforcement upon women, no woman can say I" or start to speak at all, "without being for herself a total subject, that is, ungendered, universal, whole". According to Wittig, for a woman to identify herself in public by gender alone is critically disabling, because it reinforces rather than revises the categories that have been used to oppress her' (Dykstal 1996, 34).

23. Goldsmith's comment is quoted in Adburgham 1972, 114–15. Donoghue argues that this condescension was relatively short-lived and that, by the late 1780s and 1790s prominent women, such as Mary Wollstonecraft, distinguished themselves as reviewers and that reviewing in general attempted to treat men and women authors on more equal terms (Donoghue 1996, 161).

# Part II

## Textual Conversations

# Textual Conversations: Introduction

> the community celebrated in *Tristram Shandy* is not that of the
> Shandy brothers, but rather the ingathering of authors and books,
> documents and artifacts, indeed the commentary that surrounds
> Sterne's own work, commentary he richly anticipates even as he
> mocks it.
>
> (New 1998, 8)

The textual conversations referred to in the title of this section are
examples of print responses which circled around key publications
in the eighteenth century. All three texts discussed in this section –
*The Dunciad, Gulliver's Travels* and *Pamela* – became centres of
print activity as their readings manifested themselves in further
print sequels, imitations, counter-fictions, or parodic challenges.
There are countless examples of these in the eighteenth century,
although we tend only to remember the canonical 'original' texts
which inspired the cluster of imitations and parodies. By 1760 over
40 sequels to *Robinson Crusoe* (1719) had been published. Defoe
had himself extended his book to a trilogy: *The Life and Strange
Surprizing Adventures of Robinson Crusoe of York, Mariner . . .
Written by Himself* (1719); *The Farther Adventures of Robinson
Crusoe* (1719; in which Crusoe revisits his island colony and travels
elsewhere, for example, to China, before returning to England
across Siberia and Russia); and *Serious Reflections During the Life
and Surprising Adventures of Robinson Crusoe: With His Vision of
the Angelick World* (1720; in which, in a series of moral essays,
Defoe represented the original book as an allegory of his own life).
Charles Gildon's famous critique of *Crusoe* came in the form of an
imitative parody: *The Life and Strange Surprizing Adventures of Mr
D. . . . De F . . . of London, Hosier* (1719). *Tristram Shandy* also generated a phenomenal number of imitations, burlesques, counter-
fictions and moral rejoinders. Over 20 appeared within the first
year of its first publication and included comic pieces such as *The
Clockmakers Outcry against the Author of the Life and Opinions of*

*Tristram Shandy* and *The Life and Opinions of Miss Suky Shandy of Bow-Street.*[1]

These kinds of challenges and replies are common in the history of religious and political pamphlets, with their intrinsic tendency towards provocation, polemics and debate. However, within what we now more narrowly refer to as 'literature' (fiction, poetry, drama), sequels, parodies, burlesques, keys and counter-texts also proliferated. These print conversations make these texts events, not solely books. In addition to the textual responses discussed here, there are the wide number of objects sold in the wake of the books' success. After the publication of *Gulliver's Travels*, for example, many bought fans illustrated with scenes from the books, Lilliputian wallpaper borders and tiny, boxed sets of Lilliputian books. After the phenomenal success of Gay's *The Beggar's Opera*, a whole range of memorabilia associated with the work was sold: playing cards, fans, snuff-boxes, firescreens and toys with scenes from the opera. When Pope wrote of the opera's success among the notes to *The Dunciad Variorum*, he referred, not only to its successful run of performances, but also to this extraliterary life:

> The vast success of it was unprecedented, and almost incredible . . . the ladies carried about with them the favourite songs of it in fans; and houses were furnished with it in screens. The person who acted *Polly*, till then obscure, became all at once the favourite of the town; her pictures were engraved, and sold in great numbers; her life written, books of letters and verses to her, published; and pamphlets made even of her sayings and jests. (Pope 1999, 262)

All of these texts then – *The Dunciad*, *Gulliver's Travels*, and *Pamela* – are also events in the cultural history of the eighteenth century.[2] Each one is a centrifugal force for a surrounding nexus of various kinds of texts. There are many possible similarities between these texts, not least in their reception and the ways in which they generated intense print responses. These in turn generate questions of low and high culture, questions of reading and the determining or freeing of interpretation, and the way in which this print culture encouraged textual self-reflexivity. Although an especially acute example, the pamphlet wars surrounding Pope's work, and *The Dunciad* in particular, can also be seen as representative of the wider print culture. *The Dunciad* takes as its theme the threatening (but exciting) proliferation of print and it also embodies that proliferation in its own, multiple, editions and apparatuses and in the countless replies of attack and defence. The emphasis in this chapter upon the culture wars of the early eighteenth century reverberate throughout the century, and throughout the texts discussed in this section. Each of the chapters, however, takes a different focus for its discussion of the particular text: the distinction between high and low cultures (*The Dunciad*); questions of reading and interpretation (*Gulliver's Travels*); and the representation of gender and class in narrative (*Pamela*).

As we have seen throughout this book, Habermas drew upon the model of the eighteenth century as a paradigm for a public sphere in which an 'ideal speech situation' could occur, namely, that all people might use speech freely, and could seek to be understood and to persuade. In such a context, consensus and agreed-upon truths would become possible. In this model, rational communication is transparent, and meaning is both stable and fixed. But the eighteenth century was already anxious about how print culture could fail to be meaningful and how language could obfuscate rather than clarify, confuse rather than educate. Habermas's ideal of rational discourse supposes the kind of print culture which emerges in the eighteenth century, but this same print culture calls into question the very possibility of that rational discourse. The ideal of a rational public discourse presumes the ideal of transparent communication, in which meaning can be understood and shared. But, as the study of the textual conversations in this section will suggest, meaning is always contested.

## Notes

1. See Donoghue 1996, 73–8, Bandry 1998 and Ross 2001, 15–16. For the argument that *The Clockmakers Outcry* was written by Sterne himself, see Bandry and Day 1992.
2. See Warner's 1998 discussion of the 'media event' surrounding the publication of *Pamela*, a phrase which, in this context, does not appear unduly anachronistic.

# 4 *The Dunciad:* Associating with 'Republica Grubstreetaria'

> One wonders how the legend grew up that the eighteenth century
> was impersonal, objective, dispassionate. No age ever abounded
> more in self-conscious, self-dramatizing writers.
>
> (Greene 1965, 37)

> [*The Dunciad*], . . . after I am dead and gone, will be printed with a
> large Commentary, and letterd on the back, *Pope's Dulness.*
>
> (Pope 1956, II 468)

Pope's *The Dunciad* (1728–43) is a poem which is highly self-
conscious about its own positioning within a putative literary history,
and which overtly reflects upon the status of 'competing' texts and
authors. Harold Bloom famously discussed literary history in terms
of an agonistic struggle between writers and their influential predecessors (Bloom 1973). Eighteenth-century culture, however, reveals a
struggle amongst living contemporaries. This makes debates about
literary value both more self-conscious and more vicious.

Traditionally, literary history is figured retrospectively, a 'canonical' author being one who is remembered and constantly reread.
More recent approaches to literature, especially those influenced
by cultural studies, have emphasised the embeddedness of texts
within their own culture – culture here defined in its widest sense,
so as to permit the recovery of popular and marginalised voices.
*The Dunciad* can be very easily read in either of these ways. Not
only does it continue to be read as a major work by the most canonical poet of the eighteenth century, its value celebrated by successive generations of critics, but it also gestures towards its readers of
succeeding generations and centuries. Yet it is also thoroughly
embedded in its own time and, in its attacks upon contemporary
writers, is necessarily dependent on the kind of 'popular' culture

which it ostensibly denigrates. The poem continually dramatises, ventriloquises and anticipates its own critics – particularly through the mock-scholarly notes which were added to the later 'variorum' editions. The poem's necessary association is with a corrupt, debased form of the republic of letters: the 'Republica Grubstreetaria' (Swift 1963–5, I 133). Remembering the attacks of Grub Street is crucial in thinking about *The Dunciad*, then, not only because they explain much of the poem's genesis, contemporary reception and motivation, but because they explain the tones and paradoxes of the poem: how it might be seen to be both a justified and an excessive reply to Pope's enemies, how its attitude towards the culture of the dunces is one of both derision and exuberance.

Over 150 attacks on Pope were published during his lifetime (see Guerinot 1969). Some of these were genuine critical responses to his writings but by far the greatest number were merely personally vitriolic. Pope's Catholicism, his relatively modest background and lack of a gentleman's education, his physical deformity and sexual frustration, his financial success as a writer, even his devotion to his mother – all of these were targets of attack. Pope found himself repeatedly abused, compared to a wasp (*Verses Address'd to the Imitator of . . . Horace*, 1733), to Satan (*The Blatant-Beast*, 1742), to a mad dog (*The Metamorphosis*, 1728), to Aesop's toad bursting with spleen (*Codrus*, 1728), and to a monkey (*Mr Taste, The Poetical Fop*, 1732). The literary or aesthetic value of these attacks is certainly negligible, as even one opponent, Leonard Welsted, was forced to admit:

> I cannot indeed say much in Praise of some Performances which appear'd against him, and am sorry that Voluntiers enter'd into the War, whom I could wish to have been only Spectators: But the Cause became so general, that some Gentlemen, who never aim'd at the Laurel, grew Poets merely upon their being angry. (Guerinot 1969, 191)

Welsted here recognises that important questions of literary authority are raised in the responses to *The Dunciad*. If poetic authority could be gained merely by entering into fractious exchanges of personal abuse, this would suggest a literary culture that is both an open forum and a contentious, often abusive, battleground.

Pope became a classic in his own age. This is immediately striking in the respectful portraits of Pope: in a portrait, attributed to Jonathan Richardson, in which Pope is presented as the timeless modern equivalent of the antique poet or philosopher, his head garlanded with laurel, in the profile format of medals and cameos; or in Roubiliac's sculpture in which the bust of Pope appears as that of a Roman stoic. It is also evident in Pope's literary career, one which he consciously modelled on that of the revered classical Roman writer, Virgil. Virgil's development as a poet through the writing of 'Eclogues', 'Georgics' and the epic *Aeneid* is directly paralleled in Pope's publication of *Pastorals* (1709), his georgic 'Windsor Forest' (1713) and *The Dunciad* (1728–43). The urbane and elegant classicism of Horace was also an obvious influence upon Pope, not only in the direct imitations of his satires and epistles but in the lightness of touch and humour with which Horace treated serious issues.[1] This classical culture is also an aristocratic one in tenor, if not always in personnel. (As an increasingly affluent, but disenfranchised, landless Roman Catholic, Pope's class status cannot be easily fixed.) The figure most associated with this culture in recent accounts has been Anthony Ashley Cooper, Earl of Shaftesbury, because of his ready identification with 'civic humanism' or classical republicanism. This drew its inspiration from Livy's figure of Cincinnatus, the benevolent landowner, whose personal interests, as those of the landowning class in general, are also those of the state. In the 1640s, this republican ideal opposed the monarchy, but in the later seventeenth century it became the dominant ideology of the country party which opposed commercial interests. In the rhetoric of civic humanism, virtue resides in the ability to rise above particular concerns or personal interests, the public good and individual interest are seen as inimical, and only the landowner can rise above the factionalism involved in commerce. In terms of the debates of the seventeenth and eighteenth centuries, then, it was obvious that the public sphere yielded fractious debate rather than harmonious consensus, even if some believed that these could be transcended. These political debates had their aesthetic corollaries: true art and beauty would exhort men to be virtuous, thus art should properly be idealising, rather than 'realistic'. Shaftesbury's preference, then, was for the generalising language of the classical tradition.[2]

A classical view of art is also to see art as a repository of timeless values. The work of art must transcend its own moment, must aspire towards permanence. Bolingbroke made a patriotic appeal to Pope to write 'what will deserve to be translated three Thousand years hence into Languages as yet perhaps unform'd . . . Whilst you translate [Homer] therefore you neglect to propagate the English Tongue' (1724). When Swift advised Pope that *The Dunciad* of 1728, with its veiled references to the dunces, should be reprinted with an index, he was attempting to ensure its intelligibility, not just to readers outside of London, but also to future readers: 'I have long observ'd that twenty miles from London no body understands hints, initial letters, or town-facts and passages; and in a few years not even those who live in London' (Pope 1956, II 504–5). At his suggestion, Pope had footnotes added to *The Dunciad Variorum* (1729) and because these often quoted copiously from the pamphlet wars surrounding Pope, attacks were increasingly folded within the text of *The Dunciad*. One of the most overt, and quickly registered, examples of *The Dunciad*'s capacious enfolding of its own enemies is the appendix, included in the 1729 edition, of 'A List of Books, Papers, and Verses: In which our Author was abused, before the Publication of the DUNCIAD; with the true Names of the Authors'. Many of these, the editor implies, were given renewed life by their publishers after the initial publication of *The Dunciad*, as the works of named 'dunces' are advertised under the very modern adage that 'no publicity is bad publicity': 'The Confederates, a farce. By Capt. Breval (for which he was put into the Dunciad.) An Epilogue to Powel's Puppet-Show. By Col. Ducket (for which he is put into the Dunciad.) Essays, etc. By Sir Richard Blackmore. (N.B. It was for a passage of this book that Sir Richard was put into the Dunciad.).' This indicates the momentum which *The Dunciad* generated in the proliferating print market it so disdained.

One of the many paradoxes of *The Dunciad*, then, is that, by commemorating his enemies within the text and apparatus of *The Dunciad*, Pope ensured that they would be remembered as well as he. In an extraordinarily overt manner, *The Dunciad* demonstrates the poststructuralist argument that the permanent, epic repository of value carries with it, and is defined through its opposition to, the very impermanent trash which is its conceptual opposite. While the interdependency of 'high' and 'low' cultures, or the satirist's reliance upon his target, are commonplace assumptions of contemporary literary theory, these dynamics were also being recognised from the very first. Cibber, for example, in *A Letter from Mr Cibber to Mr Pope* (1742), mocked the irony of how the *Dunciad* commemorates that which it thinks is beneath remembering:

> what have you gain'd by it? A mighty Matter! A Victory over a parcel of poor Wretches . . . Could you have let them alone, by this time, poor Souls, they had been all peaceably buried in Oblivion! But the very Lines, you have so sharply pointed to destroy them, will now remain but so many of their Epitaphs, to transmit their Names to Posterity: Which probably too they may think a more eligible Fate than that of being totally forgotten. (Cibber 1973, 11–12)

Who now might choose to study Theobald's poem *The Cave of Poetry* (1714), had Pope not mockingly alluded to it in his reference to Cibber's garret, that 'Cave of Poverty and Poetry' (I 34)?[3] Pope himself, in the *Epistle to Dr Arbuthnot* (1735), had also famously articulated this paradox: 'Pretty! In amber to observe the forms / Of hairs, or straws, or dirt, or grubs, or worms!' (ll. 169–70). Pope's own knowledge of these paradoxes is evident in the pervasive irony throughout the work. As John Sitter has argued, 'a poem recording the notorious "fame" of characters so ephemeral they need footnotes can only be written with pervasive irony' (Sitter 1971, 69).

The dunces typically have no view of literature beyond the immediacy of topical publication. Many write for a living and therefore take work where they can find it. Composing birthday odes for the monarch, writing political propaganda for whichever party will pay, rushing off 'biographies' of celebrated contemporaries by pasting together excerpts from other works, writing ephemeral prologues for plays – all of these are typical of what became known as 'Grub Street' writing. The attacks on Pope quickly became one of these ventures. The publicity which they generated was something few hacks, evidently, could resist. One pamphlet has Cibber announce to Pope: 'The more we rail, the more bespatter, / 'Twill make our *Pamphlets* sell the better' (Anon 1960, 5). The twenty-first-century book trade has little to teach the eighteenth in its business practices: elaborate puffing of books (often by 'in-house' writers), the false multiplying of 'editions' to foster sales, republishing old books under new titles or binding a new title page into unsold copies of the original edition, abridging histories and books of travel, passing off spurious poems as the work of celebrated writers – all of these were common tactics. In *An Author to be Lett* (1729) Richard Savage has his fictional hack, Iscariot Hackney, garrulously reveal the mediocrity and corruption at the heart of the Grub Street ethos:

> My Pamphlets sell many more Impressions than those of celebrated Writers; the Secret of this is, I learned from Curll to clap a new Title-Page to the Sale of every half Hundred; so that when my Bookseller has sold Two Hundred and Fifty Copies, my Book generally enters into the *Sixth Edition*. (Savage 1960, 11)

The book industry of the eighteenth century certainly illustrates the commercialisation of literature at its crudest. This is recognised by Pope throughout *The Dunciad*, as, for example, in the book-seller's race of Book II in which Curll and Lintot race after a phantom poet. The goddess Dulness fashions the poet as a lucrative prize for the rival booksellers:

> A Poet's form she plac'd before their eyes,
> And bade the nimblest racer seize the prize;
> No meagre, muse-rid mope, adust and thin,
> In a dun night-gown of his own loose skin;
> But such a bulk as no twelve bards could raise,
> Twelve starv'ling bards of these degen'rate days.
> All as a partridge plump, full-fed, and fair,
> She form'd this image of well-body'd air. (Pope 1999, 151–2)

This phantom-poet is, like the partridge, fair game for the preying booksellers. His well-fed rotundity before their eyes converts book contracts into literal meal tickets.

While many of the responses to *The Dunciad* were provoked by political and personal differences, many were simply attempts to cash in on the notoriety of the poem by publishing ostensible responses. Two examples are *The Female Dunces* (1733) and *The Female Dunciad* (1728) because their titles suggest that they will offer revisionary or parallel accounts of the world of women in Grub Street. Neither fulfil this promise, although their coming into print was probably on the basis of this connection. The title of *The Female Dunces* teases its readers with the suggestion that it might attack female pedants and hack writers (of which a few are mentioned in *The Dunciad*). But the laws of gallant concessions to women's learning and writing are as evident here as they would later be in the columns of the literary reviews. *The Female Dunces* is a catalogue of sexually improper ladies.[4] Similarly, *The Female Dunciad*, published by Curll in 1728, says nothing about women and hack writing or false taste. Instead it is a strange medley – consisting of a number of rather lewdly suggestive letters by Pope, a list of queens and consorts, an amatory narrative by Eliza Haywood and a poetic attack on Pope. *The Female Dunciad* says a lot about Curll's publishing practices. But it says little or nothing about women's relations to the culture wars depicted in *The Dunciad*.[5]

Pope's conviction that literature should transcend materialism, that the writer should be indifferent to the price of his work, caring only for its value, was an affront to the real Grub Street, the booksellers, printers and hack writers who relied upon the book industry to keep them from starving. That Pope himself made his fortune through his writings made his attacks on their commercialism all the more difficult to accept. Pope, in making considerable sums of money from his translations of the *Iliad* and *Odyssey*, can fairly be claimed as the first professional writer in English. Dr Johnson calculated that the receipts for the *Iliad* amounted to £5320. The *Odyssey*, which capitalised on the *Iliad*'s success, brought Pope almost £5000. (In 1998, Wall calculated that these sums would convert to around $1.5 million; 21.) Pope himself acknowledged: 'But (thanks to Homer) since I live and thrive, / Indebted to no prince or peer alive' (*The Second Epistle of the Second Book of Horace Imitated*, 1737, ll.68–9). The particular way in which these books were published – through subscription – mystified the relations between writing and the market in comparison to the more obvious relations between writer and patron or writer and commercial publisher. But this did not save Pope from attacks on his 'greed', and, when he inveighed against the mercantilism of the book trade, on his hypocrisy. Much of this abuse was undoubtedly motivated by envy, but Pope's sensitivities to these attacks did not help. Unhappy with the taint which making a profit through writing seemed to imply, Pope only attacked Grub Street all the more concertedly. For Pope, commercialism and corrupt taste were subverting civilised values. Art ought to be above the market. Thus Pope fashioned the image of Gay as the destitute writer, who, though unappreciated by his contemporaries, would be recognised by posterity. The facts were rather different. When John Gay died, he left an estate worth more than £6000 and was buried with state in Westminster Abbey. In the *Epistle to Arbuthnot*, however, Pope depicted Gay as perishing in poverty, a 'neglected genius' (l. 255), unsupported by benefactors or patrons (even though the Duke and Duchess of Queensbury had supported Gay for years). When he wrote of his own literary career, Pope denied all evidence of the process by which he secured financial independence.[6] For Pope, the writer was either the genius above the market, or the mercenary hack who churned out writing by order, mechanically. The poet-genius was independent of patronage or financial bribery: the poetaster prostituted his or her talent (or lack of talent). When Savage cashed in on the *Dunciad* controversy with his own defence of Pope, *An Author to be Lett* (1729), he began by stating: 'Be assured, a Scavenger of Wit is a more gainful Occupation than that of a delicate, moral Writer' (Savage 1960, 1). Such 'scavengers' did not hide the cash nexus in which they worked. At Moorfields and along the railings of Bedlam, poetasters hung up poems or broadsheets like washing. As Pat Rogers has noted in his account of the real Grub Street: 'Cheap literature was a commodity which had to be flaunted before the buyer's eyes like so much greengrocery' (Rogers 1972, 50).

That writing was becoming dangerously mechanical is satirised in Pope's 'Receit to make an Epick Poem' (*The Guardian*, 10 June 1713). Here instructions on how to write an epic are as programmatic as a recipe for pudding, so that 'even' sonneteers and ladies might compose. Thus, while an epic poem can be easily written by a man who has genius, Pope encourages his readers by adding 'the Skill lies in doing it without' genius (Stephens 1982, 287). Learning can be gleaned from indexes and a bit of ancient idiom from an imitation of Milton. In addition, a few words of old English, cribbed from any edition of Chaucer, will give the poem a venerable air of antiquity. An epic poem must have a hero, whose virtues should resemble those the poem's patron would like to think he has. A tempest, battle, burning town and 12 books are also important ingredients. Following the rules makes writing seem all too easy:

> For a Battel. Pick a large quantity of Images and Descriptions from Homer's Iliads, with a Spice or two of Virgil, and if there remain any Overplus, you may lay them by for a Skirmish. Season it well with Similes, and it will make an Excellent Battel. (Stephens 1982, 289)

When the 'Receit' was later included in *The Art of Sinking in Poetry*, or the *Peri Bathous* (1728), it followed a proposal for a Club or 'Association' of inept writers. Here each might specialise in the several arts of bathos: the 'speech by half-words' perfected by politicians, for example, or the 'diminution' at which ladies, whisperers and backbiters are expert; or 'exclamation' learnt from the Bear-garden. These specialists would pool their 'expertise' into making a rhetorical chest of drawers, containing all manner of writing, to which any work-a-day poet might apply for help (Pope 1986, 224–5). In the 'Receit' and the *Peri Bathous* formulaic writing is the target of comic vision, as it is in *The Dunciad*, but there the comedy is also marked with darker (or exuberantly mock-epic?) apocalyptic tones: 'He [the author of *The Dunciad*] lived in those days, when (after Providence had permitted the invention of Printing as a scourge for the sins of the learned) Paper also became so cheap, and Printers so numerous, that a deluge of Authors covered the land' (Martinus Scriblerus of the Poem; Pope 1999, 70).

By separating writers into hacks and authors, Pope was dividing culture into 'classic' works of literature and 'popular' or 'populist' works. In the early eighteenth century, 'literature' encompassed all texts, all forms of print culture. The eighteenth-century periodical included not just items on music, painting, the theatre and poetry or fictional prose essays, but also city gossip, political news, letters of advice, current medical and scientific topics. The London stage offered opera, tragedy, pantomime, juggling, comedy, ladder-dancing, and contortionists – often on the same evening. It is only during the eighteenth century that the distinction between that which is 'literary' and that which is not, that which is part of 'high' culture and that which is not, is drawn. Studies of romanticism have long discussed the emergence of 'Literature' as we recognise it as a result of aesthetic theories of that period: that the author is the sole originator of his work, that the literary work is imaginative, original, mysteriously inspired. More recent cultural studies' approaches to the eighteenth century are beginning to date the emergence of 'Literature' in its narrower sense much earlier in the eighteenth century than we first thought. Some commentators argue that Pope played a major role in defining the culture as we still think and talk (and disagree) about it today, establishing the categories that have been so influential in shaping our cultural perceptions, the ideas of 'good taste' within which we continue to regard art, literature and music.[7]

*The Dunciad*'s extraordinary feat is to carve these distinctions through a work which is itself a crossing of refinement and vulgarity, classicism and populism. In attacking the writing he so disdained, Pope was also perhaps compromising with it. He was certainly 'accommodating' it within his own text of *The Dunciad*. It is now a critical commonplace to argue that *The Dunciad* depends upon the very culture which it attempts to repudiate and that *The Dunciad*'s attitude towards this culture exhibits both fascination and repulsion, attraction and disgust. This ambivalence is evident everywhere in *The Dunciad*, in the general exuberance with which it excoriates duncehood of various kinds. The following excerpt from Book I illustrates the ways in which scorn, disgust, revulsion can seem surprisingly close to fascination, attraction, even allure. Here the Goddess Dulness proudly surveys her (un)creations, the works of the dunces:

> Here she beholds the Chaos dark and deep,
> Where nameless Somethings in their causes sleep,
> 'Till genial Jacob, or a warm Third day,
> Call forth each mass, a Poem, or a Play:
> How hints, like spawn, scarce quick in embryo lie,
> How new-born nonsense first is taught to cry,
> Maggots half-form'd in rhyme exactly meet,
> And learn to crawl upon poetic feet.
> Here one poor word an hundred clenches makes,
> And ductile dulness new meanders takes;
> There motley Images her fancy strike,
> Figures ill pair'd, and Similes unlike.
> She sees a Mob of Metaphors advance,
> Pleas'd with the madness of the mazy dance:
> How Tragedy and Comedy embrace;
> How Farce and Epic get a jumbled race;
> How Time himself stands still at her command,
> Realms shift their place, and Ocean turns to land.
> Here gay Description Aegypt glads with show'rs,
> Or gives to Zembla fruits, to Barca flow'rs;   <small>*Zembla* in the Arctic; *Barca* a desert in Libya</small>
> Glitt'ring with ice here hoary hills are seen,
> There painted vallies of eternal green,
> In cold December fragrant chaplets blow,
> And heavy harvests nod beneath the snow.   (Pope 1999, 106–8)

Pope's derision of Grub Street is obvious here. The hastily conceived writings of the dunces are monstrous offspring ('spawn, scarce quick', 'new-born nonsense' and 'Maggots, half-form'd') which nevertheless ape the actions of natural children (crying, playing, crawling). These 'nameless Somethings' are too worthless to be acknowledged by their parent-author, or too poorly executed to be given generic respectability. They are born prematurely, barely have the spawn begun to move than they are forced to appear, and then they are badly parented: unnaturally, they are taught to cry (or make as much noise as possible) rather than being consoled and hushed.

But the passage is not solely one of derision. The account of the crazy contradictions of the imagination, which delights in creating flowers in a desert, or fruits in a frozen expanse, is itself, paradoxically, delighting. Such images are illogical, and as such, to be scorned. (Pope's enemies reveal the literal reading habits of the day: Concanen complains that in the *Epistle to Burlington*, the lord cannot simultaneously be in his study and crossing the lawn; Dennis mocks Pope's Temple of Fame because, situated in the sky, it defies the laws of gravity and he discredits Book II of *The Dunciad* because its games could never have taken place in 'the Master Street of a populous City'; Dennis 1939–43, II 362.) But in conjuring up these transgressive poetic fictions, the poem is also articulating them. Pope's trust in the readers of the future is not always returned. The closing lines of this passage are just as 'lyrical', 'inventive' and 'imaginary' as Coleridge's 'sunny pleasure dome with caves of ice' ('Kubla Khan'). While the intention of the section may be to censure such poetic licence, readers then and now can find such indulgence attractive rather than censurable. In many of the lines here Pope is playing upon various senses of each word. The early eighteenth century would have thought of 'maggot' as we would do, thinking through the associations not just of repellent grubs and worms, but of those specifically generated through corruption. But 'maggot' then also referred to something whimsical, odd, perhaps a trifle crack-brained. As such the one word might stand for the 'grub' (street) productions of the hacks. An early publication by the commercial publisher Dunton was entitled *Maggots: or, Poems on Several Subjects, never before handled, by a Schollar* (1685).[8] But the strange fancies implied by the term 'maggot' were also strangely entrancing. It had its own allure, as Prior claimed: 'Your Horace owns, He various writ, / As wild, or sober Maggots bit' (1959, I 481). On a much wider scale, the mock-epic *Dunciad* as a whole is itself a jumble of comedy and tragedy, farce and epic. Book IV scorns collecting and antiquarianism, but as Pat Rogers has argued: 'the entire *Dunciad* has become a sort of cabinet of curiosities' (1993, 253).

The voice of this 'maggot' poem is thus by turns portentous, derisive, flippant. In its early address to Swift, it can also accommodate relative informality and geniality: 'Mourn not, my Swift, at ought our realm acquires' (I, 26). As an extravagant attack on supposedly worthless opponents, *The Dunciad* is sometimes positioned as an embarrassing work for Pope, or within Pope's canon, its savage denunciations threatening to rebound upon its author. But the poem has never been read in terms of one of Pope's explanations – that *The Dunciad* was written as a substitute conversation with Swift: 'It had never been writ but at his Request, and for his Deafness: For had he been able to converse with me, do you think I had amus'd my Time so ill?' (Pope 1956, II 523). Although some commentators have thought these remarks merely an attempt by an anxious Pope to surround himself with allies, Swift's poem, 'Dr Swift to Mr Pope' (1732; written 1726 or 1727) was probably written before these remarks (12 October 1728) and humorously suggests the same point:

> Thus, *Pope*, in vain you boast your Wit;
> For, had our deaf Divine
> Been for your Conversation fit,
> You had not writ a Line.

We know that Pope appealed to Swift to help with the variorum annotations and claimed that he was most proud of the dedication of the *Dunciad* to his friend (28 June 1728). This inscription ensured that the poem would open with an invocation to Swift in his many guises, including 'Dean, Drapier, Bickerstaff, or Gulliver'.[9] Pope sent the 12-line passage to Swift before publication with the request that he 'consider, re-consider, criticize, hypercriticize, and consult about with Sheridan, Delany, and all the Literati of (the Kingdom I mean) to render it less unworthy of you' (Pope 1956, II 468). The poem proceeds by anatomising the world of the dunces, placing their attitudes and assumptions under minute scrutiny, and opens up, in Book IV, a wider satire upon contemporary education and the Grand Tour, upon virtuosi and antiquarians, upon religious freethinking, upon opera, in short upon the entire social and cultural politics of Walpole's age. In all of these regards, the parallels with *Gulliver's Travels* are particularly resonant. There is also an allusion throughout to Swift's monstrous goddess, the Goddess Criticism in *The Battle of the Books* (1704). Perhaps himself inspired by Pope's poem on dulness, Swift would also write poetic denunciations of Grub Street venality.[10]

   In addition to these more specific connections, *The Dunciad* is always part of the Scriblerians' common endeavour to denounce false taste and learning and their tendency to do so by aping the very characteristics of those they denounce. Some time ago Gardner Stout argued that we might read Swift's *Tale of a Tub* in terms of 'an image of Swift, sitting with his fellow wits in an Augustan drawing room and saying: a Wotton, a Bentley, a bookseller, a hack, a Rosicrucian *adeptus* talks thus – and then striking a pose and personating them, while simultaneously carrying on an ironic (often sarcastic) running commentary on their absurdities' (Stout 1969, 183). *The Dunciad* might be similarly read, with Pope addressing his friends, most obviously his fellow Scriblerians, ventriloquising the dunces (whether pedants like Theobald or Bentley, or perceived dunces like Cibber, Curll, Blackmore et al.) and exposing their mediocrity. But the impersonation of one's enemies and the voice of irony directed against them are by no means exhaustive of the ways in which the poem initiates, voices, provokes, anticipates and circulates many other voices too. Pope is also, however, obviously conversing with us, as representatives of the poem's posterity. In anticipating its own canonical status, *The Dunciad* situates itself and its author as part of a literary tradition. Pope and his (mock) epic poem were fashioned then and continue to be a kind of gravitational centre of early eighteenth-century culture in the lineage of great English authors. This is to insert *The Dunciad* within a narrative of literary tradition which is consciously constructed, usually as the relationship of canonical authors across time. But inevitably simultaneous with literary tradition are the remembrances of posterity, a less controllable literary genealogy in so far as authors may be remembered without necessarily being validated. Indeed, part of the Scriblerians' anxiety concerning print culture was the likelihood that it would bequeath fame to any writing. When Swift suggested to Pope that he might annotate his poem for readers beyond London – and beyond the 1730s – he therefore initiated the poem's conscious participation in this aleatory, usually more unpredictable, kind of posterity. Future readers could not easily be satirised, incorporated or befriended. Pope was confident that literary tradition would bequeath a literary value to his work, but posterity – as the epigraph to this chapter suggests, with its self-deprecating fears that the 'Dulness' of Pope's text might be misread as its 'dullness' – was another matter.

## Notes

1. Weinbrot 1978, however, argues that Pope in particular despised the actual Augustan age, in which Virgil and Horace were leading poets, and modelled his poetry on that of Juvenal rather than Horace. Erskine-Hill 1983, in response, argues that Weinbrot's thesis (of Pope's movement from Horatian to Juvenalian satire) overlooks the complexities of works like *Epistle to Augustus*, and that Weinbrot neglects the personal, autobiographical, introspective and humorous ways in which Pope responds to Horace's example.
2. See Pocock 1975 and 1985.
3. For a consideration of Theobald's poem, see Fairer 1984, 123–35. Lonsdale's anthology (1984) reprints a number of poems by such dunces as Edward Ward, Ambrose Philips, Thomas Tickell, Colley Cibber and Leonard Welsted; Carpenter's anthology (1998) includes poems by Matthew Concanen; Ambrose Philips and Jonathan Smedley. Much recent criticism has vindicated Theobald's editing of Shakespeare over that of Pope (see Seary 1998 and Thompson 1998).
4. This poem was itself an imitation of *The State Dunces* – a catalogue of targets of political satire.
5. Only two women became openly involved in the *Dunciad* wars – Elizabeth Thomas and Lady Mary Wortley Montagu – although the *Dunciad* attacked a number of female writers, including Eliza Haywood, Susannah Centlivre, Lady Mary Wortley Montagu and the French translator Anne Dacier.
6. See Hammond 1988b and Nokes 1998.
7. See Hammond 1990, Thomas 1995 and Fabricant 1996.
8. Later Ned Ward would attack Pope in return for *The Dunciad* in 'Apollo's Maggot in his Cup' (1731).
9. Bolingbroke joked about Swift's many guises in a letter to Pope and Swift: 'the many will stare at it [*The Dunciad*], the few will smile, and all his Patrons from Bickerstaff to Gulliver will rejoice, to see themselves adorn'd in that immortal piece' (Swift 1963–5, III 264; Feb. 1728).

10. In 'The Progress of Poetry' (1727) a Grub Street writer takes flight when starving and poor. In 'Advice to the Grub Street Verse-Writers' (1735), 'On Poetry, A Rhapsody' (1733; some lines withheld) and 'Directions for a Birthday Song' (composed 1729–33; published 1765), the servile flattery of much contemporary poetry in its address to courtly patrons is satirised.

# 5 *Gulliver's Travels*: Ceding Interpretations

> you are loading our Carrier every week with Libels, and Keys, and Reflections, and Memoirs, and Second Parts; wherein I see myself accused of reflecting upon great states-folk; of degrading human nature (for so they have still the confidence to stile it) and of abusing the female sex. I find likewise, that the writers of those bundles are not agreed among themselves; for some of them will not allow me to be author of mine own Travels; and others make me author of books to which I am wholly a stranger.
>
> ('A Letter from Capt. Gulliver to his cousin Sympson', 1735; Swift 1967, 39)[1]

> But it will be much better to come over your self, and read [*Gulliver's Travels*] here, where you will have the pleasure of a variety of commentators, to explain the difficult passages to you.
>
> (Gay to Swift; Swift 1963–5, III 184)

When Swift published a later edition of *Gulliver's Travels* (1735) with George Faulkner, a Dublin publisher he could trust not to excise his work as Benjamin Motte, the work's first publisher, had done, he added a prefatory letter from his fictional captain to his (also fictional) publisher, Sympson. This letter altered the entire work in a number of significant ways. The Gulliver who speaks here is recognisably the same Gulliver who, on his return from Houyhnhnmland at the end of the book, prefers the company of horses to that of his wife. His contempt for humans is evident in the short extract which serves as an epigraph to this chapter: how could human Nature be degraded, contemptible as it already is, argues Gulliver. Reading this letter as an introduction to all of the four voyages casts doubt from the very first on his reliability as narrator. Can the Gulliver who journeys to Lilliput and Brobdingnag be in his right mind? Perhaps all of the voyages are delusional, the crazy speculations of a crazed mind?

In this excerpt we also see that, just as Gulliver-the-adventurer became estranged from himself in his encounters with exotic societies, learned to see himself as exotic and strange, so too Gulliver-the-author is estranged from his own text. Not only do commentators dispute his authorship, but they also interpret the book in ways which Gulliver cannot control. This section of the letter draws attention to the immense number of printed replies, sequels, imitations, interpretations and criticisms of *Gulliver's Travels* which appeared in the wake of its first publication, even though this letter itself, added in 1735, is also one of these 'replies'. Within months of the publication of *Gulliver's Travels*, prints of illustrated scenes from the book went on sale, one of which Swift himself bought (of Gulliver being saved from drowning in a bowl of cream in Brobdingnag, land of giants; Swift 1963–5, III 257). That Swift came to see his work reflected back at him in different guises is already apparent in the letter from Gay to Swift (17 Nov. 1726), quoted as a second epigraph to the chapter. Gay is partly playing on the conceit, popular as a joke among Swift's circle, that Swift is not the author of *Travels into Several Remote Nations*. But the letter also situates Swift and Gulliver as parallel to one another: as authors who cannot control the interpretation of their own texts. The huge number of responses and counter-fictions which *Gulliver's Travels* inspired certainly seemed to confirm this. These surrounding texts cluster around their core, noisily intervening and imitating. They reveal that the age of rationality is also an age of irrepressible information.

All of the responses to *Gulliver's Travels* have come to be called 'Gulliveriana', a term which Jeanne Welcher has popularised to describe works which are 'Gulliverian' in spirit, including imitations, parodies, and sequels. 'Lilliputian verses', written in the appropriately short line of trisyllabic verse; a magazine for children, *The Lilliputian Magazine* (c.1750); works attributed to Lemuel Gulliver, from Dublin papers relating to the election of two seats in the Irish House of Commons (1727) to a satire on marriage which parodies courtesy manuals (*The Pleasures and Felicity of Marriage*, 1745); advertisements for the exhibition of Lilliputian and Brobdingnagian souvenirs to the public (*The Weekly Journal*, 26 Nov. 1726) – all of these are examples of 'Gulliveriana'. The term 'Gulliveriana' is itself a creation of this phenomenon. It was first used by Swift's rival, Dean Smedley, who, in 1728, published *Gulliveriana* as an attack upon both Pope and Swift, provoked by the miscellanies of verse they had authored together. Although Smedley's attack is principally on the persons, rather than the writings, of Pope and Swift, even in these personal insults he uses the Gulliverian imagery of great and small to castigate the 'diminutive *Lilliputian* Poet' whom Swift has unduly placed beside him on the 'Throne of Wit' (268) and the verses which Swift has published in the *Miscellanies* are described as what 'this *Man-Mountain has brought forth of the Muses*' (xix). (Gulliver was called *Quinbus Flestrin*, or 'Great Man Mountain', by the Lilliputians.)

Welcher's list includes around 400 titles and many of these are collections containing a number of individual pieces. Welcher estimates that the total of individual items published during the eighteenth century may be closer to 700. The responses to *Gulliver's Travels* also came extraordinarily quickly. One key appeared within the first fortnight: *A Key, Being Observations and Explanatory Notes, upon the Travels of Lemuel Gulliver* (1726). Welcher even discusses a number of pamphlets which appeared in the months before the publication of *Gulliver's Travels* as 'premature Gulliveriana'. While she concedes that it is 'rare, if not unique, for a book to influence its predecessors' (Welcher 1974, viii), these pamphlets may have been responding to advance rumours concerning Swift's new book circulating among his friends. In *It Cannot Rain but it Pours* (published April 1726), for example, the account of Peter the Wild Boy, brought to London from Germany as an example of childhood without human contact, includes the description of his 'vast pleasure' in conversing with horses (Welcher 1974, 7). However, as the first response from outside of the Swift circle, the *Key* exemplifies the print culture of the eighteenth century which this book addresses in the swift opportunism of its publication, its supplementary dialogue with its 'original' and its setting in play of diverse interpretations. This first key has been linked with the infamous publisher Curll (the author is named only as 'Corolini'), whose reputation for canny commercial opportunities seems evident in the *Key* when, by the third paragraph, the author has already inserted a quick puff for Curll's publication of Pope's letters to a close friend, Henry Cromwell, and by the second page of the 'observations' proper is indexing a reference to Curll's publication of a poem by Swift.

The 1727 *Key* is interesting not only for its speed of publication, however, but for the way in which it immediately initiates 'readings' of *Gulliver's Travels*. Traditionally, the islands of Lilliput and Blefuscu have been read as allegories of the political relationship between England and France. These kinds of deductions are being made from the very first, as the 1727 *Key* makes clear:

> Mildendo, a German Critick assures me, by a Jumble of letters, is no other than *Londino*, anglicè *London*, and indeed the Description given of it, as well as of the Emperor's Palace, corresponds very much with the Royal Court at *St James's*. . . . Blefuscu . . . seems by Mr Gulliver's Map, to lye as contiguous to *Lilliput*, as *Scotland* does to *England*. (Welcher 1976, I 18 & 20)

Shortly, Corolini will also discuss Blefuscu as allegorical of France (27). Some of Corolini's other interpretations have not enjoyed such popular support. That Lilliput's position in the South Seas is an allusion to the financial shares scandal of the South Sea Bubble (1720) has not been so readily accepted. (That it is this reading which permits Corolini to allude to the poem on the Bubble by Swift, referred to above, compounds its failure to convince.) Other interpretations of Lilliput were to follow: *Gulliver Decypher'd* (1727) notes that the emperor of Lilliput is thought to represent Queen Anne, or perhaps the Pretender (Welcher 1976, I 17–18). In 'The Little Beau's Speech' (1727), Lilliput becomes Ireland, as the beau of the title celebrates the return of Carteret as Lord Lieutenant to Ireland in sycophantically pompous dimeter lines of Lilliputian verse (Welcher 1976 III). Later still, *The Gentleman's Magazine* (Feb. 1739) would defend the veracity of *Gulliver's Travels* in comparing the Lilliputians to the 'pygmy nations' referred to by Homer and Milton and it conjectured that, historically, they were a people living 'in the extremity of India' (56). (Whether this defence is ironic or genuine is difficult to tell, an uncertainty to which this chapter will return.)

To a greater extent than the *Dunciad* pamphlets, then, these imitations and references reveal eighteenth-century ways of reading and responding to their founding text in all their diversity. They suggest that *Gulliver's Travels* was already widely and differently read within the eighteenth century and that, even when they were ostensibly creative imitations or allusive versions, they were also 'critical' or 'interpretative' responses to Swift's work. Like the other texts considered in this section, *Gulliver's Travels* generates itself as the centre of numerous print conversations. While all of these texts anticipate these responses, *Gulliver's Travels* figures this prolepsis into its own text. *Gulliver's Travels* is already alluding to responses and sequels. It envisages a Brobdingnagian translation of the second voyage (154), a treatise by a Lagadan Professor in which Gulliver will appear (237) and additional, more specialised, works on the societies of Lilliput and Houyhnhnmland (83; 323–4). It is not so very surprising then, that some enterprising authors and publishers rushed into print such titles as *A Cursory View of the History of Lilliput for these last forty three Years* (1727) and *An Account of the State of Learning in the Empire of Lilliput* (1728). Gulliver's narration is always self-consciously a text, and a published text. The text of *Gulliver's Travels* is at once a later draft of an original manuscript version ('upon a strict review, I blotted out several passages of less moment which were in my first copy, for fear of being censured as tedious and trifling, whereof travellers are often, perhaps not without justice, accused.'; 133) and a flawed, censured copy of a copy text (Gulliver's 'publisher' Richard Sympson claims that he has cut the text from an original length of at least double the published version; 43–4).

Significantly too, Gulliver's account of each voyage is represented as being 'read' (or at least interpreted) differently. Captain Biddel comes to accept the story of Lilliput only when he is shown the empirical evidence of miniature sheep and cattle. Captain Wilcocks believes in Gulliver's story of Brobdingnag immediately because, in Gulliver's words, 'as truth always forceth its way into rational minds, so this honest worthy gentleman, who had some tincture of learning, and very good sense, was immediately convinced of my candour and veracity' (188). On Gulliver's return from his third voyage, the Dutch sailors are curious about his story and Gulliver obliges in making one up, one that is 'short and probable' but conceals the greatest part. Here Gulliver tells his audience only as much as he suspects they will believe and thus provides yet another fictional, this time oral, account. Something of the same control is also evident in Gulliver's initial behaviour towards Don Pedro de Mendez on his return from Houyhnhnmland. Gulliver disdains this yahoo-man but condescends to give him a 'very short' relation of his voyage. When Mendez doubts Gulliver's story, thinking it more likely a dream or vision, Gulliver's only explanation for this scepticism is Mendez's innate inferiority or ignorance.

But there is a further twist in this final encounter: Gulliver consents to answer any objections which Mendez might pose to his fuller narration. 'The captain, a wise man, after many endeavours to catch me tripping in some part of my story, at last began to have a better opinion of my veracity' (336). This suggests an ideal of transparency, by which truth-claims need only be interrogated and debated in order to convince. Its utopianism echoes that of Habermas's theories of language and its production and reception in a rational public sphere. Whether we trust this ideal will depend upon our judgement of the relationship between Gulliver and Don Pedro de Mendez, and of de Mendez himself (see the discussion below).

Whatever we make of Don Pedro de Mendez, however, the conclusion from all of these returns suggests that Gulliver has always already been read. Our attempts to understand and interpret his behaviour are always more belated than those figured within the text itself. In the first voyage, Gulliver claims he is embarrassed by having to go into the sordid details of his personal hygiene, but that he must do so in order to rebuff the slanders already greeting his story: 'I would not have dwelt so long upon a circumstance, that perhaps at first sight may appear not very momentous; if I had not thought it necessary to justify my character in point of cleanliness to the world; which I am told, some of my maligners have been pleased, upon this and other occasions, to call in question' (64). In what form have these 'maligners' heard his tale? In rumours circulating throughout Redriff, or responses to an earlier manuscript form of the account?

Partly this self-consciousness about the act of narration and its reception is due to the work's parodying of travel narratives. Gulliver's description of the King of Brobdingnag's kitchen is quickly curtailed, he argues, because he does not want to incur the critics' usual complaint of travel narratives – that they are tediously circumstantial (154). The account of the immortal Struldbruggs (260) is included because Gulliver cannot remember having read of any such race in other travel accounts, and besides, he argues, if other accounts do exist, then the veracity of his own will only be verified. When Gulliver returns from the land of truth-telling, where even the concept of lying is not understood, he redoubles his efforts to convince his readers of the truthfulness of his account, despite the deceptions of many other travel narratives (340–1).

While these references gesture towards the material, formal aspects of print conventions, they are also linked to the more epistemological concerns of interpreting difference. Gulliver's adventures in foreign lands mean that he is forced to see himself as others see him, and thus he comes, inevitably, to read himself. Within the first chapter of the voyage to Lilliput, Gulliver is already becoming his own interpreter. He remembers how he was tempted to dash a number of Lilliputians to the ground, but the remembrance of their attacks upon him, he writes, 'and the promise of honour I made them, for so I interpreted my submissive behaviour, soon drove out those imaginations' (59). When he arrives in Brobdingnag, Gulliver ventriloquises how the inhabitants see him, transposing himself into an objectified third-person form:

> It now began to be known and talked of in the neighbourhood, that my master had found a strange animal in the field, about the bigness of a *splacknuck*, but exactly shaped in every part like a human creature; which it likewise imitated in all its actions; seemed to speak in a little language of its own, had already learned several words of theirs, went erect upon two legs, was tame and gentle, would come when it was called, do whatever it was bid, had the finest limbs in the world, and a complexion fairer than a nobleman's daughter of three years old. (134)

All of these aspects might be included in what Richard Rodino calls the 'levels and loops of textuality' in *Gulliver's Travels* (1993, 171). In his letter to his cousin Sympson (which Swift added in 1735), Gulliver professes to be affronted by the 'Libels, and Keys, and Reflections, and Memoirs, and Second Parts' that have greeted the publication of his narrative. But Gulliver (or Swift) can hardly be seen as innocent of the varied readings and textual responses to his account. Swift's secrecy about his authorship of the work compounds this: Swift's letter to his publisher, Motte, prior to the publication of *Gulliver's Travels* might be included as a piece of 'Gulliveriana', especially as it is ostensibly written by 'Sympson' on behalf of his writer, Captain Gulliver (Swift 1963–5, III 152–4).[2] The projected other books cited as future intentions by Gulliver and Swift's own participation in the devising of 'Gulliveriana' provide evidence of the complicity in multiple readings of the fictional and the real authors. In Welcher's list of Gulliveriana, Swift himself is responsible for 30 pieces (of which the prefatory 'Letter' of 1735 is one).

So far in the chapter we have seen how *Gulliver's Travels* inspired a huge number of publications and even courted them. These in turn reveal a number of different ways of reading Gulliver and his adventures. They exemplify the ways in which print culture can be thought of as conversation, with published responses and sequels responding not just to the 'originary' text, *Gulliver's Travels*, but to its other possible antecedents and to each other. Even the fact that *Gulliver's Travels* had generated this kind of response was discussed and interpreted and in turn became a topic of the Gulliveriana. In the broadside verse, *The Blunder of all Blunders* (1726), for example, assembled companies at coffee houses discuss and disagree about *Gulliver's Travels*, while poetasters listen intently, waiting to turn these accounts into verse. The publisher, who advertises at the foot of the sheet that he 'will shortly publish a Pamphlet, discovering the Ignorance and Stupidity of the Decypherers and Commentators on Gulliver', inevitably compounds the proliferation (Welcher 1976 I). Publishing is becoming a habit which none can kick.

*Gulliver's Travels* and the culture of 'Gulliveriana' which it inspired are suffused with the problematic of interpretation. Gulliver is constantly read by others and is constantly reading himself. The book throughout alludes to and parodies texts of various kinds – travel accounts, the emergent novel, the scientific treatise, the political allegory, the utopian and anti-utopian romance, the fictional memoir.[3] How, then, are we to read the Houyhnhnms' lack of books? For Terry Castle the Houyhnhnms' solely oral culture is a major part of what she calls the text's 'grammaphobia', or fear of the written word (Castle 1993). It is entirely possible that Swift intended such a culture to be read as utopian. The Brobdingnagians, who are singled out for special recommendation by Gulliver at the end of his four voyages (as the 'least corrupted' of Yahoos, 'whose wise maxims in morality and government it would be our happiness to observe'; 341), share the Houyhnhnm capacity for interpretative consensus. Their laws are never disputed because their 'people are not mercurial enough to discover above one interpretation' and to comment upon any law is a capital crime (176). It is hardly surprising, then, that their libraries are described, despite the gigantism of their culture, as 'not very large' (177).

Castle was only the first to bring to bear on her study of Swift the ideas and theories of poststructuralism. Much of the critical excitement in Swift studies in the 1980s and 1990s has been created by the entwining of contemporary theory with Swiftian textual playfulness.[4] But it would certainly spoil the fun of Swift studies if a sudden consensus were to be found. Instead, predictably, there have been counter-responses. These are illuminating not only for what they suggest about *Gulliver's Travels* and *A Tale of a Tub*, but for their implications for literary theory in general. In 1990, for example, Marcus Walsh responded to what he called contemporary 'textualist' readings which position Swift as a poststructuralist *avant la lettre*. Walsh reads *A Tale of a Tub* through textual debates contemporary with Swift – namely the debates between Anglicanism, Roman Catholicism and Deism about the status of the Bible. In this reading, transmission of Faith through the spoken Word, passed down through generations of priests, is even more suspect a basis of interpretation than interpretation of the written Word. While the written Word might be misinterpreted, it is also possible to attain something of the truth of the spirit of the Word. Theological debates about the 'Word' of God apply also to all words, all printed material. In *A Tale of a Tub*, Peter and Jack misinterpret the text of their father's Will for their own ends. So too the hack, modern writer who narrates *A Tale* drowns the text of the Will in a barrage of commentary, explication, surrounding apparatus. His own demented writing is an invitation to demented readings. Within the *Tale*, then, the father's Will almost disappears under the barrage of surrounding material. The Will itself, however, 'consisted wholly in certain plain, easy Directions about the management and wearing of their Coats', such as, for example '*Item*, I charge and command my said three sons, to wear no sort of *silver fringe* upon or about their said coats' (Swift 1986, 41). That Martin obeys the spirit of his father's Will, however, is seen by Walsh as a confirmation of the Anglican belief that the word 'continues adequately to communicate even where noise intrudes' (Walsh 1999, 123). Swift's opponent, but fellow Anglican, Richard Bentley, then shares this, at least, in common with Swift: that the presence of 'a corrupt line or dubious reading' need not be thought 'to darken the whole Context' (1719; quoted in Walsh 1999, 125). Walsh's extrapolation from theological debates to literature in general is supported by the quotation he cites from Swift's *Mr C[olli]ns's Discourse of*

*Free-Thinking, put into plain English* (1713). Here Swift's narrator parodies the deism of Collins, in arguing that texts are infinitely open to interpretation:

> All *Christian* Priests differ so much about the Copies of [their Scriptures], and about the various Readings of the several Manuscripts, which quite destroys the Authority of the Bible: For what Authority can a Book pretend to, where there are various Readings? And for this reason, it is manifest that no Man can know the Opinions of *Aristotle* or *Plato*, or believe the Facts related by *Thucydides* or *Livy*, or be pleased with the Poetry of *Homer* and *Virgil*, all which Books are utterly useless, upon account of their various Readings. (Swift 1957, 33)

This passage also exemplifies the dangers of reading Swift out of context. The question 'what authority can a book pretend to, where there are various readings?' is not a rhetorical one, even though it pretends to be. Instead the speaker is ironised here, so that his question only reveals a position which Swift attacks through parodic imitation.

Swift's contemporary reception as a writer and, indeed, his own view of himself as a writer, was as much that of the political polemicist as of the playful subverter of textual fixities. In many of his works, interpretative freedom, or the textual play of writing, was to be avoided. *The Conduct of the Allies* (1711), for example, commissioned by the government to inspire popular support for its peace negotiations with France, was the best known of Swift's early works. In *A Proposal for Correcting, Improving, and Ascertaining the English Tongue* (1712), Swift advocated the establishment of an English academy, which would fix and universalise the language – the only prose document he was ever to acknowledge publicly by publishing it under his own name. In *Mr C[olli]ns's Discourse of Free-Thinking, put into plain English* (1713), Swift attacked what he perceived as the atheism of Anthony Collins's brand of deism. Later in his career *The Drapier's Letters* (1724–35), a series of seven pamphlets, successfully campaigned for the repeal of Wood's halfpence in Ireland. In all of these writings, and in many others, Swift has a clear aim. We can confidently claim, from these and other writings by Swift, that he was opposed to Britain's involvement in the War of the Spanish Succession (1701–14), supported the idea of an English academy of language, was repelled by the arguments of deism, and believed that Wood won the patent for new coinage in Ireland only because government in London was corrupt and Ireland a place which England could dump upon. Unlike *A Tale of a Tub*, *Gulliver's Travels* or *Verses on the Death of Dr Swift*, these works do not seem to invite misinterpretation. This does not mean that these texts cannot be read 'against the grain', however. This is especially the case with *Mr C[olli]ns's Discourse*, in which the speaker is a parodic persona: a friend of Collins, ostensibly defending his work. Even in the others, where the speaking voice articulates attitudes close to what we think Swift's own must have been, there are possibilities for other modes of reading. In *The Drapier's Letters*, for example, the 'drapier', commonsensical, down-to-earth man of the people, inhabits an ironic distance from Swift despite articulating a Swiftian perspective on the affair of Wood's halfpence. The *Conduct of the Allies* and the *Proposal for Correcting . . . the English Tongue* are spoken in voices closer to Swift's own, but even here there are potential 'self-contradictions and strategic silences' in these works (Palmeri 1993, 7).[5] It should not surprise a reader of this chapter that the paradoxes and inconsistencies of Swift's career were noted in his own lifetime. Opponents made much of the contradictions between professed ideals and common practice. In an attack on the *Proposal for Correcting . . . the English Language*, for example, John Oldmixon pointed out the inconsistency in Swift's arguing for 'correct' forms of language and yet writing a poem such as 'Mrs Harris' Petition', in which Swift ventriloquises a servant's voice, with all its colloquialisms and grammatical errors.[6]

While the openly polemical and even propagandistic pieces (such as *The Conduct of the Allies*) might be read against the grain, against their apparent intention, however, there are still important distinctions to be drawn between the more playful textuality of *Gulliver's Travels*, *A Tale of a Tub* and *Verses on the Death of Dr Swift* and the political commissions. Judged as a whole, Swift's career suggests a writer highly conscious of questions of reading and interpretation, who deployed a wide range of rhetorical strategies for different ends. When we talk, then, of reading 'against the grain', we need to recognise a spectrum of possibilities of reading evident across Swift's works. While all texts are potentially open to (mis)interpretations, they are not inevitably so. Textual openness towards different readings can be foreshortened or exploited. Swift was aware of the author's possible lack of control and tried to eliminate it where it was important to him. The Swift who sought the post of historiographer royal in 1714 was the same Swift who published 'Observations' on his own *Tale*. Perhaps too much emphasis can be placed upon the author's anxiety concerning his authority. Admittedly, in the new dominance of print all readers might participate in, few could be positively excluded from its domain. But readings would always reflect upon their reader. Like the example of Pedro de Mendez coming to accept Gulliver's story, open discussion and debate might persuade and convince in matters of truth. If we accept this conclusion, we accept a view of Pedro de Mendez which has long been agreed upon. Even the 'hard' and 'soft' expositors of the twentieth century agreed upon de Mendez's goodness (although they differed on the question of why he appeared only at the end of the narrative). But a short notice in *American Notes and Queries* in the mid-1980s sparked a heated exchange among Swift scholars. The name 'Pedro', Maurice O'Sullivan argued (1984), was chosen in order to satirise the Portuguese Captain, as the name is symbolically connected with Roman Catholicism. Such a reading was self-confessedly speculative: Pedro de Mendez's sheltering of Gulliver from the Inquisition certainly does not seem to fit with his character as a wily Roman Catholic. What is interesting about the exchange is the heat it generated (Real and Vienken 1986, O'Sullivan 1986). In his account of this controversy Frank Boyle argues that the anger was understandable: 'With the satiric ground shifting so constantly beneath the critical path of Swift studies, mere speculations about this rare, seemingly fixed, patch of solid earth appeared positively irresponsible' (Boyle 2000, 166). But Frank Boyle was to rub salt into the wounds of those who read Pedro de Mendez as the text's only truly good man. His name, he argued, was taken from a notoriously mendacious Portuguese sailor, one Ferdinand Mendez Pinto, whose travel narrative was held as a paradigm of the lies which sailors tend to tell of foreign encounter. Swift's audience would never have trusted such a witness of Gulliver's veracity, Boyle argues.[7]

In works like *Gulliver's Travels, A Tale of a Tub*, and *Verses*, then, Swift seems to have deliberately and playfully courted readings and misreadings. In Gulliver's encounter with the professors at Lagado, Swift satirises the tendency to discover plots and conspiracies in the most unlikely places as a form of demented read-ing. But he simultaneously traps his reader within this kind of reading by having Gulliver talk of 'Tribnia' and 'Langden' in obvi-ous code for 'Britain' and 'England' (236).[8] And many readers happily accept Gulliver's translations of the foreign languages he meets, even though we may also be deceived. (Clark suggests that the less grandiose, more correct translation of *Quinbus Flestrin* would be 'dressed in buff skin'; 1953, 603.) For ways in which Swift and his friends read *Gulliver's Travels*, we can turn to the many letters exchanged after its publication. Among the most interest-ing of these are the letters between Swift and Henrietta Howard (waiting-woman to Princess Caroline and a friend of the Scriblerians), because, in imitating and continuing the conceit of Gulliver, these letters are themselves examples of Gulliveriana. Like the examples within *Gulliver's Travels* already discussed, they demonstrate, in Rodino's phrase, Swift's 'deliberate auto-corrup-tions of his own texts and blurring of fictional levels' (Rodino, 1993, 172). Howard began the foolery by writing about Swift's gift of Irish plaid material with references to Brobdingnagian dimen-sions, Lagadan measurements and the colours of Lilliputian silks. She reports that the Princess thinks Swift ought not to be seen at court in high heels (thus declaring his Tory loyalties) and tells Swift the whole court is fascinated by how the 'big endians' could dispute about which end to crack an egg when it is served poached or buttered (Swift 1963–5, III 185). She ends by hoping that a female yahoo in England might bring forth a Houyhnhnm baby, since a woman has reportedly given birth to rabbits (an obvious allusion to the case of Mary Tofts, who was involved in just such an elaborate hoax).[9] Swift's reply was to pretend that he had had to read this unknown book in order to make sense of her letter ('I thought it hard to be forced to read a Book of seven hun-dred Pages in order to understand a Letter of fifty lines': III 187). The letter similarly weaves a dense network of allusions to the book into its own fabric, however. For example, he complains of how the lines of her letter tend either up or downwards (as Gulliver noted that ladies in England write as Lilliputians do – aslant from one corner of the page to the other; 93). His response to the allusion to Mary Tofts is similarly to pretend ignorance, while elaborately constructing a cryptic message out of what was originally a straightforward suggestion:

> I have been five days turning over old Books to discover the mean-
> ing of those monstrous Births you mention. That of the four black
> Rabbits seems to threaten some dark Court Intrigue, and perhaps
> some change in the Administration. For the Rabbit is an undermin-
> ing animal that loves to work in the dark. The Blackness denotes the
> Bishops, whereof some of the last you have made, are persons of
> such dangerous Parts and profound Abilityes. But Rabbits being
> cloathed in Furs may perhaps glance at the Judges. (Swift 1963–5, III
> 188)

The attempts end only when he reaches the end of the page and is
forced to write hasty farewells. These letters are properly
Gulliverian. Unlike the letters exchanged with Pope, Gay and
Arbuthnot, they do not evaluate the work or adjudicate upon its
popularity or political subversion.[10] Instead, they playfully engage
with it. Later letters see 'Lemuel Gulliver' (Swift) thank Howard for
defending his reputation by sending her a gift of a Lilliputian
crown, accidentally left in his pocket after the fire in the royal
palace and just now discovered (III 190–1); and a 'translation' of a
letter from a Lilliputian prince to Swift's friend 'Stella' (possibly
written by Howard, perhaps in collaboration with Princess
Caroline) in which he appeals to her to use her influence to encourage Gulliver to return and help the Lilliputian nation in its war with
Blefuscu (III 203). In these exchanges we see the author (Swift)
become a reader and, as in all of the Gulliveriana, readers become
authors.

   All of these examples counter the argument that Swift was anxious about the way in which printing a text meant ceding control of
it. Instead, they suggest that he recognised the potential playfulness of print culture and its proliferating tendencies. Partly, then,
his encouragement of different readings was a love of play, a joke.
Many commentators have argued that in *Gulliver's Travels* we see
Swift set traps for the unwary reader.[11] His own involvement in
Gulliveriana might be used as supporting evidence of how Swift
satirised the gullible, unsuspecting reader. But this would be to
underestimate the relish and pleasure so conspicuously on display
in these works (as also in all of Swift's fictional, often mock, per-
sonae). We might remember that among Swift's earliest published
work was a print-culture practical joke: in *Predictions for the Year
1708*, he predicted the death of the almanac-maker John Partridge
and in *The Accomplishment of the first of Mr Bickerstaff's*

*Predictions* (1708) he recounted Partridge's death-bed recantation of astrology. John Partridge was understandably upset but found his attempts to prove himself still alive greeted only with further derision. Swift's joking experiments in print were never merely comic, however. Swift, like all authors, may not have been able to achieve total control over the interpretation of his own work, indeed may not have been able to retain his position as 'author' of that work, but there was always the possibility that other texts could challenge those readings which were inadequate or misconceived or even just disliked. The Scriblerians were anxious about this age of proliferating texts, this age of information rather than of knowledge. But a proliferating print culture would always offer the possibility of rewriting, rereading. While Pope and Swift were clearly annoyed if not often enraged by the plagiarisers, slanderers and opportunists they saw as exploiting their own works, these hacks and competitors could always be countered by further rewritings, recyclings and textual distortions.

## Notes

1. All references in this chapter are to the Penguin Classics edition (1967) of *Gulliver's Travels*. As it largely follows the 1726 edition, it is the best edition for the purposes of a chapter in which the Gulliveriana of 1726 and thereafter are discussed. However, all the current editions of *Gulliver's Travels* conflate different parts of various editions: the Penguin includes the letter from Gulliver to Sympson of the 1735 Dublin edition, for example, and does not reproduce the frontispiece; the Oxford World's Classics edition (1986) follows Faulkner's 1735 edition of the text, but uses the frontispiece and title page of the 1726 edition.
2. For a discussion of this letter (8 Aug. 1726) and of the different frontispieces of the 1726, 1727 and 1735 editions, see Wagner 1992 and 1995.
3. See Smith 1990.
4. See, for example, Probyn 1985 and 1993, Atkins 1983, Docherty 1987, Wyrick 1988, Barnett 1990, and Rodino 1993.
5. See Kelly 1988 and Steele 1978. Kelly argues, for example, that while the language academy is to transcend political differences, the proposal would have offended the Whigs in the manner of its praise of the Tory politician and friend of Swift, Robert Harley. She also suggests that the *Proposal* is as much a work of autobiography as a

consideration of language (98) and that the modernity of the proposed academy and its putative systematisation of language troubled
the very proposer himself (100–2). There have been very few attempts
to read *The Conduct of the Allies* against the grain. However, in his discussion of this work, Peter Steele sees it as more complex than most.
He argues that it displays two contrasting emphases: 'One is on the
unscrupulous singularity of the behaviour of the party which has
manipulated the English in the war: the other is on the readiness and
thoroughness with which the English have put themselves in the
power of their manipulators' (Steele 1978, 28). While most read the
'we' of this text as an appeal to the Tory reader sympathetic to his
claims, Steele argues that Swift both aligns himself with and censures
the people he addresses.

6.  See Kelly 1988, 17.

7.  Boyle's reading is certainly supported by Gulliver's citation of Sinon,
    the most celebrated liar of antiquity, in support of his own veracity in
    the last chapter (341). Boyle's ultimate conclusion – that in satire, crit-
    ics see their own reflections – is not that drawn here, however.

8.  See Hammond 1993 on allegories and codes in Swift's work and Kropf
    1992 for the entrapment of the reader in eighteenth-century literature
    more generally, though especially in Swift.

9.  For a very interesting account of the Mary Toft case and its impor-
    tance for our reading of Pope and Swift, see Todd 1995.

10. In one letter, however, Arbuthnot tells Swift of an old gentleman who
    consulted his map to look for Lilliput and a Captain who claims that
    he knew Gulliver and that the printer has made errors in his biogra-
    phy (III 180). If these are entirely fictional anecdotes, as would be
    characteristic of Scriblerian *jeux d'esprit*, then they imitate the way in
    which Gulliver straightfacedly stresses the veracity of his account.

11. See Smith 1984, Kropf 1992, and Wagner 1992.

# 6 The Political Controversies of *Pamela*

[*Pamela*] divided the World into such opposite Judgments, that some extolled it to the Stars, whilst others treated it with Contempt. Whence arose, particularly among the Ladies, two different Parties, *Pamelists* and *Antipamelists*. . . . Some look upon this young Virgin as an Example for Ladies to follow; nay, there have been those, who did not scruple to recommend this Romance from the Pulpit. Others, on the contrary, discover in it, the Behaviour of an hypocritical, crafty Girl, in her Courtship; who understands the Art of bringing a Man to her Lure.

(Peter Shaw, *The Reflector*, 1750)[1]

[Pamela's] being eludes simple classification; her history is everywhere the history of a double identity, identity in the process of becoming something else. Like the text bearing her name, Pamela is an affront to all that is fixed, uniform, lapidary.

(Castle 1986, 136)

Within two months of its first publication, the *Gentleman's Magazine* implied that *Pamela* was being read by every Londoner with the slightest curiosity: '[It was] judged in Town as great a sign of want of curiosity not to have read PAMELA, as not to have seen the French and Italian dancers' (*The Gentleman's Magazine*, 11 Jan. 1741, 56). Within the first year the novel had appeared in six authorised editions, a number of pirated editions, an unauthorised newspaper serialisation, and Richardson had published his own sequel. A huge number of critical pamphlets, imitations and parodies had also been published. More than a 'vogue', *Pamela* had become a phenomenon; more than a 'phenomenon', *Pamela* had become a controversy, or, an 'epidemical Phrenzy now raging in Town' in the words of Parson Oliver (*Shamela*; Fielding 1980, 323). The language here of epidemic is appropriate for a publication whose effects were far-reaching and sometimes, it seemed, too radical even for its own author.[2]

*Pamela* recounts the story of a gentleman intent on seducing his maid, and of that maid just as intent on protecting her virginity. This, then, is a struggle between an aristocratic master, a Minister of Parliament, a Justice of the Peace, and a vulnerable labouring-class servant, taken from her parents at the age of 12 to be placed in service; a struggle between the ancien regime *droit de seigneur*, in which the sexualities of servant-girls are the property of their economic master, and the middle-class fantasy of romantic love; a struggle between ideas of marriage as financial power-broking between two wealthy families and marriage as based on affective feeling between two individuals; between sexual libertinism and moralised chastity. In all of these conflicts the identities of class, status, age and gender are inseparable and the designation of *Pamela* as a political novel is an obvious one. This makes the debates surrounding *Pamela* all the more acute, in making, at the very least, their political nature impossible to ignore.[3]

The novel dramatises the inherent power of social status in the eighteenth century. Mr B is able to abduct Pamela without obstacle. Her father is helpless to intervene; neighbours of Mr B's class think the issue much ado about nothing; a clergyman (Williams) who tries to help becomes himself a victim of social hierarchy (he is imprisoned for his pains on the charge of not paying debts which Mr B had previously waived); Mr B can intercept mail at the local Post Office; and Mrs Jewkes, housekeeper to Mr B in his Lincolnshire estate, is loyal to her master and aids his attacks upon Pamela. As early as the second letter in *Pamela*, we see that Pamela's father fears for her virtue: simply by being poor, she is vulnerable. Later we will see the enormous pressures which Pamela faces as Mr B attempts to bribe her with offers to make her parents financially secure (Richardson 2001, 86).[4] Mr B's power over Pamela is institutional as well as financial. After an attempted escape, Mrs Jewkes warns Pamela that had she escaped, she was provided with a warrant from Mr B to have her arrested. His power as a Justice of the Peace allows him to arrest Williams and, potentially, to waive any prosecution for rape which Pamela might threaten. Throughout the text, the appellation of 'Mr B' draws attention to this power: this man cannot be named, the text infers, because he has the power to pursue a libel charge through the courts. The use of 'Mr B' continually reminds us that this is a text which dramatises the power of the aristocracy, and that dramatising the power available to the upper classes also becomes a challenge to it.

Pamela's challenge to this power is possible through the language of morality. The commonplace libertinism of upper-class gentlemen was a 'respectable' target not only for Pamela, but for the emerging middle classes, whose self-definitions were predicated on ideals of Christian morality, and chastity in particular. Pamela's resistance to rape becomes the means by which an entire social hierarchy can be upturned: 'my Soul is of equal Importance with the Soul of a Princess' (158); 'my Virtue is as dear to me, as if I was of the highest Quality' (215). Mr B picks up on the way in which Christian conviction becomes the means of attack: 'O she can curse most heartily, in the Spirit of Christian Meekness' (185). Equality in the eyes of God permits and underpins the even more radical expressions of political equality: 'Oh! what can the abject Poor do against the mighty Rich, when they are determin'd to oppress?' (99); 'how came I to be his Property? What Right has he in me? (126). Even where there is no direct address to Christian egalitarianism, her attacks take their justification from the extremity of her situation. Pamela's pertness towards her master is psychologised as the courage of resistance under extreme pressure. Mrs Jervis upbraiding Pamela for her lack of deference towards her master reminds us that to be a servant is to be unthinking and uncomplaining, silent and submissive:

> Why, Fool, says he, won't you like to go to wait on my Sister *Davers*? Sir, said I, I was once fond of that Honour; but you was pleased to say, I might be in Danger from her Ladyship's Nephew, or he from me? – D – d Impertinence! said he; do you hear, Mrs *Jervis*, do you hear, how she retorts upon me? Was ever such matchless Assurance! –
> I then fell a weeping; for Mrs *Jervis* said, Fie, *Pamela*, fie! (58)

The pressure of the moment justifies the outspokenness of Pamela's attacks upon her master. When Mr B suddenly decides to send her home, Pamela marvels at how quickly his anger can arise and ascribes it to the kind of spoilt upbringing she sees as characteristic of his class:

> [S]ee the Lordliness of a high Condition! . . . His poor dear Mother spoil'd him at first. Nobody must speak to him or contradict him, as

I have heard, when he was a Child, and so he has not been us'd to be controul'd, and cannot bear the least Thing that crosses his violent Will. This is one of the Blessings of a high Condition! Much good may do them with their Pride of Birth, and Pride of Fortune, say I! – All that it serves for, as far as I can see, is to multiply their Disquiets, and every body's else that has to do with them. (242)

This speech moves from the particular to the general, from Mr B, whom she has heard was spoilt above measure, to all people of high condition.

The radical outspokenness of Pamela's attacks upon Mr B's behaviour is overlaid by the radicalism of the textual 'voice' of a female servant. Donna Landry identifies a tradition of lower-class women's writing which flourished between 1739 (the publication date of Mary Collier's poem *The Woman's Labour*) and 1796 (Ann Yearsley's *The Rural Lyre*), but this tradition is exclusively poetic (Landry 1990). Whereas nineteenth-century working-class women would publish predominantly autobiographical prose, most lower-class writers in the eighteenth century published poetry. Only Mary Collier, Elizabeth Bentley and Ann Candler added autobiographical introductions to their poetry, but these were rather tentatively offered only so as to authenticate their lower-class credentials. For a pseudo-autobiographical work by a labouring-class woman, however, we might turn to the ventriloquism of *Pamela*. Writing itself, particularly for a servant girl, represents social aspiration, a claim to equality effected through the act of writing. To adapt Landry's comment on Ann Yearsley, we might say that 'To write . . . at all, for [Pamela] is to enact a certain imaginary emancipation from social exigency, to take upon herself the illusory freedoms of the bourgeois subject' (1990, 125).

The pretence of Pamela's authorship is maintained through her frequent colloquialisms and homely descriptions. Margaret Anne Doody writes: 'someone who can speak of making her hands as red as a blood-pudding and as hard as a beech trencher is certainly of the servant class' (Richardson 1980, 12). And in their recent edition, Keymer and Wakely identify colloquialisms, such as the expressions 'a Mort of good Things' (18) and 'worth a Power of Money' (43), as particular to Bedfordshire (Richardson 2001, xvii). To understand the contemporary force of Pamela's linguistic 'vulgarisms', we might recall how, in translating Virgil's *Georgics*, Joseph

Warton felt it necessary to apologise for any indelicate phrases which, he fears, will 'unconquerably disgust many a delicate reader'. As John Barrell notes: 'His examples include not only such palpable barbarisms as *dung, ashes, horse,* and *cow,* but also *plough, sow,* and *wheat,* which have probably lost forever their power to shock' (Barrell 1983, 12). While poetic diction is a more exacting lexical field than prose, we can see some of the same discomfort with homely diction in the implied debate set up by one of the prefatory letters to the first edition of *Pamela.* An anonymous reader urges the 'editor' to publish these letters, but also not to alter their language:

> I could wish to see it out in its own native Simplicity, which will affect and please the Reader beyond all the Strokes of Oratory in the World; for those will but spoil it: and, should you permit such a murdering Hand to be laid upon it, to gloss and tinge it over with superfluous and needless Decorations, which, like too much Drapery in Sculpture and Statuary, will but incumber it . . . No; let us have *Pamela* as *Pamela* wrote it; in her own Words, without Amputation, or Addition. (Richardson 2001, 8–9)

This evidently responds to the argument that Pamela's language should be polished. The debate about the propriety of Pamela's voice, then, precedes the publication of the novel.[5]

Additionally, there are a significant number of references to the 'usefulness' of her writing which betray a self-consciousness about her status and its inimical relationship to the 'leisure' pursuit of writing. For example, when she is thinking about her return to her parents, she hopes there will be a little time for reading: 'Oh! I have a Power of these Things to entertain you with in Winter Evenings, when I come home. If I can but get Work, with a little Time for reading, I hope we shall be very happy, over our Peat Fires!' (77). Once she is imprisoned by Mr B, writing is redefined by Pamela as a form of 'employment': 'my Pen and Ink . . . is all that I have, besides my own Weakness of Body, to employ myself with' (170). However, Pamela displays no guilt about writing: any accusations of 'idleness' are articulated by Mr B (e.g. 'you mind your Pen more than your Needle; I don't want such idle Sluts to stay in my House'; 48), which Pamela challenges by interpreting as expressions of *his* guilt, rather than the impatience of an employer at his servant's lack of industry (26).

It is interesting to contrast Richardson's ventriloquism of a lower-class female voice with the real voices of eighteenth-century women who published poetry. Because they were always writing for a polite audience, often in anticipation of patronage, labouring-class poets can seem conventional, decorous and even obsequious in their writings. However, as Landry has shown, there are certainly moments of irony, satire and, occasionally, outspokenness in their work, which are surprising given the material circumstances of their authors. Richardson's scenario (a servant-girl under violent attack), pretended authorship (disguising himself and intervening at one point as the 'editor'), and ostensibly 'private' mode of address all permit a much more daring articulation of lower-class grievances and claims to respect. This 'lower-class voice' (albeit only ventriloquised) not only stakes a claim to be heard but positions itself firmly in the centre of its own narrative. While many critics have complained of how Mr B seems only a cipher in *Pamela*, a shadowy, elusive if not ill-defined character, this is surely also part of *Pamela*'s radicalism. It is commonplace to say that Mr B is seen only through Pamela's perspective (his occasional letters notwithstanding). But even Mr B imagines himself as Pamela as he reads her narrative and identifies with her distress. At one point he even attempts to ventriloquise her own writing:

> I beg you will write a few Lines to [your parents], and let me pre-scribe the Form for it; which I have done, putting myself as near as I can in your Place, and expressing your Sense, with a Warmth that I doubt will have too much possess'd you. (116)

Pamela, it must be noted, alters the letter, against Mr B's instructions, because it fails to articulate how she feels (97–8, 116). However, Mr B's attempt to write as Pamela would, even if he fails, demonstrates how absorbing and central Pamela's feelings and voice are to this narrative. Viewed in this way, *Pamela* represents the coming-to-full-identity of a servant girl. That eighteenth-century servants certainly read *Pamela* might well testify to the 'romance' of this narrative to those trained to expect nothing other than servitude.[6]

The labouring-class poets, in contrast to Pamela, might be seen as caught within a much more timid cultural agenda. Morag Shiach has argued that polite interest in these lower-class writers lay in the extent to which their writings 'could support particular theories about the relations between nature and poetic writing, rather than in any desire to re-evaluate the cultural and social role of the peasantry' (Shiach 1989, 6). Traditions of labouring-class poetry flourished in the eighteenth century, then, perhaps only because of the growing emphasis upon untrained spontaneity in poetic aesthetics. In these terms, and accepting, as its eighteenth-century readers were asked to do, that these letters are written by 'Pamela', *Pamela* is an extraordinary eighteenth-century text. But, of course, not all (or many?) readers were fooled by the fiction that *Pamela* is really written by 'Pamela'. The putative stability of the politics of *Pamela* presented here is then exceedingly fragile. These politics would be further shattered by the responses to the text – responses not only by readers hostile to *Pamela* and readers sympathetic to *Pamela*, but also Richardson's subsequent responses to his own text.

If we think of the novel in terms of pitting aristocrat against servant-girl, then we can read many of the counter-fictions as more conservative than *Pamela*. Fielding's Shamela displays not the composure and earnestness of the Christian Pamela, but the grasping and wily nature of, it seems, her entire class. Pamela's pious and hardworking parents are replaced with a mother who prostitutes herself at Drury Lane theatre and writes advice to her daughter on how to entrap the unwary Mr Booby, and a father who has by turns been a criminal, a mercenary soldier, and one of the despised informers against the Gin Act, before settling into work at the customs house, renowned for its corruption. Shamela is the illegitimate daughter of these scandalous figures and her 'virtue' is only feigned so as to raise her financial, not moral, value: 'seeing you have a rich Fool to deal with, your not making a good Market will be the more inexcusable', her mother writes (Fielding 1980, 328). Shamela suggests the poor will always be wise to the best chance: 'I thought once of making a little Fortune by my Person. I now intend to make a great one by my Vartue' (342). Aristocratic-husband-hunting is more lucrative than Drury Lane prostitution. Ultimately, Fielding's parody suggests that since Shamela cannot spell 'virtue', she is hardly likely to understand it. Eliza Haywood's Syrena Tricksy is equally as pragmatic. When she is forced to choose between two suitors, Sir Thomas and his son Mr L, she decides to prefer the more repulsive Sir Thomas because he has offered a financial settlement to make her his mistress. Her mother

approves of this reasoning: 'I am highly pleas'd . . . that you have
such just Notions of what is your real Interest' (83). In both of these
counter-fictions, Pamela is exposed and her 'true' story – of dupli-
city and trickery – is rewritten. In a number of other responses, in
which the servant as moral ideal is retained, romance conventions
ultimately dispel the association between virtue and poverty. In
Kelly's sequel, *Pamela's Conduct in High Life* (1741), Pamela's parents are discovered to be of genteel birth, closely related to the
neighbouring squire, and this plot twist is repeated in the anonymous *Life of Pamela*, which borrows much of its material from Kelly's
sequel. Theatrical versions by Goldoni and Voltaire also raised
Pamela's status. In Fielding's *Joseph Andrews* (1742), Joseph, it is
eventually revealed, is of aristocratic birth, a victim of a gypsy cradle-swap. Joseph's being highly born can then seem to vindicate
Lady Booby's snobbish (and lascivious) preference for him over
Pamela and Fanny (Fielding 1980, 264–5). Thus in both imitations
and counter-fictions Richardson's radical plot of metamorphosis is
replaced with the more conservative plot of discovery.[7] While there
are several Pamelist texts which retain a marriage between a virtuous servant-girl and her nobly born master – such as the ostensibly
biographical account, *Memoirs of the Life of Lady H[esilrige]* (1741)
and a dramatic version *Pamela; or Virtue Triumphant* (1741) –
Pamela's attacks upon her master are considerably more muted. In
*Memoirs . . . of Lady H-*, radical statements concerning the inherent
dignity of the lower-class servant are articulated by Sir Arthur, not
by his lowly born wife, and even here, the exceptional nature of
Pamela is highlighted: 'You are endowed with a Capacity and
Understanding, rarely to be met with in your Sex, and which shines
through the dark Clouds of a mean Birth, and the Want of
Education' (Keymer and Sabor 2001, III 49). And Peter Sabor notes
in his recent selection of dramatic versions of *Pamela*, that in
*Pamela; or Virtue Triumphant*, Pamela remains a servant throughout, excessively humble and with none of the occasional outspokenness of Richardson's heroine, even when married (Keymer
and Sabor 2001, VI xvii).[8]

These rewritings sanitise the original radicalism of *Pamela*
(1740), in which Pamela's virtue is greater than that of any other
character, not just despite but, it is suggested, because of her low
status. Richardson's *Pamela* questions that 'gentility' is equivalent
to birth. The 'gentle' Pamela is not born a lady but becomes one.

The 'ladylike' virtues which her mistress taught her and which her own moral code reinforces, suggest that a genteel nature is not the property of only one class. In *Joseph Andrews*, some of Lady Booby's arguments approach the radicalism of Pamela's sentiments, but they are too obviously motivated by self-interest: 'Is he not more worthy to Affection than a dirty Country Clown, tho' born of a Family as old as the Flood, or an idle worthless Rake, or little puisny Beau of Quality? And yet . . . we must prefer Birth, Title and Fortune to real Merit' (265). There is only irony at Lady Booby's egalitarian sentiments when, in successive pages, she turns to inveigh against low-born coarseness. Torn between desire and pride, her inconsistencies are only too obviously self-centred. In comparing the politics of *Pamela* with those of *Joseph Andrews*, we might consider the ways in which both novels use the motif of soft skin, that conventional signifier of gentility: the soft, white hands of Joseph Andrews, spotted by the maid Betty in an early hint of his genteel birth (Fielding 1980, 54, 58) and Pamela's delicate hands, which blister when she scours a pewter plate (Richardson 2001, 77). The soft skin of their hands suggests very different ideologies: Joseph's hands are soft despite his having been in service and because of his inherent gentility; Pamela's are soft because – like those of (other) genteel ladies – she has had to do no severe manual labour. In the one (*Joseph Andrews*) soft skin is accepted as an intrinsic indicator of birth; in the other (*Pamela*), soft skin is the indicator only of the lack of physical work.

To emphasise the politically radical nature of *Pamela*, however, is necessarily to focus on the first half of the novel, and on those passages where Pamela resists and challenges Mr B's brutal authority. With the exception of the lively interview between Pamela and Mr B's outraged sister, Lady Davers, and Pamela's caustic responses to some of Mr B's expectations of a wife, the second half of *Pamela* is certainly much less engaging to a modern reader than the first and Pamela's new obsequiousness and often extreme self-deprecation undoubtedly overshadow her more radical outbursts in the earlier sections. Owen Jenkins discusses the split in the novel in terms of a contest between Richardson the storyteller and Richardson the moralist (Jenkins 1965). In this reading, the novel appears inherently fractured, split between the incipiently inflammatory rhetoric of the servant-girl threatened by rape and the effusively grateful servant-girl who is married to her wealthy master. How do we resolve the contradiction between the Pamela who criticises and the Pamela who is grateful to be assimilated into the upper classes, who instructs Lord B in middle-class virtue yet is rewarded by becoming upper class? How can we reconcile the plain-speaking, homely voice of Pamela before her engagement and the much more decorous, polite (and insipid) voice of the married Mrs B? Such questions have often been read in terms of ambivalence: Richardson's own ambivalence in relation to his humble origins and prosperous career (and the aristocratic friends which that career permitted) and that of the middle classes; perpetually rising, their social elevation is on the basis of their cultural and moral confidence, even, paradoxically, their sense of superiority. In Michael McKeon's terms, this is the ideological tension between supersession and assimilation (McKeon 1987, 380). The turn in Pamela's character can also be read in terms of the desire to reform rather than revolutionise the class forces that oppress her.

To concentrate on the more radical first half of *Pamela*, however, is also to share the focus of the earliest responses. While many critics were outraged at the apparent 'morality' of the book – that a servant girl who was virtuous might marry a gentleman – most responses concentrated on the scenes prior to Mr B's marriage proposal. *Shamela* includes just one letter from Shamela written after her marriage, as the narrative ends with Mrs Booby's excitement at going up to London where she can renew her affair with Williams and spend much more extravagantly than she can in the country. The brevity of *Shamela*, itself a satire upon the prolixity of Pamela's account, is then a concentration on mostly only the first volume of Richardson's two-volume *Pamela*. Parson Oliver barely seems to have read the second volume, in which Richardson's novel becomes increasingly like the conduct books which such clergymen would be expected to find inoffensive, if, like most other readers, not particularly exciting. *Pamela Censured* devotes five pages to an extensive quotation from *Pamela* – the final assault by Mr B on Pamela when he disguises himself as his own servant Nan (55–60) – but it does not discuss any scene after Mr B's proposal to Pamela. When Eliza Haywood came to write her characteristically racy version of *Pamela*, the history of her anti-heroine Syrena Tricksy ends abruptly and without any reformation. Syrena's serial promiscuity is repeatedly thwarted (she has more than 15 lovers, 'enjoyed', to differing extents, in nine phases). She never marries, despite a succession of attempts to entrap various gentlemen into marrying, or at least settling an annuity upon her. Only when she is exiled to Wales, where, it is thought, she will be deprived of all company, does the narrative suddenly end.

The Pamela counter-fictions only began to revise the scenes of married life between Pamela and Mr B after the publication of sequels by Pamelists and by Richardson. *Joseph Andrews*, for example, has persuasively been read as a response to *Pamela in her Exalted Condition* rather than solely to *Pamela* (Sabor 1978). The Pamela of *Joseph Andrews* is haughty and proud, forgetful of her own metamorphosis from a mere servant girl. She is stridently opposed to her brother marrying his lowly born sweetheart, because such a sister-in-law is now beneath her: '"She was my Equal . . . but I am no longer *Pamela Andrews*, I am now this Gentleman's Lady, and as such am above her"' (Richardson 1980, 271). If this seems an unfair misreading of the humble Pamela of Part I, it is convincingly the same character as the married Mrs B of *Pamela*, Part II. When her parents ask if some cousins might help them in their Kentish estate, for example, the Pamela of Richardson's sequel refuses because she 'would not wish any one of them to be lifted out of his station, and made independent, at Mr B's expence, if their industry would not do it' (Richardson 1914, II 13). Similarly, she is opposed to any potential marriage between Jackey, Lady Davers's nephew, and her maid Polly Barlow, as such an alliance would be 'laid upon Mr B's example' (II 192). In both of these examples, we can see Pamela's active forgetting of her own history. As Terry Castle has persuasively argued, Richardson was himself already in the process of rewriting his original version. For Castle, *Pamela in her Exalted Condition* attempts to repress the obviously revolutionary nature of its original (Castle 1986).[9]

The retrospective defence of the politics of *Pamela*, however, begins much earlier than the composition of Richardson's sequel. The first (published) place to look is to the revisions made to the text of the second edition (1741). The vast majority of the (841) changes made to this edition were designed to elevate or correct Pamela's language. This tendency continued in the extensive revisions to the 1801 posthumous edition. Instead of Pamela saying 'my Heart went pit-a-pat', for example, she now writes 'my heart fluttered', instead of 'my Heart's turn'd into Butter', she writes 'my heart's melted'. Instead of referring to her 'sweats', she now writes of 'toil'.[10] Eaves and Kimpel argue that Richardson's tendency to alter Pamela and Mr B was also to make their characters more consistent with the idealised characters of the third and fourth volumes of the sequel, *Pamela in her Exalted Condition*. In their judgement, this reveals the fundamental flaw in the narrative:

> Richardson was evidently conscious of the gap between the servant girl and libertine of the beginning and the fine lady and gentleman of the end, and tried to bridge it. The gap proved unbridgeable, the plot of the novel forced Richardson to assume that a virtuous and intelligent girl can be made permanently blissful by marrying a man who has kidnapped her and tried hard to rape her. (Eaves and Kimpel 1967, 85)

This proves to be the double bind of the plot. Without the disparity of their status and behaviour, Pamela's sufferings would neither be as plausible nor as sympathetic. Without the closing of this gap in their marriage, Richardson cannot have his heroine rewarded with the social elevation which mirrors her spiritual and moral quality.[11] Like all fairytales, the plot of *Pamela* requires social advancement. The ending of *Pamela* – the heroine's triumphing over adversity and due reward of marriage to her master – is central to the novel's terms. This is the ending which secures the novel's radicalism: Pamela is as worthy as any highly born lady. It is also the ending which dictates all readings. Before any reading takes place, the title of *Pamela: or, Virtue Rewarded* provides a key as to how we should read. Because the title page has always already advertised the novel's ending, we inevitably read teleologically; we allow the ending of the novel to dictate how we read its beginning. Yeazell attributes Fielding's *Shamela* to this kind of reading: it is, she argues, a way 'to sort out all the contradictions and confusions in her account of herself in light of their end' (Yeazell 1991, 87).[12] It is also the way in which I have read *Joseph Andrews*: for, to read the event of the cradle-swap as making it the more conservative text, is to reread. Joseph's being highly born can seem to vindicate Lady Booby's snobbish (and lascivious) preference of him over Pamela and Fanny – but only retrospectively (Fielding 1980, 264–5). The reader of *Joseph Andrews* has been deliberately misled into thinking him a lower-class servant. At times, then, *Joseph Andrews* seems to parallel as much as it inverts *Pamela*. Just as Mr B used his legal power to tyrannise Pamela, for example, so too Lady Booby conspires with Lawyer Scout to prevent the marriage of Joseph and his childhood sweetheart Fanny. As her lawyer transparently argues:

> The Laws of this Land are not so vulgar, to permit a mean Fellow to contend with one of your Ladyship's Fortune. We have one sure Card, which is to carry him before Justice *Frolick*, who, upon hearing your Ladyship's Name, will commit him without any farther Questions. (255)

When challenged by Squire Booby, we see this same Justice of the Peace forge an ill-written deposition accusing Joseph and Fanny of stealing a twig (259). Similarly, Joseph's defence of his own dignity is comparable to that of Pamela. When Booby defends his marrying beneath him by claiming 'my Fortune enabled me to please myself', Joseph assumes an equality, echoing Booby's own words, but punning upon the idea of 'fortune': 'My Fortune enables me to please myself likewise . . . for all my Pleasure is centred in Fanny, and whilst I have Health, I shall be able to support her with my Labour in that Station to which she was born and with which she is content' (271).[13]

There are many places within *Joseph Andrews* where the class hierarchies of the eighteenth century are called into question: that the only traveller to help Joseph after he has been robbed and beaten is the poorest postillion, who, the narrator acerbically notes, was later transported for robbing a hen-roost (47); that the surgeon who is ready to come immediately when he thinks he is attending a gentleman, goes back to bed when he hears Joseph is poor and has been robbed of all he has (49); that ill-temper, avarice, unfeeling and hypocrisy might equally be found 'behind the Bar at an Inn' or sitting 'on a Throne' (169). Furthermore, these examples are legitimated by being articulated by the narrator. In contrast, where Lady Booby or Joseph question class divisions (as, for example, 294–5), the form of *Joseph Andrews* permits Fielding to dramatise points of view with which he, or the novel, does not necessarily agree. A similar 'fracturing' to that considered in *Pamela* is, then, equally evident in such responses as *Joseph Andrews*. But where the fracturing of *Pamela* occurs along the fault-line of the heroine's marriage to her master and the changes which this marriage effect in her demeanour and voice, the fracturing of *Joseph Andrews* is between the certainties of authorial intervention and comment and the uncertainties of how to judge character. Indeed, as much recent criticism of Fielding has emphasised, Fielding's narrators tend to sport with their readers, teasing and misleading them.

In the first chapters of *Joseph Andrews*, we understand that Joseph refuses Lady Booby's advances because he has learnt from Parson Adams that chastity is a male as well as a female virtue and because he keeps the model of his sister Pamela's goodness always in mind. In the eleventh chapter, however, the narrator suddenly announces an alternative motive: Joseph's love for Fanny, his childhood sweetheart. The sudden revelation reminds us that the narrator is firmly in control and that we read only what he reveals or recounts to us. For the narrator of *Joseph Andrews*, this is a measure of his book's sophistication:

> It is an Observation sometimes made, that to indicate our Idea of a simple Fellow, we say, *He is easily to be seen through*: Nor do I believe it a more improper Denotation of a simple Book. Instead of applying this to any particular Performance, we chuse rather to remark the contrary in this History, where the Scene opens itself by small degrees, and he is a sagacious Reader who can see two Chapters before him. (Fielding 1980, 42)

In contrast to the transparency of account presented by *Pamela*, *Joseph Andrews* presents narrative opacity. Both of Fielding's replies to *Pamela*, then, exemplify a hermeneutics of suspicion: *Shamela* reads Pamela as if she is hiding the truth, *Joseph Andrews* reminds us that we rarely know everything, in fiction as in real life.[14] *Pamela*, in contrast, tries to exemplify a hermeneutics of trust. There is no intentional irony in Richardson's text, although this does not prevent ironic readings, such as are evident in *Shamela*, *Anti-Pamela* and *Joseph Andrews*. Indeed, the lack of overt irony in *Pamela* may have been an invitation to ironic response in this disputatious context.

Despite the protestations and assertions of Pamela and her author, then, not all readers accepted her account, or her perspective. Why did the novel invite such critical interventions? As this chapter has argued, there is no single answer to this question. The initial 'puffing' and publicity surrounding the publication of

*Pamela* attracted censure. So too did the content of its narrative – that it disguised lasciviousness under the pretence of prudery; that it affronted social stability by teaching servant-girls to 'catch' their masters and suggesting their masters might marry whoever they chose. Richardson's coyness about his own authorship also encouraged 'spurious' sequels. The phenomenal success of *Pamela* in turn inaugurated a market frenzy in which opportunistic publishing undoubtedly played some part. There is also the inevitable indeterminacy of all texts – exacerbated in *Pamela* by the anonymous authorship and first-person narrative. *Joseph Andrews*, as I argued above, is not open to nearly so many varied readings because of its controlled narrative form. Moreover, into an already disputatious context, Richardson himself reviewed and reread his own original text (in its revisions, in its sequel, in debates about *Clarissa*, in letters to friends). The more Richardson attempted to fix his text, however, the more it slipped away from him. Indeed, Richardson's certainties were received as an invitation to rebuke:

> The positively pronouncing a Thing quite perfect, and the only good one of its Kind upon your meer *ipse Dixi*, is something so novel, and tacitly calling all Fools who shall dare to swerve from that Opinion, gives it such an Air of Consequence and assur'd Success, as may prevail on many, who feareth no farther than the Surface to believe it to *be* what it is *represented*. (*Pamela Censured*, 12)

Not only were there 'misreadings', motivated 'rereadings', and authorial emendations and revisions, but there were also rewritings. These in turn altered the terms of the debates, the perspectives on the fictional characters. Richardson wrote his continuation of *Pamela, Pamela in her Exalted Condition*, as an inevitable response to the unauthorised sequels (*Pamela's Conduct in High Life*, 1741 and *The Life of Pamela*, 1742) and to such attacks as *Shamela* and *Pamela Censured*.[15] *Joseph Andrews* responds to *Pamela in her Exalted Condition* as much as to *Pamela*. Indeed, the careers of Fielding and Richardson as novelists have been read as increasingly dialogic and even, ultimately, interchangeable (with Richardson becoming more Fieldingesque in *Sir Charles Grandison* and Fielding writing a version of *Pamela* in his last novel, *Amelia*).[16] Any discussion of the political implications of *Pamela* and its many sequels and counter-fictions, then, is caught up in the multiple refractions of alternative readings and characterisations, made by Richardson himself and by his readers and rewriters.

## Notes

1. Quoted in McKillop 1960, 101–2 who identifies this passage as plagiarised from Ludvig Holberg's *Moral Thoughts* (1744).
2. See the 'General Introduction' by Keymer and Sabor to the six volumes of *The Pamela Controversy* (2001) for an excellent account of this publishing frenzy.
3. Armstrong 1987 argues that *Pamela* exemplifies how the construction of femininity as domestic masks its significant political power. A comparison with William Godwin's novel *Caleb Williams* (1794) serves to underscore how the 'domestic' setting of *Pamela* and the respectable femininity of its heroine have disguised its subversion. The story of *Caleb Williams* is also voiced by its servant-narrator, oppressed by his aristocratic master.
4. All references to *Pamela* are to the modern reprinting of the 1740 edition, unless otherwise stated.
5. The homely diction of the 1740 heroine, however, is already in tension with her genteel accomplishments (such as embroidery and writing poetry) and her fine clothes (Mr B, for example, gives her shoes and silk stockings which belonged to his mother). Pamela's frequent fainting would also have been seen as particular to ladies of sensibility, not to robust serving girls. For the equivocal position of the ladies maid, see Bowen 1999.
6. Jan Fergus's detailed research into the accounts of one eighteenth-century bookseller (the Clays of Daventry, Rugby, Lutterworth and Warwick) found that Richardson was the only novelist to have attracted servant readers (Fergus 1996, 217).
7. The terms of this contrast are taken from Castle 1986, 360. Gooding 1995 discusses the irony that both Pamelists and anti-Pamelists serve a more conservative political agenda than the novel to which they reply in different fashions. That the ending of *Joseph Andrews* functioned conservatively can be seen in the prefatory letter to the French translation by Pierre François Guyot Desfontaines (1744). Countering those who would criticise the love of a lady for her servant, the 'English lady' (the ostensible author of the letter) attempts various defences: that Lady Booby herself condemns the thought of such a marriage and does not, in fact, marry Joseph; that the Bible described such a love in that of Potiphar's wife for Joseph; and that French paintings and theatre

have already represented such scenes. The defence ends, however, with the abrupt: 'Besides, this servant was a gentleman' (Paulson and Lockwood 1969, 129).

8. The only significant exception to these more conservative 'Pamelist' texts is Giffard's dramatic version *Pamela: A Comedy* (1741), which is truer to the spirit of Richardson's novel than most. See, for example, Longman's defence of a servant obeying his conscience rather than his master (I iv) and Pamela's bold rebuke to Belvile: countering and echoing his criticism (Belvile: 'Remember who you speak to –'. Pamela: 'Sir, do you remember who you speak to –'; 48).

9. In 1804, Barbauld wrote of how *Pamela II* was 'less a continuation than the author's defense of himself' (I, lxxvii). For a reading which counters Castle's of *Pamela*, Part II, see Gooding 1995, 113–16.

10. See Eaves and Kimpel 1967, 64; 79–80.

11. McKeon argues that this is a utopian ending within the limits of contemporary society, even if qualified in so far as Pamela's transformation leaves existing social conditions unaltered (1987, 380–81).

12. Parson Oliver's explanation for the writing of *Pamela* is that its letters were written up after the event (not 'to the moment' as Pamela claims).

13. See also Joseph's response to Lady Booby's hypothetical articulation of her desire: 'I can't see why her having no Virtue should be a Reason against my having any. Or why, because I am a Man, or because I am poor, my Virtue must be subservient to her Pleasures' (36).

14. When the narrator questions whether the Constable was bribed by the thief to help him escape, he claims that he will accept the Constable's innocence because he has been 'positively assured of it, by those who received their Informations from his own Mouth; which, in the Opinion of some Moderns, is the best and indeed only Evidence' (Fielding 1980, 63–4). But the narrator only plays the part of an innocent in order to satirise Richardson.

15. That the response is 'inevitable' is due to potential readers reading in this light, as much as to Richardson's own intentions. See Jenkins 1965 for a reading of *Pamela in her Exalted Condition* as a response to *Shamela*.

16. See Sabor 1982.

# Textual Conversations: Conclusion

The kind of historicism I outline in this book is one of tracing motifs which are general to all periods but take distinctive forms in the eighteenth century. What makes these textual exchanges or variations-on-themes distinctive to this period? Although the proliferation of texts would be familiar to a twenty-first-century reader – as, for example, in the fashion for popular science narratives which followed the publication of Dava Sobel's *Longitude* (1995), a surprise commercial success – this phenomenon is different in kind from what we see in our eighteenth-century examples. These later attempts are imitations, but they are not responses to the original text. They emulate only its success. In no sense, then, are these later imitations engaging in a conversation with the original text. This is true too of periods earlier than the eighteenth. If we take the example of Swift's *A Tale of a Tub*, we see another text that generated a significant number of keys, observations and imitations. In their edition of the *Tale*, Guthkelch and Nichol Smith name seven subsequent texts with derivative titles, published between 1705 and 1749 (Swift 1958, lxxvi–lxxvii). But the subjects of these texts rarely counter or relate to Swift's *Tale*. For example, *A Tale of a Bottomless Tub* (1723) is a poem in which Venus and Cupid debate which sex merits most applause; *A Tale of Two Tubs* (1749) is a poem on the brothers the Duke of Newcastle and Henry Pelham. Only one of the seven – *A Morning's Discourse of a Bottomless Tubb* (1712) – uses its introduction to attack the *Tale*. Of more interest to this section have been those texts which respond to, comment on or rewrite the original text.

What might account for the proliferation of these print conversations in the eighteenth century? The prevalence of keys and observations can be explained by the tendency of many satires to disguise their targets, in an age in which legislation permitted fictional aliases and the use of initials or dropped letters to 'disguise' a specific target and thus to escape prosecution for libel. Published keys therefore popularly and quickly followed any works which seemed to require or invite decoding, whether of allegorical narratives or disguised identities. All of the following texts inspired published keys: *Hudibras, The Pilgrim's Progress, Absalom and Achitophel, The Rape of the Lock, The Dunciad, A Tale of a Tub, Gulliver's Travels, The Rehearsal, The Non-Juror, The Dispensary, Law is a Bottomless Pit, Three Hours After Marriage, The What D'Ye Call It, Memoirs of the New Atalantis.* The *Eighteenth-Century Short Title Catalogue* reveals hundreds of published keys in the eighteenth century. As Paul Korshin has argued: 'The more popular the work, the more likely the key – assuming the work had enough blanks, obscure names, substitutions and strange dialects to warrant decoding' (Korshin 1985, 127). In the particular case of the Scriblerians, their dislike of such textual innovations as prefaces, footnote annotations, introductions, acknowledgements, commentaries, keys, observations and, most especially, indexes, meant that many of their works aped the very conventions they derided.[1] As early as 1715, for example, Pope published a mock commentary on his own *Rape of the Lock*, identifying an absurdly far-fetched Jacobitism in the poem: *The Key to the Lock or, a Treatise Proving beyond All Contradiction, the Dangerous Tendency of a Late Poem, Entitled, The Rape of the Lock, to Government and Religion.*[2] Legislation actually encouraged the continual exchange of satirical attacks, since evidence of counter-attacks could prevent prosecution for personal libel. In the libel laws of the eighteenth century, the defence could plead provocation as part of its evidence. Some have suspected that Pope published *Peri Bathous* (March 1728) with its obvious attack on many dunces deliberately in advance of *The Dunciad*, so as to provoke their attacks. *The Dunciad* (and the *Dunciad Variorum* of the following year) could then be justified under the plea of provocation.[3]

The significant number of imitations might also be linked to the pervasiveness of satire in the period. The Scriblerians in particular tended to attack their enemies and rivals through imitation, parody and burlesque. *Gulliver's Travels*, Pope's essay on pastoral poetry, the footnotes of the *Dunciad Variorum* editions and the mock-treatise on the 'profound' in poetry (*The Peri-Bathous: Or the Art of Sinking in Poetry*) are all well-known examples, here parodying the travelogue, the defence of the new pastoral espoused by Philips, the scholarly edition and pseudo-scientific treatise.[4]

Countless eighteenth-century writers use parody (which tends to imitate both style and subject) and burlesque (which creates comic incongruity when the imitated style is deployed for a widely different subject). A popular example of eighteenth-century burlesque is Isaac Hawkins Browne's collection of poetic parodies of Pope, Swift, Colley Cibber, Ambrose Philips, Edward Young and James Thomson, *A Pipe of Tobacco* (1736). All of their various styles are pastiched in poetic apostrophes to tobacco. Thus 'Pope's' poem crisply folds into heroic couplets and polished antitheses:

> Blest leaf! whose aromatic gales dispense
> To templars modesty, to parsons sense
> So raptured priests, at famed Dodona's shrine,
> Drank inspiration from the steam divine.

while 'Thomson's' swells in sumptuous evocations of nature:

> O thou matured by glad Hesperian suns
> Tobacco, fountain pure of limpid truth,
> That looks the very soul whence pouring thought
> Swarms all the mind; absorpt in yellow care,
> And at each puff imagination burns. (Quoted in Kitchin 1931, 120)

The competitive play of parodies and burlesques is a particular feature of the Nonsense Club. In the *Drury-Lane Journal*, for example, Bonnell Thornton attacked the dullness of *The Covent-Garden Journal* through imitation. *The Drury-Lane Journal* made no pretence of being a 'real' periodical. Even its advertisements were fakes. Its sole purpose was to make its rival seem ridiculous. Similarly, Colman and Lloyd's *Two Odes* (1760) burlesqued the poetry of William Mason and Thomas Gray. In the disputatious print culture of the eighteenth century, parodies, burlesques and absurd imitations were deployed more frequently than any other form of attack.

The transition from manuscript to print culture in the eighteenth century might account for the variety of texts involved in these kinds of print activity. As all of these chapters show, authors themselves were involved in the responses to their own work. Publication was rarely a once-for-all moment in the composition of each of these, and other, texts. Instead, constant revisions are a remarkably consistent feature of many eighteenth-century texts. In addition to the examples discussed in this chapter are countless others. Swift's addition of an 'Apology' to the fifth edition of his *Tale* (1710), six years after its first edition, drew a much more orthodox reading out of the text than many readers had originally found there. Sarah Fielding's *The Adventures of David Simple, Volume the Last* (1753), her sequel to her own novel (1744), was a much darker exploration of the possibility of virtue in a corrupt society. Now the innocent David would witness the suffering of his family, powerless to protect them. Constant self-revisions, then, might be the consequence of the author's own change of perspective, or a response to the first receptions of his or her text. That authors were so ready to rush into print responses to their own works might be a feature of a culture in which the fixity of print is only just being understood. A second aspect of this transition from a predominantly manuscript to a print culture is also the generic playfulness of the period. Jeanne Welcher argues that the enabling assumptions of readers responding to a familiar genre and the misunderstandings which innovations to those genres generate is the cause of the phenomenal number of textual replies to *Gulliver's Travels*.

The commercial opportunism evident in the twentieth-century imitations of *Longitude* is obviously part of the narrative of these print phenomena too. Many of the printed responses are rather plodding, 'hack' work, produced to order, to make a quick profit rather than to please aesthetically. This is especially true of the attacks on and responses to Pope, many of which are personally abusive and far from pleasant reading. In one of the sequels to *Pamela*, the anonymously written *Pamela in High Life: or, Virtue Rewarded*, the life of the married Pamela is so uneventful that its author expatiates instead on such diverse topics as explaining what functions an alderman performs, the marvellous economy of ants and bees, the motion of the earth and the tides of the Thames, and whether the Flood covered the entire earth. It also includes a sermon on the Gunpowder Plot and a substantial amount of geographical information: sketches of English cities, a 37-page description of Russia, and a 10-page description of the rest of Europe, a third of it devoted to the clock of Strasbourg. Eaves and Kimpel view this compendia of accounts as illustrating the difficulty of 'making a novel out of Pamela's married life' (1971 141).[5] It also suggests that the cachet of the *Pamela* title was sufficient to sell any kind of text. Certainly many of the imitations flaunted allusions to *Pamela* in their titles only so as to increase the chances of their sale. Richard Gooding notes, for example, that Parry's *The True Anti-Pamela* seems to have been written before the publication of *Pamela* and thus displays 'a blatantly adventitious title' (Gooding 1995, 110 n2). At their worst, then, these 'textual conversations' resemble the book machine which Gulliver discovers in the Academy of Lagado. Writing here is thoroughly mechanised, writers are without education, artistry, or talent and words proliferate for their own sake. The vision of the book machine is a nightmare one, presenting a view of print as ultimately anarchic.

That this is a culture of proliferating print is also reflected in the tendency of texts to refer to putative sequels and spin-offs. In *Moll Flanders* (1722), Defoe seems constantly tempted by the story of Jemy, and avoids being digressive only by repeatedly suggesting another book might tell his story (Defoe 1981, 5, 301, 339). In *Tom Jones*, Fielding suggests a conversation between Squire Western and the Squire he meets hunting when he is chasing Sophia might be related in 'an appendix, or on some other occasion' (1996, 544). Additional texts might thus be welcomed as continuing the 'histories' of characters. Alternatively, they are rivals. In the final paragraph of *Volume the Last*, Sarah Fielding's narrator imagines that false sequels might attempt to drag David Simple back from the grave and warns that this would only be to renew his sufferings (432). Negative accounts of imitations and sequels might also be seen as part of the increasing valorisation of originality in the eighteenth century. The 'Essay on the New Species of Writing Founded by Mr Fielding' (1751), probably written by Francis Coventry, discusses imitations as reflecting the power of an original text and their own inability to emulate that power: 'so infatuated are the modern Tribe of Imitators that they imagine all the Commendations due to their great Masters, equally the Desert of them, their Followers: and that the same Road that led the first to Glory will guide them also, without ever reflecting whether they are equally furnish'd for the Journey' (Coventry 1962, 37). Sequels and imitations might flourish in a literary culture which is only just beginning to identify and celebrate the concept of literary originality.

This aesthetic debate is also part of the history of the rise of literary criticism as an institution and profession. Professional literary criticism may be said to start in Button's coffee house, with the circle around Addison, many of whom wrote for the *Spectator* and *Guardian* periodicals. By the mid-century, a sudden growth in book reviewing is largely due to the founding of specifically literary periodicals, especially the rival *Monthly Review* (1749) and *Critical Review* (1756). Throughout the period, however, literary criticism can be found as much in 'creative' literature – novels, plays, poems – which discusses books and the theatre as in the formal reviews. In *Evelina*, for example, the company discusses Congreve's *Love for Love* at some length (Burney 2000, 181–4). In *The Expedition of Humphry Clinker*, Tabitha and Quin discuss the ghost of Hamlet (or the 'Ghost of Gimlet' as Tabitha insists on calling him; Smollett 1984, 53). And Charles Macklin's *The New Play Criticiz'd* (1747) dramatises an account of the first performance of Benjamin Hoadly's *The Suspicious Husband*.[6] Clifford Siskin has explored the historicity of the distinction between 'creative' and 'critical' (1998, 37–63) and a number of his conclusions about eighteenth-century writing precipitate the point argued here, that all of these print conversations made writing necessarily self-reflexive and tended to erase the distinction between the 'creative' and the 'critical':

> that concern *with* writing . . . . articulated *in* writing, made writing as much an object of inquiry as a means: writing about writing produced more writing in a self-reflexive proliferation. All writing became, in that sense, critical. (Siskin 1998, 176)

The parodies and burlesques discussed above often served as forms of literary criticism. Parodies might be written in admiration or in contempt of an originating work. Whichever of these perspectives were adopted, the parody often served as a commentary upon its original. The burlesques of Mason and Gray in *Two Odes* repeat many of the criticisms made by Lloyd in *The Monthly Review*, the excessive use of adjectives in their modern odes in particular: 'The *cloud-built height*, the *pebbled shore*, the *surging brook, flower-hid path*, pellucid stream, moss-grown bed, and quivering beam, are infinitely too pretty for the poetry of nature; a profusion of such epithets cloys the taste' (quoted in Bertelsen 1986, 98). The 'New Chapter in Amelia' which Bonnell Thornton published in *The Drury-Lane Journal* (13 Feb. 1752), depicts the sentimental scene of Booth's family waiting for his return, in which Amelia's extreme tenderness, her children's simplicity, the drunken learnedness of Mrs Atkinson, the boorishness of Booth and the coarseness of Fielding's style are all exaggerated for comic and satiric effect. Elevated diction is juxtaposed vertiginously with slang: 'All hands were now aloft in assisting to sweeten poor Booth, who, after having puk'd awhile, recover'd his senses sufficiently to remember how he came in this condition' (Paulson and Lockwood 1969, 323). In Bertelsen's reading of this parody, it is one of the best contemporary pieces of criticism on *Amelia* (Bertelsen 1986, 21).

The kinds of social sphere – of literary clubs and networks of friends, writers and readers – sketched in the introduction and first chapter of this book also account for some of these replies and responses. True of all of the literary clubs in the eighteenth century, for example, is the tendency to write works addressed to each other, continuations of each other's work and works directly inspired by others' ideas and writings. The chapters in Part II indicate the ways in which literature was often produced out of the conversation between authors in eighteenth-century culture. In the case of *The Dunciad* and *Gulliver's Travels*, the personal friendship of Pope and Swift and the literary creativity and strong opinions which circulated around their associated club, the Scriblerians, make the issues discussed in each chapter equally applicable to the other. Many of the responses to these works also link Swift and Pope, demonstrating the importance of their friendship and of the group known as the Scriblerians, in the reading of their contemporaries. Richardson's circle of readers, many of them women, indefatigably discussed and wrote letters on his fiction, especially *Clarissa* and *Sir Charles Grandison*, which were published serially and thus permitted Richardson to counter and (more rarely, alter) his text according to their views. Readers such as Lady Bradshaigh, Edward Young and the teenage daughters of Aaron Hill were given bound copies of his novels in which interleaved blank pages encouraged them to intersperse their comments.[7] And, as we have seen in chapter 2, Richardson claimed that debate among his readers was an important means of making them as much authors as readers: 'It is not an unartful Management to interest the Readers so much in the Story, as to make them differ in Opinion as to the Capital Articles, and by Leading one, to espouse one, another, another, Opinion, make them all, if not Authors, Carpers' (Richardson 1964, 296).

Richardson's ideal for readers might be seen to be embodied in the huge number of texts which succeeded his own work and that of other significant eighteenth-century writers. There are therefore a great many possible explanations for the distinctiveness of eighteenth-century print culture, all of which take us to the heart of key debates in the period (such as questions of originality, or of what constitutes libel) and key issues for our study of the period (the pervasiveness of satire, the nature of literary criticism, the significance of literary groups). These textual exchanges reinforce the sense in which eighteenth-century literary culture constitutes a 'republic of letters'. Writers used these responses for a variety of reasons: perhaps to challenge a rival faction or to defend or forge an allegiance with the group surrounding the original text; to prolong the sense of speaking to a community of readers, or to refuse the false closure which ending a text represents.[8] They remind us that, even when eighteenth-century texts do not openly thematise dialogues and debates or necessarily use aspects of conversational style, their own culture situated them within a context of public conversation.

## Notes

1. For the Scriblerians' disapproval of many modern textual innovations, see Lund 1998.
2. Pope published this work under the pseudonym of 'Esdras Barnivelt', which comically suggested associations with apothecaries and the Dutch, both of which were suspect to the English. The *Key* was a pre-emptive strike on Pope's part, in an atmosphere of political tension. (On the accession of George I in August 1714, Tory politicians, and friends of Pope such as Bolingbroke and Oxford, were removed from office. Bolingbroke fled to France: Oxford was imprisoned in the Tower in July 1715.) This is not, of course, to say that possible political interpretations are not 'there'. See Paul Hammond's comment that: '*A Key* seems simultaneously to alert readers to *The Rape*'s political implications and to suggest that Pope himself can carry no responsibility for whatever political significance his readers find there' (Hammond 1987, 73).
3. See, for example, Sutherland in Pope 1963, xvi–xvii. The *Peri Bathous* could have been defended in court as not specifically naming the apparent victims – Pope claimed that he picked the initials given there at random. For details on libel legislation in the eighteenth century, see Kropf 1974–5.

4. See Brean Hammond 1988a.
5. Kelly's sequel *Pamela's Conduct in High Life* is also capacious enough to include its narrator's reflections upon spreading scandal, the iniquities of criticising the clergy, the truthfulness of the Book of Job, the ways in which George Herbert's poetry had been underestimated, the importance of trade to the nation, why the doctrine of Election through Grace was wrong, why clergymen should not hold many livings and so on. (See Eaves and Kimpel 1971, 139.)
6. See the list of 'Plays about the Theatre, 1737–1800' included as an appendix in Smith and Lawhon 1979, 213–25.
7. See Eaves and Kimpel 1971, 120. In *Pamela in her Exalted Condition*, Pamela talks of her intention to print and bind her letters on education, offering her reader (Mr B) 'one side of the leaf blank for your corrections and alterations' (Richardson 1914, II 420). For accounts of the composition of *Pamela, Clarissa* and *Sir Charles Grandison* through Richardson's correspondence with a circle of friends, see Sabor 1981, Eaves and Kimpel 1968 and Jocelyn Harris's introduction to the 1972 edition respectively.
8. See Schellenberg's argument that in writing sequels, Sarah Fielding, Sarah Scott and Frances Sheridan won 'a faceless audience over to the role of old friends' (1996 97) and J. Paul Hunter's essay on how eighteenth-century writers in general refused closure (1997).

# 7 Afterword: Continuing the Conversation

This study has situated eighteenth-century literature in the context of ideas of coteries and communities of various kinds: literary groups, informal networks of support and collaboration; the communities of readers and spectators and the particular literary forms which seek to call such communities into existence; and the textual communities which surround texts when works are pulled into debates and defences by imitations and parodies. In doing so, it has joined an increasing number of studies which attempt to move beyond traditional paradigms of the period, such as the 'age of reason' or 'Augustan literature' giving way to an age of 'sensibility'. No paradigm can totally explain a literary period in all its variety. If we think of the eighteenth century as an age of 'sociability' or of literary coteries, then we also need to remember the ways in which these ideas were contradicted by their own culture. This book has thus also emphasised the way in which many writers feared the fracturing of literary communities in the wake of print culture with its anonymous, unknown readers; how representations of community were as likely to reflect upon disputation and noise as upon acts of rational communication and amicable persuasion. At the heart of this book, then, is an ideal model of conversation as debate. The conversation initiated by this study needs to be supplemented with other stories and voices.

The model of the period as one in which the author as an identifiable individual emerges, for example, is the reverse image of the attempts discussed here – to incorporate oneself and one's readers into a known community. The modern idea of the writer as an inspired individual can certainly be traced to changes evident within eighteenth-century culture. Edward Young's *Conjectures on Original Composition* (1759), for example, is often read as originating the 'Romantic' criteria of originality, or Samuel Johnson's *Lives of the Poets* (1779–81) is the work which consolidates the importance of the individual, named and understood, author. Both of these moments refuse the importance of convention and tradition, or, in the terms of this book, conversation and debate with predecessors, contemporaries and putative heirs. Much recent criticism has also mapped these changes persuasively. Martha Woodmansee (1984, 1994) and Mark Rose (1993) have written of how changes in copyright legislation during the century reflect as they also constitute the idea of literary genius. Barbara Benedict (1996) and Clifford Siskin (1998) have written of how the naming of authors becomes increasingly important as the century progresses, how, in Siskin's terms, the concept of 'Author-before-Work' gains in importance. Their research suggests that the importance of group identity and formations is true of the early period, but that the century witnesses a shift to a much more individualistic culture which anticipates what we tend to associate with Romanticism. The evidence they offer for this shift is certainly persuasive. But it is equally possible to see the coterie formations of the earlier century continuing across the century. A number of recent studies explore the sociable communities and public conversations out of which Romantic literature is also formed.[1] These challenge the stereotypical image of the solitary Romantic writer and the argument that the 1790s witnessed the disintegration of community and consensus in the heat of Revolutionary debate.[2] If eighteenth-century literature was for a long time constructed as the antithetical foil to ideas of 'Romanticism' (as discussed in the preface), then new studies of Romantic sociability teach us that 'Romanticism' has similarly been misconstrued as the individualistic, solitary other of the eighteenth century.

Putting accounts of the eighteenth century together with those of the Romantic period, in what the academy now recognises under the designation of the 'long eighteenth century', is one way of countering these kinds of interested constructions. This kind of larger paradigm also permits other stories of the eighteenth century to be told. This book has had little to say about eighteenth-century escapes of various kinds – to dusky twilight and lonely churchyards (in the popularity of night-pieces and graveyard poetry); to the retreat of the countryside (in the significant number of descriptive poems such as Thomson's *The Seasons*); to explorations of introspection (as in Collins's rhapsodic preoccupation with subjectivity); to antiquarianism (in the forgeries of medieval poetry by Macpherson, Chatterton and in the imitations of

Spenser, such as Akenside's *The Castle of Indolence*); to religious enthusiasm (in the hymn-writing of Watts and the Wesleys, the accounts of Methodist conversion or Smart's ecstatic piety). In important work by Sitter (1982) and Bogel (1984), poetry from the 1750s is characterised by a turning away from society, towards poetic introspection and, sometimes, alienation. Perhaps like all dominant paradigms, however, their arguments have also been increasingly questioned. Dustin Griffin (2002) argues that we have neglected the considerable body of patriotic poetry in which the poet assumes a public role, written by, for example, Thomson, Akenside, Collins, Gray, Dyer, Goldsmith and Smart. This tradition certainly includes the social visions of patriotic georgic (largely recovered to us through John Goodridge's readings of such poems as Dyer's *The Fleece* and Grainger's *The Sugar-Cane*). Similarly, Linda Zionkowski (2001) argues that William Mason's construction of Gray as a 'melancholy' poet in his posthumous edition of Gray's poems (1775), ignores the satiric work and Heidi Thomson (1998), in reading his letters, argues that we have exaggerated the isolation of Gray. In other recent studies of Thomas Gray, an interest in his poetry's homoeroticism and the homosocial contexts in which he wrote predominates.[3] And throughout the editorial apparatus of *Eighteenth-Century Poetry*, Fairer and Gerrard foreground the continuity between poetry of the early and later eighteenth centuries. Thus, poetry on the contemplation of ruins is not reserved to the so-called 'graveyard' school (such as Robert Blair's *The Grave*, 1743), but extends from Pope (*Windsor-Forest*), through Dyer ('Grongar Hill') before gaining the notoriety of traditional literary history in the fashion for Gothic (as in Walpole's *The Castle of Otranto*, 1764) and antiquarianism (in the forgeries and Spenserian and romance revival of the 1750s and 1760s).[4]

The motifs of conversations and circles engaged throughout this book might include these other kinds of literature as part of its narrative. Gray and Macpherson, like countless other writers, found themselves imitated and parodied in the manner of the texts considered in Part II: William Whitehead's parody of Ossian in *Gisbal* (1762) and the anonymous parody of Gray's Eton ode, 'Ode on Ranelagh, Addressed to the Ladies' (1763), are just two examples.[5] But we might also think of the importance of Shaftesbury and Hutcheson to the poetry of Thomson and Akenside, such that, for example, spring is praised for its social benevolence: 'Great Spring, before, / Green'd all the Year; and Fruits and Blossoms blush'd, / In social Sweetness, on the self-same Bough' (Thomson, 'Spring', ll. 320–2).[6] We might think too of how Macpherson and Chatterton were attempting to reconstruct the voices and the *communities* of the past. Indeed, the poems of isolation which Sitter and Bogel discuss are simultaneously laments for dispersed and disappearing communities. Peter Manning's discussion of Gray's 'Sonnet' on the death of Richard West situates it in the kind of context sketched in chapter 1 of this book: the echoes of West's own poem 'Ad Amicos', of Tibullus and a letter from Pope to Steele printed in *The Guardian*, all 'place Gray's lament within the exchanges of a circle of men of letters. . . . The reader who recognizes the allusions is urbanely complimented, drawn into the band of initiates' (Manning 1982, 517). A number of other recent critics have drawn attention to Gray's attempt to construct a community of readers for his work. Linda Zionkowski, for example, discusses the ways in which Gray's *Odes* of 1757 ('The Bard' and 'The Progress of Poetry') are written to exclude certain kinds of reader and to construct an idealised, elite audience, and she argues that all of Gray's work is written to combat the incipient vulgarity and debasement which he sees infecting the literary market (Zionkowski 2001). This makes him just as close to the concerns of Pope and Swift as to the 'flight from society' which Sitter sees as characteristic of mid-century poetry.

However, it would be wrong to seek to bend all literature to one model, even one which permits various conclusions and arguments. Eighteenth-century literature displays a huge diversity of forms, in an age which does not yet recognise the 'literary' as only the imaginative or fictional, an age, moreover, characterised by continual formal experimentation and revision. Under the auspices of new historicism, Stephen Greenblatt has argued that there is no 'whole reading', nor even the illusion of one, possible any more: 'the impression created by powerful critics that had they but world enough and time, they could illuminate every corner of the text and knit together into a unified interpretative vision all of their discrete perceptions' (Greenblatt 1988, 4). No vision of a period can be a totalising one. No single reading of a text is possible. The paradigms of this book, the motifs of conversations and communities, do not impose a single vision upon the period or a single reading on any text. Instead, they have been chosen because they permit and historicise the operation of consensus and dissensus in the reception of literary works, evident in eighteenth-century readings as much as twenty-first-century ones; because they figure literature as a site of social and cultural contention; because they permit canonical and non-canonical writers to be discussed together and encourage us to raise questions of how literature participates in processes of inclusion and exclusion. In the spirit of the eighteenth-century ideals of interaction and rationality as *process* rather than *product*, this book hopes, in considering eighteenth-century literature through ideas of conversations and communities, to have engaged in the wider conversations about how, why and if we might characterise literature of this period. And it looks to students and other studies to keep the conversation going.

## Notes

1. See, for example, Haefner 1994, Magnuson 1998, Russell and Tuite 2002.
2. This argument can be found in the focus on the 1790s as the period in which reading audiences fragmented (Klancher 1987), radical circles constituted a counter public sphere (Eagleton 1984), or the 'republic of letters' became discredited through its association with political radicalism (Cook 1996).
3. See Bentman 1992; Haggerty 1999; Gleckner 1997. For an early discussion, see Hagstrum 1974.
4. See Fairer and Gerrard 1999, 225n.
5. See Mack 1998 for the anonymous 'Ode on Ranelagh'. The earliest parody of Gray is John Duncombe's parody of the *Elegy*, *Evening Contemplation in a College* (1753).
6. See Inglesfield 1986, Fabel 1997 and Sambrook's introduction and annotations to *The Seasons* (Thomson 1972).

# Chronology 1714–1779

| Births and deaths | Principal publications and theatre productions | Cultural and scientific events | Historical and political events |
|---|---|---|---|
| **1714** | | | |
| | Centlivre, *The Wonder*; Gay, *Shepherd's Week*; Mandeville, *Fable of the Bees*; Manley, *History of Rivella*; Pope, *Rape of the Lock* (5-canto version) | Addison & Steele, *The Spectator* (2nd series); John Rich opens theatre at Lincoln's Inn Fields | Death of Queen Anne; accession of George I; Tory government is dismissed |
| **1715** | | | |
| | Defoe, *Family Instructor* (–1718); *Iliad*, trans. Pope (–1720); Watts, *Divine Songs for the Use of Children* | Nicholas Rowe, poet laureate; Society of Ancient Britons founded to promote Welsh culture; Leoni, *Architecture of A. Palladio*; Richard Temple begins building and garden work at Stowe; book club established in Doncaster | 1st Jacobite rebellion aiming to overthrow the Hanoverian succession fails; Tory defeat in general election; Robert Harley, Earl of Oxford, imprisoned and impeached; Bolingbroke flees to France |
| **1716** Thomas Gray b. | Gay, *Trivia*; Wortley Montagu, *Court Poems* | Hanover Square, London, begun; St Paul's Cathedral completed; | Septennial Act lengthens the maximum duration of a |

| Births and deaths | Principal publications and theatre productions | Cultural and scientific events | Historical and political events |
|---|---|---|---|
| | | London Grand Lodge of Free-masons formed | parliament from three to seven years; Whig split: Walpole v Townshend |
| **1717** David Garrick b. Horace Walpole b. (d.1797) Elizabeth Carter b. (d.1806) | Gay, *Three Hours After Marriage*; Jacob, *Rape of the Smock*; Pope, *Eloisa to Abelard* in Collected Works | Heidegger organises weekly masquerades at the Haymarket theatre (–1730s); Handel, *Chandos Anthems* (–18); *Water Music*; Newton, *Opticks*; Society of Antiquaries founded | |
| **1718** Thomas Parnell d. (b.1679) | Centlivre, *A Bold Stroke for a Wife*; *The Ladies Miscellany*, published by Curll; Prior, *Poems on Several Occasions* | Eusden, poet laureate; Gay & Handel, *Acis and Galatea*; *Esther*; Welsh language press established at Trerhedyn (Ceredigion) | |
| **1719** Joseph Addison d. (b.1672) | Defoe, *Robinson Crusoe*; Haywood, *Love in Excess*; Watts, *Psalms of David Imitated* | Royal Academy of Music is established to promote opera (–1728) | War with Spain declared; Jacobite invasion in Scotland |
| **1720** Anne Finch d. (b.1661) Elizabeth Montagu b. Charlotte | Defoe, *Captain Singleton*; *Memoirs of a Cavalier*; Gay, *Collected Poems* | Little Theatre in the Haymarket is built; Cavendish Sq, London, begun; Westminster | South Sea Bubble: many investors ruined after speculation in South Sea stock; |

| Births and deaths | Principal publications and theatre productions | Cultural and scientific events | Historical and political events |
|---|---|---|---|
| Lennox b. (d.1804) | | Hospital founded, the 1st subscription hospital | Declaratory Act |
| **1721** | | | |
| Matthew Prior d. (b.1664) Mark Akenside b. Hester Chapone b. William Collins b. Tobias Smollett b. | Penelope Aubin, *Count de Vinevil*; Montesquieu, *Lettres persanes* | The Honourable Society for Improvement in the Knowledge of Agriculture; 1st smallpox inoculations introduced by Lady Mary Wortley Montagu | Walpole in power, the first 'prime minister' in all but name |
| **1722** | | | |
| Susanna Centlivre d. (b.1669) Christopher Smart b. Mary Leapor b. | Defoe, *Moll Flanders*; *Journal of the Plague Year*; *Colonel Jack*; Haywood, *British Recluse*; Parnell, *Poems*; Steele, *Conscious Lovers* | Guy's Hospital founded | Atterbury Plot, the most notable Jacobite plot: Walpole exposes Bishop Atterbury |
| **1723** | | | |
| | Barker, *Patchwork Screen for the Ladies*; Mandeville, *Fable of the Bees* (2nd, expanded edition); Ramsay, *Tea-Table Miscellany* (–1737) | The Roman Club founded (–1742) | Bishop Atterbury goes into exile; Wood's halfpence controversy in Ireland; Act for construction of workhouses; Black Acts attempt to limit poaching |
| **1724** | | | |
| Frances Sheridan b. | *Venus in the Cloyster: or the Nun in her Smock* | Handel, *Giulio Cesare*; *Tamerlano* | 'Leveller's revolt' v enclosures in south-west |

| Births and deaths | Principal publications and theatre productions | Cultural and scientific events | Historical and political events |
|---|---|---|---|
| | publ. Curll; Davys, *Reform'd Coquet*; Defoe, *Roxana*; *Tour through Great Britain* (–1726); Haywood, *A Wife to be Lett*; *Works*; Ramsay, *Evergreen*, collection of early Scots poems; Swift, *Drapier's Letters* | | Scotland |
| **1725** | Davys, *Works*; Haywood, *Fantomina*; *The Tea Table*; 'Hillarian' circle, *Miscellaneous Poems*; Hutcheson, *Inquiry into Beauty and Virtue*; Pope, edition of Shakespeare; trans. *Odyssey* (–1726) | 1st circulating libraries open in Bath and in Edinburgh; Grosvenor Sq, London, begun; Blenheim Palace completed; Handel, *Rodelina* | |
| **1726** Jane Barker d. (fl.1668) | Barker, *Lining of the Patch-Work Screen*; Haywood, *City Jilt*; *Mercenary Lover*; Swift, *Gulliver's Travels*; *Cadenus and Vanessa*; Thomson, *The Seasons: Winter* | Voltaire in England (–1729); Mary Toft convinces many, including the Royal Surgeon, that she has given birth to rabbits; Bolingbroke's opposition paper, *The Craftsman* begun; the Temple of the Four Winds, designed by Vanbrugh, is built at Castle Howard | |

| Births and deaths | Principal publications and theatre productions | Cultural and scientific events | Historical and political events |
|---|---|---|---|
| | | (–28); Academy of ancient Music founded | |
| **1727** | | | |
| | Mary Davys, *Accomplish'd Rake*; Gay, *Fables*; Pope, Swift, Arbuthnot, *Miscellanies* (–1732); Thomson, *The Seasons: Summer* | Kent, *Designs of Inigo Jones*; Heidegger condemned by royal proclamation | Death of George I; accession of George II; Royal Bank of Scotland founded |
| **1728** | | | |
| | Defoe, *Captain Carleton*; Fielding, *Love in Several Masques*; Gay, *Beggar's Opera*; Pope, *The Dunciad*; Elizabeth Rowe, *Friendship in Death*; Thomson, *The Seasons: Spring* | Jonathan Tyers acquires Vauxhall and begins to remodel the gardens and gentrify the clientele; Queen Sq, Bath, begun; Sedbergh book club inaugurated (–1928); the Royal Academy closes; weekly concerts begin in Edinburgh | |
| **1729** Richard Steele d. (b. 1672) Ignatius Sancho b. Clara Reeve b. (d. 1807) | Gay, *Polly*; *Mother Goose* (English translation of Perrault); Pope, *Dunciad Variorum*; Swift, *Modest Proposal*; Savage, *An Author to be Lett* | Thomson, *Britannia*; Heidegger condemned by the Middlesex Grand Jury; Parliament House, Dublin, begun; regular subscription concerts begin at | Wesley's Holy Club begins meeting |

| Births and deaths | Principal publications and theatre productions | Cultural and scientific events | Historical and political events |
|---|---|---|---|
| | | Hickford's Room, London | |
| **1730**<br>Oliver Goldsmith b. | Duck, *Thresher's Labour*; Fielding, *Tom Thumb*; *Modern Husband*; Thomson, *The Seasons* (inc. *Autumn* and *Hymn*) | Colley Cibber, poet laureate; *The Grub Street Journal* (–1737); Lindsey's Assembly Rooms, Bath, opened; Assembly Rooms, York, designed by Burlington (–1732) | Fall of Townshend; Methodist society formed in Oxford |
| **1731**<br>Daniel Defoe d. (b.1660) | Fielding, *Grub Street Opera*; Lillo, *London Merchant*; Pope, *Epistle to Burlington* | *The Gentleman's Magazine* launched, edited by Edward Cave (–1914); Hogarth, *Harlot's Progress*; Dublin Society formed | Treaty of Vienna with Austria |
| **1732**<br>John Gay d. (b.1685), Mary Davys d. (b.1674) | Berkeley, *Dialogues of Alciphron*; Fielding, *Covent Garden Tragedy*; Pope, *Epistle to Bathurst*; Swift, 'The Ladys Dressing Room' | *The London Magazine* (–1785); John Rich opens new Opera House at Covent Garden with proceeds of *The Beggar's Opera*; Jonathan Tyers opens Vauxhall gardens to the public; Kay invents flying shuttle; Burlington's Assembly Rooms, York, opened; the | Act requiring property qualification for English and Welsh county JPs |

| Births and deaths | Principal publications and theatre productions | Cultural and scientific events | Historical and political events |
|---|---|---|---|
| | | Dilettante Society established | |
| **1733** John Dunton d. (b.1659) | Haywood, *Opera of Operas*; Pope, *Essay on Man* (–1734); *Horace's Satire, II.i.*; Wortley Montagu, *Verses Address'd to the Imitator of Horace* | George Cheyne, *The English Malady*; The Opera of the Nobility is formed to rival the dominance of Handel (–1737) | Excise crisis: Walpole has to abandon his plans to reorganise the customs and excise; Secession Church in Scotland formed |
| **1734** | Pope, *Horace's Satire, II, ii.*; *Epistle to Cobham* | The Society of Dilettanti established, a dining society for gentlemen Grand Tourists, many of whom prided themselves on their connoisseur-ship of the arts; Handel, *Ariodante* | Walpole's majority reduced at general election |
| **1735** John Arbuthnot d. (b.1667) | Pope, *Epistle to Dr Arbuthnot*; *Epistle to a Lady*; Thomson, *Liberty* (–1736) | Hogarth, *Rake's Progress*; Handel, *Alcina*; Tyers builds a raised orchestra at Vauxhall | |
| **1736** | Browne, *A Pipe of Tobacco*; Duck, *Poems on Several Subjects*; Haywood, *Adventures of* | The 'Shakespeare Ladies Club' wages a campaign to promote performances of Shakespeare; | Statutes against witchcraft repealed; Porteous Riots, Edinburgh |

| Births and deaths | Principal publications and theatre productions | Cultural and scientific events | Historical and political events |
|---|---|---|---|
| | *Eovaii*; Swift, 'The Legion Club' | subscription concerts organised in Newcastle upon Tyne (–1770) | |
| **1737** Elizabeth Rowe d. (b.1674) | Cooper, *Muses Library*; Green, *The Spleen*; Pope, *Horace's Epistles, I.i., vi; II. I, ii*; Shenstone, *Poems upon Various Occasions* | Theatre Licensing Act gives a patent to only two theatres and compels all plays to be submitted to the Lord Chamberlain before performance; Wortley Montagu, *The Nonsense of Common Sense* (–1738) | Death of Queen Caroline; Frederick, Prince of Wales, forms Leicester House opposition |
| **1738** | Carter, *Poems*; Duck, *Poems*; Johnson, *London*; Pope, *Epilogue to Satires*; Swift, *Polite Conversation* | Ware's edition of Palladio; Handel, *Saul*; *Israel in Egypt* | Wesley's 'conversion' to Methodism |
| **1739** | Collier, *Woman's Labour*; Swift, *Verses on the Death of Dr Swift* [Faulkner's edition with Swift's own notes] | Circulating library opens in London; rooms to allow concerts and balls are built at Marylebone Gardens; London Foundling Hospital opens | War of 'Jenkins' Ear': Anglo-Spanish naval war; Gaming Act; Country-Rate Act gives JPs the power of local taxation |
| **1740** James Boswell b. (d.1795) | Cibber, *Apology for the Life of* | Mallet and Thomson, | War of the Austrian |

| Births and deaths | Principal publications and theatre productions | Cultural and scientific events | Historical and political events |
|---|---|---|---|
| | *Mr Colley Cibber*; Dyer, *Ruins of Rome*; Richardson, *Pamela*; Wetenhall Wilkes, *Letter of Genteel and Moral Advice to a Young Lady* | masque *Alfred* ('Rule Britannia'); Stukeley, *Stonehenge*; Goodman's Fields Theatre reopens (–1742); London Hospital is founded | Succession begins: Britain allies with Maria Theresa of Austria against France, Spain, Bavaria, Prussia, and Saxony; Horse-Racing Act |
| **1741** | Arbuthnot et al. *Memoirs of Martinus Scriblerus*; Fielding, *Shamela*; Hume, *Essays, Moral and Political* (–1742); Richardson, *Letters Written to and for Particular Friends*; *Pamela* (Part II) | Garrick's London debut as Richard III begins a movement towards more naturalistic acting styles; Ned's Music Hall, Dublin, built; Madrigal Society founded in London | Attack on Cartagena fails; Famine in Ireland; Grain riots in England and Scotland |
| **1742** | Collins, *Persian Eclogues*; Fielding, *Joseph Andrews*; Pope, *New Dunciad*; Young, *Night Thoughts* (–1745) | Handel, *Messiah*, first performed in Dublin; Huntingdon book club established; Ranelagh Rotunda and Gardens open and begin to offer masquerades | Walpole resigns |
| **1743** Anna Laetitia Barbauld b. (d.1824) | Robert Blair, *The Grave*; Fielding, *Miscellanies: Jonathan Wild the Great*; *Journey from this World to* | Catherine Clive's pamphlet attacking the management of the two patent theatres | George II defeats the French at the Battle of Dettingen in War of the Austrian Succession; Britain at war |

| Births and deaths | Principal publications and theatre productions | Cultural and scientific events | Historical and political events |
|---|---|---|---|
| | the Next; Pope, Dunciad in Four Books | | with France in America and India |
| **1744** Alexander Pope d. (b.1688) | Akenside, Pleasures of Imagination; Sarah Fielding, David Simple; Johnson, Life of Mr Richard Savage; Thomson, The Seasons (rev.); Joseph Warton, The Enthusiast | Haywood, The Female Spectator (–1746) | Ministry of Pelham; formal declaration of war with France; 1st Methodist Conference |
| **1745** Jonathan Swift d. (b.1667) | Akenside, Odes on Several Subjects | Hogarth, Marriage-à-la-Mode engravings; Lying-In Hospital, Dublin, founded; Shenstone creates his ferme ornée at Leasowes | Jacobite Rebellion led by 'Bonnie Prince Charlie' takes Edinburgh and wins Battle of Prestonpans |
| **1746** Mary Leapor d. | Collins, Odes on Several Descriptive and Allegoric Subjects; Joseph Warton, Odes on Various Subjects | Handel, Judas Maccabaeus | Jacobites retreat from Derby; Battle of Culloden: the duke of Cumberland routs the Jacobite army |
| **1747** | Gray, Ode on . . . Eton College; Richardson, Clarissa (–1748); | Walpole acquires lease of Strawberry Hill and plans its tranformation; |

| Births and deaths | Principal publications and theatre productions | Cultural and scientific events | Historical and political events |
|---|---|---|---|
| | Thomas Warton, *Pleasures of Melancholy* | Hogarth, *Industry and Idleness* | |
| **1748** James Thomson d. (b.1700) | Cleland, *Memoirs of a Woman of Pleasure* (–1749); Dodsley (ed.), *Collection of Poems by Several Hands* (–1758); Hume, *Enquiry concerning Human Understanding*; Leapor, *Poems upon Several Occasions*; Pilkington, *Memoirs*; Smollett, *Roderick Random*; Thomson, *The Castle of Indolence* | Ruins of Pompeii discovered; Handel, *Solomon* | Treaty of Aix-la-Chapelle concludes War of the Austrian Succession |
| **1749** | Henry Fielding, *Tom Jones*; Sarah Fielding, *The Governess, Remarks on Clarissa*; Hartley, *Observations of Man*; Johnson, *The Vanity of Human Wishes* | *The Monthly Review*, the 1st periodical dedicated to literary reviewing; Jubilee masquerade at Ranelagh, at which Elizabeth Chudleigh as Iphigenia wore a scandalous semi-nude costume; Handel, *Music for the Royal Fireworks* to commemorate the | Embezzlement criminalised |

| Births and deaths | Principal publications and theatre productions | Cultural and scientific events | Historical and political events |
|---|---|---|---|
| | | Peace of Aix-la-Chapelle: the public rehearsal at Vauxhall gardens is a huge success, the royal performance a disaster | |
| **1750** | | | |
| | Mary Jones, *Miscellanies in Prose and Verse*; Robert Paltock, *Peter Wilkins* | Johnson, *The Rambler* (–1752); Westminster Bridge built, the first classical bridge of its size in Britain | |
| **1751** Richard B. Sheridan b. (d. 1816) | Cleland, *Memoirs of a Coxcomb*; Henry Fielding, *Amelia*; Gray, *Elegy in a Country Churchyard*; Haywood, *The History of Miss Betsy Thoughtless*; Leapor, *Poems*, Vol.II; Smollett, *Peregrine Pickle* | Hogarth, *The Four Stages of Cruelty; Beer Street; Gin Lane*; Lancelot Brown sets up in London as independent garden designer; Giardini's subscription concerts begin; Handel's composition of *Jephtha* interrupted by problems with eyesight | Death of Frederick, Prince of Wales; Gin Act forbids sale of spirits by small shopkeepers |
| **1752** Thomas Chatterton b. Frances Burney b. (d. 1840) | Ballard, *Memoirs of Several Ladies of Great Britain;* Lennox, *Female Quixote*; Smart, | Act requiring licensing of all places of popular entertainment in | Britain adopts new (Gregorian) calendar; Bawdy House Act; Murder Act |

| Births and deaths | Principal publications and theatre productions | Cultural and scientific events | Historical and political events |
|---|---|---|---|
| | Poems on Several Occasions | London; Fielding, Covent-Garden Journal | |
| **1753** | | | |
| | Jane Collier, Essay on the Art of Ingeniously Tormenting; Sarah Fielding, David Simple, Volume the Last; Designs by Mr R Bentley for Six Poems by Mr T Gray; Richardson, Sir Charles Grandison (–1754); Smollett, Ferdinand Count Fathom | The British Museum is founded; Hogarth, Analysis of Beauty | Hardwicke's Marriage Act attempts to formalise marriage and prevent clandestine marriages; Jewish Naturalisation Bill attempts to accord Jewish population equal status; Apostolicum Ministerium of Benedict XIV organising Catholic Church in England |
| **1754**<br>Henry Fielding d. (b.1707) | Jane Collier & Sarah Fielding, The Cry; Duncombe, The Feminiad | The Connoisseur (–1756) ed. Colman & Thornton; King's Circus, Bath, begun; London Society for the Encouragement of Arts, Manufactures, and Commerce founded | Newcastle ministry; Jewish Naturalisation Bill revoked due to public clamour; Franco-British hostilities in Ohio valley |
| **1755** | Amory, Memoirs; Charlotte Charke, Narrative of the | | Lisbon earthquake |

| Births and deaths | Principal publications and theatre productions | Cultural and scientific events | Historical and political events |
|---|---|---|---|
| | *Life of;* Colman & Thornton, eds. *Poems by Eminent Ladies;* Fielding, *Voyage to Lisbon;* Hutcheson, *System of Moral Philosophy;* Johnson, *Dictionary of the English Language;* Smollett's translation of *Don Quixote* | | |
| **1756**<br>Stephen Duck d. (b.1705) Eliza Haywood d. (b.1693?) | Amory, *Life and Opinions of John Buncle;* Joseph Warton, *Essay on the Writings and Genius of Pope,* Vol I. | *The Critical Review* (–1763) rivals the *Monthly Review* as an excusively literary periodical and introduces a more evaluative style of literary reviewing | Seven Years War begins: Britain allied with Frederick the Great of Prussia against France, Austria and Russia |
| **1757** | Burke, *Philosophical Enquiry into . . . the Sublime and the Beautiful;* Dyer, *The Fleece;* Gray, *Odes* ('The Progress of Poetry' and 'The Bard'); Smollett's *Complete History of England* (–1758) | William Whitehead, poet laureate; Walpole's private printing press at Strawberry Hill is established with Gray's *Odes* as its first publication; Rotunda Hospital, Dublin, founded | Pitt–Newcastle ministry; Militia Act riots; East India Company victory at Battle of Plassey |
| **1758** | Carter's translation of Epictetus; John | Johnson, *The Idler* (–1760); | |

| Births and deaths | Principal publications and theatre productions | Cultural and scientific events | Historical and political events |
|---|---|---|---|
| | Upton and Ralph Church's edition of Spenser's *The Faerie Queene* | Subscription library in Liverpool; Aberdeen Philosophical Society founded; Magdalen House for Penitent Prostitutes, London, founded | |
| **1759** William Collins d. | Sarah Fielding, *Countess of Dellwyn*; Johnson, *Rasselas*; Smith, *Theory of Moral Sentiments*; Sterne, *Tristram Shandy* Vols I & II; Young, *Conjectures on Original Composition* | British Museum opens | Capture of Quebec: British victory over the French; victories also at Guadeloupe, Minden, Goree, Lagos, Quiberon Bay |
| **1760** | Colman & Lloyd, *Two Odes*; Goldsmith, *Citizen of the World* (–1762); Lyttleton & Elizabeth Montagu, *Dialogues of the Dead*; Macpherson, *Fragments of Ancient Poetry* ('Ossian'); Smollett, *Sir Launcelot Greaves* | Subscription library in Warrington; Wedgwood opens pottery works in Staffordshire; Society of Artists of Great Britain founded | Death of George II; accession of George III; conquest of Canada completed; Battle of Wandewash and capture of Pondicherry, destroying French power in India |
| **1761** | Churchill, *Rosciad*; Macpherson, | Bridgwater Canal opens; the | Resignation of elder Pitt |

| Births and deaths | Principal publications and theatre productions | Cultural and scientific events | Historical and political events |
|---|---|---|---|
| | *Fingal;* Sarah Pennington, *An Unfortunate Mother's Advice to her Absent Daughters;* Frances Sheridan, *Memoirs of Miss Sidney Bidulph;* Sterne, *Tristram Shandy,* Vols III & IV; V & VI | Noblemen and Gentlemen's Catch Club founded to promote early music | |
| **1762** Lady Mary Wortley Montagu d. (b.1689) | Carter, *Poems;* Churchill, *The Ghost;* Falconer, *The Shipwreck;* Hurd, *Letters on Chivalry and Romance;* Lord Kames, *Elements of Criticism;* Scott, *Millenium Hall* | *The North Briton,* a radical political weekly; suppressed after 45 issues; George III buys Buckingham House; Garrick expands Drury Lane and attempts to ban spectators from the stage; Poke Club, Edinburgh, founded; Merrion Sq, Dublin begun; Horace Walpole, *Anecdotes of Painting in England,* the first history of British art | Bute's ministry; war with Spain; capture of Havana and Manila |
| **1763** | Hugh Blair, *On the Poems of Ossian;* Frances Brooke, *Lady Julia Mandeville;* Churchill, | | Treaty of Paris concludes Seven Years War and consolidates British rule over Canada and |

| Births and deaths | Principal publications and theatre productions | Cultural and scientific events | Historical and political events |
|---|---|---|---|
| | *Prophecy of Famine*; Catherine Macaulay, *History of England* (–1783); Macpherson, *Temora*; Smart, *Song to David*; Wortley Montagu, *Letters* | | India; Grenville ministry; John Wilkes and general warrants case; cider tax |
| **1764** | | | |
| | Churchill, *The Times*; Evans, *Specimens of Ancient Welsh Bards*; Goldsmith, *The Traveller*; Grainger, *The Sugar Cane*; Ridley, *Tales of the Genii*; Walpole, *The Castle of Otranto* | Formation of the 'Literary Club'; attempts to bar people from the 'dark walks' of Vauxhall prove ineffective; James Hargreaves invents the spinning jenny; James Watt perfects the steam engine | Wilkes expelled from government |
| **1765** | | | |
| | Collins, *Poetical Works*; Johnson, edition of Shakespeare; Macpherson, *The Works of Ossian*; Percy, *Reliques of Ancient English Poetry*; Smollett, *Travels through France and Italy*; Sterne, *Tristram Shandy*, Vols VII & VIII | Almack's Club opens as London's first private club for mixed sexes; Foote granted a patent for Little Theatre, Haymarket, for summer months; Harrison wins prize for fixing longitude at sea; J.C. Bach and Abel begin their subscription concerts in London (–1781) | Rockingham ministry; American Stamp Act attempts to make the defence of the American colonies self-financing: repealed 1766; grant of 'diwanni' of Bengal to East India Company; 'Whiteboy' disturbances in Ireland |

| Births and deaths | Principal publications and theatre productions | Cultural and scientific events | Historical and political events |
|---|---|---|---|
| **1766** Frances Sheridan d. | Amory, *Life and Opinions of John Buncle* Vol II; Anstey, *New Bath Guide*; Colman & Garrick, *Clandestine Marriage*; Goldsmith, *Vicar of Wakefield* | Rousseau in England (–1767); Stubb's engraved plates, *The Anatomy of the Horse* | Chatham (formerly Pitt) ministry; grain shortages and riots |
| **1767** | Frances Sheridan, *History of Nourjahad*; Sterne, *Tristram Shandy*, Vol IX | James Craig's plan for New Town, Edinburgh, chosen; Royal Crescent, Bath, begun (–1775); first Gaelic New Testament published | Townshend duties provoke American protests |
| **1768** Laurence Sterne d. Sarah Fielding d. (b.1710) | Goldsmith, *The Good-Natur'd Man*; Gray, *Poems*; Wortley Montagu, *Poems*; Sterne, *Sentimental Journey*; *Encyclopaedia Britannica* (–1771) | Royal Academy of Art opens; Sarah Scott attempts to found a female community at Hitcham, Berkshire; Joseph Wright, *An Experiment on a Bird in the Air Pump* | Grafton ministry; Middlesex election crisis; Priestley, *Essay on the First Principles of Government* |
| **1769** | Montagu, *Essay ... on Shakespear*; Smollett, *Adventures of an Atom* | *The Morning Chronicle* (–1862); Shakespeare Jubilee is celebrated at Stratford; Reynolds is made president | Wilkes expelled from House of Commons and is re-elected three times |

| Births and deaths | Principal publications and theatre productions | Cultural and scientific events | Historical and political events |
|---|---|---|---|
| | | of the Royal Academy and delivers first of 15 *Discourses* (–1790); James Watt's steam engine patented; Captain Cook's first voyage to Australia and New Zealand | |
| **1770** Mark Akenside d. Thomas Chatterton d. | Goldsmith, *Deserted Village*; Talbot, *Reflections on the Seven Days of the Week* | *The Lady's Magazine*; subscription library in Macclesfield | Lord North's ministry; Falkland Islands crisis |
| **1771** Thomas Gray d. Christopher Smart d. Tobias Smollett d. | James Beattie, *Minstrel* (–1774); Cumberland, *West Indian*; MacKenzie, *Man of Feeling*; Smollett, *Humphry Clinker* | Pantheon opens in London, an important venue for public concerts; subscription library in Sheffield; Upper Assembly Rooms, Bath, opened; Benjamin West, *Death of Wolfe* | Somerset case (–1772): Lord Mansfield decides that a slave cannot be removed from England against his/her will; Wilkesite challenge to parliamentary control of publication of debates |
| **1772** | Sir William Jones, *Poems, Consisting Chiefly of Translations from the Asiatic Languages* | *The Morning Post* (–1936); Chambers, *Dissertation on Oriental Gardening* | Grain shortage and riots |

| Births and deaths | Principal publications and theatre productions | Cultural and scientific events | Historical and political events |
|---|---|---|---|
| **1773** | | | |
| | Barbauld, *Poems*; Cook, *Account of a Voyage round the World*; James Boswell, *Journal of a Tour to the Hebrides*; Chapone, *Letters on the Improvement of the Mind*; Fergusson, *Poems*; Goldsmith, *She Stoops to Conquer*; Phillis Wheatley, *Poems* | Subscription library in Bristol | Boston Tea Party: American colonists protest against the East India Company's monopoly of tea exports to America; New Stock Exchange |
| **1774** Oliver Goldsmith d. | Mary Scott, *Female Advocate*; *Letters Written by the Earl of Chesterfield to His Son* | Perpetual copyright is declared invalid (maximum now 28 years); Thomas Warton, *History of English Poetry* (–1781), the first extensive literary history from the Norman Conquest to early 17th century; subscription library in Bradford; Omai in London; The Humane Society founded | Coercive Acts passed in retaliation for Boston Tea Party |
| **1775** | Hester Chapone, *Poems*; Gray, | Subscription libraries in | American War of Independence |

| Births and deaths | Principal publications and theatre productions | Cultural and scientific events | Historical and political events |
|---|---|---|---|
| | *Poems*; Johnson, *Journey to Western Islands*; *Poetical Amusements at a Villa near Bath* (also 1776, 1777 & 1781); Mary Robinson, *Poems*; Sheridan, *The Duenna*; *The Rivals*; *St Patrick's Day*; Sterne, *Letters* | Whitby and Hull; Drury Lane Theatre redesigned by Robert Adam; Lunar Society meets in Midlands for scientific discussion and experiment | begins; hostilities in Lexington and Concord |
| **1776** | | | |
| | Gibbon, *Decline and Fall of the Roman Empire*, Vol I; Paine, *Common Sense*; Smith, *Wealth of Nations* | Charles Burney, *General History of Music*, Vol 1; Colman opens Little Theatre; Concert of Ancient Music promotes music repertory by earlier composers | Declaration of American Independence |
| **1777** | | | |
| | Chatterton, *Poems . . . by Thomas Rowley and others*; Chapone, *Letter to a New-Married Lady*; Cook, *Voyage towards the South Pole*; Sheridan, *School for Scandal*; *Trip to Scarborough*; Thomas Warton, *Poems* | | Philadelphia captured but British defeated at Saratoga |

| Births and deaths | Principal publications and theatre productions | Cultural and scientific events | Historical and political events |
|---|---|---|---|
| **1778** | Barbauld, *Lessons for Children*; Burney, *Evelina*; Mary Hamilton, *Munster Village*; Clara Reeve, *Old English Baron* | Marylebone Gardens close; subscription libraries in Leeds, Halifax & Carlisle; Highland Society formed in London | France joins the Americans in war against Britain |
| **1779** David Garrick d. | Alexander, *History of Women*; Cowper, *Olney Hymns*; Elizabeth Griffiths, *The Times*; Hume, *Dialogues concerning Natural Religion*; Johnson, *Lives of the Poets* (–1781); Mungo Park, *Travels in the Interior Districts of Africa*; Sheridan, *The Critic* | Samuel's *The Nine Living Muses of Great Britain* exhibited at the Royal Academy exhibition; the 'Ladies of Llangollen' settle in north Wales (–1829); Cook murdered by natives in Hawaii; 1st iron bridge built at Coalbrookdale | War with Spain; invasion threat in Channel; Wyvill's Association movement; Dissenters' Relief Act |

# Key Concepts and Contexts

## Augustan literature

The term 'Augustan' was first used to describe English literature by Francis Atterbury, writing in 1690 of the 'refinements' Edmund Waller had introduced in poetic style during the reign of Charles II. By 1756, Joseph Warton refuted that Restoration England was the English Augustan age and located it in the later reign of William and throughout that of Anne. Both writers were agreed in using the term 'Augustan' to signify a time of ideal culture, a golden age of writing which emulated the original 'Augustan' age under the reign of the Roman Emperor Augustus (27 BC–AD 14), when the Latin writers Ovid, Juvenal, Horace, Virgil, Propertius, Tibullus and Livy all flourished and excelled. Twentieth-century literary criticism continued to use the term 'Augustan', partly because a major part of the writing of the late seventeenth and early eighteenth centuries modelled itself upon, or imitated, Augustan writers, Virgil and Horace in particular. The term was then used to describe literature written from Dryden to Johnson, or from about 1680 to 1750. More recently, however, the term has been questioned, because many eighteenth-century writers repudiated Augustus and viewed him as tyrannous, cruel, and fond of sycophancy. Virgil and Horace are then interpreted as sycophants who celebrated Roman imperial destiny for their own interests, in contrast to Juvenal, who fearlessly pointed out the evils of imperial society. (For this argument, see Weinbrot 1978 and, for a critique of Weinbrot's thesis, Erskine-Hill 1983.) Another reason could be because the Hanoverian kings, George I and George II, failed to emulate Augustus, particularly in his patronage of the arts. The term also excludes other influences on culture of the period – not just ancient Greek, which was equally revered, but the influence of contemporary popular culture, an influence much discussed in recent research.

## The Enlightenment

Eighteenth-century Europe and America witnessed a movement, known even then as 'the Enlightenment', which might be defined as the passion for rational enquiry, religious toleration, political liberalism and universal human values. Enlightenment thinkers believed that human reasoning could be used to combat ignorance, superstition, and tyranny and to build a better world. Their principal targets were religion (embodied in France in the Catholic Church) and the domination of society by a hereditary aristocracy. Although the Enlightenment has been attacked in the twentieth century for its perceived instrumentalism and tyranny – the tyranny of reason being used to oppress and dominate rather than to emancipate – the concept of universal human rights it developed continues to be the most important value in the modern world, the guarantee of equality and freedom irrespective of difference. An important celebration of the British Enlightenment is found in Roy Porter's recent book (2000), a good place to start in thinking about the Enlightenment in general.

## The novel

Among the most significant eighteenth-century studies have been examinations of the 'rise of the novel'. Recent work has explored the importance of early women writers and the genre which they dominated, amatory fiction, to the development of the novel (for example, Ballaster 1992 and Warner 1998). More unusually, Margaret Doody has traced the novel's emergence to texts of antiquity (1996). In his 1957 study, Ian Watt developed the broadly sociological approach to the eighteenth-century novel that largely continues today. His book examined the impact that social and economic issues had upon the development of the novel, most obviously in his linking of the rise of a middle class with the emergence of the novel. The important critical interventions of the 1980s and 1990s have continued to be largely responses to Watt's book: questioning or refining, for example, his broad-brush analogy between the 'rise of the middle classes' and the 'rise of the novel' (McKeon, Armstrong) or the book's narrow focus on Defoe, Richardson and Fielding (Todd, Warner, Ballaster). It is important to note that few of the eighteenth-century writers we would now call 'novelists' would themselves have accepted this term. Eighteenth-century prose fiction tends to insist on its veracity, often with titles such as 'the history of . . .' or 'the life and adventures of . . .' and with the author posing as editor of the text.

### The public sphere

For Jürgen Habermas, the bourgeois public sphere developed in Europe in the late seventeenth century as a sphere separated from both the state and from civil society, the realm of private life. Because of its autonomy, it could criticise both these spheres and this critique propelled the democratic revolutions of the eighteenth century. For Habermas this independence has been eroded, the modern media, for example, having lost its critical distance from the state and civil society. Habermas implies that the first public sphere was a literary public sphere. Newspapers, novels, art criticism and magazines are the literary equivalents of the coffee houses, debating societies and literary salons where men met as equals. This book argues, however, that the idealised consensus of Habermas's public sphere is under challenge even in the eighteenth century, its putative moment of inception, as writers fear the splintering as much as they celebrate the consolidation of community and recognise that language could obfuscate rather than clarify, confuse rather than educate. Chapter 3 of this book follows many feminist challenges to Habermas in arguing that his idealisation of a theoretical public sphere, in which an abstract humanity makes all equal, blinds him to its historical exclusions. Despite this, however, the theoretical ideal which Habermas offers remains attractive, as one in which women writers might be recognised primarily as writers rather than as *women* writers.

### Satire

In literary terms, satire is a mode in which a polemical, critical challenge is waged against a specific or general target. Satire is often driven by contempt or anger, feelings which many satirists defend as part of their reforming zeal. Despite Swift's definition of satire as 'a sort of glass, wherein beholders do generally discover everybody's face but their own', we might think of satire as a mode which attempts to make us see ourselves and the world just as much as it attempts to reform the world. Critical debates on eighteenth-century satire have tended to discuss the extent to which Horatian, polite forms of satire, or Juvenalian, more angry forms, predominated, although the question of which was the more correct model was also an eighteenth-century debate. Much eighteenth-century satire is highly 'unstable' because, frequently parodying the thing it attacks, it makes it possible to miss the satire in reading the text literally. Satire is specifically important to the ideas contained in this book because, to paraphrase Goldsmith, satire fools the many for the entertainment of the few, and thus might more properly be called 'coterie satire' (Goldsmith 1975, xii). However, Swift defined two kinds of satire: one, to mock coxcombs, for 'no other Reward than that of laughing with a few Friends in a Corner'; the second, representing 'a *publick Spirit*, prompting Men of *Genius* and Virtue, to mend the World as far as they are able' (Swift 1955, 34). In this way, satire embodies the same kind of tension between the specific, exclusive example and the universal ideal which fractures the work of Habermas on the public sphere.

## Sensibility

Traditionally, the latter half of the eighteenth century is seen to be under the sway of the cult of 'sensibility' in which people are encouraged to be tender-hearted, compassionate to others and sensitive to the beauties of nature and fine art, particularly poetry, painting and music. There are thus a variety of meanings (moral, political, sexual and aesthetic) and associated concepts (such as virtue, landscape, benevolence, feeling, delicacy, enthusiasm, imagination, compassion, and taste) which accrued around this key term, all of which are neatly characterised in Jane Austen's depiction of Marianne in *Sense and Sensibility*. At its most radical, sensibility was an oppositional movement, which challenged aristocratic hegemony on the grounds of community and sociality, and which promoted the spread of philanthropic movements, including the campaign against slavery and the care of former prostitutes. At its most conservative, it merely indulged the complacency of the middle classes, permitting them, in shedding a tear for the distresses of another, to feel good about their own tender feelings without actually changing anything (see Ellis 1996). Among the most significant work on sensibility is that of John Mullan, who writes, for example, that 'sentimentalism in eighteenth-century novels seems much more like the consequence of an anxiety about the sociability of individuals, than the assertion of a faith in human benevolence' (1996, 250).

# Annotated Bibliography

Brewer, John. *The Pleasures of the Imagination: English Culture in the Eighteenth Century*. London: Harper Collins, 1997.

A hugely enjoyable study, encompassing literature, visual art, music, popular entertainments and more besides. Brewer gives an excellent overview of eighteenth-century culture but combines this with interesting studies of specific examples and case studies. While the final chapters of the book are specific studies of exemplary 'provincial' artists (the engraver Thomas Bewick, the amateur musician John Marsh, and the poet Anna Seward) which demonstrate the cultural life of Britain beyond London, there are countless insights among its pages. The discussions of *The Beggar's Opera*, the Royal Fireworks of 1749 and the fashioning of the cult of Shakespeare are just a few of many highlights. Definitely my top recommendation.

Castle, Terry. *Masquerade and Civilization: The Carnivalesque in Eighteenth-Century English Culture and Fiction*. Stanford, CA: Stanford University Press, 1986.

Castle's work exemplifies the work of cultural studies at its best. A social history of the masked assembly and its importance to eighteenth-century culture, this is also a literary study of the eighteenth-century imagination, particularly the way in which the collective meditations on the self and other which the masquerade permitted were appropriated by fiction. Her study is a corrective to such simplistic designations as 'an age of reason' in discussing how the masquerade as a cultural phenomenon 'institutionalized dreams of disorder' and how, while satirists condemned such dreams, novelists embraced them.

Cook, Elizabeth Heckendorn. *Epistolary Bodies: Gender and Genre in the Eighteenth-Century Republic of Letters*. Stanford, CA: Stanford University Press, 1996.

Although this considers only one English language text, *Clarissa*, it is an excellent discussion of epistolarity, and beyond that of the wider concerns of how eighteenth-century writers negotiate the transformation of manuscript into print and how a culture actively redefines its notion of public and private in relation to print culture. It also contains a very lucid discussion and critique of Habermas.

Doody, Margaret Anne. *The Daring Muse: Augustan Poetry Reconsidered.* Cambridge: Cambridge University Press, 1985.

Essential reading for those interested in eighteenth-century poetry, this study encourages us to jettison the stereotype of Augustan poetry as a conventional and traditional form and recognise the self-reflexivity, experimentation and desire for liberty which this poetry represented to its readers. Doody argues her case persuasively and with an enthusiasm which is infectious.

Fairer, David and Christine Gerrard, eds. *Eighteenth-Century Poetry: An Annotated Anthology.* Oxford: Basil Blackwell, 1999.

Although an anthology of primary texts, this is also an excellent critical introduction to eighteenth-century poetry. A good range of canonical and lesser-known poems is included and each poem is accompanied with a headnote and annotations which provide invaluable support for individual readings. The editors usefully suggest continuities across poetry written throughout the century and thus avoid the divisions of 'Augustan' and 'pre-Romantic' poetry which have dominated studies until recently. In doing so, they begin to remap how we might read the diversity and liveliness of eighteenth-century poetic styles and themes.

Hammond, Brean, ed. *Pope.* Longman Critical Reader. London: Longman, 1996.

This collection of essays reprints many of the most influential and controversial readings of Pope in the last two decades, including, for example, critiques of Pope from feminist (Pollak) and largely marxist (Fabricant and Brown) perspectives. Hammond's introduction discusses postwar trends in Pope criticism and the headnotes to each section helpfully situate the essays in terms of literary theory and make explicit the implications of the stances taken. An additional feature of this excellent collection is the responses to Hammond's own comments by a number of critics included within the book (Fabricant, Bygrave and McLaverty).

—— *Professional imaginative writing in England, 1670–1740:'hackney for bread'.* Oxford: Clarendon Press, 1997.

Combining the best of cultural studies critique with scrupulous historicism, this study resituates literature of the late seventeenth and early eighteenth centuries. It revisits arguments about the rise of the novel by situating poetry and drama, and especially the work of the Scriblerians, in the context of 'novelization', defined by Hammond as the shift in commercial publishing, authorship and readership which led to the novel's ascendancy. An indispensable read for those particularly interested in issues of 'high' and 'low' culture as defined by the eighteenth century.

Jones, Vivien, ed. *Women and Literature in Britain, 1700–1800*. Cambridge: Cambridge University Press, 2000.

This collection of specially written essays allows its contributors to reflect upon developments in the study of women's writing and to challenge some misperceptions in danger of becoming commonplace. Jan Fergus, for example, questions whether women really were the dominant readers of eighteenth-century fiction and Clare Brant considers the miscellaneous writings by women (including life-writings, letters, and dialogues) which have tended to be overlooked because their generic hybridity does not fit our definitions of the literary as poetry, fiction, and drama. Margaret Doody writes on poetry, Ros Ballaster on the novel, Isobel Grundy on the implications of acts of rediscovery, Angela Smallwood on the theatre, Dianne Dugaw on popular culture and Paula McDowell on aspects of literary production. All are excellent starting places for these issues and suggest ways in which future work might extend our knowledge.

Lonsdale, Roger, ed. *The New Oxford Book of Eighteenth-Century Verse*. Oxford: Oxford University Press, 1984.
—— ed. *Eighteenth-Century Women Poets*. Oxford: Oxford University Press, 1989; repr.1990.

Both of these anthologies have transformed the study of eighteenth-century poetry in reminding us of its significant range and variety. The work of re-evaluation which they inspired continues and these collections are still unrivalled for their recovery of many eighteenth-century voices. Both, for example, reprint Frances Greville's poem 'A Prayer for Indifference', the most celebrated poem by a woman writer in the eighteenth century, but not found in other modern editions. The anthology of women poets contains a very useful introduction which discusses why women writers were subsequently neglected.

Maurer, Shawn Lisa. *Proposing Men: Dialectics of Gender and Class in the Eighteenth-Century English Periodical*. Stanford, CA: Stanford University Press, 1998.

One of the few full-length studies of masculinity in the eighteenth century, this book questions the traditional distinction of the public/private spheres according to gender in its analysis of the construction of the sentimental family. As such, it is of significance beyond the form of the periodical, containing useful insights for the study of literary sensibility too, for example.

Mullan, John. *Sentiment and Sociability: The Language of Feeling in the Eighteenth Century*. Oxford: Clarendon Press, 1988; repr. 1990

In my view, this remains the most important study of sensibility. It examines how the novel came to be legitimised through its increasing sentimentalism and how that sentimentalism expressed an anxiety about the nature of social relations. The novelists Richardson and Sterne and the philosophers Hume and Smith are the writers discussed in detail – an important pairing of disciplines ('fiction' and 'philosophy') which were not nearly so distinct in the eighteenth century as they can seem today.

Porter, Roy. *Enlightenment Britain and the Creation of the Modern World*. London: Allen Lane, Penguin Press, 2000.

Porter's book argues that the British Enlightenment – once thought a contradiction in terms – preceded and shaped those of the continent, differing only from continental Enlightenments in its adherence to pragmatism and practicality, rather than abstract thought. For the literary scholar, the book provides an excellent context in its comprehensive discussions of social history, philosophy, scientific and religious thinking and the development of print culture. The society he sketches is sceptical, pleasure-seeking, innovative, garrulous and meritocratic.

Richetti, John, ed. *The Cambridge Companion to the Eighteenth-Century Novel*. Cambridge: Cambridge University Press, 1996.
—— *The English Novel in History, 1700–1800*. London: Routledge, 1999.

Richetti's collection of essays includes specially commissioned essays on major aspects of eighteenth-century fiction by recognised experts in their fields (thus, Novak on Defoe; Doody on Richardson; Rawson on Fielding; Epstein on Burney; Spencer on women novelists and Mullan on novels of sensibility, to name a few). This book is probably the best place to start in considering eighteenth-century novelists, with important introductory essays by J. Paul Hunter and Richetti himself.

Richetti's own book on the eighteenth-century novel is part of a series written for student readers. However, it is as much an intervention in debates about the novel as it is an introduction to them. His broad theme, of social change and social representation, is an important one for the concerns of this book and permits him to discuss a wide range of novelists, canonical and non-canonical (hence, there are full discussions of Defoe, Richardson, Fielding, Smollett and Sterne but also of Behn, Manley, Haywood, Sarah Fielding, Lennox, Burney and Henry Brooke).

Schellenberg, Betty A. *The Conversational Circle: Rereading the English Novel, 1740–1775*. Lexington, KY: University Press of Kentucky, 1996.

Schellenberg focuses on fictional portrayals of the 'conversational circle' in mid-century novels as expressing a longing for (lost) social consensus. The novels discussed at length are *The Adventures of David Simple, Pamela Part II, Sir Charles Grandison, Amelia, Millenium Hall* and *The Adventures of Humphry Clinker*, novels not always seen as key to our definition of eighteenth-century fiction. An important study for the consideration of the importance of the idea of community to the period, as sketched in this book.

Sitter, John, ed. *The Cambridge Companion to Eighteenth-Century Poetry.* Cambridge: Cambridge University Press, 2001.

Like the other 'Cambridge Companion' (Richetti 1996), Sitter's collection of essays consists of new essays by leading experts in respective areas of eighteenth-century poetry (Gerrard on political poetry; Benedict on the material concerns of reading and publishing poetry; Fulford on poems of natural description; Fairer on the links with earlier traditions of English poetry and Spacks on the poetry of sensibility, among many others). J. Paul Hunter's essay on 'Couplets and Conversation' and Sitter's on 'why and how [eighteenth-century] poetry matters' are especially recommended starting places.

Todd, Janet. *The Sign of Angellica: Women, Writing and Fiction, 1660–1800.* New York: Columbia University Press, 1989.

Although one of the first books to address eighteenth-century women's writing at length, this book continues to be the most important and useful overview of fiction by women. The period 1660–1800 is mapped according to three phases: Restoration and early eighteenth century (a period of sexual frankness in writing, when the status of female fiction remained dubious); mid-eighteenth century (when sentimentalism and the cult of sensibility flourished, giving a new respectable image and restricted subject matter to the woman writer); and the last two decades (which witnessed in part a reaction to this restriction and in part a conscious and public embracing of it).

Warner, William. *Licensing Entertainment: The Elevation of Novel Reading in Britain, 1684–1750.* Berkeley, CA: University of California Press, 1998.

Warner refuses the narrative of Ian Watt's influential account of the rise of the novel (1957) as a story of heroic authorial innovation and argues instead that the 'elevation' of the novel did not so much institute a new type of literature ('the novel') as attempt to reform reading practices. Thus the elevation of novels was a creative early modern response to the onset of market-driven media culture. Warner's thesis makes important and interesting links between our own literary culture and that of the eighteenth century and his arguments are important to the concerns traced in the second section of this book.

Wood, Nigel, ed. *Jonathan Swift.* Longman Critical Reader. London: Longman, 1999.

Like the other Longman Critical Reader selected above (Hammond 1996), Wood's collection both selects key essays on Swift published in the 1980s and

1990s and situates these explicitly in relation to each other and to contemporary literary theories. A wide range of approaches to Swift is included here – poststructuralist, feminist, historicist and new historicist. An indispensable guide to contemporary readings of Swift.

# Bibliography

Adburgham, Alison. *Women in Print: Writing Women and Women's Magazines From the Restoration to the Accession of Victoria*. London: George Allen & Unwin, 1972.

Aitkin, George A., ed. *The Tatler*, 4 vols (1898), facsimile edition. New York and Hildesheim: Georg Olms, 1970.

Alexander, William. *The History of Women from the Earliest Antiquity, to the Present Time; giving some Account of almost every interesting Particular concerning that Sex, among all Nations, Ancient and Modern*, 2 vols. London: 1779.

Allen, Emily. 'Staging Identity: Frances Burney's Allegory of Genre', *Eighteenth-Century Studies*, 31.4 (1998): 433–51.

Allen, Robert J. *The Clubs of Augustan London*. Cambridge, MA: Harvard University Press, 1933.

Amory, Thomas. *Memoirs of Several Ladies of Great Britain. Interspersed with Literary Reflexions and Accounts of Antiquities and Curious Things in Several Letters*. London: John Noon, 1755.

—— *The Life and Opinions of John Buncle, Esquire*, ed. Ernest A. Baker. London: George Routledge & Sons, 1904.

Anderson, Benedict. *Imagined Communities: Reflections on the Origin and Spread of Nationalism*. London: Verso, 1983; revised edn 1991.

Anon. *The Petticoat Plotters, or the D[uches]s of M[arlboroug]h's Club*. London: T. Wellard, 1712.

Anon. *Critical Remarks on the Four Taking Plays of this Season; by Corinna, a Country Parson's Wife*. London: James Bettenham, 1719.

Anon. *The Female Dunces. Inscrib'd to Mr Pope*. London: J. Dormer, 1733.

Anon. *Biographium Faemineum, The Female Worthies: or, Memoirs of the most Illustrious Ladies of all Ages and Nations*, 2 vols. London: 1766.

Anon. *Sawney and Colley* (1742) *and other Pope pamphlets*, facsimile edition. The Augustan Reprint Series No.83. Los Angeles: University of California Press, 1960.

Armstrong, Nancy. *Desire and Domestic Fiction: A Political History of the Novel*. Oxford: Oxford University Press, 1987.

Astell, Mary. *A Serious Proposal to the Ladies*, ed. Patricia Springborg. London: Pickering and Chatto, 1996.

Atkins, G. Douglas. 'Allegory of Blindness and Insight: Will-ing in *A Tale of a Tub*' in *Reading Deconstruction/Deconstructive Reading*. Lexington, KY: University Press of Kentucky, 1983, 105–17.

—— 'A Matter of Difference: Deconstruction and Eighteenth-Century Studies', *The Eighteenth Century: Theory and Interpretation*, 28 (1987): 264–9.

Austen, Jane. *Sense and Sensibility*, ed. James Kinsley. Oxford: Oxford World's Classics, 1980.

Avery, Emmet L. 'The Shakespeare Ladies Club', *Shakespeare Quarterly*, 7 (1956): 153–8.

Backscheider, Paula R. 'Introduction' in *The Intersections of the Public and Private Spheres in early modern England*. London: Frank Cass, 1996, 1–21.

—— 'The Novel's Gendered Space' in *Revising Women: Eighteenth-Century 'Women's Fiction' and Social Engagement*, ed. Paula Backscheider. Baltimore, MD and London: Johns Hopkins University Press, 2000, 1–30.

—— and John Richetti, eds. *Popular Fiction by Women, 1660–1730*. Oxford: Clarendon Press, 1996.

Ballard, George. *Memoirs of Several Ladies of Great Britain, who have been Celebrated for their Writings or Skill in the Learned Languages Arts and Sciences*, 2 vols. Oxford: W. Jackson, 1752.

Ballaster, Ros. *Seductive Forms: Women's Amatory Fiction from 1684–1740*. Oxford: Clarendon Press, 1992.

Bandry, Anne. 'Imitations of *Tristram Shandy*' in *Critical Essays on Laurence Sterne*, ed. Melvyn New. New York: G. K. Hall, 1998, 39–52.

Bandry, Anne and W. G. Day. 'The Third Edition of the *Clockmakers Outcry*', *Shandean*, 4 (1992): 153–66.

Barker, Jane. *The Galesia Trilogy and Selected Manuscript Poems*, ed. Carol Shiner Wilson. Oxford: Oxford University Press, 1997.

Barnett, Louise K. 'Deconstucting *Gulliver's Travels*' in *The Genres of Gulliver's Travels*, ed. Frederik N. Smith. Newark: University of Delaware Press; London: Associated University Presses, 1990, 230–45.

Barney, Richard A. *Plots of Enlightenment: Education and the Novel in Eighteenth-Century England*. Stanford, CA: Stanford University Press, 1999.

Barrell, John. *English Literature in History, 1730–1780: an equal, wide survey*. London: Hutchinson, 1983.

—— and Harriet Guest. 'On the Use of Contradiction: Economics and Morality in the Eighteenth-century Long Poem' in *The New Eighteenth Century*, ed. Felicity Nussbaum and Laura Brown. London: Routledge, 1987, 121–43.

Barry, Jonathan. 'Bourgeois Collectivism? Urban Association and the Middling Sort' in *The Middling Sort of People: Culture, Society and Politics in England, 1550–1800*, ed. Jonathan Barry and Christopher Brooks. Basingstoke: Macmillan – now Palgrave Macmillan, 1994, 84–112.

Bellamy, Liz. *Commerce, Morality and the Eighteenth-Century Novel*. Cambridge: Cambridge University Press, 1998.

Bender, John. *Imagining the Penitentiary: Fiction and the Architecture of Mind in Eighteenth-Century England*. Chicago: University of Chicago Press, 1987.

Benedict, Barbara M. *Framing Feeling: sentiment and style in English prose fiction, 1745–1800*. New York: AMS Press, 1994.

—— *Making the Modern Reader: cultural mediation in early modern literary anthologies*. Princeton, NJ: Princeton University Press, 1996.

Bentman, Raymond. 'Thomas Gray and the Poetry of "Hopeless Love"', *Journal of the History of Sexuality*, 3 (1992): 203–22.

Berry, Helen. '"Nice and Curious Questions": Coffee Houses and the Representation of Women in John Dunton's *Athenian Mercury*', *The Seventeenth Century*, 12 (1998): 257–76.

Bertelsen, Lance. *The Nonsense Club: literature and popular culture, 1749–1764*. Oxford: Clarendon Press, 1986.

Black, Scott. 'Social and Literary Form in the *Spectator*', *Eighteenth-Century Studies*, 33.1 (1999): 21–42.

Bloom, Harold. *The Anxiety of Influence: a theory of poetry*. New York: Oxford University Press, 1973.

Bogel, Fredric. *Literature and Insubstantiality in Later Eighteenth-Century England*. Princeton, NJ: Princeton University Press, 1984.

Bond, Donald F., ed. *The Spectator*, 5 vols. Oxford: Clarendon Press, 1965.

Borsay, Peter. *The English Urban Renaissance: Culture and Society in the Provincial Town, 1660–1760*. Oxford: Clarendon Press, 1989.

Boswell, James. *Life of Johnson*. Oxford: Oxford University Press, 1980.

Bowen, Scarlett. '"A Sawce-box and Boldface Indeed": Refiguring the Female Servant in the Pamela-Antipamela Debate', *Studies in Eighteenth-Century Culture*, 28 (1999): 257–85.

Bowers, Toni O'Shaughnessy. 'Sex, Lies and Invisibility: Amatory Fiction from Restoration to Mid-century' in *The Columbia History of the Novel*, ed. John Richetti. New York: Columbia University Press, 1994, 50–65.

Boyle, Frank T. *Swift as Nemesis: modernity and its satirist*. Stanford, CA: Stanford University Press, 2000.

Boyle, John, Earl of Orrery. *Remarks on the Life and Writings of Dr Jonathan Swift*. London: 1752.

Brant, Clare. 'Varieties of women's writing' in *Women and Literature in Britain, 1700–1800*, ed. Vivien Jones. Cambridge: Cambridge University Press, 2000, 285–305.

Bree, Linda. 'Sisterhood and Sarah Fielding' in *Female Communities 1600–1800: Literary Visions and Cultural Realities*, ed. Rebecca D'Monté and Nicole Pohl. Basingstoke: Macmillan – now Palgrave Macmillan, 2000, 184–98.

Brewer, Daniel. 'The Philosophical Dialogue and the Forcing of Truth', *Modern Language Notes*, 98 (1983): 1234–47.

Brewer, John. 'This, that and the other: Public, Social and Private in the Seventeenth and Eighteenth Centuries' in *Shifting the Boundaries: Transformation of the Languages of Public and Private in the Eighteenth Century*, ed. Dario Castiglione and Lesley Sharpe. Exeter: University of Exeter Press, 1995, 1–21.

—— *The Pleasures of the Imagination: English Culture in the Eighteenth Century*. London: Harper Collins, 1997.

Brissenden, R. F. *Virtue in Distress: Studies in the Novel of Sentiment from Richardson to Sade*. London: Macmillan – now Palgrave Macmillan, 1974.

Brown, Laura. *English Dramatic From 1660–1760: An Essay in Generic History*. New Haven, CT: Yale University Press, 1981.

Brückmann, Patricia Carr. *A Manner of Correspondence: A Study of the Scriblerus Club*. Montreal and Kingston: McGill–Queen's University Press, 1997.

Burney, Frances. *The Early Journals and Letters of Fanny Burney*, ed. Lars E. Troide and Stewart J. Cooke. 3 vols. Oxford: Clarendon Press, 1994.

—— *The Complete Plays*, ed. Peter Sabor, 2 vols. London: Pickering & Chatto, 1995.

—— *Evelina; or, A Young Lady's Entrance into the World in a series of letters*, ed. Susan Kubica Howard. Ontario, Canada: Broadview Press, 2000.

Campbell, Gina. 'How to Read Like a Gentleman: Burney's Instructions to Her Critics in *Evelina*', *English Literary History*, 57 (1990): 557–84.

Campbell, Jill. 'Fielding and the Novel at Mid-Century' in *The Columbia History of the British Novel*, ed. John Richetti. New York: Columbia University Press, 1994, 102–26.

—— *Natural Masques: Gender and Identity in Fielding's Plays and Novels*. Stanford, CA: Stanford University Press, 1995.

Carlson, C. Lennart. 'Edward Cave's Club and its Project for a Literary Review', *Philological Quarterly*, 17 (1938): 115–20.

Carnell, Rachel K. 'Clarissa's Treasonable Correspondence: Gender, Epistolary Politics, and the Public Sphere', *Eighteenth-Century Fiction*, 10.3 (1998): 269–86

Carpenter, Andrew, ed. *Verse in English from Eighteenth-Century Ireland*. Cork: Cork University Press, 1998.

Carretta, Vincent. 'Olaudah Equiano or Gustavus Vassa? New Light on an Eighteenth-century Question of Identity', *Slavery and Abolition*, 20.3 (1999): 96–105.

Carter, Elizabeth. *Letters from Mrs Carter to Mrs Montagu between the Years 1755 and 1800*, 3 vols. London: F. C. & J. Rivington, 1817.

Castle, Terry. 'Why the Houyhnhnms Don't Write; Swift, Satire and the Fear of the Text' (1980) in *Critical Essays on Jonathan Swift*, ed. Frank Palmeri. New York: G.K. Hall, 1993, 57–71.

—— *Masquerade and Civilization: The Carnivalesque in Eighteenth-Century English Culture and Fiction*. Stanford, CA: Stanford University Press, 1986.

Centlivre, Susanna. *The dramatic works of the celebrated Mrs Centlivre*, 3 vols. London: J. Pearson, 1872.

—— *A Bold Stroke for a Wife*, ed. Nancy Copeland. Ontario, Canada: Broadview Press, 1995.

Cibber, Colley. *A Letter from Mr Cibber to Mr Pope* (1742), facsimile edition. The Augustan Reprint Series No. 158. Los Angeles: University of California Press, 1973.

Clark, P. O. 'A Gulliver Dictionary', *Studies in Philology*, 1 (1953): 592–624.

Clark, Peter. *British Clubs and Societies, 1580–1800: The Origins of an Associational World*. Oxford: Clarendon Press, 2000.

Clery, E. J. 'Women, Publicity and the Coffee-House Myth', *Women: a cultural review*, 2.2 (1991): 168–77.

Colley, Linda. *Britons: Forging the Nation, 1707–1837*. New Haven, CT and London: Yale University Press, 1992.

[Colman, George and Bonnell Thornton]. *The Connoisseur. By Mr Town, Critic and Censor-General. Volume the Second.* 3rd edition: London: 1757a.

—— eds. *Poems by Eminent Ladies*, 2 vols. Dublin: D. Chamberlaine, 1757b.

Colman, George and David Garrick. 'The Clandestine Marriage' in *The Beggar's Opera and other eighteenth-century plays*. London: Everyman, 1928, 268–337.

Cook, Elizabeth Heckendorn. *Epistolary Bodies: Gender and Genre in the Eighteenth-Century Republic of Letters*. Stanford, CA: Stanford University Press, 1996.

Cope, Kevin L. ed. *Compendious Conversations: The Method of Dialogue in the Early Enlightenment*. New York: Peter Lang, 1992.

Copley, Stephen. 'Commerce, Conversation and Politeness in the Early Eighteenth-Century Periodical', *British Journal for Eighteenth-Century Studies*, 18.1 (Spring 1995): 63–77.

[Coventry, Francis.] 'An Essay on the New Species of Writing Founded by Mr Fielding' (1751), ed. A. D. McKillop. Los Angeles: William Andrews Clark Memorial Library, University of California, 1962.

Damrosch, Leopold, ed. *The Profession of Eighteenth-century Literature: reflections on an institution*. Madison, WI: University of Wisconsin Press, 1992.

Davys, Mary. *The Works of Mrs Davys: Consisting of Plays, Novels, Poems and Familiar Letters*, 2 vols. London: H. Woodfall, 1725.

Defoe, Daniel. *Moll Flanders*, ed. G. A. Starr. Oxford: Oxford Worlds Classics, 1981.

—— *Robinson Crusoe: A Norton Critical Edition*, ed. Michael Shinagel. New York: Norton, 1994.

DeMaria Jr, Robert, ed. *British Literature 1640–1789: An Anthology*. Oxford: Blackwell, 1996.

Dennis, John. *The critical works of John Dennis*, ed. Edward Niles Hooker, 2 vols. Baltimore, MD and London: Johns Hopkins University Press, 1939–43.

Diderot, Denis. *Selected Writings on Art and Literature*, transl. by Geoffrey Bremner. Harmondsworth: Penguin, 1994.

D'Monté, Rebecca and Nicole Pohl, eds. *Female Communities 1600–1800: Literary Visions and Cultural Realities*. Basingstoke: Macmillan – now Palgrave Macmillan, 2000.

Docherty, Thomas. *On Modern Authority: The Theory and Condition of Writing, 1500 to the Present Day*. Brighton: Harvester, 1987.

Dodsley, Robert, ed. *A Collection of Poems by Several Hands*, facsimile edition (1781), 6 vols, intro. Michael Suarez. London: Routledge/Thoemmes Press, 1997.

Donoghue, Frank. 'Colonizing readers. Review criticism and the formation of a reading public' in *The Consumption of Culture, 1600–1800: Image, Object, Text*, ed. Ann Bermingham and John Brewer. London: Routledge, 1995, 54–74.

—— *The Fame Machine: Book Reviewing and Eighteenth-Century Literary Careers*. Stanford, CA: Stanford University Press, 1996.

Doody, Margaret Anne. *The Daring Muse: Augustan Poetry Reconsidered*. Cambridge: Cambridge University Press, 1985.

—— *The True Story of the Novel*. New Brunswick, NJ: Rutgers University Press, 1996.

Doughty, Oswald. *English Lyric in the Age of Reason*. London: D. O'Connor, 1922.

Douglas, Aileen. 'Britannia's Rule and the It-Narrator', *Eighteenth-Century Fiction*, 6.1 (1993): 65–82.

—— *Uneasy Sensations: Smollett and the Body*. Chicago: University of Chicago Press, 1995.

Dowling, William C. *The Epistolary Moment: The Poetics of the Eighteenth-Century Verse Epistle*. Princeton, NJ: Princeton University Press, 1991.

Duncombe, John. *The Feminiad, a poem*. The Augustan Reprint Series No. 207. Los Angeles: University of California Press, 1981.

Dunton, John. *Petticoat-Government; In a letter to the Court Ladies*. London, 1702.

Dykstal, Timothy. 'Introduction' in *The Intersections of the Public and Private Spheres in early modern England*, ed. Paula Backscheider and Timothy Dykstal. London: Frank Cass, 1996, 22–40.

Eagleton, Terry. *The Function of Criticism: from 'The Spectator' to poststructuralism*. London: Verso, 1984.

Eaves, T.C. Duncan and Ben D. Kimpel. 'Richardson's Revisions of *Pamela*', *Studies in Bibliography*, 20 (1967): 61–88.

—— 'The Composition of *Clarissa* and its Revision before Publication', *PMLA*, 83 (1968): 416–28.

—— *Samuel Richardson: A Biography*. Oxford: Clarendon Press, 1971.

Eger, Elizabeth. 'Representing culture: "The Nine Living Muses of Great Britain" (1779)' in *Women, Writing and the Public Sphere, 1700–1830*, ed. Elizabeth Eger, Charlotte Grant, Clíona Ó Callchoir, Penny Warburton. Cambridge: Cambridge University Press, 2001, 104–132.

Ellis, Markman. *The Politics of Sensibility: Race, Gender and Commerce in the Sentimental Novel*. Cambridge: Cambridge University Press, 1996.

—— 'Coffee-women, *The Spectator* and the public sphere in the early eighteenth century' in *Women, Writing and the Public Sphere, 1700–1830*, ed. Elizabeth Eger, Charlotte Grant, Clíona Ó Callchoir, Penny Warburton. Cambridge: Cambridge University Press, 2001, 27–52.

Epstein, Julia L. 'Jane Austen's Juvenilia and the Female Epistolary Tradition', *Papers on Language and Literature*, 21.4 (1985): 399–416.

Erskine-Hill, Howard. *The Augustan Idea in English Literature*. London: Edward Arnold, 1983.

—— *Poetry of Opposition and Revolution: Dryden to Wordsworth*. Oxford: Clarendon Press, 1996.

Ezell, Margaret J. M. *Social Authorship and the Advent of Print*. Baltimore, MD and London: Johns Hopkins University Press, 1999.

Fabel, Kirk M. 'The Location of the Aesthetic in Akenside's *Pleasures of Imagination*', *Philological Quarterly*, 76.1 (1997): 47–68.

Fabricant, Carole. 'Pope's Moral, Political and Cultural Combat' in *Pope*, ed. Brean Hammond. Longman Critical Reader. London: Longman, 1996, 41–57.

Fairer, David. *Pope's Imagination*. Manchester: Manchester University Press, 1984.

—— '"Sweet Native Stream": Wordsworth and the School of Warton' in *Tradition in Transition: Women Writers, Marginal Texts and the Eighteenth-Century Canon*, ed. Alvaro Ribeiro and James G. Basker. Oxford: Clarendon Press, 1996, 314–38.

—— 'Chatterton's Poetic Afterlife, 1770–1794: A Context for Coleridge's Monody' in *Thomas Chatterton and Romantic Culture*, ed. Nick Groom. Basingstoke: Macmillan – now Palgrave Macmillan, 1999, 228–52.

Fairer, David and Christine Gerrard, eds. *Eighteenth-Century Poetry: An Annotated Anthology*. Oxford: Basil Blackwell, 1999.

Fawcett, Trevor. 'An Eighteenth-Century Book Club at Norwich', *The Library: A Quarterly Journal of Bibliography*, 23 (1968): 47–50.

Fergus, Jan. 'Provincial servants' reading in the late eighteenth century' in *The Practice and Representation of Reading in England*, ed. James Raven, Helen Small and Naomi Tadmor. Cambridge: Cambridge University Press, 1996, 202–25

—— 'Women readers: a case study' in *Women and Literature in Britain, 1700–1800*, ed. Vivien Jones. Cambridge: Cambridge University Press, 2000, 155–76.

Fielding, Henry. *The Works of Henry Fielding*, ed. Leslie Stephen, 10 vols. London: Smith, Elder and Co, 1882.

—— *Joseph Andrews and Shamela*, ed. Douglas Brooks-Davies. Oxford: Oxford World's Classics, 1980.

—— *Amelia*, ed. J. M. Morrell. Harmondsworth: Penguin, 1987.

—— *The Covent-Garden Journal* and *A Plan of the Universal Register-Office*, ed. Bertrand A. Goldgar. Oxford: Clarendon Press, 1988.

—— *The History of Tom Jones*, ed. John Bender and Simon Stern. Oxford: Oxford Worlds Classics, 1996.

Fielding, Sarah. *The Adventures of David Simple and Volume the Last*, ed. Malcolm Kelsall. Oxford: Oxford University Press, 1969.

—— *Remarks on Clarissa*. The Augustan Reprint Series, 231–2. Los Angeles: University of California Press, 1985.

—— *The Governess: or Little Female Academy*. London: Pandora Press, 1987.

Finberg, Melinda, ed. *Eighteenth-Century Women Dramatists*. Oxford: Oxford University Press, 2001.

Fordyce, David. *Dialogues concerning Education*. 2 vols. London: 1745.

Foreman, Amanda. *Georgiana: Duchess of Devonshire*. London: HarperCollins, 1998.

Foxon, David. Revised James McLaverty. *Pope and the Early Eighteenth-Century Book Trade.* Oxford: Clarendon Press, 1991.

Fraser, Nancy. 'Rethinking the Public Sphere: A Contribution to the Critique of Actually Existing Democracy' in Craig Calhoun, ed. *Habermas and the Public Sphere.* Cambridge, MA: MIT Press, 1992, 109–42.

Frye, Northrop. 'Towards Defining an Age of Sensibility', *English Literary History*, 23 (1956): 144–52.

Gay, John. *The Beggar's Opera*, ed. Bryan Loughrey and T. O. Treadwell. Harmondsworth: Penguin, 1986.

Gerrard, Christine. *The Patriot Opposition to Walpole: Politics, Poetry, and National Myth, 1725–1742.* Oxford: Clarendon Press, 1994.

Gill, James, ed. *Cutting Edges: Postmodern Critical Essays on Eighteenth-Century Satire.* Knoxville: University of Tennessee Press, 1995.

Gleckner, Robert. *Thomas Gray and Masculine Friendship.* Baltimore, MD: Johns Hopkins University Press, 1997.

Goldgar, Bertrand A. *Walpole and the Wits: The Relation of Politics to Literature, 1722–1742.* Lincoln: University of Nebraska Press, 1976.

Goldsmith, Michael M. 'Public Virtue and Private Vices, Bernard Mandeville and English Political Ideologies in the Early Eighteenth Century', *Eighteenth-Century Studies*, 9 (1975): 477–510.

—— ed. *Essays in The Female Tatler: By A Society of Ladies.* Durham: Thoemmes Press, 1999.

Goldsmith, Oliver. *The Citizen of the World; or Letters from a Chinese Philosopher residing in London to his friends in the East.* London: The Folio Society, 1969.

—— *Poems and Plays*, ed. Tom Davis. London: J. M. Dent, 1975.

Gooding, Richard. '*Pamela, Shamela,* and the Politics of the *Pamela* Vogue', *Eighteenth-Century Fiction*, 7 (1995): 109–30.

Goodridge, John. *Rural Life in Eighteenth-Century English Poetry.* Cambridge: Cambridge University Press, 1995.

Gordon, Scott Paul. 'Voyeuristic Dreams: Mr Spectator and the power of the spectacle', *The Eighteenth Century: Theory and Interpretation*, 26 (1995): 3–23.

Gordon, Thomas. *The Humourist.* London: W. Boreham, 1720.

Gray, Thomas. *Correspondence of Thomas Gray*, 3 vols. Oxford: Clarendon Press, 1971.

Greenblatt, Stephen. *Shakespearean Negotiations: The Circulation of Social Energy in Renaissance England.* Oxford: Oxford University Press, 1988.

Greene, Donald. '"Dramatic Texture" in Pope' in *From Sensibility to Romanticism*, ed. F. W. Hilles and Harold Bloom. Oxford University Press, 1965, 31–53.

—— 'An anatomy of Pope-bashing' in *The Enduring Legacy: Alexander Pope Tercentenary Essays*, ed. Pat Rogers and and G. S. Rousseau. Cambridge: Cambridge University Press, 1988, 241–81.

Greene, Richard. *Mary Leapor; A Study in Eighteenth-Century Women's Poetry.* Oxford: Clarendon Press, 1993.

Griffin, Dustin. 'Fictions of Eighteenth-Century Authorship', *Essays in Criticism*, 43 (1993): 181–94.

—— *Literary Patronage in England, 1650–1800*. Cambridge: Cambridge University Press, 1996.

—— *Patriotism and Poetry in Eighteenth-Century Britain*. Cambridge: Cambridge University Press, 2002.

Griffin, Robert J. *Wordsworth's Pope: A Study in Literary Historiography*. Cambridge: Cambridge University Press, 1995.

Grundy, Isobel. *Lady Mary Wortley Montagu: Comet of the Enlightenment*. Oxford: Oxford University Press, 1999.

Guerinot, Joseph V. *Pamphlet Attacks on Alexander Pope, 1711–1744: a descriptive bibliography*. London: Methuen, 1969.

Habermas, Jürgen. *The Structural Transformation of the Public Sphere: An Inquiry into a Category of Bourgeois Society*, transl. by Thomas Burger and Frederick Lawrence. Cambridge: Polity Press, 1989.

—— 'Further Reflections on the Public Sphere' in Craig Calhoun, ed. *Habermas and the Public Sphere*. Cambridge, MA: MIT Press, 1992, 421–61.

Haefner, Joel. 'The Romantic Scene(s) of Writing' in *Re-visioning Romanticism: British Women Writers, 1776–1837*, ed. Carol Shiner Wilson and Joel Haefner. Philadelphia: University of Pennsylvania Press, 1994, 256–73.

Haggerty, George E. *Men in Love: Masculinity and Sexuality in the Eighteenth Century*. New York: Columbia University Press, 1999.

Hagstrum, Jean. 'Gray's Sensibility' in *Fearful Joy: Papers from the Thomas Gray Bicentenary Conference at Carleton University*, ed. James Downey and Ben Jones. Montreal: McGill-Queen's University Press, 1974, 6–19.

Hamilton, Alexander. *The Tuesday Club: A Shorter Edition of The History of the Ancient and Honorable Tuesday Club*, ed. Robert Micklus. Baltimore, MD and London: Johns Hopkins University Press, 1995.

Hamilton, Mary. *Munster Village*. London: Pandora Press, 1987.

Hammond, Brean. 'Scriblerian Self-Fashioning', *Yearbook of English Studies*, 18 (1988a): 108–22.

—— '"A Poet, and a Patron, and Ten Pound": John Gay and Patronage' in *John Gay and the Scriblerians*, ed. Peter Lewis and Nigel Wood. London: Vision, 1988b, 23–43.

—— '"Guard the sure barrier": Pope and the partitioning of culture' in *Pope: New Contexts*, ed. David Fairer. Hemel Hempstead: Harvester Wheatsheaf, 1990, 225–40.

—— 'Applying Swift' in *Reading Swift: Papers from the Second Munster Symposium on Jonathan Swift*, ed. Hermann J. Real and Richard H. Rodino. Munich: Wilhelm Fink Verlag, 1993, 185–98.

—— ed. *Pope*. Longman Critical Reader. London: Longman, 1996.

—— *Professional Imaginative Writing in England, 1670–1740: 'hackney for bread'*. Oxford: Clarendon Press, 1997.

Hammond, Paul, ed. *Selected Prose of Alexander Pope*. Cambridge: Cambridge University Press, 1987.

Harris, Michael. *London Newspapers in the Age of Walpole*. Rutherford: Fairleigh Dickinson University Press, 1987.

Hawes, Clement. 'The Utopian Public Sphere: Intersubjectivity in *Jubilate Agno*' in *Christopher Smart and the Enlightenment*, ed. Clement Hawes. New York: St Martins Press, 1999, 195–212.

Hawley, Judith. 'Margins and Monstrosity: Martinus Scriblerus his "Double Mistress"', *Eighteenth-Century Life*, 22 (February 1998): 31–49.

Haywood, Eliza. *The History of Miss Betsy Thoughtless*, ed. Beth Fowkes Tobin. Oxford: Oxford World's Classics, 1997.

Heller, Deborah. 'Bluestocking Salons and the Public Sphere', *Eighteenth-Century Life*, 22 (May 1998): 59–82.

Hill, Bridget. 'A Refuge from Men: The Idea of a Protestant Nunnery', *Past and Present*, 117 (November 1987): 107–30.

Hill, Peter Murray. *Two Augustan Booksellers: John Dunton and Edmund Curll*. Library Series no 3. Lawrence: University of Kansas Publications, 1958.

Hillis Miller, J. 'Reading and Periodization: Wallace Stevens' "The Idea of Order at Key West"' in *The Challenge of Periodization: Old Paradigms and New Perspectives*, ed. Lawrence Besserman. New York: Garland, 1996, 197–215.

Hume, David. *Enquiries Concerning Human Understanding and Concerning the Principles of Morals*, ed. L. A. Selby-Bigge. Oxford: Clarendon Press, 1966.

—— *Selected Essays*, ed. Stephen Copley and Andrew Edgar. Oxford: Oxford University Press, 1996.

Hunter, J. Paul. 'The Loneliness of the Long-Distance Reader', *Genre* 10 (1977): 455–84.

—— 'The World as Stage and Closet' in *British Theatre and the Other Arts, 1660–1800*, ed. Shirley Strum Kenny. London and Toronto: Associated University Presses, 1984, 271–87.

—— *Before Novels: The Cultural Contexts of Eighteenth-Century English Fiction*. New York: W. W. Norton, 1990.

—— 'The novel and social/cultural history' in *The Cambridge Companion to the Eighteenth-Century Novel*, ed. John Richetti. Cambridge: Cambridge University Press, 1996, 9–40.

—— 'Serious Reflections on Further Adventures: Resistances to Closure in Eighteenth-Century English Novels' in *Augustan Subjects: Essays in Honor of Martin C. Battestin*, ed. Albert Rivero. Newark, DE: University of Delaware Press, 1997, 276–94.

—— 'Couplets and Conversation' in *The Cambridge Companion to Eighteenth-Century Poetry*, ed. John Sitter. Cambridge: Cambridge University Press, 2001, 11–36.

Inglesfield, Robert. 'Shaftesbury's Influence on Thomson's *Seasons*', *British Journal for Eighteenth-Century Studies*, 9.2 (1986): 141–56.

Ingrassia, Catherine. *Authorship, Commerce, and Gender in Early Eighteenth-Century England: A Culture of Paper Credit*. Cambridge: Cambridge University Press, 1998.

Jenkins, Owen. 'Richardson's *Pamela* and Fielding's "Vile Forgeries"', *Philological Quarterly*, 44 (1965): 200–10.

Johnson, Charles. *The Wife's Relief, or the Husband's Cure*. London: Jacob Tonson, 1712.

Johnson, Samuel. *The Yale Edition of the Works of Samuel Johnson*, ed. E. L. McAdam Jr, with Donald and Mary Hyde, and others, 16 vols. New Haven, CT: Yale University Press, 1958–.

—— *The Rambler*, ed. W. J. Bate and Albrecht B. Strauss, 3 vols. New Haven, CT: Yale University Press, 1969.

Jones, Vivien, ed. *Women and Literature in Britain, 1700–1800*. Cambridge: Cambridge University Press, 2000.

Kaufman, Paul. 'English Book Clubs and Their Social Import', in *Libraries and their Users: Collected Papers in Library History*. London: Library Association, 1969, 36–64.

Kelly, Ann Cline. *Swift and the English Language*. Philadelphia: University of Pennsylvania Press, 1988.

Kelly, Gary, general ed. *Bluestocking Feminism: Writings of the Bluestocking Circle, 1738–1785*, 6 vols. London: Pickering and Chatto, 1999.

—— 'Bluestocking Feminism' in *Women, Writing and the Public Sphere, 1700–1830*, ed. Elizabeth Eger, Charlotte Grant, Clíona Ó Callchoir, Penny Warburton. Cambridge: Cambridge University Press, 2001, 163–80.

Kerber, Linda. 'Separate Spheres, Female Worlds, Women's Place: The Rhetoric of Women's History', *Journal of American History*, 75.1 (1988): 9–39.

Kerby-Miller, Charles, ed. *The Memoirs of the Extraordinary Life, Works and Discoveries of Martinus Scriblerus*. Oxford: Oxford University Press, 1988.

Kernan, Alvin B. *Samuel Johnson and the Impact of Print*. Princeton, NJ: Princeton University Press, 1989.

Ketcham, Michael. *Transparent Designs: Reading, Performance, and Form in the* Spectator *Papers*. Athens, GA: University of Georgia Press, 1985.

Keymer, Thomas. *Richardson's* Clarissa *and the Eighteenth-Century Reader*. Cambridge: Cambridge University Press, 1992.

—— and Peter Sabor, eds. *The Pamela Controversy: Criticisms and adaptations of Samuel Richardson's Pamela, 1740–1750*, 6 vols. London: Pickering and Chatto, 2001.

Kitchin, George. *A Survey of Burlesque and Parody in English*. New York: Russell and Russell, 1931.

Klancher, Jon P. *The Making of English Reading Audiences, 1790–1832*. Madison, WI: University of Wisconsin Press, 1987.

Klein, Lawrence E. 'Gender, Conversation and the Public Sphere in Early Eighteenth-Century England' in *Textuality and Sexuality: Reading Theories and Practices*, ed. Judith Still and Michael Warton. Manchester University Press, 1993, 100–15.

—— *Shaftesbury and the Culture of Politeness: Moral Discourse and Cultural Politics in Early Eighteenth-Century England*. Cambridge: Cambridge University Press, 1994.

Korshin, Paul J. 'Deciphering Swift's Codes' in *Proceedings of the First Munster Symposium on Jonathan Swift*, ed. Hermann Real and Heinz J. Vienken. Munich: Wilhelm Fink Verlag, 1985, 123–34.

Kropf, Carl R. 'Libel and Satire in the Eighteenth Century', *Eighteenth-Century Studies*, 8 (1974–5): 153–68.

—— ed. *Reader Entrapment in Eighteenth-century Literature*. New York: AMS Press, 1992.

Landes, Joan B., ed. *Feminism, the Public and the Private*. Oxford: Oxford University Press, 1998.

Landry, Donna. *The Muses of Resistance: Laboring-class women's poetry in Britain, 1739–1796*. Cambridge: Cambridge University Press, 1990.

Law, Alexander. 'Allan Ramsay and the Easy Club', *Scottish Literary Journal*, 16.2 (1989): 18–40.

Lennox, Charlotte. *The Female Quixote*, ed. Margaret Dalziel. Oxford: Oxford World's Classics, 1980.

Lew, Joseph. 'Lady Mary's Seraglio', *Eighteenth-Century Studies*, 24.4 (Summer 1991): 432–50.

Lillywhite, Bryant. *London Coffee Houses*. London: George Allen & Unwin, 1963.

Lonsdale, Roger, ed. *The New Oxford Book of Eighteenth-Century Verse*. Oxford: Oxford University Press, 1984.

—— ed. *Eighteenth-Century Women Poets*. Oxford: Oxford University Press, 1989; repr. 1990.

Love, Harold. *Scribal Publication in Seventeenth-Century England*. Oxford: Clarendon Press, 1993.

Lund, Roger D. '*Res et Verba*: Scriblerian Satire and the Fate of Language', *The Bucknell Review*, 27.2 (1983): 63–80.

—— 'The Eel of Science: Index Learning, Scriblerian Satire, and the Rise of Information Culture', *Eighteenth-Century Life*, 22 (1998): 18–42.

Lynch, Deirdre Shauna. *The Economy of Character: Novels, Market Culture, and the Business of Inner Meaning*. Chicago: University of Chicago Press, 1998.

Mack, Maynard. *Alexander Pope: A Life*. New Haven, CT and London: Yale University Press, 1985.

Mack, Robert L. 'From Eton to Ranelagh', *English Language Notes*, 36 (1998): 38–48.

Mackenzie, Henry. *The Man of Feeling*, ed. Brian Vickers. Oxford: Oxford World's Classics, 2001.

Mackie, Erin. *Market à la Mode: Fashion, Commodity, and Gender in* The Tatler *and* The Spectator. Baltimore, MD and London: Johns Hopkins University Press, 1997.

Magnuson, Paul. *Reading Public Romanticism*. Princeton, NJ: Princeton University Press, 1998.

Manley, Delarivier. *The New Atalantis*, ed. Ros Ballaster. London: Pickering & Chatto, 1991.

Manley, K. A. 'Rural Reading in Northwest England: The Sedbergh Book Club, 1728–1928', *Book History*, 2 (1999): 78–95.

Manning, Peter. 'Wordsworth and Gray's Sonnet on the Death of West', *Studies in English Literature*, 22.3 (1982): 505–18.

Marshall, David. *The Figure of Theater: Shaftesbury, Defoe, Adam Smith, and George Eliot*. New York: Columbia Press, 1986.

Maurer, Shawn Lisa. *Proposing Men: Dialectics of Gender and Class in the Eighteenth-Century English Periodical*. Stanford, CA: Stanford University Press, 1998.

McDowell, Paula. *The Women of Grub Street: Press, Politics and Gender in the London Literary Marketplace 1678–1730*. Oxford: Clarendon Press, 1998.

McGann, Jerome. *Poetics of Sensibility: A revolution in literary style*. Oxford: Oxford University Press, 1996.

McKeon, Michael. *The Origins of the English Novel, 1600–1740*. Baltimore, MD and London: Johns Hopkins University Press, 1987.

McKillop, Alan Dugald. *Samuel Richardson: Printer and Novelist*. Chapel Hill: University of North Carolina Press, 1936; repr. 1960.

McLaverty, James. 'The First Printing and Publication of Pope's Letters', *Library*, 2 (1980): 264–80.

—— 'The Mode of Existence of Literary Works of Art: The Case of the *Dunciad Variorum*', *Studies in Bibliography*, 37 (1984): 82–105.

Michaelson, Patricia Howells. 'Women in the Reading Circle', *Eighteenth-Century Life*, 13. ns3 (1989): 59–69.

Montagu, Elizabeth. *Mrs. Montagu, "Queen of the blues": her letters and friendships from 1762 to 1800*, ed. Reginald Blunt, 2 vols. London: Constable and Company Limited, 1923.

Morgan, Fidelis, ed. *The Female Tatler*. London: J. M. Dent, 1992.

Morrissey, Lee. '"To invent in art and folly": Postmodernism and Walpole's *Castle of Otranto*', *Bucknell Review*, 41 (1998): 86–99.

Mullan, John. *Sentiment and Sociability: The Language of Feeling in the Eighteenth Century*. Oxford: Clarendon Press, 1988; repr. 1990

—— 'Sentimental Novels' in *The Cambridge Companion to the Eighteenth-Century Novel*, ed. John Richetti. Cambridge: Cambridge University Press, 1996, 236–54.

Myers, Sylvia Harcstark. *The Bluestocking Circle: Women, Friendship, and the Life of the Mind in Eighteenth-Century England*. Oxford: Clarendon Press, 1990.

New, Melvyn, ed. *Critical Essays on Laurence Sterne*. New York: G. K. Hall, 1998.

Nicholson, Colin. *Writing and the Rise of Finance*. Cambridge: Cambridge University Press, 1994.

Nicoll, Allardyce. *The Garrick Stage: Theatres and Audience in the Eighteenth Century*. Manchester University Press, 1980

Nokes, David. *John Gay: a profession of friendship*. Oxford: Oxford University Press, 1995.

—— 'The Ambitious Pursuit: Pope, Gay and the Life of Writing' in *Alexander Pope: World and Word*, ed. Howard Erskine-Hill. Oxford: Oxford University Press, 1998, 135–146.

Novak, Maxmillian E. *Defoe and the Nature of Man*. Oxford: Oxford University Press, 1963.

Nussbaum, Felicity and Laura Brown, eds. *The New Eighteenth Century*. London: Routledge, 1987.

Ogude, S. E. 'Facts into Fiction: Equiano's Narrative Reconsidered', *Research in African Literatures*, 13 (1982): 31–43.

Oldfield, J. R. 'An Eighteenth-Century Hampshire Book Club', *The Library: The Transactions of the Bibliographical Society*, 11.1 (1989): 52–7.

Ong, Walter. 'The Writer's Audience is Always a Fiction', *PMLA*, 90 (1975): 9–21.

O'Sullivan, Maurice J. 'Swift's Pedro de Mendez', *American Notes & Queries*, 22 (May–June 1984): 131–3.

—— 'How Now? What Means the Passion at His Name?', *American Notes & Queries*, 24 (May–June 1986): 140–2.

Palmeri, Frank, ed. *Critical Essays on Jonathan Swift*. New York: G. K. Hall, 1993.

Pateman, Carole. 'Feminist Critiques of the Public/Private Dichotomy' in *The Disorder of Women: Democracy, Feminism and Political Theory*. Cambridge: Polity Press, 1989, 118–40.

Patey, Douglas Lane. 'The Eighteenth Century Invents the Canon', *Modern Language Studies*, 18 (Winter 1988): 17–37.

—— '"Aesthetics" and the Rise of the Lyric in the Eighteenth Century', *Studies in English Literature*, 33 (1993): 587–609.

Paulson, Ronald and Thomas Lockwood, eds. *Henry Fielding: The Critical Heritage*. London: Routledge & Kegan Paul, 1969.

Pilkington, Laetitia. *Memoirs of Laetitia Pilkington*, ed. A.C. Elias, Jr. Athens, GA: University of Georgia Press, 1997.

Piozzi, Hester Lynch. *Thraliana: the diary of Mrs Hester Lynch Thrale (later Mrs Piozzi), 1776–1809*, ed. Katharine C. Balderston, 2 vols. Oxford: Clarendon Press, 1942.

Pincus, Steven. '"Coffee politicians does create": coffeehouses and Restoration political culture', *Journal of Modern History*, 67 (1995): 807–34.

Pocock, J. G. A. *The Machiavellian Moment: Florentine political thought and the Atlantic republican tradition*. Princeton, NJ, and London: Princeton University Press, 1975.

—— *Virtue, commerce, and History: essays on political thought and history, chiefly in the eighteenth century*. Cambridge: Cambridge University Press, 1985.

Pointon, Marcia. *Hanging the Head: Portraiture and Social Formation in Eighteenth-Century England*. New Haven, CT and London: Yale University. Press, 1993.

Pope, Alexander. *The Prose Works of Alexander Pope: Vol. I The Earlier Works, 1711–1720*, ed. Norman Ault. Oxford: Basil Blackwell, 1936.

—— *The Correspondence of Alexander Pope*, ed. George Sherburn, 5 vols. Oxford: Clarendon Press, 1956.

—— *The Twickenham Edition of the Poems of Alexander Pope*, ed. John Butt et al., 11 vols. London: Methuen, 1939–69: I, *Pastoral Poetry and an Essay on Criticism*, ed. E. Audra and Aubrey Williams (1961).

—— *The Dunciad*, ed. James Sutherland. (Vol V of the *Twickenham Edition of the Poems of Alexander Pope*.) London: Methuen, 1963.

—— *The Prose Works of Alexander Pope: Volume II*, ed. Rosemary Cowler. Hamden, CT: Archon Books, 1986.

—— *The Oxford Authors: Alexander Pope*, ed. Pat Rogers. Oxford: Oxford University Press, 1993.

—— *The Dunciad in Four Books*, ed. Valerie Rumbold. Harlowe: Longman, 1999.

Porter, Roy. *English Society in the Eighteenth Century*. Harmondsworth: Penguin, 1982.

—— *Enlightenment Britain and the Creation of the Modern World*. London: Allen Lane, Penguin Press, 2000.

Prescott, Sarah and Jane Spencer. 'Prattling, tattling and knowing everything: public authority and the female editorial persona in the early essay-periodical', *British Journal of Eighteenth-Century Studies*, 23.1 (Spring 2000): 43–58.

Price, Leah. *The Anthology and the Rise of the Novel: from Richardson to George Eliot*. Cambridge: Cambridge University Press, 2000.

Prince, Michael. *Philosophical Dialogue in the British Enlightenment: Theology, aesthetics, and the novel*. Cambridge: Cambridge University Press, 1996.

Prior, Matthew. *The Literary Works of Matthew Prior*, ed. H. Bunker Wright and Monroe K. Spears, 2 vols. Oxford: Clarendon Press, 1959.

Probyn, Clive. 'Haranguing upon Texts: Swift and the Idea of the Book' in *Proceedings of the First Munster Symposium on Jonathan Swift*, ed. Hermann Real and Heinz J. Vienken. Munich: Wilhelm Fink Verlag, 1985, 187–97.

—— 'Swift and Typographic Man: Foul Papers, Modern Criticism, and Irish Dissenters' in *Reading Swift: Papers from the Second Munster Symposium on Jonathan Swift*, ed. Richard H. Rodino and Hermann J. Real. Munich: Wilhelm Fink Verlag, 1993, 25–44.

Raven, James, Helen Small and Naomi Tadmor, eds. *The Practice and Representation of Reading in England*. Cambridge: Cambridge University Press, 1996.

Raven, James. 'From promotion to proscription: arrangements for reading and eighteenth-century libraries' in *The Practice and Representation of Reading in England*, ed. James Raven, Helen Small and Naomi Tadmor. Cambridge: Cambridge University Press, 1996, 175–201.

Real, Hermann and Heinz J. Vienken, eds. *Proceedings of the First Munster Symposium on Jonathan Swift*. Munich: Wilhelm Fink Verlag, 1985.

—— 'What's in a Name: Pedro De Mendez Again', *American Notes & Queries*, 24 (May–June 1986): 136–40.

Real, Hermann J. and Richard H. Rodino, eds. *Reading Swift: Papers from the Second Munster Symposium on Jonathan Swift*. Munich: Wilhelm Fink Verlag, 1993.

Redford, Bruce. *The Converse of the Pen: Acts of Intimacy in the Eighteenth-Century Familiar Letter*. Chicago: University of Chicago, 1986.

Richardson, Samuel. *The Correspondence of Samuel Richardson*, ed. Anna Laetitia Barbauld, 6 vols. London: R. Phillips, 1804.

—— *Pamela*. 2 vols, ed. George Saintsbury. London, 1914.

—— *Selected Letters of Samuel Richardson*, ed. John Carroll. Oxford: Clarendon Press, 1964.

—— *Sir Charles Grandison*, ed. Jocelyn Harris, 3 vols. Oxford: Oxford University Press, 1972.

—— *Pamela*. (1801 edition) ed. Peter Sabor and with an introduction by Margaret Doody. Harmondsworth: Penguin Classics, 1980.

—— *Clarissa; or, The History of a Young Lady*, ed. Angus Ross. Harmondsworth: Penguin, 1985.

—— *Pamela*. (1740 edition) ed. Thomas Keymer and Alice Wakely. Oxford: Oxford World's Classics, 2001.

Richetti, John. 'The Public Sphere and the Eighteenth-Century Novel: Social Criticism and Narrative Enactment', *Eighteenth-Century Life*, 16 (November 1992): 114–29.

—— ed. *The Cambridge Companion to the Eighteenth-Century Novel*. Cambridge: Cambridge University Press, 1996.

—— *The English Novel in History, 1700–1800*. London: Routledge, 1999.

Rizzo, Betty. *Companions Without Vows: Relationships Among Eighteenth-Century British Women*. Athens and London: The University of Georgia Press, 1994.

Roberts, Marie Mulvey. 'Pleasures Engendered by Gender: Homosociality and the Club' in *Pleasure in the Eighteenth Century*, ed. Roy Porter and Marie Mulvey Roberts. Basingstoke: Macmillan – now Palgrave Macmillan, 1996, 48–76.

Rodino, Richard H. '"Splendide Mendax": Authors, Characters, and Readers in *Gulliver's Travels*' in *Reading Swift: Papers from The Second Münster Symposium on Jonathan Swift*, ed. Richard H. Rodino and Hermann J. Real. Munich: Wilhelm Fink Verlag, 1993, 167–84.

Rogers, Pat. *Grub Street: Studies in a Subculture*. London: Methuen, 1972.

—— *An Introduction to Pope*. London: Methuen, 1975.

—— 'Introduction: the writer and society' in *The Eighteenth Century*, ed. Pat Rogers. London: Methuen, 1978, 1–80.

—— *Essays on Pope*. Cambridge: Cambridge University Press, 1993.

—— and G. S. Rousseau, eds. *The Enduring Legacy: Alexander Pope Tercentenary Essays*. Cambridge: Cambridge University Press, 1988.

Rose, Mark. *Authors and Owners: the invention of copyright*. Cambridge, MA: Harvard University Press, 1993.

Ross, Ian Campbell. *Laurence Sterne: A Life*. Oxford: Oxford University Press, 2001.

Rumbold, Valerie. *Woman's Place in Pope's World*. Cambridge: Cambridge University Press, 1989.

Russell, Gillian and Clara Tuite, eds. *Romantic Sociability: Social Networks and Literary Culture in Britain, 1770–1840*. Cambridge: Cambridge University Press, 2002.

Sabor, Peter, '*Joseph Andrews* and *Pamela*', *British Journal for Eighteenth-Century Studies*, 1 (1978): 169–81.

—— 'Samuel Richardson's Correspondence and His Final Revision of *Pamela*', *Transactions of the Samuel Johnson Society of the Northwest*, ed. Ann Messenger, 12 (1981): 114–31.

—— '*Amelia* and *Sir Charles Grandison*: The Convergence of Richardson and Fielding', *Wascana Review*, 17.2 (Fall 1982): 3–18.

Saintsbury, George. *The Peace of the Augustans: A Survey of Eighteenth Century Literature as a place of rest and refreshment.* London: G. Bell and Sons, 1916.

Sambrook, A. J., ed. *The Scribleriad and The Difference Between Verbal And Practical Virtue.* The Augustan Reprint Society, No. 125. Los Angeles: University of California, 1967.

Sancho, Ignatius. *The Letters of Ignatius Sancho*, ed. Paul Edwards and Polly Rewt. Edinburgh: Edinburgh University Press, 1994.

Savage, Richard. *An Author to be Lett*, ed. James Sutherland. The Augustan Reprint Society, No. 84. Los Angeles: University of California, 1960.

Schakel, Peter J. '"Friends Side by Side": Theme, Structure, and Influence in the Swift-Pope *Miscellanies* of 1727' in *Reading Swift: Papers from the Second Munster Symposium on Jonathan Swift*, ed. Hermann J. Real and Richard H. Rodino. Munich: Wilhelm Fink Verlag, 1993, 103–12.

Schellenberg, Betty A. *The Conversational Circle: Rereading the English Novel, 1740–1775.* Lexington, KY: University Press of Kentucky, 1996.

Scott, Joan. '"La Querelle des Femmes" in the Late Twentieth Century', *New Left Review*, 226 (1997): 3–19.

Scott, Mary. *The Female Advocate; a Poem. Occasioned by Reading Mr Duncombe's Feminead.* The Augustan Reprint Series, 224. Los Angeles: University of California, 1984.

Scott, Sarah. *A Description of Millenium Hall*, ed. Gary Kelly. Ontario, Canada: Broadview Press, 1995.

Scouten, Arthur H. 'Jonathan Swift's Progress from Prose to Poetry' in *The Poetry of Jonathan Swift: Papers Read at a Clark Library Seminar.* Los Angeles: University of California, 1981. Repr. in Frank Palmeri, ed. *Critical Essays on Jonathan Swift.* New York: G. K. Hall, 1993, 38–56.

Seary, Peter. 'Lewis Theobald, Edmond Malone, and Others' in *Reading Readings: Essays on Shakespeare Editing in the Eighteenth Century*, ed. Joanna Gondris. Madison, NJ: Fairleigh Dickinson University Press, 1998, 103–22.

Seidel, Michael. 'Strange Dispositions: Swift's *Gulliver's Travels*' in Frank Palmeri, ed. *Critical Essays on Jonathan Swift.* New York: G. K. Hall, 1993, 75–90.

Sherburn, George. *The Early Career of Alexander Pope.* Oxford: Clarendon Press, 1934.

Sheridan, Frances. *Memoirs of Miss Sidney Bidulph*, ed. Patricia Köster and Jean Coates Cleary. Oxford: Oxford Worlds Classics, 1995.

Sheridan, Richard Brinsley. *The School for Scandal and Other Plays*, ed. Michael Cordner. Oxford: Oxford World's Classics, 1998.

Sherman, Sandra. *Finance and Fictionality in the early Eighteenth Century: accounting for Defoe.* Cambridge: Cambridge University Press, 1996.

Shevelow, Kathryn. *Women and Print Culture: The Construction of Femininity in the Early Periodical.* London: Routledge, 1989.

Shiach, Morag. *Discourse on Popular Culture: Class, Gender and History in Cultural Analysis, 1730 to the Present.* Cambridge: Polity Press, 1989.

Shields, David. *Civil Tongues and Polite Letters in British America.* Chapel Hill: University of North Carolina Press, 1997.

Siskin, Clifford. *The Work of Writing: Literature and Social Change in Britain, 1700–1830.* Baltimore, MD and London: Johns Hopkins University Press, 1998.

Sitter, John. *The Poetry of Pope's Dunciad.* Minneapolis and London: University of Minnesota Press and Oxford University Press, 1971.

—— *Literary Loneliness in Mid-Eighteenth-Century England.* Ithaca, NY: Cornell University Press, 1982.

—— ed. *The Cambridge Companion to Eighteenth-Century Poetry.* Cambridge: Cambridge University Press, 2001.

—— 'Questions in poetics: why and how poetry matters' in John Sitter, ed. *The Cambridge Companion to Eighteenth-Century Poetry.* Cambridge: Cambridge University Press, 2001, 133–56.

Skinner, Gillian. *Sensibility and Economics in the Novel, 1740–1800: The Price of a Tear.* London: Macmillan – now Palgrave Macmillan, 1999.

Smith, Dane Farnsworth and M. L. Lawhon. *Plays about the Theatre in England, 1737–1800 or The Self-Conscious Stage from Foote to Sheridan.* Lewisburg and London: Bucknell University Press and Associated University Presses, 1979.

Smith, Frederik N. 'The Danger of Reading Swift: The Double Binds of *Gulliver's Travels*', *Studies in the Literary Imagination,* 17 (Spring 1984): 35–47.

—— ed. *The Genres of Gulliver's Travels.* Newark: University of Delaware Press; London: Associated University Presses, 1990.

Smollett, Tobias. *The Expedition of Humphry Clinker,* ed. Lewis M. Knapp. Oxford: Oxford World's Classics, 1984.

Sobel, Dava. *Longitude: The True Story of a Lone Genius Who Solved the Greatest Scientific Problem of his Time.* London: Fourth Estate, 1996.

Solkin, David. H. *Painting for Money: The Visual Arts and the Public Sphere in Eighteenth-Century England.* New Haven, CT: Yale University Press, 1992.

Somerville, Wilson. *The Tuesday Club of Annapolis (1745–1756) as Cultural Performance.* Athens and London: University of Georgia Press, 1996.

Spacks, Patricia Meyer. *Desire and Truth: functions of plot in eighteenth-century English novels.* Chicago: University of Chicago Press, 1990.

—— 'The poetry of sensibility' in *The Cambridge Companion to Eighteenth-Century Poetry,* ed. John Sitter. Cambridge: Cambridge University Press, 2001, 249–69.

Stallybrass, Peter and Allon White. 'The Grotesque Body and the Smithfield Muse: Authorship in the Eighteenth Century' in *The Politics and Poetics of Transgression.* London: Methuen, 1985, 80–118.

Stanton, Judith Phillips. '"This New-Found Path Attempting": Women Dramatists in England, 1660–1800' in *Curtain Calls: British and American women and the theater, 1660–1820*, ed. Mary Anne Schofield and Cecilia Macheski. Athens, GA: Ohio University Press, 1991, 325–54.

Starr, George A. 'Sentimental Novels of the Later Eighteenth Century' in *The Columbia History of the Novel*, ed. John Richetti. New York: Columbia University Press, 1994, 181–98.

Stauffer, Donald Alfred. *The Art of Biography in Eighteenth-Century England*, 2 vols. Princeton, NJ: Princeton University Press, 1941.

Steele, Peter. *Jonathan Swift: Preacher and Jester*. Oxford: Clarendon Press, 1978.

Stephens, John Calhoun, ed. *The Guardian*. Lexington, KY: University Press of Kentucky, 1982.

Sterne, Laurence. *Letters of Laurence Sterne*, ed. Lewis P. Curtis. Oxford: Clarendon Press, 1935.

—— *The Life and Opinions of Tristram Shandy*, ed. Ian Campbell Ross. Oxford: Oxford World's Classics, 1983.

—— *A Sentimental Journey with The Journal to Eliza and A Political Romance*, ed. Ian Jack. Oxford: Oxford World's Classics, 1984.

Stout, Gardner. 'Speaker and Satiric Vision in Swift's *Tale of a Tub*', *Eighteenth-Century Studies*, 3 (1969): 175–99.

Suzuki, Mika. '*The Little Female Academy* and *The Governess*', *Women's Writing*, 1.3 (1994): 325–39.

Swift, Jonathan. *The Complete Prose Works*, ed. Herbert Davis. 14 vols. Oxford: Basil Blackwell, 1939–68.

—— *Irish Tracts, 1720–23 and Sermons*, ed. Herbert Davis. Vol 9. Oxford: Basil Blackwell, 1948.

—— *Irish Tracts, 1728–1733*, ed. Herbert Davis. Vol 12. Oxford: Basil Blackwell, 1955.

—— *A Proposal for Correcting the English Tongue, Polite Conversation etc*, ed. Herbert Davis. Vol IV. Oxford: Basil Blackwell, 1957.

—— *A Tale of a Tub, To which is added the Battle of the Books and the Mechanical Operation of the Spirit*, ed. A. C. Guthkelch and D. Nichol Smith. Oxford: Clarendon Press, 1958.

—— *Correspondence*, ed. Harold Williams, 5 vols. Oxford: Clarendon Press, 1963–5.

—— *Gulliver's Travels*, ed. Peter Dixon and John Chalker. Penguin Classics, 1967.

—— *The Complete Poems*, ed. Pat Rogers. London: Penguin, 1983.

—— *A Tale of a Tub and other works*, ed. Angus Ross and David Woolley. Oxford: Oxford University Press, 1986.

—— *A Collection of Genteel and Ingenious Conversation* (1750), facsimile edition. Bristol: Thoemmes Press, 1995.

Tadmor, Naomi. '"In the even my wife read to me": women, reading and household life in the eighteenth century' in James Raven, Helen Small and Naomi

Tadmor, eds. *The Practice and Representation of Reading in England.* Cambridge: Cambridge University Press, 1996, 162–74.

Thomas, Claudia N. *Alexander Pope and His Eighteenth-Century Women Readers.* Carbondale and Edwardsville: Southern Illinois University Press, 1994.

—— 'Pope and his *Dunciad* Adversaries: Skirmishes on the Borders of Gentility' in *Cutting Edges: Postmodern Critical Essays on Eighteenth-Century Satire,* ed. James E. Gill. Knoxville: University of Tennessee Press, 1995, 275–300.

Thomas, David, ed. *Restoration and Georgian England, 1660–1788: Theatre in Europe: a documentary history.* Cambridge: Cambridge University Press, 1989.

Thompson, Ann. '"Making Him Speak True English": Grammatical Emendation in Some Eighteenth-Century Editions of Shakespeare, with particular reference to *Cymbeline*' in *Reading Readings: Essays on Shakespeare Editing in the Eighteenth Century,* ed. Joanna Gondris. Madison, NJ: Fairleigh Dickinson University Press, 1998, 71–85.

Thompson, James. *Models of Value: eighteenth-century political economy and the novel.* Durham and London: Duke University Press, 1996.

Thomson, James. *The Seasons and The Castle of Indolence,* ed. James Sambrook. Oxford: Clarendon Press, 1972.

Thomson, Heidi. 'The Poet and the Publisher in Thomas Gray's Correspondence', *The Yearbook of English Studies,* 28 (1998): 163–80.

Todd, Dennis. *Imagining Monsters: Miscreations of the Self in Eighteenth-Century England.* Chicago: University of Chicago Press, 1995.

Todd, Janet. *Sensibility: An Introduction.* London and New York: Methuen, 1986.

—— *The Sign of Angellica: Women, Writing and Fiction, 1660–1800.* New York: Columbia University Press, 1989.

Turner, James Grantham. 'Novel Panic: Picture and Performance in the Reception of *Pamela*', *Representations,* 48 (Fall 1994): 70–96.

Van Sant, Ann Jessie. *Eighteenth-Century Sensibility and the Novel: The Senses in Social Context.* Cambridge: Cambridge University Press, 1993.

Vattimo, Gianni. *The End of Modernity,* transl. by Jon R. Snyder. Cambridge and Oxford: Polity Press and Blackwell, 1988; repr. 1991.

Vickery, Amanda. 'Golden age to separate spheres? A review of the categories and chronology of English women's history', *Historical Journal,* 36 (1993): 383–414.

—— *The Gentleman's Daughter: Women's Lives in Georgian England.* New Haven, CT and London: Yale University Press, 1998.

—— *In Pursuit of Pleasure.* Milton Keynes: Open University, 2001.

Wagner, Peter. 'Swift's Great Palimpsest: Intertextuality and Travel Literature in *Gulliver's Travels*', *Dispositio,* 17. 42–3 (1992): 107–32.

—— *Reading Iconotexts: From Swift to the French Revolution.* London: Reaktion, 1995.

Wahl, Elizabeth Susan. *Invisible Relations: Representations of Female Intimacy in the Age of Enlightenment.* Stanford, CA: Stanford University Press, 1999.

Wall, Cynthia, ed. *Alexander Pope: The Rape of the Lock.* Boston, New York: Bedford Books, 1998.

Walsh, Marcus. 'Text, "Text", and Swift's *A Tale of a Tub*', *The Modern Language Review*, 85 (1990): 290–303; repr. in *Jonathan Swift.* Longman Critical Reader, ed. Nigel Wood. London: Longman, 1999, 110–29.

Warner, William. *Reading Clarissa: The Struggles of Interpretation.* New Haven, CT: Yale University Press, 1979.

—— *Licensing Entertainment: The Elevation of Novel Reading in Britain, 1684–1750.* Berkeley, CA: University of California Press, 1998.

Warren, Leland E. 'Turning Reality Round Together: Guides to Conversation in Eighteenth-Century England', *Eighteenth-Century Life*, 8 (May 1983): 65–87.

Watt, Ian. *The Rise of the Novel: Studies in Defoe, Richardson and Fielding.* London: Hogarth Press, 1957; repr. 1987.

Weinbrot, Howard. *Augustus Caesar in 'Augustan' England: the decline of a classical ideal.* Princeton, NJ: Princeton University Press, 1978.

Welcher, Jeanne K. and George E. Bush, eds. *Gulliveriana V: Shorter Imitations of* Gulliver's Travels. Delmar, New York: Scholars' Facsimiles & Reprints, 1974.

—— *Gulliveriana VI: Critiques of* Gulliver's Travels *and Allusions Thereto.* 3 vols. Delmar, New York: Scholars' Facsimiles & Reprints, 1976.

Welcher, Jeanne. *An Annotated List of Gulliveriana, 1721–1800.* Delmar, New York: Scholars' Facsimiles & Reprints, 1988.

Welsted, Leonard. *One Epistle to Mr A Pope* (1730) and anonymous, *The Blatant Beast* (1740), facsimile edition. The Augustan Reprint Society, No. 114. Los Angeles: University of California Press, 1965.

Williams, Aubrey. *Pope's Dunciad: A Study of its Meaning.* London: Archon, 1968; orig. 1955.

Wiseman, Susan. 'Catharine Macaulay: history, republicanism and the public sphere' in *Women, Writing and the Public Sphere, 1700–1830*, ed. Elizabeth Eger, Charlotte Grant, Clíona Ó Callchoir, Penny Warburton. Cambridge: Cambridge University Press, 2001, 181–99.

Wood, Nigel. 'Mocking the Heroic? A Context for *The Rape of the Lock*' in James Gill, ed. *Cutting Edges: Postmodern Critical Essays on Eighteenth-Century Satire.* Knoxville: University of Tennessee Press, 1995, 233–55.

—— ed. *Jonathan Swift.* Longman Critical Reader. London: Longman, 1999.

Woodman, Thomas, ed. *Early Romantics: Perspectives in British Poetry from Pope to Wordsworth.* Basingstoke: Macmillan – now Palgrave Macmillan, 1998.

Woodmansee, Martha. 'On the Author Effect; Recovering Collectivity' in *The Construction of Authorship: textual appropriation in law and literature*, ed. Martha Woodmansee and Peter Jaszi. Durham, London: Duke University Press, 1994, 15–28.

Woolf, Virgina. *Orlando*, ed. Brenda Lyons. Harmondsworth: Penguin, 1993.

Wortley Montagu, Lady Mary. *The Complete Letters of Lady Mary Wortley Montagu*, ed. Robert Halsband, 3 vols. Oxford: Clarendon Press, 1965–7.

—— *Essays and Poems and Simplicity, a Comedy,* ed. Robert Halsband and Isobel Grundy. Oxford: Clarendon Press, 1977.

Wyrick, Deborah Baker. *Jonathan Swift and the Vested Word.* Chapel Hill: University of North Carolina Press, 1988.

Yeazell, Ruth Bernard. *Fictions of Modesty: Women and Courtship in the English Novel.* Chicago: University of Chicago Press, 1991.

Zionkowski, Linda. *Men's Work: Gender, Class and the Professionalization of Poetry, 1660–1784.* Basingstoke: Palgrave, 2001.

# Index

Addison, Joseph 10, 11, 24, 35, 38, 39, 44, 45, 121, 124, 137n.24, 161, 231; *see also The Tatler* and *The Spectator*
Akenside, Mark 237
Alexander, William 157
Allestree, Richard 126–7
Amherst, Nicholas 45
Amory, Thomas 157–8, 170n.10
Anderson, Benedict 50–1
Angellis, Peter 26
anthologies, poetry 16, 17, 115, 158, 167, 170n.11
Arbuthnot, John 7–8, 14, 36–40, 45–6, 163, 171nn.18, 19, 206, 208n.10
Armstrong, Nancy 88, 96, 263
Astell, Mary 28, 146, 153, 156, 158
Atterbury, Francis 38, 262
Augustan literature xii, xiii, xiv, xvi, xviin.4, 191n.1, 262
Austen, Jane xv, 265

Backscheider, Paula 85
Ballard, George 157, 170n.10
Ballaster, Ros 263
Bancks, John 54–5
Barbauld, Anna Laetitia 138, 225n.9
Barber, Mary 12
Barker, Jane 148–50, 156, 158
Barney, Richard 69, 89, 93, 98
Barrell, John 213
*Bee, The* 122
Behn, Aphra 71, 90
Bellamy, Liz 89
Bender, John 79, 85
Benedict, Barbara 21, 25, 89, 236

Bennet, John 54
Bentley, Elizabeth 54, 212
Bentley, Richard 190, 201
Berkeley, George 120
Berry, Helen 141, 142
Bertelsen, Lance 232
Black, Scott 121–2, 125, 130–1
Blackmore, Richard 181, 190
black writers 3, 54, 103–7, 132–3
Blair, Hugh 137n.24
Blair, Robert 237
Blake, William xiv
Blamire, Susanna 107–8
Blandy, Mary 51
Bloomfield, Robert 54
bluestockings 4, 7, 8–10, 12, 29nn.2, 4, 40–1, 52, 133–4, 138–9, 143, 147, 166, 169
Bogel, Fredric 237, 238
Bolingbroke, Henry St John, Viscount 109, 171n.18, 181, 191n.9, 233n.2
book clubs 24–5, 51, 85, 121, 161
Boscawen, Frances 40
Boswell, James 12, 117–18
Bowers, Toni O'Shaughnessy 63
Boyle, Frank 204
Boyle, John, Earl of Orrery 99
Bradshaigh, Lady 21, 71, 110, 232
Brereton, Jane 108
Brewer, Daniel 120
Brewer, John 114
Bridges, Thomas 5
*British Mercury, The* 68–9
Browne, Isaac Hawkins 228
Bryant, John 54
Burgh, James 19
Burke, Edmund 11, 40
Burlington, Lord 20, 109